World Yearbook of Education 2016

This latest volume in the World Yearbook of Education series examines the global education industry both in OECD* countries and in developing countries, and presents the works of scholars based in different parts of the world who have significantly contributed to this area of research. Focusing on the areas of crossover in public–private partnerships in education, *World Yearbook of Education 2016* critically examines the actors and factors that have propelled the global rise of the education industry.

Split into three key sections: Part I explores how education agendas are shaped; Part II considers the private financing of education and the export of school improvements to professional consultancies; and Part III analyses new market niches, such as low-fee private schooling and for-profit education provisions.

The book draws upon case studies of many global organizations, including:

- The Bill and Melinda Gates Foundation
- Pearson Affordable Learning Fund
- Bridge International Academies
- Teach for All
- Omega Schools

Co-edited by three internationally renowned scholars, Antoni Verger, Christopher Lubienski and Gita Steiner-Khamsi, *World Yearbook of Education 2016* will be a valuable resource for researchers, graduates and policy makers who are interested in the global education industry.

* Organisation for Economic Co-operation and Development.

Antoni Verger is Associate Professor at the Department of Sociology of the Universitat Autònoma de Barcelona.

Christopher Lubienski is Professor of Education Policy at the University of Illinois, and a fellow with the National Education Policy Center.

Gita Steiner-Khamsi, PhD, is Professor of International and Comparative Education and Chair of the Department of International and Transcultural Studies at Teachers College, Columbia University.

World Yearbook of Education Series

Series editors: Terri Seddon, Jenny Ozga, Gita Steiner-Khamsi and Agnes van Zantén

World Yearbook of Education 2016

The Global Education Industry

Edited by

Antoni Verger, Christopher Lubienski and Gita Steiner-Khamsi

Routledge
Taylor & Francis Group

LONDON AND NEW YORK

First published 2016
by Routledge
2 Park Square, Milton Park, Abingdon, Oxon OX14 4RN

and by Routledge
711 Third Avenue, New York, NY 10017

Routledge is an imprint of the Taylor & Francis Group, an informa business

British Library Cataloguing in Publication Data
A catalogue record for this book is available from the British Library

Library of Congress Cataloging in Publication Data
World Yearbook of Education ISSN 0084-2508

ISBN: 978-1-138-85539-7 (hbk)
ISBN: 978-1-315-72035-7 (ebk)

Typeset in Minion Pro
by Swales & Willis Ltd, Exeter, Devon, UK

Printed and bound by CPI Group (UK) Ltd, Croydon, CR0 4YY

Contents

Illustrations

Figures

Tables

Boxes

Contributors

Wayne Au is an associate professor in the school of educational studies at the University of Washington Bothell, and an editor for the social justice teaching magazine, *Rethinking Schools*. His work focuses on critical education theory, critical policy analysis, and teaching for social justice. He has engaged in scholarship about high-stakes testing, social studies education, curriculum studies, and multicultural education. Au's scholarly articles have appeared in *Educational Researcher, Harvard Educational Review,* and *Teachers College Record,* among others, and he has authored or edited multiple volumes including the four-volume Routledge *Major Works in Critical Education* (with Michael Apple) and *Mapping Corporate Education Reform: Power and Politics in the Neoliberal State* (with Joseph J. Ferrare).

Stephen J. Ball is a distinguished service professor of sociology of education at the University College London, Institute of Education. He was elected Fellow of the British Academy in 2006; and is also Fellow of the Academy of Social Sciences; he has honorary doctorates from the Universities of Turku (Finland), and Leicester. He is co-founder and Managing Editor of the Journal of Education Policy. His main areas of interest are in sociologically informed education policy analysis and the relationships between education, education policy and social class. He has written 20 books and had published over 140 journal articles. Recent books: *How Schools do Policy* (2012), *Global Education Inc.* (2012), *Networks, New Governance and Education* (with Carolina Junemann)(2012), and *Foucault, Power and Education* (2013).

Gili S. Drori is an associate professor of sociology and anthropology at the Hebrew University of Jerusalem, Israel. She undertook her academic education at Tel Aviv University (BA 1986; and MA 1989) and Stanford University (PhD, 1997, sociology), where she taught until 2011. Drori's research interests include the comparative study of science and innovation, globalization, and rationalization. She also studies branding, the digital divide, world culture, technology entrepreneurship, higher education, and global health – analysing all from an institutionalist and comparative perspective. These interests are expressed in her five books and numerous journal articles. Specific to the study of worldwide university branding and marketization, Drori co-authored several articles and chapters with Giuseppe Delmestri and Achim Oberg and, together with Janne Tienari and Arild Wæraas, co-edited a 2015 special issue of the journal *International Studies of Management and Organization.*

Shailaja Fennell is a university lecturer in development studies attached to the Department of Land Economy, University of Cambridge, research director of the Cambridge Central Asia Forum at the Centre of Development Studies, University of Cambridge and a fellow of Jesus College, Cambridge. She is also a visiting professor at the Graduate Institute, Geneva. She has a UGC-UKIERI grant for a collaborative research initiative with the Indian Institute of Technology–Madras for 2014–16 that aims to understand how bottlenecks limit Internet access for rural agricultural production and could improve youth education and employment outcomes. She is also principal investigator on a UK Department for International Development commissioned study on activity-based learning in India that looks closely at not just what children learn, but how they learn. She was a consultant on inequality and rural development with Oxfam GB (2014–15), and on evidence-based policy with the World Bank (2013–15).

Daniel Friedrich is an assistant professor of curriculum at Teachers College, Columbia University. Friedrich is currently interested in the system of thought behind the travelling of teacher education reforms around the world. He has recently edited a special issue of *Education Policy Analysis Archives* on the global network Teach For All (with Rolf Straubhaar). He has published in the *Journal of Curriculum Theorizing, Comparative Education Review,* and the *Journal of Curriculum and Pedagogy,* among others. His book *Democractic Education as a Curricular Problem* was published by Routledge in 2014.

Helen Gunter is a professor of educational policy and Sarah Fielden professor of education in the Manchester Institute of Education, University of Manchester, UK, and is a fellow of the Academy of Social Sciences. She co-edits the *Journal of Educational Administration and History.* Her work focuses on the politics of education policy and knowledge production in the field of school leadership. Her most recent books are: *Leadership and the Reform of Education,* published in 2012 by Policy Press; *Educational Leadership and Hannah Arendt,* published in 2014 by Routledge; and *An Intellectual History of School Leadership Practice and Research,* published in 2016 by Bloomsbury Press.

Eva Hartmann is an assistant professor in sociology and political economy at the Department of Business and Politics, Copenhagen Business School. She has widely published in German, English and French on the internationalization of higher education, cross-border labour mobility, international social policy, international economic sociology and the role of law in international political economy. Her current research project examines the role of multinational companies in promoting an internationalization of qualification policy and standards.

Anna Hogan is a lecturer of pedagogy, curriculum and assessment in the School of Human Movement and Nutrition Sciences at the University of Queensland. Anna is interested in the privatization of education and has been researching the emerging role of edu-business on global education policy and practice. She is currently involved in projects investigating the external provision of school curriculum, the impacts of 'outsourcing' on teachers' work and, more broadly, young people's health and wellbeing, and the future of schooling.

Carolina Junemann is a researcher at the UCL Institute of Education, London. Her research interests focus on education policy analysis, the social impacts of policy and more broadly the relationship between educational and social inequalities. She is co-author (with Stephen J. Ball) of *Networks, New Governance and Education* (Policy Press, 2012).

Susan Kippels is a research associate at the Sheikh Saud bin Saqr Al Qasimi Foundation for Policy Research, where she has researched Arab migrant teachers, access and equity in private education in the Gulf region, and the role of philanthropic institutions in the United Arab Emirates. Prior to joining the Al Qasimi Foundation, Kippels conducted research for UNICEF and a non-governmental organization in Sri Lanka. Kippels has a dual bachelor's degree (Economics and Arabic) from the University of Notre Dame and a master's (International Education Policy) from the Harvard Graduate School of Education.

Janja Komljenovic is a Marie Curie doctoral research fellow at the University of Bristol, where she is part of the project 'Universities in the Knowledge Economy (UNIKE)', an EU Marie Curie Initial Training Network. Her current research is on the processes of market making and marketization, focusing on the higher education sector. She is particularly interested in the diversity and complexity of markets in and around universities, including the variety of actors that have entered the sector, their strategies, ways of working, and consequences for higher education and societies at large. Before joining the University of Bristol, Komljenovic has been actively involved in higher education policy making in Slovenia, and in the Bologna Process in Europe. She has also published internationally on higher education, universities and transformations in governance.

Nora Rut Krawczyk holds a Ph.D. degree in education from the Universidade Estadual de Campinas – Unicamp (Brazil), and a master's degree in state, education and society from the Facultad Latinoamericana em Ciencias Sociales – Flacso (Argentina). She is currently a professor and researcher at the Faculty of Education, teaching graduate and postgraduate levels. She is co-founder and member of the Research Group in Public Policy and Education of Unicamp (Brazil) and research scholar of the Brazilian National Research Council. Her work focuses on public education and inequalities in Latin America. She researches issues related to educational policy in a comparative perspective: educational reform, changing scenarios for public action, structures of educational systems and the school, new forms of governance in the educational sphere in Latin American societies. At present, she focuses on high school education.

Bob Lingard is a professor in the School of Education at The University of Queensland, Brisbane, Australia. His work is situated within the sociology of education and focuses on education policy, with a particular focus on the impacts of globalization and on the education work of the OECD. He is an editor of the journal *Discourse: Studies in the Cultural Politics of Education* and a member of the editorial board of the *British Journal of Sociology of Education*. His most recent book, co-authored with Wayne Martino, Goli Rezai-Rashti and Sam Sellar, is *Globalizing Educational Accountabilities* (Routledge) and he has a forthcoming edited book with Greg Thompson and Sam Sellar, *National Testing in Schooling: An Australian Assessment* (Routledge). His most recent published books include, *Politics, Policies and Pedagogies in Education* (Routledge, 2014) and *Globalizing Education Policy* (Routledge, 2010), co-authored with Fazal Rizvi.

Christopher Lubienski is professor of education policy, and director of the Forum on the Future of Public Education at the University of Illinois. He is also a fellow with the National Education Policy Center at the University of Colorado, and Sir Walter Murdoch Visiting Professor at Murdoch University in Australia. His research focuses on the political economy of education and education policy making. Lubienski held post-doctoral fellowships with the National Academy of Education and the Advanced Studies Program at Brown University, and was a Fulbright Senior Scholar in New Zealand. His previous book, *The Public School Advantage: Why Public Schools Outperform Private Schools* (with co-author Sarah Theule Lubienski, University of Chicago Press), won the 2015 PROSE Award for Education Theory from the American Publishers Awards for Professional and Scholarly Excellence.

Rabea Malik is a research fellow at the Institute of Development and Economic Alternatives. Rabea's substantive interests lie in the areas of sociology of education and political economy of education reform in low-income country contexts. With a background in policy analysis using mixed methods (MPhil Ed. University of Cambridge) and research on markets, and inequities in school choice and parental participation (PhD University of Cambridge), Rabea's current research interests include marketization of primary and secondary education; inclusive education; and school based management.

Erika Moreira Martins holds a Master's degree in education and social sciences and is currently a doctoral student in the College of Education, State University of Campinas – Unicamp (Brazil). She has studied the new forms of governance in the educational sphere, the influence and action strategies used by civil society movements and corporate movements in public education of Latin American countries. Her master's dissertation was entitled *"All for Education!" Movement: the influence on Brazilian education policies* (2013).

She is a member of the Research Group in Public Policy and Education and is awarded a FAPESP - São Paulo Research Foundation fellowship.

Francine Menashy is an assistant professor in the Department of Leadership in Education at the University of Massachusetts Boston. Her research focuses on aid to education, private sector engagement, and the educational policies of international financial institutions. She has published on these topics in such journals as the *International Journal of Educational Development, the Journal of Human Development and Capabilities,* and *Discourse: Studies in the Cultural Politics of Education,* among others. Menashy was selected as a 2013 National Academy of Education/Spencer Foundation postdoctoral fellow. She (with co-author Karen Mundy) received the 2015 George Bereday Award for best article in the *Comparative Education Review.*

Colin Mills is a senior teaching fellow at the University of Manchester Institute of Education. His major research interests reflect his past experience as a school leader in primary schools in England, the USA and in Canada, as well as work as an adviser in several local authorities in England. These focus on the role and work of consultants as agents of policy and pedagogical changes in schools and on shifts and influences on the literacy curriculum in schools. His publications include seminal works in language and literacy, including *Language and Literacy in the Primary School* (with M. Meek, Falmer Press), which has been in print since 1988. Recent publications include *Education Policy Research* (edited with Gunter and Hall, Bloomsbury Press 2014). Mills has also published in journals including the *Journal of Education Policy, British Education Research Journal* and *Discourse.*

Antonio Olmedo is a reader in education policy at the University of Roehampton, UK. He is also an Honorary Reader at the UCL Institute of Education, UK, and a visiting lecturer at the University of Granada, Spain. His research rests within the fields of education policy analysis and the sociology of education and, more specifically, he is interested in aspects related to education policy and social class: the role of the private sector in education; neoliberal policies and the creation of quasi-markets; and global networks, international organizations, policy advocacy, philanthropy and edu-businesses: international education policy and emerging patterns of access, opportunity and achievement in education. Together with Professor Stephen J. Ball, Olmedo has currently completed a research project funded by the British Academy, as part of his Newton International Fellowship, entitled: 'Philanthropy, business and education: Market-based solutions to educational problems in developing countries'. He is also involved in a research project funded by the Spanish Ministry of Education, with colleagues from the University of Granada, which focuses on processes of privatization and the creation of quasi-markets in the Spanish educational system.

Stefano Ponte is a professor of international political economy at the Department of Business and Politics, Copenhagen Business School. He is interested in how the global economy is governed and in how developing countries and emerging economies fare in it. His work examines how standards, labels and certifications on social and environmental conditions of production shape agro-food value chains. In recent research, he has been examining the increasing importance of celebrities and branding in mobilising 'compassionate consumption' and new forms of corporate social responsibility that are 'distant and disengaged'. His most recent books are *Brand Aid: Shopping Well to Save the World* (co-author with Lisa Ann Richey, 2011) and *Governing through Standards: Origins, Drivers and Limitations* (co-editor with Peter Gibbon and Jakob Vestergaard, 2011).

Lisa Ann Richey is a professor of international development studies and director of the Doctoral School of Society and Globalisation at Roskilde University (Denmark). She also serves as vice-president of the Global South Caucus of the International Studies Association (ISA). She is the author of the books *Brand Aid: Shopping Well to Save the World* with Stefano Ponte (2011), *Population Politics and Development: From the Policies to the Clinics* (2008), and the co-editor with Stefano Ponte of *New Actors and Alliances in Development* (2014). She works on new actors in international aid, citizenship and body politics, and gender and the global South. She leads the Research Network on Celebrity and North–South Relations: https://celeb-northsouth.wordpress.com/.

Natasha Ridge is a the executive director of the Sheikh Saud bin Saqr Al Qasimi Foundation for Policy Research. Prior to this, she was the acting director of research at the Dubai School of Government (DSG). Ridge has a number of publications including a book entitled *Education and the Reverse Gender Divide in the Gulf States: Embracing the Global, Ignoring the Local*. Her additional research includes a chapter in the 2012 World Education Yearbook and publications with the Emirates Centre for Strategic Studies and UNESCO as well as working papers for DSG and the Al Qasimi Foundation. Natasha holds a Doctorate of Education in international education policy from Columbia University and a Master's in international and community development from Deakin University, Australia. Her latest research focuses on the educational aspirations and choices of young men in the Gulf Cooperation Council (GCC), Arab migrant teachers, and access and equity in private education in the GCC.

Susan Robertson is a professor of sociology of Education at the University of Bristol, UK. Susan is director of the Centre for Globalisation, Education and Social Futures. She is also founding co-editor of the journal *Globalisation, Societies and Education*. Susan has published widely on transformations of the state and education, as well as spatial projects – including globalization and region building and the role of education in this. She has a long-standing interest in the governance of education, including privatization initiatives and new forms of market-making as well as the social justice implications of these developments. Her recent books include *Public Private Partnerships and* *the Global Governance of Education* (with Mundy, Verger and Menashy) and *Privatisation, Education and Social Justice* (with Macpherson and Walford).

Diego Santori is a senior lecturer in education at the University of Roehampton. His research interests include the relationships between education policy, economics and subjectivity and the ways in which their interpenetration produce new cultural forms and practices. Together with Professor Stephen J. Ball and Carolina Junemann, he has recently completed a Leverhulme Trust-funded research on the role of philanthropy in education policy, with a focus on the development of chains of low-cost, private schools for the poor in sub-Saharan Africa. His most recent work has been published in the books *Mapping Corporate Education Reform: Power and Policy Networks* (Routledge) and the *Handbook of Global Education Policy* (Wiley-Blackwell), as well as and in academic journals such as *Journal of Education Policy*.

Sam Sellar is a postdoctoral research fellow in the School of Education at the University of Queensland. Sellar draws on social theory in empirical studies of education policy and pedagogy. He is currently involved in projects investigating large-scale assessments, new accountabilities and data infrastructure in schooling; globalization and equity in higher education; and the aspirations of young people. He is editor of *Critical Studies in Education* and associate editor of *Discourse: Studies in the Cultural Politics of Education*. His recent books include *Globalizing Educational Accountabilities* (with Lingard, Martino and Rezai-Rashti) and *National Testing in Schooling: An Australian Assessment* (with Lingard and Thompson).

Soha Shami is a research associate at the Sheikh Saud bin Saqr Al Qasimi Foundation for Policy Research, where she has conducted qualitative and quantitative education research on secondary school male dropouts in the UAE, gender and education in the GCC, and teachers in the UAE. She holds a BA in economics from the American University of Sharjah (AUS) with a minor in international studies and her background includes economic policy, labour economics, and development. Prior to joining the Foundation, Soha was a teaching assistant in the Economics Department at AUS, wherein she employed her background in economics to assist in teaching coursework to undergraduate students. She also conducted qualitative market research and consumer studies in the UAE and Qatar for the Nielsen Company.

Prachi Srivastava is a associate professor at the School of International Development and Global Studies, University of Ottawa, and visiting senior research fellow, Centre for International Education, University of Sussex. She holds a doctorate from the University of Oxford. She has held visiting appointments at Columbia University, the University of Oxford, and the National University of Singapore. Srivastava is credited as coining the term 'low-fee private schooling', and is among the first researchers to conduct work on the subject. She has published widely on low-fee private schooling, non-state private actors in education in the Global South, the right to education and privatization, and global education policy. Her latest co-edited book is, *Low-fee Private Schooling: aggravating equity or mitigating disadvantage?* (Symposium Books, 2013). She is currently leading a major international collaborative research project on the role of non-state private actors and the right to education in India and the Global South, funded by the Canadian Social Sciences and Humanities Research Council.

Gita Steiner-Khamsi is a professor of comparative and international education at Teachers College, Columbia University in New York. Her most recent books are *World Yearbook of Education 2012 – Policy Borrowing and Lending in Education* (co-edited with Florian Waldow, Routledge, 2012) and *South–South Cooperation in Education and Development* (co-edited with Linda Chisholm, Teachers College Press and HSRC Publisher, 2009). She published several books and articles on globalization, transnational policy borrowing and lending as well as school reform and teacher policy in developing countries, mostly in post-Soviet Central Asia and Mongolia. She was 2009–10 president of the Comparative and International Education Society.

Antoni Verger is an associate professor at the Department of Sociology of the Universitat Autònoma de Barcelona. A former post-doctoral fellow at the Amsterdam Institute for Social Science Research (University of Amsterdam), Verger's research has specialized in the study of the relationship between global governance institutions and education policy, with a focus on the dissemination, enactment and effects of education privatization, public–private partnerships and quasi-market policies in education. He has published more than four dozen journal articles, book chapters and books on these themes, including *WTO/GATS and the Global Politics of Higher Education* (Routledge, 2010), *Public–Private Partnerships in Education: New Actors and Modes of Governance in a Globalizing World* (Edward Elgar 2012), *Global Education Policy and International Development* (Bloomsbury, 2012), and *The Global Education Policy Handbook* (Wiley-Blackwell 2016).

Series Editors' Introduction

The 2016 title of the *Routledge World Yearbook of Education* analyses a phenomenon that leaves many of us puzzled: the fast pace with which the private sector is conquering the world of public education as providers, test developers, publishers, policy analysts, and consultants. This volume extends the exploration of globalization and education that began in 2005, with the publication of *Globalization and Nationalism in Education*. Since then, the *Routledge World Yearbook of Education* has built up a series of cutting edge analyses that offer detailed empirical insights into worlds of education as they re-spatialise, re-scale and re-culture with the effects of global transitions.

As the composition of the authors of this volume demonstrates, the global education industry is omnipresent across all levels of education and everywhere in the world. What is needed are sophisticated and empirically solid analyses of this phenomenon: what does the spread of the global education industry tell us about the changing relationship between business, national governments, and civil society organizations? What is the association between for-profit companies and their non-profit foundations that do work in education? How do profit-oriented education businesses manage to present themselves as charitable organizations that do good? The book presents inspiring analyses on an emerging research field: the rise, the strategies, and the scope of the global education industry.

Drawing on case studies of the Bill and Melinda Gates Foundation, Pearson Affordable Learning Fund, Bridge International Academies, Teach for All, Omega Schools, GEMS, LinkedIn, and many other organizations that went global, the authors not only describe in depth the phenomenon but also explore how the rise of the global education industry has changed the way we conceive education, how privatization in education operates compared with that in other sectors of public life, and who the new actors are in the sphere of education.

Three internationally renowned scholars are the co-editors of this volume: Antoni Verger, Autonomous University of Barcelona, author of seminal books on public–private partnership in education, Christopher Lubienski, University of Illinois, renowned expert on the charter school movement in the United States, and Gita Steiner-Khamsi, Teachers College, Columbia University, dedicated to understanding policy borrowing and globalization in education. These editors have secured contributions from scholars who have established the study of education business as a research field and greatly advanced this area of research that with certainty will attract tremendous attention and stir important debates in educational research.

Finally, the title editors Antoni Verger, Christopher Lubienski and Gita Steiner-Khamsi would like to express their appreciation for copy editing and formatting by Raisa Belyavina and Emily Richardson, which greatly facilitated their work of producing this volume.

Julie Allan, *Birmingham*
Terri Seddon, *Melbourne*
Gita Steiner-Khamsi, *New York*

Introduction

1 The Emergence and Structuring of the Global Education Industry

Towards an Analytical Framework

Antoni Verger, Christopher Lubienski, and Gita Steiner-Khamsi

Introduction

In an era characterized by globalization across myriad sectors, industries, technologies and social movements, it may come as no surprise that we are also seeing the rise of an education industry on a global scale. Of course, the participation of private interests in education is hardly a new phenomenon. Parents and students seek individual advantage through education, and their interests are evident in activities such as paying tuition fees, fundraising, or taking up residence near a "better" school. Yet, even as a largely state-maintained sector, schools are not run on the philanthropic impulses of teachers, administrators, education software developers, or textbook publishers, since each also seeks some personal return in exchange for his or her efforts at educating children. One is reminded that Adam Smith's famous observation – "It is not from the benevolence of the butcher, the brewer, or the baker that we expect our dinner, but from their regard to their own interest" – applies to the education sector as well.

But what is new here is the conception of education as a sector that is increasingly globalized and managed by private organizations. That is, we are seeing the emergence of the idea of education as a sector for investment and profit making, where organizations, practices and networks engaged in these endeavors take on an increasingly global scale. Even though – or perhaps, because – education is often funded through public resources, substantial avenues are available for penetration by private actors and organizations. Now we are witnessing the emergence of whole trade associations dedicated to optimizing opportunities for investors looking to capitalize on the education sector.

Such interest from investors makes sense, since, in most countries, education spending makes up a significant portion of GDP. Thus, as a discernable set of activities, investments and policies, education has long been considered as an industry sector, with its distinct set of services and economic transactions. Of course, this sector, at least in most developed nations, is dominated by state actors in terms of provision, regulation and spending. Actors in the global education industry – or GEI – see this spending as too often ineffective, wasteful, and poorly leveraged by bureaucracies. Thus we are seeing with the GEI an increasing attention from private, often for-profit organizations and investors across a range of levels and activities, including an interest in investment, ownership, servicing and management of education at different levels, which have traditionally been within the purview of the state. The emergence of the GEI has also meant the development of new market niches that are often outside of traditional state control, such as test preparation, edu-marketing, the provision of curriculum packages or school improvement services.

The rise of the GEI is not an isolated phenomenon, of course, as other sectors have witnessed globalizing and marketizing trends as well. Indeed, in many ways it represents the apparently inexorable growth of the market into many areas of life (Kuttner 1999; Sandel 2012). And, as with other sectors, many of the economic and institutional trends we are seeing around are shaped by political actors, often influenced by the economic interests in the globalizing sector. That is, the GEI is not simply an organic phenomenon in the economic sphere. Instead, it is shaped and enabled by public policy making. But that policy making itself is often influenced by the private interests in the GEI as they seek to set policy agendas, frame policy problems, and refashion regulatory regimes to their advantage. While many of these political and policy efforts traditionally played out at the national (or even more local) levels, as a global creature, GEI actors are increasingly able to exert their influence on a transnational basis. GEI actors include multi-national corporations and philanthropies with a global reach. The global scale of their influence is evident in the scale of the networks in which they operate. At the same time, local actors are often formally or informally subsumed into these larger networks, so that an autonomous school in Malaysia may be adopting some of the same policies and curricular packages as a school district in suburban Washington, DC. As transnational organizations replicate their practices across borders, they are also building their infrastructure both formally through corporate acquisitions, or informally, through partnerships and contracts that broaden the scope of their activities. Thus, the GEI is the site of increasing horizontal and vertical integration.

In this introductory chapter, we survey the rise, shape, and impact of the GEI, providing a conceptual and theoretical framework to help us consider the GEI as a truly global phenomenon proliferating across a discernable education sector. This approach helps us to conceptualize the changing nature and the structural forces underpinning the GEI.

Definition, Facts, and Figures

The GEI is an increasingly globalized economic sector in which a broad range of educational services and goods are produced, exchanged and consumed, often on a for-profit basis. The GEI is constituted by its own sets of processes, systems of rules, and social forces, which interact in the production, offer and demand of educational services and goods. Nonetheless, despite its particularities, as with other industry sectors, education is becoming increasingly subject to:

- the participation of actors and firms (the so-called "edu-businesses"), from both the non- and for-profit sectors, in the provision of education goods and services;
- interactions and operations happening at a global scale, including the cross-border supply of educational services (on-line courses, establishment of campuses abroad, marketing in pursuit of international students, etc.);
- competitive dynamics between edu-businesses, but also between edu-businesses and conventional public providers, with the sometimes-intended potential to incentivize competitive behaviors of conventional providers. In fact, to become more efficient and competitive within the global education market, public providers behave (and are being managed) similarly to business actors;
- for-profit motives as the main driving force behind the participation of private actors (but also some state actors) in educational activities;
- access to financial capital markets as a way to support the activities of the GEI and its territorial and institutional expansion, including equity funds, venture capital and so on;
- vertical and horizontal integration of edu-businesses, as well as mergers and acquisitions between companies involved in the education sector, with Pearson as the most clear illustration of this tendency (see Hogan et al. in this volume).

The GEI can be considered as an industry sector in expansion. Merrill Lynch-Bank of America calculated in 2014 that the value of the education sector, globally speaking, is $4.3 trillion (see Robertson and Komljenovic in this volume). And GSV Advisors (2012) consider that the market size of the education for-profit sector is expected to grow by 17 percent in the next five years. In the US alone, the for-profit education industry revenues more than doubled in the last decade, going from $60 billion in 1999 to $125 billion in 2012 (BMO Capital Markets 2014). Traditionally, there have been more market opportunities in those sub-sectors and educational levels, such as pre-kindergarten and post-secondary education, where the state is not so present. Nonetheless, in the last decade, we have witnessed a significant penetration of primary and secondary education levels by the for-profit sector as well. In fact, this is a development that has been apparent in both the global north and the global south.

The GEI is involved in the production of a broad variety of educational services and goods. Some sources, however, tend to use the concept of the GEI to refer to a rather delimited set of activities. For instance, James Tooley (2001), in *The Global Education Industry* likens this concept to the expansion of private schooling into developing contexts.[1] More recently, the Organisation for Economic Cooperation and Development (OECD) has also adopted the notion of the GEI, basically to refer to Information Technology (IT) edu-businesses. In particular, for the OECD (2014), the GEI is represented by those companies selling educational resources and services of a technological nature to schools, including e-books, software, courseware, learning devices, learning platforms or dedicated IT solutions. Nonetheless, and despite the centrality and emergence of both the IT industry and for-profit private schools, in this book we consider that the GEI also involves other rising sub-sectors, activities and modalities of educational provision that transcend them. They include school improvement services, on-line education, tutoring or supplemental/ "shadow education," edu-marketing, consultancy services for governments and schools, testing preparation services, and so on.

Thus, one of the more recent developments that reflect the strength and dynamism acquired by the GEI is the penetration of business actors in new market niches such as those mentioned. However, there are at least two other developments that reflect the major centrality being acquired by education industry actors in contemporary societies and economies that deserve to be highlighted. They are, first, the increasing role of GEI actors in educational politics, including their capacity to settle education policy agendas and frame education regulation at different scales (Ball 2012); and, second, the intensification of the links between financial markets and the GEI. In relation to the latter, private investors seem to consider the education industry as a sector in which it is more and more worthwhile to operate. In fact, operations in the stock market (and in NASDAQ in particular) concerning the education industry have increased rapidly in the last decade. According to GSV Advisors, only eight of these operations were active in 2002, whereas 127 operations were identified in 2011.

Conditions for the GEI's Emergence and Expansion

While factors such as private interests in education have been at play for ages, recent years have seen the emergence of a global education industry that is qualitatively distinct from anything that preceded it. Certainly, the scope and scale of the GEI is new, as is its degree of both horizontal and vertical integration. The relatively recent emergence of this phenomenon raises questions as to why it is happening at this point in history, and why it is taking the shape that it is.

Multiple reasons are behind the emergence and expansion of the education industry in a broader range of activities and territories. In this section, we focus on those that we consider to be more relevant or to have a more direct effect in the GEI's expansion. They include: economic globalization as a driving force of both an increasing educational demand and an intensification of cross-border supply of educational services; the commodification of schooling as a positional good for families; the financialization of the education sector (from both the demand and the supply sides); recent changes in the governance of education (including education decentralization and the adoption of global education policies such as accountability and curricular standards); the emergence of an evidence-based policy paradigm; and the intensification of the IT to learning relationship.

The Globalization of the Economy: Increasing Educational Demand and Cross-Border Supply

In a globalized economic environment, in which competition between economic actors and territories intensifies, education is treated as a key instrument of international competitiveness. In fact, education and training are among the few public policy instruments that, in a more open and liberalized economy, states can legitimately activate in an effort to promote their industry, without being accused of altering the rules of free trade (Fernandez and Hayward 2004). At the same time, many countries and world regions aspire to become "knowledge economies" (e.g. to adopt an economic development model that is more intense in knowledge products and services) and logically see education as a key asset to this purpose. To some extent, the knowledge economy has currently become a powerful economic imaginary (see Jessop et al. 2008) that makes governments, but also private companies, more willing to invest in education, as well as to presume that the strengthening of the effectiveness of their education systems is desirable and, on occasions, urgent. Overall, companies and governments operating at multiple scales (national, regional and local) consider education as a strategic asset to develop their economies and to provide the labor market with the new skills and human-power profiles that are more aligned with the current economic environment. Yet, even as the causal link between a nation's educational and economic development might not be as clear as is commonly assumed, especially in education reform rhetoric, there are clear benefits to individuals and families from investing resources and effort into education (Benavot 1992; Labaree 2007; Ramirez et al. 2006). Indeed, beyond states and companies, for those individual citizens who do not want to be left behind in an increasingly flexible and dualized labor market, education is also more and more perceived both as a positional good – a symbol or site of competition for prestige – and as a worthwhile investment. All these forces converge in a higher demand for education at all levels, a demand from which a broad range of edu-businesses directly benefit.

The globalization of the economy promotes interdependence and openness to trade among a broad range of national territories and economic sectors. Since the 1990s, with the constitution of the General Agreement on Trade in Services (GATS) in the Uruguay Round, the international trade regime contemplates and favors the liberalization of all sorts of services, including education services. According to some observers, the constitution of the GATS became an inflexion point in the development of the global education industry (Robertson et al. 2002). This is due to the fact that the GATS, as well as other regional and bi-lateral trade-in-services agreements that came after, have given enormous facilities (of a fiscal, legal and administrative nature) for edu-business when it comes to accessing education markets abroad, and selling their education services internationally (Verger 2010). In international trade jargon, the modes of educational services commerce that are being promoted by free trade agreements are:

- *cross-border supply*: provision of a service between countries at a distance. In the case of education, this mode is seen in e-learning or all types of distance learning programs;
- *consumption abroad*: students move to a foreign country to consume educational services;

- *commercial presence:* the service provider sets up a subsidiary abroad. Examples of this are universities or international chains of schools with headquarters in one country setting up a branch campus/school in another country;
- *presence of natural persons:* a researcher or a lecturer moves to a foreign country to provide a service.

Economic competitiveness is promoting educational demand at higher education levels. However, we cannot forget that, especially in low-income countries, the number of children without any access to the most basic education is still high. According to the *Education for All* Global Monitoring Report, in 2011, 57 million children were still not in school (UNESCO 2014). Due to the passivity of both governments from the South and the international community in the face of this reality, the not-in-school children represent a huge market opportunity for private education providers and investors, including the so-called low-fee private schools chains. This private schooling modality, which differentiates itself from more conventional private education in the sense that is supposed to be "affordable" for the poor even while it is for-profit, is expanding in sub-Saharan Africa and South-East Asia, but also to a less extent in several Latin American countries (Srivastava in this volume).

The Commodification of Schooling

Even as nations often treat education as a key element in increasing their economic competitiveness in a globalized world, individuals and families are apparently embracing the idea of education as a privatized, individual good. As noted, the rhetoric surrounding global education reform often conflates the individual and collective economic benefits of schooling. Thus, just as nations strive to increase their competitive advantage in the global marketplace through improved education, families in those nations often compete for sought-after spots for their children in what are perceived as relatively better schools. Even open-access education systems often see families competing to place their children higher up in the hierarchy of schools, as education becomes a positional good with social cachet connected to one's particular consumption, and not only a route to enhanced employment prospects.

As scholars such as David Labaree (2007) have demonstrated, this is not necessarily a new phenomenon, as education systems often reflect a self-contradictory mix of individual and collective goals. However, as education policy has increasingly emphasized the market mechanisms of choice and competition, which are evident in the growing global education industry, the "good" of schooling itself is often commodified, as "consumers" vie for the better services. Arguably, the education system itself is not "privatized" as nations open up their systems to the GEI. After all, it is not clear the degree to which schooling exhibits the classic characteristics of both rivalry and exclusivity associated with private goods, since governments may still play a role in funding, ensuring access, or otherwise regulating the sector. However, the fact is that parents and policymakers appear to be perceiving education as a privatized good for which they must use their resources and advantages to compete for desirable spots, at the expense of other consumers.

Education Financialization

As mentioned above, private investors and commercial banks are willing to invest in education businesses due to their potential profitability. Such an availability of national and international credit comes also from public finance initiatives, among which the International Finance Corporation (IFC), the World Bank credit facility for the private sector, stands out. In 2001, the IFC declared education, together with health, as a priority sector by establishing the "Health and Education Group" (see Robertson and Komljenovic, and Srivastava in this volume). This organization justified this shift toward "public services" after detecting, on the one hand, a "gap left by the public sector" and, on the other, that families were "more willing to pay for education than in the past, understanding its contribution to a child's future success and associated family stability" (Mundy and Menashy 2012: 86). In 2011, the IFC reported cumulative investments of over $500 million to 63 education projects, most of them focusing on postsecondary education, in a broad range of Southern countries (Mundy and Menashy 2012). Similarly, as Santori, Ball, and Junemann demonstrate in this volume, companies like Pearson purport to straddle the for-profit and civic sectors by creating publicly-facing, civic-minded learning corporations using business capital and techniques.

But not only do private providers resort to financial markets to develop their activity. Many public universities, in the context of the relative public spending decline of the last decade, have become increasingly involved in financial operations. Thus, an important portion of the university finances is derived from derivatives purchases, debt management affairs and even in complex real estate operations. In countries such as the Netherlands, the deepening of the financialization of the economy of some of the most emblematic universities has generated important cash flow issues that have put at risk the "core businesses" of these universities, such as research and education (Engelen et al. 2014).

Finally, it is not only education providers, including universities and schools, that resort to financial markets to sustain or expand their activity. Demand for credit also comes from students and their families. This is especially true in those countries where governments have tended to substitute scholarships for students' loan policies and/or where the college or university fees have tended to increase (Metcalf 2005).

International Trends in the Governance of Education

The rapid dissemination and adoption of a range of global education policies including accountability systems and common core standards are opening market opportunities to a broad range of edu-businesses. The establishment of common core standards at the curricular level is helping companies selling school materials to enjoy a broader market in territorial terms, since their books, software or other type of materials – as far as they ascribe to the standards in question – will have validity on a broader scale. Accountability policies are putting pressure on schools and districts to deliver educational results aligned to monolithic metrics, especially when these policies are accompanied by the application of rewards and sanctions according to results. As a response to accountability pressures, many schools and/or districts are more willing to resort to consultancy firms and to other types of experts offering school improvement and testing preparation services (see Gunter in this volume).

On many occasions, analogous pressures come from international education assessments such as the OECD Programme for International Student Assessment (PISA). It has been generally seen how these international assessments result in political and media pressures on many governments (Waldow et al. 2014; Sellar and Lingard 2014). As a consequence, these governments are temped to adopt short-term fixes and solutions to their performance issues, such as those being offered and sold within the global education industry (Kamens 2013).

Finally, countries that have witnessed higher levels of education decentralization tend to be more conducive to education privatization trends of a different nature (Lubienski 2014). Especially in developing countries, the municipalization of education has meant the underfunding and devaluation of public education in multiple locations, and consequently the private sector has expanded. The fact that local governments do not always have the appropriate technical and political capacity to deliver education in an effective way leads to middle class families exiting the public sector and enrolling their children in private schools. Furthermore, as shown by Adrião et al. (2009) in the case of Brazil, local governments tend to supplement such technical and political weaknesses by buying "reform packages" and other education consulting services from private consultancy firms.

Evidence-Based Policy

In an era where policy embraces a discourse of evidence-based decisions, policy-makers purportedly rely more than before on what scientific evidence says when it comes to their policy decisions, although there can be substantial variation by country, sector, and scientific discipline – and the use of research evidence in education policy is often one of the weaker connections (Oreskes and Conway 2010; Specter 2010). This approach has also been appropriated as a key strategy of the GEI. Although often in a selective way, evidence is strategically used by edu-businesses and/or their philanthropic arms to frame and package their preferred policy solutions for governments and other education stakeholders. For instance, as Hogan, Lingard, and Sellar show in this volume, Pearson often uses the images and language of experimental sciences (including laboratories, researchers with data, microscopes, etc.) in the promotion of its products such as the so-called *Education Efficacy Framework*. These authors use the metaphor of the "medicalization" of educational research to refer to this promotional strategy, through which edu-businesses present their products as rigorous and make them accordingly more appealing.

Technology and Learning

Currently, information technologies are often seen – correctly or not – as key drivers of quality learning processes and better access and learning outcomes, often by tech entrepreneurs interested in reforming and marketizing education. This, together with the importance that many governments and international organizations give to promoting digital skills through education as a way to raise the employability of their population, is contributing significantly to facilitating the penetration of the IT industry into educational systems and schools. This is a trend not only affecting developed countries, but also developing ones through policy programs such as the one-to-one computing program (Valiente 2010). In fact, in many developing countries technology is seen as a cost-effective way to compensate for teacher shortages and insufficient teacher training.

Despite the global dimension this phenomenon is acquiring, according to the OECD, in most countries the relationship between IT firms and the education system is still too informal and ruled by a sort of "'wild west' of commercial practice" (OECD 2014: 3). This tends to end up with expensive and/or inappropriate purchases, which do not necessarily fit the schools' educational needs. Because of this, the OECD has started promoting a partnership approach between the IT industry and governments as a more effective way to bring technological innovations and devices into the everyday practices of schools. These new developments and normative debates are clear indicators, in any case, of the rise of the IT sector, which is mainly in the hands of transnational private firms in the global education policy field, often with demonstrable ties to political actors.

Researching the GEI: Conceptual and Heuristic Tools

For neoclassic economics, industry sectors are mainly seen as constituted by interactions between rational and self-interested actors offering and/or looking for goods and services. In a free market economy, these relations are conceived as competitive and as (self-) regulated by agents' access to information and choice, and by the mechanism of price – a mechanism not typically mediated by competition in the state-run education sector. Nonetheless, our perspective on the GEI phenomenon is substantially different and rather builds on sociological and political science approaches. These approaches put emphasis on non-economic and non-material factors in the configuration and structuring of markets. In particular, these approaches emphasize the role of institutional contexts and social relations (and relations of power in particular) as key drivers in the making, maintaining and transforming of industry sectors such as the GEI (Berndt and Boeckler 2009). It is from this perspective that we find it appropriate and useful to conceptualize the GEI as a social field.

The concept of field, in the way it was advanced by Pierre Bourdieu (1993), forces us to think of the GEI as a structured social space with its specific institutions, forms of agency and power practices; in this space, different actors struggle for the expansion, transformation and/or reproduction of the field, as well as for having an advantageous or dominant position in it. Despite being open to the participation and involvement of a broad range of actors, a field is far from a flat terrain but is a three-dimensional space. Not all the actors have the same power and capacity to mobilize the different types of capital (social, economic, symbolic, etc.) that are necessary to achieve their objectives within the field in question (Lingard et al. 2005).

As with any other social field, the GEI should be seen as a quasi-autonomous field with its own logics of action and practice, but one that at the same time is embedded in broader social and economic structures. Overall, the GEI field interacts and to some extent depends on the events and on the configuration of other fields, including the field of politics, the international development field, the global education policy field and the global economy field, to name the most relevant.

Main Actors in the Field

The GEI field includes a broad range of actors. At the center of the field, we find the so-called edu-businesses, a very broad category of economic actors involved in the production of educational goods and services that includes:

- chains of private schools, such as GEMS, ARK, Bridge International Academies, and the Omega schools. Many of these chains operate under for-profit motives and are contributing to the diversification of the private schooling sector, which has been traditionally in the hands of religious or NGO-based providers;
- big education corporations and conglomerates, with companies such as Pearson, which provides a broad range of publishing and educational services, and IT/software companies, such as Microsoft, Intel, Hewlett Packard or Blackboard standing out;
- consultancy firms, which go from big transnational corporations such as PriceWaterhouseCoopers or McKinsey, which have broad portfolios and apply business logic to education, to a wide but disparate constellation of individual consultants, some of whom focus more exclusively on education;
- philanthropic foundations, such as the Bill and Melinda Gates Foundation or the Hewlett Foundation, which are formally autonomous from the corporate matrices, but are usually implicitly aligned with the business strategy of their funders and founders;
- advocacy networks, which emerge when edu-businesses and other types of private corporations come together in a more or less formal, more or less stable way to advocate for educational changes. An example of a well-organized corporate-based advocacy network in education is *Todos pela Educacao* in Brazil (see Martins and Krawczyk in this volume), or the Gates-funded effort to bring charter schools to Washington (see Au and Lubienski in this volume).

So far, we have referred mainly to corporative (or collective) actors. However, the GEI field is fertile with individual policy entrepreneurs and boundary spanners, who tend to play a key role in promoting education "innovations" that favor the expansion of the GEI, in part due to their capacity to strategically connect different organizations and to transit across different fields. Michael Barber and James Tooley are probably two of the most renowned actors of this type in the GEI literature. Barber was a close advisor of Tony Blair in the UK in the 1990s, whose role is key to understanding the market-oriented nature of the New Labour policies in education at the time (Fitz and Hafid 2007). In the 2000s, Barber was hired by McKinsey, where he produced the well-known 2007 report *How the World's Best-Performing Schools Come Out on Top*, and is currently the chief education adviser of the Pearson corporation. Apart from being located in powerful organizations, Barber's policy influence relies on his personal contacts and on his strategic situation as a "broker" on a broad range of policy networks. For his part, James Tooley, a professor at Newcastle University, is deeply involved in the low-fee private school business from multiple angles: as a researcher, as an advocate, as a funder and, more recently, as the owner of a chain of low-fee private schools called Omega. Tooley's presence as a speaker is remarkable in all types of international events on private education, and he has also received numerous awards from organizations such as the Templeton Foundation and the International Finance Corporation. According to Stephen J. Ball, one of the keys of Tooley's success is that he "is a persuasive storyteller who is able to put faces and figures into the neo-liberal imaginary" (2012: 40).

In the GEI field, as happens in any other industry sector, business actors do not operate in an isolated manner. They depend on a broad range of other actors, with whom they can interact in a cooperative or a conflicting way. Among them, we find regulators (including national and sub-national governments, and international organizations), public providers, workers (and their organizations), private capital and clients (including governments, students and families). In fact, the interaction of edu-businesses with these other actors is fundamental to understanding their position in the GEI hierarchy as well as the configuration and evolution of the field itself.

Despite all the non-business actors, even in an era of withdrawal of formal government structures, the role of the state is still quite relevant here. The state is a key institution in the making, maintenance and modification of industry sectors. Welfare regime literature tends to think about the state vs. the market in the provision of public services, often in a zero-sum conception, where more of one means less of the other. However, far from this dichotomist thinking, we conceive of the state, especially in a neoliberal context, as a key ally in market-making processes. In a global marketplace, the role of the state focuses on maintaining and promoting economic competitiveness at different scales. To this purpose, states can create the space in which markets can thrive, regulating entry to the marketplace for providers and consumers, often providing funding, compelling use, enforcing contracts, protecting competitors (and competition), and often being "captured" by the competitors themselves. They promote pro-market regulation in different spheres as well as "the international competitiveness of domestically based (although often transnationally organized) industries" (Cerny 2010: 17). As stated similarly by Au and Lubienski (in this volume), the competition state "supports the creation of markets in all areas in which they do not yet exist, including in state-administered goods and services" such as education.

Analyzing the GEI as a Social Field

According to Bourdieu (1993), any social field is a *field of forces*. In his view, such forces are activated by social actors who compete against each other, on the basis of the powers at their disposal, to achieve a position of relative dominance in the field. This idea, which is very actor-centered, has been further developed by sociologists of markets, such as Jens Beckert (2010). According to Beckert, there are three main forces that, from an analytical point of view, are particularly relevant in structuring fields. These are *networks, cognitive frames* and *institutions. Networks* refer to the more or less stable sets of relationships between political, social and/or economic actors, which work as channels of influence and, in many cases, as more or less formal governance mechanisms. *Cognitive frames* refer to the types of ideas that social, political and economic actors mobilize to advance their vision of societal problems and preferred solutions. And *institutions* can be broadly defined as sets of rules, norms and procedures in which actors develop their economic activity and their political strategies (Campbell 2004; Ball 2012).

Networks, cognitive frames and institutions, due to their ability to constitute any industry field, shape the conditions of competition in which edu-businesses operate, and are key elements to understanding the social and economic stratification of the GEI field. However, it is also important to consider that not only governments, but also business actors can try to activate and shape these elements for different reasons. In fact, several chapters in this book focus on how edu-businesses activate networks and ideas to shape institutional rules and normative frameworks, usually for their economic interest, but also to advance their ideological agenda (see Au and Lubienski in this volume). Networks, cognitive frames and institutions are three social forces that can be analyzed separately, but it needs to be acknowledged that they exert their influence simultaneously. According to Beckert (2010: 611):

> Network positions can be used to influence institutional rules and dominant cognitions; institutions can be a resource to force changes in networks and to influence mental maps; ideas that are influential in the field can be used to advocate changes in institutional rules and network composition.

Networks seem to play an important role in the GEI literature, to a great extent due to their properties as sites of policy influence. According to Fligstein (2007), if firms are embedded within the right networks and have the appropriate connections, they can solve their resource dependence problems more easily, and have more chances to reproduce or expand their business activity successfully. Businesses actors and their representatives tend to be inserted in a range of policy networks, usually in a casual or informal way. Networks are often sustained through social and personal relationships, conversations, face-to-face meetings, social events, discussions, consultations and so on. At a global level, for instance, social events, annual meetings or international conferences – such as the IFC *Private Education Conference* or Qatar's Foundation *World Innovation Summit Education* (WISE) – are key spaces to connect companies, investors, policy entrepreneurs and governments within the GEI. It is worth bearing in mind that this informality might result in a virtually invisible and inaccessible infrastructure, which is something that generates serious concerns among network analysts (see Olmedo in this volume). Nonetheless, despite this apparent informality, private players are organizing themselves more openly and are even being accepted as legitimate participants in national and global governance structures (see for instance Menashy in this volume on the inclusion of the private sector in the Global Partnership for Education board).

Finally, we would like to note that the GEI is a dynamic and constantly changing field. Furthermore, this is a fluid field that, as we have highlighted in this chapter, is expanding and globalizing. However, the globalization of the education industry does not mean that it can be isolated from its closer social and institutional context. On the contrary, the configuration of the social forces that make up the education industry varies according to mediating factors such as the welfare regime, the administrative tradition or the political culture that prevails in particular contexts. Hence, the configuration, dynamism and implications of the GEI field vary accordingly in different places.

Writing about the Global Education Industry: The Chapters in the Book

As editors of this volume, we invited authors from different research areas to consider the rise of the GEI. One group of contributors represents policy studies scholars with a keen interest in understanding the role of business in shaping and selling educational reforms. The other group of contributors is composed of comparativists who ponder the breath-taking pace with which privatization, public–private partnership, and the business complex have expanded across the globe, penetrating arenas as vast as education and aid. For this group, education constitutes one of many niches in which multinational companies managed to find a lucrative market. As a corollary, investigating how business operates in the education sector enables them to dig deeper and understand the logic of the global education industry. One of the research questions they set out to address is whether doing business in education is in any way different in terms of agency, rationale, or operationalization, than buying and selling goods and services in other sectors. The list of interesting research questions is too long to enumerate in this introductory chapter. Moreover, the authors are context-specific in their analyses and represent a wide range of theoretical orientations. At the same time, they share a common interest in investigating GEI empirically and understanding the different facets of the phenomenon conceptually. In this section, we briefly sketch out the three parts of the book in order to identify a few common threads as well as differences among the authors of this volume.

Part I of the book deals with the role of the GEI in *Shaping Education Agendas*. Business involvement in education is not a new phenomenon, as we have noted. Some scholars in fact would argue that business influence comes and goes cyclically (Tyack and Cuban 1995). It disappears periodically, typically because of public outrage over some scandal, and then reappears after a while. Yet it seems that the most recent wave of business involvement has a greater systemic impact and is more global in nature. Without any doubt, the universal belief in the right to education and lifelong learning explains why the most recent iteration of education business could expand to every corner of the world. Long before entrepreneurs discovered education as a commodity that functions as an economy of scale, the term "policy entrepreneurs" was coined in policy studies. The term denotes professionals who propagate or lobby for a particular reform agenda with the intention of having political impact. Some of the questions that the emergence of policy entrepreneurship raises in the education sector are: What if the policy entrepreneurs are first and foremost business entrepreneurs and only secondarily policy experts? Are they likely to advocate for particular educational reforms that are good (for) business? If they do so, how do they manage to make governments "buy" into their private vision of public education? The first chapters of the book examine the impact that business has had in a number of areas, including on the charter school movement in the United States (Wayne Au and Christopher Lubienski), curriculum reform and teacher education in the United Kingdom (Antonio Olmedo), the organization Global Partnership for Education (Francine Menashy), and the "Todos pela Educação" movement in Brazil (Erika Moreira Martin and Nora Rut Krawczyk). Finally, the authors of "Better (Red)™ than Dead? Celebrities, Consumption and International Aid" (2008) and *Brand Aid: Shopping well to save the world* (2011), Lisa Richey and Stefano Ponte, reflect on how brand aid and glamor aid shape conceptions of education and development and how they "market" the people in developing countries to consumers in the global north.

Wayne Au and Christopher Lubienski disprove the myth that the global education industry is exclusively interested in "for-profit business models for schooling" (see Chapter 2). In their empirical study of the Bill and Melinda Gates Foundation, they trace the role of the Foundation in advocating for, funding and creating networks, and supporting legislative changes, first in the Foundation's home state (Washington State) and then nationwide for the charter school reform movement. They find, for example, that the Yes On 1240 campaign (Washington Coalition for Public Charter Schools) was in great part funded either directly by the Gates Foundation or by donors connected with Gates. A total of nine Gates-connected donors donated just over $8.32 million of the $10.9 million campaign to promote public charter schools in the State of Washington.

"Philanthro-capitalist" policy advocacy is also the subject of analysis in the chapters written by Antonio Olmedo (Absolute Return for Kinds) and Francine Menashy (Global Partnership for Education). Olmedo's chapter contributes to the scholarship on "philanthro-capitalism" or "charitable business" which by now is an established research field with critical analyses on how businesses either set up their own facilities or attempt to shape public services, including education, in their microcosmos, that is, in the regions or districts in which they produce or do business.

Olmedo's chapter focuses on the "charitable business" Absolute Return on Kids, which bundles up with businesses, including the GEI giant Pearson, to offer teacher training courses (titled "Teaching Leaders") that focus heavily on measurement and accountability. Needless to say, businesses such as Pearson, Cambridge Education, PWC, Mattrix Knowledge Group or A4e have put a value chain in operation that is lucrative for each and every element in the chain: they reap profit from providing training to teachers by selling modules, books that accompany the training, testing of teachers and – to illustrate the big numbers the education industry is dealing with – testing the 20 students or so per teacher at each grade and each subject throughout their education career because they made us believe in the great value of lifelong testing.

In her chapter, Francine Menashy investigates how foundations attempt to advocate for more private sector involvement in the world's largest public–private partnership in education: the multilateral aid organization Global Partnership for Education (GPE). She analyzes key documents from the GPE Board of Directors for the period from 2009 to 2014 and carried out interviews with former and current board members and staff. During that period, the foundations and companies held a single seat in the GPE Board of Directors.

In the chapter on entrepreneurship in the Brazilian education sector, Erika Moreira Martin and Nora Rut Krawczyk Erika trace the history of private sector involvement in the administration of President Fernando Henrique Cardoso (1995–2002), which encouraged the corporate sector to assume more responsibility for public welfare, especially in educational matters. With the same argument of social responsibility, Brazilian businesses launched in 2006 the initiative "Todos pela Educação" (All for Education), with financial backing from the Inter-American Development Bank. Considered a powerful think tank in education, its influence is today much larger than merely disseminating in script and media their vision of education in the form of "good practices." Todos pela Educação uses the entire repertoire of influencing education policy in Brazil, ranging from monitoring progress to lobbying politicians for changes in legislation.

Lisa Richey and Stefano Ponte focus on the marketing aspect of business and scrutinize what marketing does to those for whom "charitable businesses" supposedly collect or spend money – that is, for the child, the poor, and the underdeveloped. They show that, in Brand Aid, the problems themselves and the people who experience them are branded and marketed to Northern consumers (through celebritized multi-media story-telling) just as effectively as the products that will "save" them (Richey and Stefano, Chapter 6).

Part II of the book focuses on the ambition of GEI to improve the public education system by privatizing it, that is, by using public funds for contracting the services of private providers of a different nature, often education corporations and consultancy firms. We entitled Part II as *Selling School Improvement*. Anna Hogan, Sam Sellar and Bob Lingard start out Part II of the book with a succinct analysis of the business strategy of the largest global education company: Pearson plc. They zoom in on the 2013 Efficacy Framework of Pearson to understand how "Pearson is looking for and creating opportunities in the education market *globally* and with a stated *social purpose* for this investment" (see Chapter 7, italics by chapter authors). However, Pearson CEO John Fallon commented in the 2012 annual report on the great prospects for business when Pearson starts expanding into developing countries:

Our growth prospects are also fuelled by a remarkable socio-economic trend: in this decade, the global middle class will almost double in size to more than three billion people. Nearly all of that growth will be in the developing world. That's important to many industries but especially to ours, because, as consumers join the middle class and earn higher incomes, they tend to invest more in education – either to advance their careers or give their children a good start in life.

(Joe Fallon, cited in Chapter 7: 110)

It is important to keep in mind that, as banal as this may sound, business-minded policy entrepreneurs do truly believe in the salutary effect of having multiple, competing providers in education. For them, privatization of education resolves the three challenges in education: access, equity and quality. The bottleneck in supply, negatively affecting the poor and those in remote areas, will supposedly get remedied by opening education up for non-state providers who *happily* get involved in the education sector because they see a lucrative business awaiting them. Perhaps the boldest move in this regard is the advice given by the McKinsey Company, financed by the UK Department for International Development and taken by the Government of Punjab, to invite entrepreneurs to step forward, establish new schools and claim vouchers, provided that the new school is in a location without a school or with a "failing school." Pakistan and Chile have been early laboratories for the education industry. We therefore invited Rabea Malik and Shailaha Fennell to consider the experience in Pakistan and Daniel Friedrich the new developments in Latin America. Fennell and Malik examine how, with the passage of time, private actors have been increasingly involved in education politics and policies in Pakistan. They demonstrate it by looking at three main spaces:

- the service delivery space, where the emergence of low-fee private actors has been particularly noticeable;
- the policy space, traditionally inhabited by multi- and bi-lateral donors and where the emergence of the international development consultancies (IDCs) is becoming evident; and
- the public–private partnership space, that has seen the rise of contracts between the state and both national and international business actors to provide, deliver and manage education.

(Chapter 9)

Friedrich makes a fascinating comparison: he contrasts the success of *Teach for All* in Chile and the failure of the same program in Argentina. In Chile, a country notorious for its voucher system that is foundering after many years of experimentation, privatization and deregulation, *Teach for All* was enthusiastically embraced as the new herald that would fix a fragmented and unequal school system. This was not the case at all in Argentina; *Teach for All*, established in 2007 and already working in more than 35 countries, set up operations in Argentina too but lacked clients. Friedrich's chapter focuses on the local encounters with global reform packages, notably with *Teach for All*.

Finally, two of the chapters in Part II deal with backstage as well as front stage advisors of governments and institutions: "consultocracy" in England (Helen Gunter and Colin Mills) and business consultancy in higher education (Gili S. Drori). Gunter and Mills present a nuanced contextual analysis of the consultancy business in UK education by dissecting in compelling detail what is "offered, what is taken, and what is used" in terms of advice given by over 50 consultants in the National Literacy Strategy. Drori draws on two empirical studies on branding in academia, in which she and her associates collected the emblems of over 1,000 universities worldwide, complemented with a case study of universities in Israel to investigate the advance of managerialism in higher education.

Part III of the book presents novel research on *new market niches*. It comprises noted scholars who have shaped the study of education businesses in major ways. Part III starts out with a chapter written by Diego Santori, Stephen J. Ball and Carolina Junemann. Without any doubt, their classification of business enterprises in education, presented in Chapter 12, is a foundation for future generations of scholars to delve into this new and fascinating area of educational research. They differentiate between specialized non-profit investment ventures (e.g. New Schools Venture Fund), specialized financial advisors (e.g. Global Silicon Valley Advisors), specialized education private equity investors (e.g. Kaplan Ventures), specialized incubators and accelerators (e.g. Imagine K–12), and specialized funds (e.g. the World Bank, with a $150 million equity stake in Laureate Education, Inc. through the International Finance Corporation). Using the Pearson Affordable Learning Fund as a case, the authors lay out a succinct sociological analysis of global business actors that benefit from, and propel, globalization in education.

Higher education is starting to become the "United States," "Chile" and "Pakistan" of the education sector: the vast territory where business is able to expand rapidly and with little regulation. In their chapter "Unbundling the University and Making Higher Education Markets," Susan L. Robertson and Janja Komljenovic observe and interpret remarkable new phenomena in higher education, such as, for example: INTO University Partnerships Ltd that created its first two joint ventures in 2006 with the University of East Anglia and the University of Exeter to attract international students. By 2015, it had expanded to 22 ventures, assisting universities in the United Kingdom, United States and China to recruit students from abroad. The sky seems to be the limit for profits made in such higher education businesses. INTO, for example, sold a 25 percent stake of its business for more than USD $100 million in 2013. Other businesses analyzed in the chapter are Laureate Education, Quacquarelli Symonds Limited, and LinkedIn. In 2015, LinkedIn made headlines in the media for setting up a business in which it sells data on the job placement and careers of its graduates. The next step is setting up a university ranking system based on employment criteria, challenging the current systems that focus on academic issues such as selectivity, research grants, publications, etc.

Also focusing on tertiary education, Eva Hartmann investigates the "parallel universe" of information and communication technology (ICT) certifiers. Hers is an interesting theoretical argument: "In order to study ICT certifiers in the context of privatization, we need to go beyond a notion of privatization that merely focuses on the opening up of public education to private, for-profit providers" (Hartmann, Chapter 14). Hartmann presents a sophisticated analysis of "endogenous privatization" (Ball) and provides a classification of different types of certifiers to demonstrate that today's certification industry represents a decentralized, fragmented and diversified field of transnational certifiers that no longer requires a government, a legislative body, or a profession for accreditation or legitimization.

The final two chapters of the book bring us full circle back to the first entry point for business: schools. Prachi Srivastava, one of the first authors to publish on low-fee public schools in developing countries, explores the evolution of low-fee private schools from "one-off mom-and-pop teaching shops" in schooling micro-ecosystems (e.g. individual villages, slum communities, and urban neighborhoods), to their coexistence with corporate-backed school chains and service providers (Srivastava, Chapter 15).

A manifestation of this second wave of corporate-run or corporate-backed low-fee private schools, Pearson's Affordable Learning Fund targets specifically low-fee private schools where the tuition ranges from USD $0.65 a day (Omega Schools) to USD $5 a month. Some of these enterprises, such as Bridge International Academies, are business conglomerates that operate in a dozen countries or more of sub-Saharan Africa and South Asia and receive funding from venture capital and private investment firms, personal investors as well as bilateral aid. Contrary to the expectations of GEI, Srivastava expresses doubt as to whether the corporate model of low-fee private schools is likely to be scaled up.

The edited volume ends with a chapter on GEMS (formerly known as Global Education Management Systems), written by Natasha Ridge, Susan Kippels and Soha Shami. As the authors point out, the GEMS corporation has been compared to a hotel chain for using a differentiated fee structure with different levels of service. In fact, GEMS founder and Managing Director Sunny Varkey himself unabashedly points out the philosophy of "you get what you pay for" as one of the key features of the GEMS business strategy: "We adopted the airline model of economy, business, and first class to make top-notch education available based on what families could afford" (Sunny Varkey, cited in Chapter 16). In its home city, Dubai, it enrolls one-quarter of all private school students. In 2014, GEMS ran 70 schools (in UAE, United States, United Kingdom, Kenya, India) and employed over 11,000 people worldwide. Throughout the book one cannot help but wonder: how do business tycoons in the GEI manage to make their business look like a charitable organization? The last chapter in this book provides a succinct answer: GEMS hooks up with UNESCO, OECD, the Clinton Global Initiative, the Brookings Institute and other reputable organizations. The Varkey Foundation granted, for example, USD$ 1 million to UNESCO's Global Partnership for Women's and Girl's Education program in Kenya and Lesotho and another undisclosed amount for UNESCO's school principal leadership programs in India, Ghana, and Kenya. These programs did not benefit GEMS but rather enabled UNESCO to receive funding for its programs. In the case of the GEMS corporation, UNESCO replicated the favor and appointed Varkey as Goodwill Ambassador for Education Partnerships. Ridge, Kippels and Shami round up this book with several social network analyses that demonstrate the kinship of the global education industry with governments, international organizations, think tanks, and charitable organizations.

To Conclude

Of course, proponents in favor of increasing the participation of private interests in education see advantages to the rise of GEI. Certainly, the sets of policies manifested in GEI allow for and encourage the use of private resources and capital in public education – a state-run sector that is often starved of funding. At the same time, proponents see advantages not just in accessing private resources for the public sector, but also in management approaches and principles that have proven successful for businesses and could conceivably be applied to schools as well. As we will see, this is not only an argument coming from businesses themselves, but also from private philanthropies built on business success, which then try to aid education both with investments and ideas. Another apparent advantage to the sets of policies represented in the GEI is that it thus allows the participation of new entrants – individuals and organizational forms – in educating a wider swath of the population than is typically served effectively by state systems. For example, online providers, teacher cooperatives, or education entrepreneurs are thought to offer new and innovative ideas that could afford opportunities for students underserved in the current system.

Still, there are obvious concerns voiced by critics and skeptics of the GEI in general, or of some of its individual actors. To the well-known concerns on market segmentation and educational inequalities as a consequence of education commodification, several scholars refer also to the challenges posed by the GEI in terms of democracy and accountability. The shift in authority from the state to private actors could arguably make sense on grounds of efficiency, but also necessarily entails some degree of undermining democratic control of public education (Lubienski 2006). Moreover, the professional autonomy and rights of teachers, as well as the local control of communities over their schools, may be undercut by the shift in authority to private, corporate, and global actors. Similarly, it is reasonable to question whether the shift in accountability structures away from democratic modes to corporate/consumer arrangements reshapes the orientation of education as a public good. That is, corporations are legally accountable primarily to their stockholders and must work first and foremost to create returns for those investors (Bakan 2004). Yet the interests of investors are not always aligned with those of clients or customers, or – in this case – those of students, their families, or their communities. As Bakan notes (cited in Ridge et al. in this volume):

> Unlike public institutions, whose only legitimate mandate is to serve the public good, corporations are legally required to always put their own interest above everyone else's. They may act in ways that promote the public good

when it is to their advantage to do so, but they will just as quickly sacrifice it – it is their obligation to do so – when necessary to serve their own ends.

Thus, between apparent advantages and pronounced concerns about the GEI, there is much that remains to be known. While there have been multiple studies on individual aspects of the GEI, often as it is manifested in individual countries, researchers need to better understand the conditions – both globally and nationally – which promote the expansion of GEI. This could entail cross-case analyses focusing on different countries, regions or localities. But it might also involve more in-depth studies of transnational organizations themselves, or include examinations of their partnerships, collaborations, or networks. Perhaps most importantly, researchers will need to conduct rigorous analyses of the effects of GEI actors, with particular focus not only on the claims made on their behalf – for example, in terms of increasing investment, innovation, and effectiveness – but also on the impacts on the education of *all* children, and particularly those from marginalized and disadvantaged communities.

Note

1 The only reference that this author makes in this book to something similar to a definition of the GEI is when he writes: "This monograph aims to give a flavor of the private education sector in developing countries – what I call the 'global education industry'" (Tooley 2001: 27).

References

Adrião, T., T. Garcia, R. Borghi and L. Arelaro. (2009). Uma Modalidade Peculiar de Privatizacão Da Educacão Pública: a Aquisicão de 'Sistemas de Ensino' Por Municípios Paulistas. *Educacão & Sociedade* 30 (108): 799–818.

Bakan, J. (2004). *The Corporation: The Pathological Pursuit of Profit and Power*. New York: Free Press.

Ball, Stephen. (2012). *Global Education Inc: New Policy Networks and the Neo-Liberal Imaginary*. London: Routledge.

Beckert, J. (2010). How Do Fields Change? The Interrelations of Institutions, Networks, and Cognition in the Dynamics of Markets. *Organization Studies* 31 (5): 605–627.

Benavot, A. (1992). Educational Expansion and Economic Growth in the Modern World, 1913–1985, in B. Fuller and R. Rubinson (eds) *The Political Construction of Education: The State, School Expansion, and Economic Change*. New York: Praeger, pp. 117–134.

Berndt, C. and Boeckler, M. (2009). Geographies of Circulation and Exchange: Constructions of Markets. *Progress in Human Geography* 33 (4): 535–551.

BMO Capital Markets (2014). *Education and Training*. Available at www.research-us. bmocapitalmarkets.com/.../EducationandTraining2012.pdf.

Bourdieu, P. (1993). *The Field of Cultural Production*. Cambridge: Polity Press.

Campbell, J. L. (2004). *Institutional Change and Globalisation*. Princeton, NJ: Princeton UP.

Cerny, P. G. (2010). The Competition State Today: From Raison d'État to Raison du Monde. *Policy Studies* 31 (1): 1, 5–21.

Engelen, E., R. Fernandez and R. Hendrikse (2014). How Finance Penetrates Its Other: a Cautionary Tale on the Financialization of a Dutch University. *Antipode* 46 (4): 1072–1091. doi: 10.1111/anti.12086.

Fernandez, R. M. and G. Hayward (2004). Qualifying for a Job: an Educational and Economic Audit of the English 14–19 Education and Training System, in G. Hayward and S. James (eds) *Balancing the Skills Equation: Key Issues for Policy and Practice.* Bristol: Policy Press, pp. 77–100.

Fitz, J. and T. Hafid (2007). Perspectives on the Privatization of Public Schooling in England and Wales. *Educational Policy* 21: 273 DOI: 10.1177/0895904806297193.

Fligstein, N. (2007). The Sociology of Markets. *Annual Review of Sociology* 33: 105–128.

GSV Advisors (2012). *Fall of the Wall: Capital Flows to Education Innovation.* Available at: http://gsvadvisors.com/wordpress/wp-content/themes/gsvadvisors/GSV%20Advisors_Fall%20of%20the%20Wall_2012-06-28.pdf.

Jessop, B., N. Fairclough and R. Wodak (2008). *Education and the Knowledge-Based Economy in Europe.* Rotterdam: Sense Publishers.

Kamens, D. H. (2013). Globalization and the Emergence of an Audit Culture: PISA and the Search for 'Best Practices' and Magic Bullets, in H. D. Meyer and A. Benavot (eds) *PISA, Power, and Policy: the Emergence of Global Educational Governance.* Oxford: Symposium, pp 117–140.

Kuttner, R. (1999). *Everything for Sale: The Virtues and Limits of Markets.* New York: University of Chicago Press.

Labaree, D. F. (2007). *Education, Markets, and the Public Good: The Selected Works of David F. Labaree.* New York: Routledge.

Lingard, B., S. Rawolle and S. Taylor (2005). Globalizing Policy Sociology in Education: Working with Bourdieu. *Journal of Education Policy* 20 (6): 759–777.

Lubienski, C. (2006). School Choice and Privatization in Education: An Alternative Analytical Framework. *Journal for Critical Education Policy Studies* 4 (1).

Lubienski, C. (2014). Re-Making the Middle: Dis-Intermediation in International Context. *Educational Management Administration and Leadership* 42 (3): 423–440. doi: 10.1177/1741143214521594.

Metcalf, H. (2005). Paying for University: the Impact of Increasing Costs on Student Employment, Debt and Satisfaction. *National Institute Economic Review* 191 (1): 106–117.

Mundy, K. and F. Menashy (2012). The Role of the International Finance Corporation in the Promotion of Public–Private Partnerships for Educational Development, in Robertson, S., K. Mundy, A. Verger and F. Menashy (2012). *Public Private Partnerships in Education: New Actors and Modes of Governance in a Globalizing World.* London: Edward Elgar, pp. 81–103.

OECD (2014). *Proposal for an Annual Summit of the Global Education Industry.* CERI Governing Board Document, code EDU/CERI/CD(2014)19.

Oreskes, N. and E. M. Conway (2010). *Merchants of Doubt: How a Handful of Scientists Obscured the Truth on Issues from Tobacco Smoke to Global Warming.* New York: Bloomsbury Press.

Ramirez, F. O., X. Luo, E. Schofer and J. W. Meyer (2006). Student Achievement and National Economic Growth. *American Journal of Education* 113 (1): 1–29.

Robertson, S., X. Bonal and R. Dale (2002). GATS and the Education Services Industry: The Politics of Scale and Global Reterritorialisation. *Comparative Education Review* 46 (4), 472–496.

Sandel, M. J. (2012). *What Money Can't Buy: The Moral Limits of Markets.* New York: Farrar, Straus and Giroux.

Sellar, S. and B. Lingard (2014). The OECD and the Expansion of PISA: New Global Modes of Governance in Education. *British Educational Research Journal* 40 (6): 917–936.

Specter, M. (2010). *Denialism: How Irrational Thinking Hinders Scientific Progress, Harms the Planet, and Threatens Our Lives.* New York: Penguin Press.

Tooley, J. (2001). *The global education industry: Lessons from private education in developing countries.* (2nd ed.). Washington, DC: The International Finance Corp.

Tyack, D. and L. Cuban (1995). *Tinkering toward Utopia: A Century of Public School Reform.* Cambridge, MA: Harvard University Press.

UNESCO (2014). Teaching and Learning: Achieving Quality for All, *EFA Global Monitoring Report 2013/14.* Paris: UNESCO.

Valiente, O. (2010). 1-1 in Education: Current Practice, International Comparative Research Evidence and Policy Implications *OECD Education Working Papers,* No. 44. Paris: OECD.

Verger, A. (2010). *WTO/GATS and the Global Politics of Higher Education.* New York: Routledge.

Waldow, F., K. Takayama and Y. K. Sung (2014). Rethinking the Pattern of External Policy Referencing: Media Discourses over the 'Asian Tigers'. PISA Success in Australia, Germany and South Korea. *Comparative Education* 50 (3): 302–321.

Part I

Shaping Education Agendas

2 The Role of the Gates Foundation and the Philanthropic Sector in Shaping the Emerging Education Market

Lessons from the US on Privatization of Schools and Education Governance

Wayne Au and Christopher Lubienski

Introduction

The emerging global education industry is not necessarily based in for-profit business models for schooling. While profit-seeking corporations have certainly had a significant role in the rise of the global education industry, non-profit entities have played a substantial role in shaping emerging education markets at the local and global levels. While these philanthropies, foundations, and advocacy organizations do not themselves explicitly pursue profits, many have in fact been established and funded by capital accumulated through business enterprises. Indeed, as we demonstrate in this chapter, civic-minded philanthropists are pursuing reform of state-funded school sectors as a way of applying business principles to school governance and operations, with important implications for the role of democratic processes in both schooling and policymaking.

As a case in point, with its fragmented education governance structures, the United States has been a prime site for the growth of corporate influence on education policymaking. In recent reforms, though, further changes to the governance schemes that *centralize* authority have led to the even greater influence of interest groups. In these concurrent processes of centralization and decentralization, meso-level governance is weakened, allowing these interest groups access to cash-starved localities as well as centralized policymaking processes (Lubienski 2014). While corporate interests have certainly taken advantage of these opportunities to marketize the public school sector, in this chapter we demonstrate that "non-profit" groups such as philanthropic interests have been leading the way in this restructuring, and in exerting greater authority over American schools in ways that can also advance corporate interests. In this chapter we use the Bill and Melinda Gates Foundation as an example of one particularly powerful actor within public education policy development and implementation in the US. We start here with a brief overview of neoliberalism, the role of the state, and the concept of network governance. We then move onto a brief history of the Gates Foundation and its education reform efforts, paying specific attention to the role of Bill Gates Jr. and the Foundation's disproportionate influence over the passage of charter school law in Washington State – as an example of network governance in the neoliberal state. The concluding discussion considers the implications of these models both for school governance and for democratic forms of policymaking.

Governance and the Rise of the Neoliberal State

Neoliberal economic and social policy has become hegemonic in the world today. The first large-scale, neoliberal experiment took place in Chile when, in 1973, with the help of the United States' Central Intelligence Agency, Augosto Pinochet violently overthrew the democratic socialist government of Salvador Allende, and the Chilean economy was subsequently restructured in ways that privatized public assets, loosened trade restrictions, allowed foreign investments, and enabled natural resources to be exploited by private entities (Klein 2007). In the more than four decades since, policies and international agreements supporting neoliberal free trade and the privatization of public goods and services have exploded around the globe (Harvey 2007).

As a basic definition, Harvey (2007) explains that neoliberalism is "a theory of political economic practices proposing that human well-being can be best advanced by the maximization of entrepreneurial freedoms within an institutional framework characterized by private property rights, individual liberty, unencumbered markets, and free trade" (Harvey 2007: 22). Similarly, but with slightly different nuance, Lipman (2011) defines neoliberalism as:

> an ensemble of economic and social policies, forms of governance, and discourses of ideologies that promote self-interest, unrestricted flows of capital, deep reductions in the cost of labor, and sharp retrenchment of the public sphere. Neoliberals champion privatization of social good and withdrawal of government from provision for social welfare on the premise that competitive markets are more effective and efficient.
>
> (Lipman 2011: 6)

For our purposes, we consider neoliberalism as an approach that, while it can endorse liberal values such as equity and even equality, elevates economic individualism and market mechanisms as policy mechanisms preferable to state action for achieving those – or almost any other – ends. Because of its ideological and economic commitment to free markets, neoliberalism places high value on deregulation, private competition, and the reduction of collective interests often expressed through government institutions whose express purpose is to serve the broader public – institutions such as state-provided public education. Thus it is critical to also address the role of the state government within the neoliberal framework.

Neoliberalism, and its academic iteration as "public choice theory," views state regulation and state intervention as obstacles to free market competition (Lubienski 2006b). The public-choice critique targets public administration of public goods and services as inherently untenable due to the susceptibility of state power to private interests. As such, neoliberals desire the existence of a very small state government with limited function, and with those entities that remain under state control adopting principles of management to the greatest extent possible. In this regard the neoliberal state exists to help maintain the integrity of currency, maintain defense and police forces, and keep some semblance of a judiciary system, all in support of maintaining rights to private property and keeping the markets free and open. Further, the neoliberal state must support the creation of markets in all areas in which they do not yet exist, including in state-administered goods and services (Harvey 2007).

In addition to shifting public assets into the purview of private interest, another critical outcome of the shrinking neoliberal state is a shift in public power and the responsibilities of governing from citizens, taxpayers and voters into the hands of "customers" or service "users" and unelected private interests unaccountable to the voting and tax-paying public. Lipman (2011) explains this as a fundamental shift from *government* to *governance*:

> The "triumph of market ideology" is coupled with an erosion of the idea that informed citizens should make decisions based on the general welfare. The shift from *government* by elected state bodies and a degree of democratic accountability to *governance* by experts and managers and decision making by judicial authority and executive order is central to neoliberal policy making ... Public–private partnerships, appointed managers, and publicly unaccountable bodies comprised of appointed state and corporate leaders make decisions about urban development, transportation, schools, and other public infrastructure using business rationales. In these arrangements, the state acts as an agent of capital.
>
> (Lipman 2011: 13)

Thus, as part of the movement towards privatization, the neoliberal state concentrates power in private, unaccountable interests that operate through systems of network governance (Ball 2012). In these systems of network governance, wealthy elites, foundations, NGOs, non-profit and for-profit organizations, publishing companies, professional consultants, and corporate leaders are relied upon to shape policy and are paid for direct services to the public, including public education (Au and Ferrare 2014; Burch 2006; Fabricant and Fine 2013; Scott and Jabbar 2014). In recent years, the system of public education in the United States has witnessed the rise in network governance in education policy and reform.

Since the 2002 passage of the *No Child Left Behind Act* during the Bush II Administration, and with continued support through President Obama's and Secretary of Education Arne Duncan's "Race to the Top" initiative, private interests have seen their power over public education increase exponentially, and this power has largely manifest through systems of network governance (Au and Ferrare 2015; Barkan 2011, 2012; Buras 2014; Lipman 2011). In the US, large philanthropic foundations, particularly the Eli and Edythe Broad Foundation, the Walton Family Foundation, and the Bill and Melinda Gates Foundation (Barkan 2011; Ravitch 2010, 2013; Reckhow 2013), have become powerful actors in these networks.

In what follows we turn to arguably the most powerful philanthropic actor in network governance, the Bill and Melinda Gates Foundation (hereafter referred to as the Gates Foundation) as a case and starting point for understanding the power of the non-profit philanthropic sector in shaping education markets and playing a role in the privatization of public education. Our analysis starts in the State of Washington, home of the Gates Foundation, to illustrate its outsized influence in advancing charter schools there, but then traces the efforts of Gates and other major philanthropies in advocating at the national and international levels for neo-liberal education reforms that push back the position of democratic institutions in favor of corporate-style institutions and environments for education.

The Gates Foundation represents an appropriate subject for this analysis, since it is the largest philanthropy in the US and the world, is the largest philanthropy with a stated focus on education issues, and has become the dominant player in setting both the philanthropic and policymaking agendas on many issues. The Foundation has been active in a number of areas, including childhood vaccinations and the eradication of disease. But some of its most controversial work has been in education reform – controversial not just for the contested nature of the policies it promotes, but also because of the pre-eminent role the Foundation enjoys in policymaking processes (Layton 2014).

The Gates Foundation and Education Reform

The US has seen a series of private philanthropies and foundations seeking to reform public education, from the Annenberg Challenge to the Carnegie Unit. Typically, these were seen as efforts to "give back" by fixing or strengthening public schools; more recent efforts from philanthropists such as the Gates, Broad, and Walton Foundations have leveraged unprecedented amounts of money to shape education policymaking, often embracing business-style market mechanisms for public schools (Lubienski et al. in press). The Gates Foundation started in 2000 with roughly $30 billion (USD) of Gates' own money, which was then supplemented with roughly another $30 billion from Warren Buffet. The Gates Foundation increased its giving to education advocacy groups from $276,000 in 2002 to nearly $57 million in 2005, and this giving was made almost exclusively to neo-liberal, corporate education reform non-profits, which included Education Trust, Achieve, the Progressive Policy Institute, and the National Alliance for Public Charter Schools, amongst others (Ravitch 2010). According to the National Committee for Responsive Philanthropy, in 2005 the Gates Foundation was also the fourth-largest donor to organizations promoting vouchers to send children from public schools to private schools, granting them $2.6 million (Klonsky 2011). In their study, Kovacs and Christie (2011) found that, between 1999 and 2007, the Gates Foundation gave 441 organizations – neoconservative think tanks (Fordham Foundation and the Manhattan Institute), neoliberal think tanks (Education Trust and Education Sector), various state departments, public school districts and charter (publicly funded but privately or independently managed) school organizations – over $3 billion for a range of education-related activities.

It is important to note that this number is low, considering the accelerated activity of the Gates Foundation in education since 2007. For instance, since roughly 2009, when the Common Core State Standards initiative was first spearheaded, the Gates Foundation has spent $233 million on not just the development of the standards, but also creating political support for the adoption and implementation of the standards through the funding of a range of organizations that includes both major teachers unions in the US, liberal and conservative think tanks, nonprofit organizations, and research centers (Layton 2014).

The Gates Foundation agenda did not originally have so much of a focus on charter schools, but, like many other neoliberal reformers, came to embrace the model, likely because they represented a relatively easy, politically palatable route for introducing market mechanisms such as choice and competition to public education (Lubienski and Weitzel 2010). In 1999, Gates hired Tom VanderArk to run the Foundation's $6 billion education program, and specifically to reform the traditional, comprehensive high school into small schools/small learning communities (Klonsky 2011). From 2000 to 2008, the Gates Foundation spent $2 billion on the small schools effort, reaching 2,600 schools in 45 states and the District of Columbia. The small schools reform generally did not produce the promised increases in achievement; for instance, it failed miserably in Denver and outside of Seattle, and supposed gains in places such as New York City turned out to be elusive (Ravitch 2010). The Gates-led effort failed because, contrary to the more successful, community-based small school reforms that came before it, the Gates-backed small schools movement was an outside-in, top-down reform that viewed teachers as needing to be controlled instead of consulted/included, and typically left parents and students out of the process entirely (Klonsky and Klonsky 2008).

Having found mostly failure in its small schools effort, the Gates Foundation quietly shifted gears towards other reforms, including an increased emphasis on charter schools. As Klonsky explains:

> Several of the largest foundations, including Gates, began advising school districts and state departments of education to steer clear of SLCs [small learning communities] and concentrate instead on closing low-performing schools and replacing them exclusively with new start-ups or charter schools.
> (2011: 25)

For instance, the Gates Foundation became a primary financial supporter of Renaissance 2010 in Chicago, giving over $90 million to a reform effort which included closing 100 schools with the intent of re-opening two-thirds of them as charter schools or schools managed by outside agencies (Barkan 2011; Hursh 2011).

This shift, of course, did not happen overnight. As early as 2000, the Gates Foundation gave almost $100 million to charter management organizations, including the NewSchools Venture Fund, Communities Foundation of Texas, New Visions for Public Schools in New York City, and the Alliance for Education in Seattle, among others (Ravitch 2010). Indeed, as former Gates Foundation education head VanderArk points out regarding the more recent push for charter schools:

The "new" education agenda didn't get written last month: it's been a decade in the making … Since 2001, the charter school movement has become a powerful force backed by funding from Gates, Broad, Walton, Fisher, and Robertson foundations. Active charter school advocates include The National Alliance of Public Charter Schools, Center for Education Reform, and funding coalitions including New Schools and Charter School Growth Fund.

(2012: n.p.)

This shift has also been welcomed with open political arms, as prominent Gates staffers have taken key jobs with both Democratic and Republican administrations. For example, under President Obama's administration, the Chief of Staff for Secretary of Education Arne Duncan, Margot Rogers, was a special assistant to the director of education at the Gates Foundation. Similarly, James Shelton, who had earlier been the program director for the education division of the Gates Foundation, now serves as the Assistant Deputy Secretary for Innovation and Improvement in the Obama Administration (Klonsky 2011). While not nearly as expansive as searching for specific charter management organizations, advocacy groups, and research centers, a simple search for "charter school" in the Gates Foundation grant database produces 54 grants totaling $188,740,147.00 (Bill and Melinda Gates Foundation 2015).

The Case of the Gates Foundation and Charter School Reform in Washington State

The campaign to legalize charter schools in the US state of Washington clearly illustrates how Bill Gates Jr. and the Gates Foundation both construct and use forms of network governance to advance their policy agenda and provides an example of how policy is increasingly developed in the neoliberal state more generally. Additionally, this case further illustrates how philanthropies and wealthy elites use network governance more generally to advance their policy agendas.

Charter School Policy in Washington State and Initiative 1240

While 42 states and the District of Columbia in the US have charter school legislation, in virtually all cases, these schools have been established by lawmakers and not by voters. Indeed, voters often reject them. Washington State has a unique history when it comes to the issue of charter schools. The state system allows for popular votes on whether or not various initiatives (put on the ballot by petition) become law, and there have been four opportunities for the public to decide if charter schools would be allowed in the state. Three times voters have rejected charter schools: in 1996, only 36 percent voted in favor of charters; in 2000, 48.2 percent voted in favor of charters; and in 2004 only 41.7 percent voted in favor of charters (Corcoran and Stoddard 2011).

Functionally, the lead up to I-1240 began in Washington in January 2012, when two companion charter school bills were introduced into the state house and senate (Rosenthal 2012). Among other details, these laws set a specific number of charter schools to be authorized over five years, established three charter school authorizers, established "transformational zone districts" allowing for state takeover of low performing schools, and included a parent–teacher charter conversion trigger that would allow a majority of teachers or parents to petition to convert an existing public school into a charter school (Westbrook 2012). In early 2012, legislation allowing charter schools in Washington State was killed in committee by state Democratic Party leadership (Seattle Times Editorial Board 2012). Charter school advocates in the state soon after drafted Initiative 1240, which was filed with the State of Washington by Tania de Sa Campos, a staff worker for a local non-profit advocacy organization, the League of Education Voters (League of Education Voters 2012a; Sa Campos 2012).

Similar to the state-level legislative bills introduced earlier in 2012, I-1240 was structured to establish 40 charter schools over five years, create two charter authorizers (local school boards or an appointed state level charter school commission), set up appointed individual charter school boards for individual charter oversight, and allow for a parent–teacher charter conversion trigger, among other details (Au 2012). Bill Gates Jr., along with members of Amazon. com's Bezos family, venture capitalist Nick Hanauer, and Microsoft co-founder Paul Allen, among others, contributed $2.26 million in donations to collect signatures to successfully put I-1240 on the Washington ballot for November 2012 (Callaghan 2012).

I-1240 supporters Stand for Children, League of Education Voters, Partnership for Learning, and Democrats For Education Reform (DFER) coalesced to co-found the Washington Coalition for Public Charter Schools (Washington Coalition for Public Charter Schools 2012b), publicly taking responsibility for directing the Yes On 1240 campaign (Washington Coalition for Public Charter Schools 2012a) – a role verified by state databases cataloguing their "in-kind" donations of staff time and resources to all aspects of the campaign (Washington State Public Disclosure Commission 2012c). By election day, November 6, 2012, the Yes On 1240 campaign had amassed $10.9 million in donations (Washington State Public Disclosure Commission 2012a). At the time, the amount donated to the Yes On 1240 Campaign was the third most money spent on an initiative campaign in state history (Washington State Public Disclosure Commission 2012d). The Yes On 1240 campaign used these millions for phone banking, direct mailing, on-the-ground field organizing, and signs, and they were able to devote over $5 million specifically for web, radio, and television advertising (Washington State Public Disclosure Commission 2012b).

Three weeks before election day, in conjunction with researchers from the Gates-funded Center on Reinventing Public Education (CRPE) at the University of Washington, Partnership for Learning (2012a) published *Examining Charters: How Public Charter Schools Can Work in Washington State* (Lake et al. 2012), a report which makes several explicit references to I-1240 as a good charter school law. CRPE founder and charter school advocate Paul Hill was also prominently featured in a Yes On 1240 television advertisement advocating for the passage of

I-1240 (Yes on 1240 2012). In November 2012, citizens of Washington State voted to approve I-1240 with a 50.69 percent majority, or 41,682 votes out of just over 3,020,000 total cast (Reed 2012).

Bill Gates Jr. and the Gates Foundation have made a concerted effort to lay the groundwork for charter schools in Washington State primarily through three means: (1) large donations from Bill Gates Jr. individually (as well as other charter school supporters from the technology sector and former Microsoft employees) to the Yes On 1240 campaign; (2) the select funding of local non-profit organizations to lend community credibility to their policy agenda; and (3) the select funding of a pro-charter research center to attempt to lend empirical credibility to their policy agenda. Tracing the flow of resources around and through the Yes On 1240 campaign provides us with the opportunity to see exactly how Bill Gates Jr. and his philanthropic arm, the Gates Foundation, as well as other wealthy elites and their associated philanthropies, were able to utilize network governance to influence charter school policy in the State of Washington.

Yes On 1240 Campaign Contributions

For our analysis we looked at publicly available campaign records for the US state of Washington. Table 1 indicates the contributions to the Yes On 1240 campaign at an amount of $100,000 or greater:

These 17 contributions constitute over 95 percent of the $10.9 million total donated to the Yes On 1240 campaign. Of those 17 donors, 9 were connected either to Bill Gates Jr. through Microsoft or to the Gates Foundation through simultaneous funding of charter-related non-profits and research centers. These Gates-connected donors accounted for just over $8.32 million or just over 76 percent of the total Yes On I-1240 campaign donations (Washington State Public Disclosure Commission 2012a). Even for the donors without a Gates-specific connection, it is worth highlighting that several come from the technology sector as well, as opposed to, say, having a background in education.

Funding of Local, Pro-Charter Non-Profit and Advocacy Organizations

In addition to direct cash contributions to the Yes On 1240 campaign, Bill Gates Jr.'s philanthropic arm, the Bill and Melinda Gates Foundation, also funds the locally based non-profits directly responsible for coordinating the campaign. In what follows, we list the funding each organization has received from the Gates Foundation. However, while our focus is primarily on the specific influence of Bill Gates Jr. and the Gates Foundation on the campaign to legalize charter schools in Washington State, we also include both the Broad Foundation's and the Walton Foundation's support for these organizations, for two reasons. First, representatives of both the Broad and Walton family fortunes made major individual contributions to the Yes On I-1240 campaign (see Table 2.1). Second, together with the Gates Foundation, the Broad and Walton Foundations constitute the "big three" philanthropies currently involved with shaping education policy reform

Table 2.1 Yes on I-1240 campaign contributions of $100,000 and over

	Yes on I-1240 Donor	Donation Amount
1	Bill Gates Jr. – Microsoft co-founder and current chairman, co-founder of the Bill and Melinda Gates Foundation	$3,000,000.00
2	Alice Walton – Heiress daughter of Wal-Mart founder Sam Walton; board member of the Walton Family Foundation	$1,700,000.00
3	Vulcan Inc. – Founded by Paul Allen, Microsoft co-founder	$1,600,000.00
4	Nicolas Hanauer – Venture capitalist, early investor in Amazon.com, Board of Directors at LEV	$1,000,000.00
5	Mike Bezos – Father of Amazon.com founder Jeff Bezos	$500,000.00
6	Jackie Bezos – Mother of Amazon.com founder Jeff Bezos	$500,000.00
7	Connie Ballmer – Wife of Microsoft CEO Steve Ballmer	$500,000.00
8	Anne Dinning – Managing director of hedge fund giant, D. E. Shaw Investments	$250,000.00
9	Michael Wolf – Yahoo! Inc. Board of Directors	$250,000.00
10	Katherine Binder – EMFCO Holdings Chairwoman	$250,000.00
11	Eli Broad – Real estate mogul, founder of the Eli and Edythe Broad Foundation	$200,000.00
12	Doris Fisher – Gap co-founder	$100,000.00
13	Reed Hastings – CEO of Netflix, founding investor of the New Schools Venture Fund	$100,000.00
14	Microsoft Corporation	$100,000.00
15	Gabe Newell – formerly of Microsoft, co-founder of video game developer Valve Corporation	$100,000.00
16	Benjamin Slivka – formerly of Microsoft, co-founder of DreamBox Learning	$124,200.00
17	Kemper Holdings LLC – local Puget Sound developer	$110,000.00

Source: Washington State Public Disclosure Commission (2012a).

in the United States, and their agendas have converged in recent years (Barkan 2011; Lubienski *et al.* in press; Ravitch 2010). Thus, the individual contributions of the Broad and Walton families, as well as their respective foundations' material support of non-profit organizations and research that are both directly and indirectly related to the Yes On I-1240 campaign represent how, even in a limited case such as that of Washington State and I-1240, the big three venture philanthropies leverage their education policy agenda by developing mutually sustaining networks of charter school advocacy (see also Scott *et al.* 2009). As such, both the Broad and Walton Foundations are present and affiliated to Bill Gates Jr. and the Gates Foundation through their respective campaign contributions and shared reform efforts.

LOCAL PRO-CHARTER NON-PROFIT: THE LEAGUE OF EDUCATION VOTERS

The League of Education Voters (LEV) is a local non-profit advocacy group that has a history of working for a wide range of education reforms, including lowering class sizes, increasing opportunities for early learning, interrupting the schools-to-prisons pipeline, and pushing for increases in Washington State's funding for public education (League of Education Voters 2012b). In recent years, LEV has also shifted its focus to embrace aspects of the national, corporate-driven educational reform movement including Race to the Top and charter schools. LEV has received nearly $8 million from the Gates Foundation since 2002 (Bill and Melinda Gates Foundation 2015). This funding included a 2011 grant for LEV to write an education reform platform based on Washington State's Race to the Top application.

LOCAL (AND NATIONAL) PRO-CHARTER NON-PROFIT: STAND FOR CHILDREN

Stand for Children is a national organization with chapters in multiple states, including Washington. They originated in the late 1990s with an expressed commitment to improving the lives of poor children through fighting for healthcare for the uninsured, for affordable, high quality child care, for safe and productive after-school activities, and for classrooms with lower class sizes, well trained teachers, and increased parent involvement. Similar to LEV, Stand for Children has made a shift in recent years, including a change in leadership, and its agenda has come to embrace charter schools and undermining the teachers unions as part of the broader, bipartisan corporate education reform movement (Libby and Sanchez 2012). The Gates Foundation has given Stand for Children $9 million in grants and contracts for a range of education reform-related activities (Bill and Melinda Gates Foundation 2013; Foundation Center 2013). While it is not clear exactly how much of this money comes directly to the Washington State chapter, it is clear that Stand for Children is now organizationally aligned with the Gates agenda for public education reform. Stand for Children has also received just over $2.8 million from the Walton Family Foundation (Foundation Center 2013; Stand for Children 2013).

LOCAL PRO-CHARTER NON-PROFIT: PARTNERSHIP FOR LEARNING

Partnership For Learning is a local non-profit that sees its role as working to prepare high school graduates "for the demands of today's global society" (Partnership For Learning 2012b np). Partnership For Learning received $4.7 million in Gates Foundation funding 1999–2009 mostly to focus on common core and increasing test scores (Bill and Melinda Gates Foundation 2013). They consider themselves to be partners with LEV and Stand for Children, and together they lead the Excellent Schools Now Coalition (Partnership For Learning 2012a).

Democrats for Education Reform (DFER) is a national political action committee with branches in multiple states, including Washington. DFER has supported education reforms that include using high-stakes, standardized tests to evaluate teachers, merit pay schemes for teachers, mayoral control, and the promotion of charter schools, among others (Democrats for Education Reform 2012b; Harris 2012; Libby 2012). More relevant to the current analysis is that Lisa Macfarlane, a co-founder of LEV, was the State Director of DFER Washington during the Yes On 1240 campaign (Democrats for Education Reform 2012a). While, as a political action committee, DFER is not funded by the Gates Foundation, it has received over $2.4 million from the Broad Foundation and $600,000 from the Doris and Donald Fisher fund (Foundation Center 2013; Libby 2012; New York State Office of the Attorney General 2013), which as noted above are both prominent donors to the Yes On 1240 campaign.

Funding the Pro-Charter Research Center

In terms of educational research, the major Washington-based research center funded by the Gates Foundation is the Center on Reinventing Public Education (CRPE), which is fiscally housed at the University of Washington, but is physically located off campus in the city of Seattle (Center on Reinventing Public Education 2012). The CRPE does education policy research, including studies and reports largely in support of charter schools, and its former and current directors Paul Hill and Robin Lake, respectively, regularly speak on charter school "success" in increasing the achievement of low income and students of color (see Washington State Parent Teachers Association 2012).

University of Washington internal records indicate that the CRPE has received over $8,578,000 in grants and contracts total since its founding (University of Washington Bothell Office of Sponsored Programs 2013). The pro-charter bent of the CRPE research agenda secures the support of the Gates Foundation, and in turn the CRPE-produced reports and staff of the CRPE lend an air of research expertise to the Gates Foundation charter school policy agenda.

Together, these three elements of (1) focusing philanthropic interests to (2) fund local (and national) political advocacy (3) supported by hired advocacy researchers represent an effective strategy for influential funders like Gates. And it is a strategy we see replicated at the national and international levels as market-based school reform serves as a key conduit for the emerging global education industry.

The Implications of Philanthropic Policy Advocacy

In this chapter, we have highlighted the ways that groups such as the Gates Foundation have exercised their influence in effecting policy change. This case is particularly interesting because the Gates Foundation succeeded in promoting its agenda on a broader basis, through the electorate, in a way that decentralizes school authority. But at the same time, Gates funds many charter school management organizations that are positioned to benefit from that devolution of authority to the school level. At the same time, Gates has exerted influence on centralized modes of authority, for example, through close connections to federal administrations that promulgated or supported the No Child Left Behind Act, the Race to the Top initiative, and the Common Core State Standards. Notably, the results are not simply a matter of shifting to a more privatized school system, but privatizing the policymaking process itself, as philanthropists such as Gates re-write the rules in their own favor, and then distribute resources in ways that advance their agendas in those new policy landscapes (Scott et al. 2009). Thus, these private philanthropies are not just influencing public policy, but are private policymakers, unaccountable to the broader public.

As we have shown, there is a discernable strategy in this case of the Washington charter school initiative. The Gates Foundation was a big player in getting this issue on the policy agenda, and was assisted by other philanthropies that shared this interest, even when they may have disagreed on other policy particulars such as, say, vouchers or merit pay. So it was not simply a matter of Gates's funding driving the issue, but leadership from the Gates Foundation apparently motivating other interests to follow suit. Similarly, Gates's funding appears to have been a crucial element in re-orienting and driving the efforts of local (and state/national) intermediary organizations that advanced this initiative (Lubienski et al. 2011). Finally, these philanthropies provided support for the production of research to lend empirical legitimacy for this cause. In this case, it was a university-based research outfit – something we are witnessing when similar policy proposals are championed by university-based outfits such as PEPG at Harvard, or the Department of Education Reform at the University of Arkansas, both of which have received funding from the Gates or an allied philanthropy (Lubienski and Weitzel 2008).

Of course, the Gates Foundation is but one – albeit the major – player in education reform in the world today. And the efforts of Gates and its philanthropic partners in Washington State, as well as in Washington DC, Davos, and the halls of power around the globe, are effectively contributing to the nurturing of a global education industry. For instance, the fingerprints of these US philanthropists are very clearly evident on national-level reforms in the US such as the Common Core State Standards (Layton 2014), as well as on international efforts such as PISA-based tests for schools and Teach For All (TFAll) (Goel La Londe et al. in press). Such efforts together represent important elements of the neoliberal reform agenda, as they promote the market mechanisms of competition, consumer-style choice, and alternatives to state-administered schooling.

Of course, there are many valid concerns with state administration of schools, as aptly expressed in neoliberal or public-choice theory critiques of state education systems (Chubb and Moe 1990). Such systems can be prone to inefficiency, can be unresponsive to the needs of students and their families, and can be "captured" by special interests such as bureaucracies and teachers' unions. Consequently, moving away from the state-administered model by letting new entrants such as charter schools access public monies, or new non- and for-profits such as TFAll or Pearson offer services previously provided only by the state represents an attractive alternative. In many cases, these new approaches do not necessarily "privatize" the system, as some critics contend (Ravitch 2013). Instead, they can rely primarily on the non-profit sector to advance reforms of the state system.

Certainly, though, the non-profit philanthropists pushing these types of reforms are leveraging policies that enhance the market-style environment in the school sector. Even if these policies do not "privatize" schools, they serve to elevate market mechanisms that offer competition for the state sector, creating quasi-markets, as is prescribed by public-choice theorists. For instance, charter schools are designed as choice-based schools that must attract families or "go out of business" (Gilder 1999; Gove 2012; Ravitch 2010). As such, they are positioned to draw students away from "failing" state schools in order to induce those schools to improve, or themselves lose funding, thereby injecting market-style competition into the publicly funded sector (Lubienski and Weitzel 2010). Moreover, such schools are modeled largely on business principles such as operational autonomy and managerial entrepreneurialism – reflecting the business-world experiences of the philanthropists who promote them. Thus, even if they do not privatize public education, these policies effectively marketize the system by giving the public sector a more market-like institutional environment. And, as economists of the non-profit sector have shown, that can often have similar consequences (Kapur and Weisbrod 2000; Lubienski 2006a; Weisbrod 1998). That is, even non-profit entities can adopt more profit-seeking behaviors when faced with competition from for-profits; evidence of this is appearing in a mixed sector of education markets (Lacireno-Paquet et al. 2002; Lubienski et al. 2013).

The philanthropic interests, such as the Gates Foundation, that are pushing these models for education are certainly having an impact in changing the institutional orientation of schools (Scott 2008; Scott and DiMartino 2010). And there are legitimate questions about how this might be reshaping education governance in ways that crowd out traditional forms of democratic voice schooling (Lubienski and Lubienski 2014). But another concern is the degree to which these philanthropic interests are exercising influence through policy networks in ways that may be detrimental to democratic control of policymaking processes (Au and Ferrare 2015).

Indeed, frustrated by the ineffectiveness of the political control of state schooling, philanthropies have taken the lead in creating network governance structures that they see as a opportunity to apply managerial or business approaches to intractable problems in education, often under a rhetoric of equal educational opportunity. Yet, as these networks become permeated by and oriented toward private, philanthropic interests, these corporate models often emerge by supplanting democratic forms of governance in education systems.

References

Au, W. (2012, October 22). Policy memo on Washington State Initiative 1240. Retrieved May 31, 2015 from: http://seattleducation2010.wordpress.com/2012/10/22/policy-memo-on-washington-state-initiative-1240/.

Au, W. and Ferrare, J. J. (2014). Sponsors of policy: A network analysis of wealthy elites, their affiliated philanthropies, and charter school reform in Washington State. *Teachers College Record, 116*(8), 1–24. Retrieved May 31, 2015 from: http://crecord.org/content.asp?contentid=17387.

Au, W. and Ferrare, J. J. (Eds). (2015). *Mapping corporate education reform: Power and policy networks in the neoliberal state.* New York: Routledge.

Ball, S. J. (2012). *Policy networks and new governance.* New York: Taylor & Francis.

Barkan, J. (2011). Got dough? How billionaires rule our schools. *Dissent, 58*(1), 49–57.

Barkan, J. (2012). Hired guns on astroturf: How to buy and sell school reform. *Dissent, 59*(2), 49–57.

Bill and Melinda Gates Foundation. (2015). How we work: Awarded grants. Retrieved May 31, 2015 from: http://www.gatesfoundation.org/How-We-Work/Quick-Links/Grants-Database.

Buras, K. L. (2014). *Charter schools, race, and urban space: Where the market meets grass-roots resistance.* New York: Routledge.

Burch, P. (2006). The new educational privatization: Educational contracting and high stakes accountability. *Teachers College Record, 108*(12), 2582–2610.

Callaghan, P. (2012, July 3). Might be a record: Sponsors of charter schools initiative say they have enough signatures. Retrieved May 31, 2015 from: http://blog.thenewstribune.com/politics/2012/07/03/might-be-a-record-sponsors-of-charter-schools-initiative-say-they-have-enough-signatures/.

Center on Reinventing Public Education. (2012). Home. Retrieved May 31, 2015 from: http://crpe.org.

Chubb, J. E. and Moe, T. M. (1990). *Politics, markets, and America's schools.* Washington, DC: Brookings Institution.

Corcoran, S. P. and Stoddard, C. (2011). Local demand for a school choice policy: Evidence from the Washington charter school referenda. *Education Finance and Policy, 6*(3), 323–353.

Democrats for Education Reform. (2012a). DFER Washington staff and advisors. Retrieved May 31, 2015 from: http//dfer.org/branches/wa/staff/.

Democrats for Education Reform. (2012b). Home. Retrieved May 31, 2015 from http://dfer.org.

Fabricant, M. and Fine, M. (2013). *The changing politics of education: Privatization and the dispossessed lives left behind.* Boulder, CO: Paradigm Publishers.

Foundation Center. (2013). 990 finder. Retrieved May 31, 2015 from: http://foundationcenter.org/findfunders/990finder/.

Gilder, V. (1999). Want better public education? Support private vouchers. *Imprimis, 28*(9), 5–6.

Goel La Londe, P., Brewer, T. J., and Lubienski, C. (in press). The proliferation of Teach for America around the globe: Cloning corporate reform through Teach for All. *Education Policy Analysis Archives.*

Gove, M. (2012, June 14). *Michael Gove at the National College Annual Conference.* Paper presented at the National College annual conference, International Convention Centre, Birmingham.

Harris, R. (2012). For the record: Democrats for Education Reform. *Catalyst Chicago*. Retrieved May 31, 2015 from: http://catalyst-chicago.org/notebook/2012/06/28/20239/record-democrats-education-reform.

Harvey, D. (2007). Neoliberalism as creative destruction. *Annals of the American Academy of Political and Social Science, 610* (1), 22–44.

Hursh, D. (2011). The Gates Foundation's interventions into education, health, and food policies: Technology, power, and the privatization of political problems. In P. E. Kovacs (Ed.), *The Gates Foundation and the future of US "public" schools*, 39–52. New York: Routledge.

Kapur, K. and Weisbrod, B. A. (2000). The roles of government and nonprofit suppliers in mixed industries. *Public Finance Review, 28*(4), 275–308.

Klein, N. (2007). *The shock doctrine: The rise of disaster capitalism* (1st ed.). New York: Metropolitan Books/Henry Holt.

Klonsky, M. (2011). Power philanthropy: Taking the public out of public education. In P. E. Kovacs (Ed.), *The Gates Foundation and the future of US "public" schools*, 21–38. New York: Routledge.

Klonsky, M. and Klonsky, S. (2008). *Small schools: Public school reform meets the ownership society*. New York: Routledge.

Kovacs, P. E. and Christie, H. K. (2011). The Gates' Foundation and the future of US public education: A call for scholars to counter misinformation campaigns. In P. E. Kovacs (Ed.), *The Gates Foundation and the future of US "public" schools*, 145–167. New York: Routledge.

Lacireno-Paquet, N., Holyoke, T. T., Moser, M., and Henig, J. R. (2002). Creaming versus cropping: Charter school enrollment practices in response to market incentives. *Educational Evaluation And Policy Analysis, 24*(2), 145–158.

Lake, R., Gross, B., and Maas, T. (2012). *Examining charters: How public charter schools can work in Washington state*. Seattle, WA: Partnership For Learning; Center for Reinventing Public Education.

Layton, L. (2014, June 7). How Bill Gates pulled off the swift common core revolution. *Washington Post*. Retrieved May 31, 2015 from: http://washingtonpost.com/politics/how-bill-gates-pulled-off-the-swift-common-core-revolution/2014/06/07/a830e32e-ec34-11e3-9f5c-9075d5508f0a_story.html.

League of Education Voters. (2012a). Staff. Retrieved May 31, 2015 from: http://www.educationvoters.org/about-2/staff/.

League of Education Voters. (2012b). Who we are. Retrieved May 31, 2015 from http://educationvoters.org/about-2/.

Libby, K. (2012). Education reform now advocacy committee. Retrieved May 31, 2015 from: http://dferwatch.wordpress.com/connections-2/education-reform-now-advocacy-inc/.

Libby, K. and Sanchez, A. (2012). For or against children? The problematic history of Stand for Children. *Rethinking Schools, 26*(1). Retrieved May 31, 2015 from: http://rethinking schools.org/archive/26_01/26_01_sanchez.shtml.

Lipman, P. (2011). *The new political economy of urban education: Neoliberalism, race, and the right to the city*. New York: Routledge.

Lubienski, C. (2006a). Incentives for school diversification: Competition and promotional patterns in local education markets. *Journal of School Choice, 1*(2), 1–31.

Lubienski, C. (2006b). School diversification in second-best education markets: International evidence and conflicting theories of change. *Educational Policy, 20*(2), 323–344.

Lubienski, C. (2014). Re-making the middle: Dis-intermediation in international context. *Educational Management Administration and Leadership, 42*(3), 423–440. doi: 10.1177/1741143214521594.

Lubienski, C. and Lubienski, S. T. (2014). *The public school advantage: Why public schools outperform private schools*. Chicago: University of Chicago Press.

Lubienski, C. and Weitzel, P. (2008). The effects of vouchers and private schools in improving academic achievement: A critique of advocacy research. *Brigham Young University Law Review, 2008*(2), 447–485.

Lubienski, C. and Weitzel, P. (Eds). (2010). *The charter school experiment: Expectations, evidence, and implications*. Cambridge, MA: Harvard Education Press.

Lubienski, C., Brewer, T. J., and Goel La Londe, P. (in press). Orchestrating policy ideas: Philanthropies and think tanks in US education policy advocacy networks. *Australian Education Researcher*.

Lubienski, C., Gordon, L., and Lee, J. (2013). Self-managing schools and access for disadvantaged students: Organisational behavior and school admissions. *New Zealand Journal of Educational Studies, 48*(1), 82–98.

Lubienski, C., Scott, J., and DeBray, E. (2011). The rise of intermediary organizations in knowledge production, advocacy, and educational policy. *Teachers College Record*, http://tcrecord.org ID Number: 16487.

New York State Office of the Attorney General. (2013). Charities nys.com. Retrieved May 31, 2015 from: http://charitiesnys.com/RegistrySearch/show_details.jsp?id={4D9E71F8-0188-4433-9D6C-4892837A401C.

Partnership For Learning. (2012a). Partnership for learning: Partners in reform. Retrieved May 31, 2015 from www.partnership4learning.org/node/2860.

Partnership For Learning. (2012b). Who we are. Retrieved May 31, 2015 from http://partnership4learning.org/who-we-are.

Ravitch, D. (2010). *The death and life of the great American school system: how testing and choice are undermining education* (e-book). New York: Basic Books.

Ravitch, D. (2013). *Reign of error: The hoax of the privatization movement and the danger to America's public schools*. New York: Alfred A. Knopf.

Reckhow, S. (2013). *Follow the money: How foundation dollars change public school politics*. Oxford: Oxford University Press.

Reed, S. (2012, November 27). November 6, 2012 general election results: Initiative measure no. 1240 concerns creation of a public charter school system. Retrieved May 31, 2015 from: http://vote.wa.gov/results/current/Initiative-Measure-No-1240-Concerns-creation-of-a-public-charter-school-system.html.

Rosenthal, B. M. (2012). Charter schools on legislative agenda: "Worth the fight": Many say we can't wait longer for solution; others worry. *The Olympian*. Retrieved from http://theolympian.com/2012/01/13/1946994/charter-schools-on-legislative.html.

Sa Campos, T. de. (2012). *Initiative measure No. 1240 concerns creation of a public charter school system*. Olympia, Washington. Retrieved May 31, 2015 from: http://sos.wa.gov/_assets/elections/initiatives/FinalText_274.pdf.

Scott, J., Lubienski, C., and DeBray-Pelot, E. (2009). The politics of advocacy in education. *Educational Policy, 23*(1), 3–14.

Scott, J. T. (2008). Managers of choice: Race, gender, and the political ideology of the "new" urban school leadership. In W. Feinberg and C. Lubienski (Eds), *School choice policies and outcomes: Empirical and philosophical perspectives*, 149–176. Albany, NY: SUNY Press.

Scott, J. T. and DiMartino, C. (2010). Hybridized, franchised, duplicated, and replicated: Charter schools and management. In C. Lubienski and P. Weitzel (Eds), *The charter school experiment: Expectations, evidence, and implications*. Cambridge, MA: Harvard Education Press.

Scott, J. T. and Jabbar, H. (2014). The hub and the spokes: Foundations, intermediary organizations, incentivist reforms, and the politics of research evidence. *Educational Policy, 28*(2), 233–257.

Seattle Times Editorial Board. (2012). Washington's legislative education chairs stalled reform to improve education: The failure of Democratic leaders in the state Legislature to move on charter schools and teacher evaluations is all the more disappointing because of the urgency for school reforms. *The Seattle Times*. Retrieved May 31, 2015 from: http://seattletimes.com/html/editorials/2017417952_edit05education.html.

Stand for Children. (2013). Annual report and financial statement. Retrieved May 31, 2015 from: http://stand.org/national/about/annual-report-financial-statement.

University of Washington Bothell Office of Sponsored Programs. (2013). Request for information. Retrieved May 31, 2015 from: http//uwb.edu/research/reports/current-awards.

VanderArk, T. (2012). A long trek before a race to the top. *Huffington Post*. Retrieved May 31, 2015 from: http://huffingtonpost.com/tom-vander-ark/a-long-trek-before-a-race_b_254979.html.

Washington Coalition for Public Charter Schools. (2012a). WA public charter schools initiative now state law. Retrieved May 31, 2015 from: http://wacharters.org/wa-public-charter-schools-initiative-now-state-law/.

Washington Coalition for Public Charter Schools. (2012b). Yes on 1240. Retrieved May 31, 2015 from: http://yeson1240.com.

Washington State Parent Teachers Association. (2012). Charter public school forum now online. Retrieved May 31, 2015 from: http://wastatepta.org/advocacy/session_2012/charter.html.

Washington State Public Disclosure Commission. (2012a). Washington State Public Disclosure Commission: 40 years of shining light on Washington politics: Cash contributions for Yes On 1240 WA Coalition for Public Charter Schools. Retrieved May 31, 2015 from: http://pdc.wa.gov/MvcQuerySystem/CommitteeData/contributions?param=WUVTIFdDIDUwNw====&year=2012&type=initiative.

Washington State Public Disclosure Commission. (2012b). Washington State Public Disclosure Commission: 40 years of shining light on Washington politics: Expenditures for Yes On 1240 WA Coalition for Public Charter Schools. Retrieved May 31, 2015 from: http://pdc.wa.gov/MvcQuerySystem/CommitteeData/contributions?param=WUVTIFdDIDUwNw====&year=2012&type=initiative.

Washington State Public Disclosure Commission. (2012c). Washington State Public Disclosure Commission: 40 years of shining light on Washington politics: In-kind contributions for Yes On 1240 WA Coalition for Public Charter Schools. Retrieved May 31, 2015 from: http://pdc.wa.gov/MvcQuerySystem/CommitteeData/contributions?param=WUVTIFdDIDUwNw====&year=2012&type=initiative.

Washington State Public Disclosure Commission. (2012d). *Washington State Public Disclosure Commission's "most money" journal*. Olympia, Washington: Washington State Public Disclosure Commission. Retrieved May 31, 2015 from: http://pdc.wa.gov/archive/home/historical/pdf/MostMoneyJournal.pdf.

Weisbrod, B. A. (1998). Institutional form and organizational behavior. In W. W. Powell and E. S. Clemens (Eds), *Private action and the public good*, 69–84. New Haven, CT: Yale University Press.

Westbrook, M. (2012). Why the Washington State charter bills are flawed. Retrieved May 31, 2015 from: http://saveseattleschools.blogspot.com/2012/02/why-washington-state-charter-bills-are.html.

Yes on 1240. (2012). *Yes On 1240: Prof. Hill*. Retrieved May 31, 2015 from: https://youtube.com/watch?v=tGLNzlImRNY.

3 Philanthropic Governance

Charitable Companies, the
Commercialization of Education
and *That Thing* Called "Democracy"

Antonio Olmedo

Even before the recent economic meltdown of the "nth" phase of capitalism, the winds that propelled the expansion of neoliberal modes of governance had already begun to change direction. As Ong suggests, "in recent years, shake-ups in global events and in the social sciences have required a shift away from models of stabilized world arrangements to the analysis of heterogeneous situations contingently shaped by global forces" (Ong 2012: 25). As an example, the World Bank's new impetus in promoting public–private partnership (PPP) schemes in all domains of public policy was accompanied by calls for novel reformulations and readjustments of traditional capitalist logics and mechanisms, and new political frameworks where such changes could take place (Bishop and Green 2010). Gates's *Creative capitalism* is a good example of the former. According to the billionaire businessman, who has recently metamorphosed into a "global" philanthropist:

> The genius of capitalism lies in its ability to make self-interest serve the wider interest (…) but to harness this power so it benefits everyone, we need to refine the system; and, to do so, we need to develop an approach where governments, businesses, and nonprofits work together to stretch the reach of market forces so that more people can make a profit, or gain recognition, doing work that eases the world's inequities.
>
> (Gates in Kinsley 2010: 9–10)

Creative capitalism calls for new political sensitivities and forms of governance that orbit around the traditional capitalist binary axis: profit (recognition)/market (competition). David Cameron, the UK Prime Minister, picked up the gauntlet and, in his first major speech after winning the 2010 election, he sketched a straightforward response to Gates's challenge. At the heart of his coalition government strategy, the *Big Society* championed a new form of governmentality in which the government is not at the center and gives away its role as the most substantive player in the provision of public services. In his own words:

> we have got to open up public services, make them less monolithic, say to people: if you want to start up new schools, you can; if you want to set up a

co-op or a mutual within the health service, if you're part of the health service, you can (…) I don't believe that you just sort of roll back the state and the Big Society springs up miraculously. There are amazing people in our country, who are establishing great community organizations and social enterprises, but we, the government, should also be catalysing and agitating and trying to help build the Big Society.[1]

(Cameron 2011)

Both Gates' *creative capitalism* and Cameron's *Big Society* aim to extend neoliberal sensitivities into places and spaces where they had not had access before. Indeed, the argument is now being made that the disciplines of competition and profit are what is needed to reform and re-energize the provision of public sector services. On the one hand, governing within this new paradigm entails a redefinition of the relationship between the domains of the economy and the social. It also involves the design of new ways of addressing social problems in which the boundaries between government and state, public and private, processes and results, common wealth and individual profit, charity and benefit, are made increasingly indistinguishable. However, as Ong (2012: 26) reminds us, "it is especially a mistake to fuse political sovereignty with capitalist might, as these are separate technologies of power that interact in complex ways." It is this space of interaction, where the economy invites the state to adapt and the state responds by "recycling" capitalist solutions to do so, that concerns us here. In short, both schemes sketch a scenario where, as Jessop (1998: 43) portrayed it, "the invisible hand will be combined with a visible handshake." On the other hand, they require building up a set of conceptions, new policy technologies and apparatuses intended to operate in complex networked contexts. As the advocates of the new model of governance suggest, in order to achieve gains in efficiency and innovation, those "policy solutions" that traditionally fell under the domains and responsibilities of the government should now be shared by a new set of social, political, and economic actors. Far from past roles and duties as a warrantor of equality and welfare for all its citizens, the government becomes a "croupier assistant," a facilitator, a broker, or, as Ball (2007) aptly puts it, a "market-maker." In other words, there is a reconfiguration of the field of policy and a shift from a focus on "*correcting* for" to "*connecting to* the market*" (Brooks et al. 2009). As a consequence, during the last decade of the twentieth century, a new group of political actors, including "new" venture philanthropists, social entrepreneurs, and neoliberal policy advocates, among others, have repopulated the policy arena.

The mistake at this stage would be to focus merely on the structural dimension of neoliberalism, what Ong (2007) calls "N"eoliberalism (with a capital N). This refers to Neo-Marxist formulations of Neoliberalism that conceive it as a "dominant structural condition [characterised by private property rights, individual liberty, free markets, and free trade] that projects totalizing social change across a nation" (2007: 4). However, as Ong suggests, "n"eoliberalism (with small "n") could be also seen as "a technology of governing 'free subjects' that co-exists with other political rationalities" (2007: 4). This second perspective, closer to Foucauldian approaches, understands neoliberalism as a set of "traveling" and flexible practices that adapt to the contexts in which it operates. In Springer's (2015: 3) words, "neoliberalizing practices are thus understood as necessarily and always over-determined, contingent, polymorphic, open to intervention, reconstituted, continually negotiated, impure, subject to counter-tendencies, and in a perpetual process of becoming." Making a free paraphrase of Foucault's mantra, it could be argued that there is not such a thing as "neoliberalism" but "neoliberal practices." This is what Springer means when he stresses the need to treat neoliberalism as a verb, which implies focussing on its "processual, unfolding, and action oriented sense" (Springer 2015: 3). Here, the focus becomes to identify the subject (in terms of interchanging "subjector"/subjected relationships) of such processes and actions.

This chapter sketches some of the new ways through which these changes are being enacted. More specifically, it analyzes the new methods of policy linked to what is known as *philanthrocapitalism* (Edwards 2008). This new philanthropic approach has gained an increasingly important political dimension, becoming a central explanatory variable to understand the recent changes and directions of national and international political agendas in different parts of the world (see Ball and Olmedo 2012). These transformations represent new forms of governmentality and power regimes and are deeply rooted within the political economy and political philosophy of neoliberalism. According to Jessop (2002), they also facilitate the transition to a new political framework characterized by new forms of coordination, or "heterarchies." The analytical approach to what is referred to here as "the global" responds to the set of discrete, identifiable and traceable practices (connections, transactions, meetings, travels, influences, and impositions, etc.), through which international economic and political relationships are enacted. In Dicken and his colleagues' words:

> Instead of conceiving of the global economy as a disembodied and disembedded set of supra-human forces, the network understanding of how commodities and services are produced, distributed and consumed highlights the *grounded* mechanisms through which the web of international economic relationships is actually created and reproduced.
>
> (Dicken et al. 2001: 106)

More specifically, the following sections reflect on a set of "new" edu-enterprises, their connections, ideological influences, and agendas on the ground. Within the field of policy analysis,

> policy network analysis seeks to identify the important actors – governmental and nongovernmental organizations (NGOs), interest groups, and persons involved in policymaking institutions – to describe and explain the structure of their interactions during policymaking processes, and to explain and predict collective policy decision and outcomes.
>
> (Knoke 2011: 210)

To do so, the chapter furthers previous analysis (see Olmedo 2013) on the organizational configuration and international operations of the English charitable company: ARK (Absolute Return for Kids). More concretely, the sections below focus on the new policy solutions promoted by and through the members that configure ARK's policy network. It will be suggested that the role and nature of profit is not only blurred but is also blurring other dimensions in the realm of policy and politics. The aim of the chapter is to raise a number of questions and concerns on the potential impact that these new policy actors could be exerting over democratic processes and political practices.

New Philanthropy: Philanthrocapitalism and Philanthro-Policymaking

By coining the term "philanthropic governance" in previous papers (Ball and Olmedo 2012; Olmedo 2013), we aimed to highlight the important changes that can be acknowledged in the nature and the subject of processes of policy enactment in the field of education. Although philanthropy is not a new phenomenon (see Arnove 1980), its functions and position within the social space have changed substantially. Within the aforementioned reorganization of the architecture of regulation and policy production, philanthropic involvement in the public arena has shifted from an initial role as "cooling-out agencies" (Arnove 1980: 1) into a more "hands-on" approach, where "new" philanthropists have become key political actors involved in the design, negotiation, promotion, and delivery of policy processes, including the reorganization and enactment of public services, civic action, and community development.

There are two main characteristics of what has been denominated as "philanthropy 3.0" (The Bellagio Initiative 2011). On the one hand, new philanthropists bring into play new "methods" of policy. As suggested in the initial quotation above, "new" philanthropists such as Gates, Omidyar, Broad, Bertelsmann, Agnelli, etc. are willing to "give back" that which they generated in the form of profit from their businesses. However, they want to use their donations in a business-like way – that is, in the form of "strategic investments" that should lead to "good" measurable results. The rationale behind it is led by the new social enterprise slogan: "do good while doing well." In this sense, social enterprise is being developed as a new "economic rationalization of giving" (Saltman 2010). These new sensibilities of charity, understood now as social "investment," have led to increasing use of commercial and enterprise models of practice within new forms of philanthropic organization and investment (e.g. venture philanthropy, due diligence, accountable donations, micro-finance, etc. (see Stewart et al. 2011). This is what is known as "philanthrocapitalism" (Bishop and Green 2010).

ARK is a good example of these nascent philanthropic enterprises. Registered both as a charity and as a company limited by guarantee in England, ARK takes the shape of what are known as "charitable companies." As such, ARK is entitled to own property and generate profit. However, the economic surplus generated from the

provision of the services that they provide should be "reinvested" within the organization. That does not exclude the alternative possibility of using their economic
assets to trade and purchase services and goods with other public and private providers. Once again, within these novel philanthropic enterprises, the already thin
line between profit and social altruism becomes even more diffused. Their ethos and
methods are attuned with the corporate roots and organograms of their parental
organizations. As the business leaders who founded ARK over a decade ago stated
in their introduction to the charitable company's 2012 Annual Report:

> We created ARK in 2002, convinced that our combined efforts could have a
> greater effect on children's lives than if we each supported individual chari-
> ties. We wanted to apply the same robust measurement and accountability
> to philanthropy as we do to business, in order to deliver programmes that
> transform the lives of the most disadvantaged children.
>
> (ARK Annual Report 2012)

"New" philanthropy is taking a more protagonist role in political terms, which
is already contributing to the re-dispersal of political and moral authority.
Business actors, in their new role as charitable philanthropists, feel the "need"
to take action outside the sphere of the economy, assuming key roles in the
organization of the societies where their companies operate. This new dimension of philanthropy responds to dynamics of what Shamir (2008: 4) understands as the "moralization of economic action," whose aim is to roll out a "a
kind of rehabilitation for forms of capital that were subject to 'ill repute' in the
public imagination" (Ball and Junemann 2012: 32). As an example, in 2011,
the president and Chief Executive Officer (CEO) of Starbucks Coffee Company
Howard Schultz stated that:

> As corporate citizens of the world, it is our responsibility – our duty – to serve
> the communities where we do business by helping to improve, for example,
> the quality of citizens' education, employment, health care, safety, and overall
> daily life, plus future prospects.
>
> (Schultz 2011)

Portraying themselves as morally compromised agents, the new philanthro-
capitalists thin out the relationships between, on the one hand, the processes
through which they amass their fortunes and, on the other, the roots of the
social problems that they seem willing to address. That is, there seems to be no
critical reflection on the "contribution" of capitalism, and, within it, the business practices of their own companies in the worsening of old and the creation of new forms of inequality and social injustice across the globe. Instead,
promoters of this new role of philanthropy have begun to advocate for an even
clearer "new division of labour (...) between governments, businesses, charitable NGOs, and philanthropists" in order to solve "the stagnant problems of the
world" (Bishop and Green 2010: 12).

On the other hand, some of these organizations are becoming global behemoths. Their organizational configurations spread over complex networked structures, where once well-established boundaries between public and private goods, charity and profit-making activities, citizenship and self-interest, and local and foreign players, are blurred. These networks, as Ong (2012: 25) suggests, "invoke 'the global' not as a metaphorical or achieved instantiation of a singular logic, but as a historically contingent concept that points to configurations shaped by the interaction of global and situated components." One again, ARK exemplifies the new "global" character of philanthropic governance:

> Originally set up by leaders of the alternative investment industry, we deliver high social returns on our philanthropy, leveraging intellectual, financial and political investment. We are headquartered in the UK and our work focuses on health, education and child protection around the globe.
>
> (ARK website)

Figure 3.1 shows the dense assemblage of connections of different nature (economic transactions, in-kind donations, intellectual contributions, partnerships "on the ground," etc.) that constitutes ARK's network.[2]

The remaining sections focus on some of the programs and actors that comprise ARK's network.

"Connecting People": The Role of Network Capital in "Doing Neoliberalism"

As ARK's policy network diagram shows, "new" philanthropy is facilitating access to new players to the field of social and education policy, repopulating and reworking existing policy networks, and giving legitimacy to the role of business in the solution of social problems. As Ball and Junemann's research concludes, "strategically, philanthropy has provided a 'Trojan horse' for modernizing moves that opened the 'policy door' to new actors and new ideas and sensibilities" (Ball and Junemann 2012: 32). As an example, within Pearson Education's endless portfolio of edu-products and activities,[3] of both a for-profit and philanthropic nature, the company is involved with ARK in the development of their Teaching Leaders program. This consists of three sub-programs aimed at middle-leaders, or teachers who show "high potential" to be so, and trains them in three different fronts: managing pupil data; holding teachers accountable; and motivating their teams. Once again, Teaching Leaders rests on ARK's compromise with the principles of accountability and measurement. The program is funded by the National College for Teaching and Leadership (an executive agency of the UK's Department for Education), the Future Leaders Trust, and Teach First (though the network of supporters and partners is broader – see Figure 3.1). Through their participation in ARK's Teaching Leaders, Pearson is not only donating altruistically but also gaining back access to important "hot knowledge" and situated and

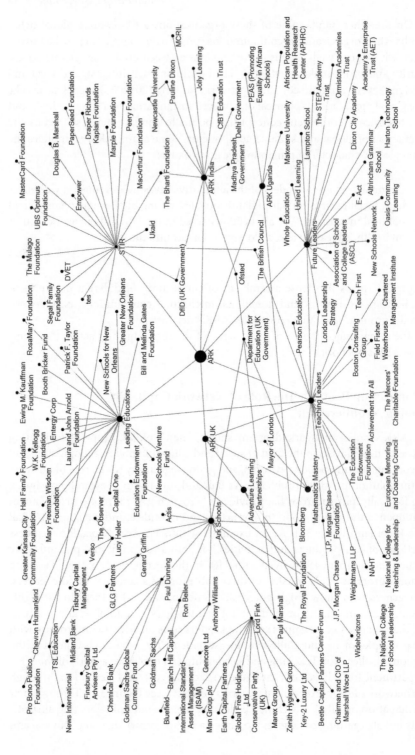

Figure 3.1 Extract of ARK's programs and policy network

local experiences that would inform the company's operations in other fronts. As stated on the program's website:

> Pearson has kindly sponsored our Graduation Ceremony for the past 3 years and established the Pearson Excellence Awards for Teaching Leaders. All graduating Alumni and Fellows at the end of their first year are eligible to apply for this award. The judging panel looks at a wide range of criteria reflecting both the quality of the thinking behind and execution of the individual's Impact Initiative as well as their impact on the staff and pupils within their school.
>
> We also look at innovative ways for Fellows on our programmes to share experiences of leadership and a view from within schools with the Pearson team to aid them with their policy work.
>
> (Teaching Leaders website)

Here, it can be seen how it is not only profit, or, more accurately, profit in its monetary form, that these charitable companies and those who support them are seeking. Money and ideas work to join up advocacy activities to policy proposals and to programs of reform. Businesses, through their philanthropic foundations, are also investing in the work of think tanks, advocacy networks and policy entrepreneurs with the hope of future political "returns." Ball (2012: 139) has given clear evidence of a "growing global market in policy ideas" and stresses that policy itself has become a commodity and a profit opportunity that can now be bought and sold (Ball 2007). As a consequence, policy work is increasingly being out-sourced to profit-making organizations, which bring their skills, discourses, and sensibilities to the policy table. International companies (Pearson, Cambridge Education, PriceWaterhouseCoopers, Mattrix Knowledge Group, or A4e) are now offering a broad portfolio of "policy products" that range from school improvement programs through Continuing Professional Development and training courses, to "evidence-based" policy knowledge and performance-based evaluation toolkits, design and brokering of outsourcing contracts, and, more recently, even writing education policy themselves for local and national governments.[4]

ARK's network works as a "connective tissue" (Ball and Junemann 2012: 12), comprising the "circulatory systems that connect and interpenetrate the local and the national" (Peck 2003: 229). It generates and accumulates what could be considered as *political* "network capital" (Larsen et al. 2006), with the potential of being "traded" into other forms of capital when required (Bourdieu 1986). As an example, back to our diagram, ARK also works in partnership with the Chartered Management Institute (CMI). The CMI is a registered charity in England, Wales, and Scotland whose "charitable mission is to promote the art and science of management" (Chartered Management Institute website). Through a network of accredited centers, it offers a wide portfolio of standard and tailored training courses to professionals operating in the field of management and leadership. It also conducts research and works as a political consultant and government lobbyist. As stated on their website, CMI is:

A POWERFUL ALLY

CMI enjoys an authoritative mandate from the management community. So you can be sure that we can make your voice heard in government, education and business. When we speak, people listen.

INFLUENCING PUBLIC POLICY

We set the standards for management and leadership throughout the UK and our policy agenda ensures that managers' voices are heard by government.
(Chartered Management Institute website)

ARK is involved with the CMI in the construction of:

generative nodes, that is, spaces aimed at facilitating new connections and linking opportunities between public and private actors. These are "new sites of policy mobilisation" and "globalising microspaces" that operate between and beyond traditionally defined areas of policy formulation, such as localities, regions and nations.
(Ball and Olmedo 2012: 86)

Teaching Leaders and the CMI have partnered to create a round table between business and education leaders.[5] Bringing actors together in meetings and conferences, training present and future leaders, carrying out research and promoting ideas, lobbing government at different levels, amongst other activities, configure the everyday practices of "doing neoliberalism" (Ball and Olmedo 2012) and, as can be seen through previous examples, ARK plays a key role in this.

Operating Between the Trenches: ARK's Public–Private Partnership Model

A second dimension in the role of new philanthropy focusses on their direct involvement in the design and delivery of policy programs. As mentioned above, in general terms, the move from government to governance, or, more accurately, to neoliberal governance, involves moving away from previous top-down forms of imperative coordination and points toward new modes of what Rhodes (1996) captured as "governing without government." This form of governance encompasses processes of continuous dialogue and the creation of alliances between political and other actors from different fields. That is the move towards a "polycentric state" (Rhodes 1996). In policy practice, all this translates into changes in the way in which public services are designed and delivered. More and more, education, health, and other social services are enacted through a mix of "strategic alliances, joint working arrangements, networks, partnerships and many other forms of collaboration across sectoral and organizational boundaries" (Williams 2002: 103) based upon "relations involving mutuality and interdependence" (Peterson 2003: 1). This new form of "network governance" involves new governing mechanisms, what Rose and Miller (1992) identified as processes of "governing at a distance" which rely "on a dense fabric of lasting ties and networks that provide key resources of expertise, reputation and legitimization" (Grabher 2004: 104). As a result, governments are increasingly "catalyzing all sectors – public, private and voluntary – into action to solve their community's problems" (Osborne and Gaebler 1992). Public–private partnerships (PPPs) are a good example of this. They are presented as a "new programmatic idea" (Verger 2012: 110) and imply "a form of relational contracting between the public and the private sector for the organization and delivery of services that involve risk sharing and mutual learning between the parties involved" (Verger 2012: 114).

Back to our case, ARK Schools runs one of the largest Academy chains in England (see Gunter 2011). The academies program is similar to the US charter schools counterpart. Through it, schools become independent from local authorities' control and receive funding directly from the Department for Education on a per pupil basis (like any other maintained school). The program, launched by the Labour party, was revitalised by the following Conservative government as part of David Cameron's "all-out war on mediocrity" in schools (Watt 2015). Currently, ARK is operating 31 primary and secondary schools. Two Prime Ministers and their Secretaries of State for Education, from the Labour and Conservative parties, have publicly praised the charitable company for its contribution to the program and the positive results in driving up standards in challenging areas (Junemann and Ball 2013).

The application of market-based principles does not only relate to the already mentioned structural and organizational dimensions of ARK, but it is also instilled in the charitable company's methodological "innovations." Their model is based on six pillars: high expectations; exemplary behavior; excellent teaching; depth before breadth; more time for learning; and knowing every child (ARK website). Running through the capillaries and connecting each one of those, there is a strong focus on measurement and performance indicators: "to ensure no child is left behind, we have developed data management tools which allow teachers to monitor pupils' progress and quickly identify when children, or indeed teaching staff, need extra support" (ARK website).

Accountability is coupled with a broader set of corporate strategic methods that ARK is developing with the support of partner organizations in order to bring "innovation" into their teaching. An example of it is Mathematics Mastery, a teaching framework and approach "that will enable every student to reach their true mathematics potential" (Mathematics Mastery website). The program consists of a full curriculum for teaching mathematics that spreads across primary and secondary education, based on the Singaporean model: "the programme is based on the world leading curriculum and pedagogy of Singapore, which has consistently been amongst the highest performers in the Trends in International Mathematics and Science Study (TIMSS) since 1995" (Mathematics Mastery website).

Mathematics Mastery is being supported by the Department for Education, the Mayor of London and the Education Endowment Foundation. The Foundation is expected to invest more than £200m over a period of 15 years on innovative schemes to improve attainment, particularly among the poorest students in England (Mathematics Mastery website). With the economic support of its funders, ARK launched the program in 2009 and is expanding it with the aim of reaching sustainability:

> We will continue to act as a seedbed for innovation beyond ARK Schools. For example, we will grow Mathematics Mastery to sustainability. A £600,000 grant from the Education Endowment Foundation will enable us to expand the programme to over 100 schools in 2013. We will also launch a new corporate mentoring partnership with Bloomberg and its support will help us to pilot new initiatives across our network.
>
> (ARK website)

However, a recent independent external evaluation conducted by researchers from the Institute of Education (IOE), University of London, and funded by the Education Endowment Foundation suggests that the program does not seem to be offering the level of outcomes expected from ARK's "innovative" and expensive curriculum. As the IOE's report summarizes:

Key Conclusions

1   On average, Year 7 pupils in schools adopting Mathematics Mastery made a small amount more progress than pupils in schools that did not. However, the effect detected was not statistically significant, meaning that it is not possible to rule out chance as an explanation.
2   There is no strong evidence that the approach had a greater impact on lower-attaining pupils than on higher-attaining pupils.
3   Combining the findings from this study and a second randomised controlled trial of Mathematics Mastery involving Year 1 pupils may strengthen the overall evidence for the approach.
4   Given the low per-pupil cost, Mathematics Mastery may represent a cost-effective change for schools to consider. However, teachers would need to resolve tensions related to differentiation to provide support for all groups of children.
5   It would be worthwhile to track the medium- and long-term impact of the approach, to assess whether there is a cumulative effect to the approach and whether it has an impact on performance in high-stakes tests.

Source: Education Endowment Foundation.

Back to ARK's Academies program, the charitable company is embracing existing models based on the sustainability of chains of private schools through the attainment of economies of scale (Tooley 2007, 2009). They are expecting to expand into a full network of 50 schools by 2017 and envisage the possibility of becoming fully independent of extra funding (apart from that coming from the UK government) in the near future:

GROWING OUR NETWORK OF SCHOOLS

Our target is to establish a network of around 50 schools by 2017. These schools will provide 23,500 places for the 2015/16 academic year, rising to over 35,000 pupils at full capacity. As our network grows, we will realise further economies of scale and aim to become self-sustaining on funding from the Department for Education by 2017/18.

(ARK website)

This quotation clearly shows an intention to keep growing on a "sustainable" basis, or at least as sustainable as traditional local authority schools were. If their aim is to reach that benchmark, this implies that at least at the moment they are more expensive to run than their counterparts in the public sector. The charitable company's accounts (at least for their academies program) can be easily traced; however, the sources and use of the extra philanthropic contribution and economic donations are difficult to follow. Also, it could be questionable whether the costs and bureaucratic burden of running a chain of 50 schools would not result in the same issues and alleged "inefficiencies" experienced by the local authorities, which seem to be the root of all the current problems.

Running schools is just the first step. In 2012, ARK formed a partnership with Canterbury Christ Church University, an Anglican public university affiliated with the Church of England, to develop its own teacher-training scheme:

Research shows that a teacher's performance doesn't vary much after their first three years in the job. So, the training they have in those early years is crucial. In 2012 we created our own teacher-training programme in collaboration with Canterbury Christ Church University, and have now become an accredited teacher-training institution in our own right ... By 2020 we want half of our teachers to have come through our programme – and by 2015 we want all of them to be using our training resources as part of their ongoing professional development.

(ARK Annual Report 2012)

Brewing their own teachers is a controversial move that has important implications on different fronts. It creates a potential conflict of interest or, at least, dynamics of unfair competition against other Initial Teacher Education providers who do not own schools, and therefore are not in a position to be able to offer jobs directly to their graduates. Furthermore, it raises questions on whether those graduates would be ready to work in all kinds of environments, and not only in those schools that follow the ARK model. Finally, it could be questioned whether public money should be used to fund such enterprises.

Going the "Extra Mile": From Local Charity to International Player

Based on their experiences in England, ARK has in recent years expanded its operations into Asia and Africa. In India, the charitable company has run two projects since 2009: ENABLE and ASPIRE. The former is a phonics-based program for teaching English, designed with the help of Dr. Pauline Dixon (University of Newcastle) and developed through partnerships with two state governments and the Bharti Foundation (one of India's largest education foundations). It is now being used in 335 schools across 9 Indian states. The latter consists of a voucher scheme developed in Delhi:

> We are piloting an education voucher scheme in the poorest areas of Delhi to encourage families to claim their entitlement to free private school places. ARK uses picture guides to inform parents about the quality of schools available; to ensure children from all backgrounds have an equal chance, we allocate places with a lottery system. Our corruption-proof vouchers cover tuition fees, uniforms, textbooks and lunch for the full five years of primary school.
>
> (ARK website)

The first cohort consisted of 635 pupils across 69 schools and ARK is already "looking ahead":

> Generating robust evidence on the difference the voucher system can make to children's learning is a priority for 2013. Ark is collaborating with Newcastle University to compare the results of pupils with and without vouchers. Our aim is to offer state governments a one-stop solution for implementing the Right to Education Act; two Indian state governments have already shown interest.
>
> (ARK website)

ASPIRE ran between 2009 and 2014 and ENABLE will cease in 2016. Over the last five years, the charitable company has acquired enough expertise and knowledge to move one step forward. As a result, ARK has developed two new schemes. The first one consists of a School Quality Assurance (SQA) program initially piloted in the Indian state of Madhya Pradesh. SQA was developed with the input of former inspectors from the Office for Standards in Education, Children's Services and Skills (Ofsted) – England's inspectorate service and in collaboration with partners: UK's Department for International Development, Centre for British Teachers, Education Trust, and Micro-Credit Ratings International Limited. SQA offers a quality assurance framework and a set of tools to automate the inspection process to make it easier for stakeholders to analyze school data. Though the program started as a small-scale pilot scheme, it has now become "officially adopted policy" and it is expanding into other Indian states:

> Following the project's success, it has now gone from being a small-scale pilot to an officially adopted policy. Our framework will be scaled up across all Madhya Pradesh schools in the next five years, after being praised as "a special and excellent step for the enhancement of education" by the state's Chief Minister … As a result, thousands of schools will be held to higher standards, and will therefore be more likely to deliver good results for their pupils. We're now working with the

authorities in Delhi to do the same work for them. This is a huge step for us, and for all the pupils who will now enjoy a better quality of education ... In just three months, Ark and the Madhya Pradesh School Education Department inspected 2,000 schools. Our framework will be used in over 120,000 schools by 2019.

(ARK website)

ARK's second program in India is the result of a public–private partnership with the Indian government. Through it, the charitable company will be launching its own chain of primary schools in 2015:

Combining the education experience and expertise we have gained through working in India and the UK, Ark now plans to set up a network of high quality primary schools in partnership with the government, which will provide an excellent education for disadvantaged children. Ark's plans are ambitious; we ultimately aim to grow a network of high-performing schools which could impact the entire education system as demonstration models, proving what can be done using the right educational approaches. Our education approach is based on our six pillars of education, which have underpinned the success of our network of schools in the UK.

(ARK website)

In a similar fashion, ARK has recently expanded its operations into Uganda. In partnership with Promoting Equality in African Schools (PEAS), ARK is running a network of state-funded secondary schools in rural Uganda (ARK website). Once again, the aim is to champion the PPP model through which their other school programs in the UK and India operate:

Our goal is to work with Uganda's Ministry of Education and Sports to support improvements across the education system, using proven, effective elements of our model in other secondary schools. We also aim to pilot another type of public–private partnership model, where we contract-manage new government-built schools ... By 2014, combining PEAS's local expertise with Ark's focus on measurement and quality, we hope to show that public–private partnerships can deliver academic achievement greater than the national average, at a lower cost to the government.

(ARK website)

What we can see here are the fingerprints of new forms of what Ozga and Jones (2006) understand as "traveling" and "embedded" policies. As McCann (2011: 107) suggests, the idea of conceiving policy in terms of "mobilities" facilitates the operationalization of approaches that intend to explain what he defines as the "'local globalness' of urban policy transfer." More than straightforward and lineal exercises of policy borrowing (see Steiner-Khamsi and Waldow 2012), the analysis of ARK's network and the programs analyzed in this section help us identify the surface traces of policy flows or instances of circulating policies.

Implications Over that Thing that Some Used to Call "Democracy"

As suggested at the beginning of this chapter, the new forms of political and eco-nomic coordination are redefining the apparent incompatibility between anar-chic (market-based) and hierarchic (state-centered) forms of co-ordination. The resulting model consists of more flexible structures (heterarchies), where relation-ships, responsibilities and processes of decision making are shared at different instances by old and new actors (Jessop 1998). Such new models of global govern-ance imply the development of new "methods for co-ordinating actions across different social forces with different identities, interests, and meaning systems, over different spatio-temporal horizons, and over different domains of action" (Jessop 1998: 37). The dominant mode of governance is characterized by networks that are formed by a hybrid mix of actors (individuals, companies, foundations, NGOs, governments, etc.) embedded in a system of national, sub-national, supra-national, intergovernmental, and transnational relations. As Besussi (2006: 6) sug-gests, policy networks represent "a real change in the structure of the polity." Such networks open spaces "of attraction and meaning, in which soft power is at work, creating a space in which actors are drawn to work within it and to produce it" (Lawn 2006: 272).

However, far from the mirage proclaimed by some scholars (Sørensen and Torfing 2007) of a more democratic space where actors operate through horizon-tal and balanced power-relations, "alongside the introduction of new actors and organizations, the shift to polycentrism also involves the displacement of some others, like trade unions and professional associations" (Junemann and Ball 2013: 425). It could be suggested that network governance creates a "democratic deficit" as the processes of policy and governance become more dispersed and less trans-parent, and political spaces are "governed softly and by persuasion" (Lawn and Grek 2012). From this second perspective, policy networks are intentionally blur-ring the line between business, enterprise, development, and the public good, and pose fundamental questions about the methods and future role of government and other traditional political agents. As a result of this, states around the world could be ceding the ability to design and steer their education systems.

The cases and examples presented throughout the chapter illustrate Horne's (2002) claims of the existence of a "parapolitical sphere" within which new phi-lanthropists would be operating and developing their own policy agendas. The direct involvement of these new players in the political sphere implies changes in the steering of democratic societies, and, most importantly, in terms of social accountability and control. As Frumkin suggests,

> unlike government, which has elections to set policy directions, and unlike corporations, which have shareholders to whom they must be responsive, philanthropy is able to operate across the boundaries of public and private and to do so with little or no accountability to its many stakeholders.
>
> (2006: 26–27)

This reconfiguration rests upon a double moral shift in the conception of the relationship between charity, policy, and profit. On the one hand, corporate and family foundations and philanthropic individuals are beginning to "assume socio-moral duties that were heretofore assigned to civil society organizations, governmental entities and state agencies" (Shamir 2008: 4). On the other, these new philanthropists do not completely renounce the possibility of profit; indeed, in their own words, it is possible to "do good and have their profit, too."

The programs, initiatives, enterprises, and schemes presented throughout the previous pages are examples of policy flows and policy advocacy within and beyond the state reach. Their connections and alliances, agendas and methods, cross-border movements, and local implementations, constitute new sites of policy within what Peck and Tickell (2003: 22) call "emergent geographies of neoliberalisation." What we are dealing with here are new ways of "neoliberalism in action," that is a set of practices and processes, structures, and relationships, which constitute what could be understood as "doing neoliberalism." At the same time, the work of the philanthropists and foundations sketched here also represent a different spatial dimension that challenges the principles and theoretical scaffolding in which contemporary education policy research is framed. Therefore, there is the need for a "second generation of governance research" (Sørensen and Torfing 2007: 14) which will bring "clarity and rigour" to what is currently "a somewhat eclectic and confusing theoretical landscape" (Sørensen and Torfing 2007: 7).

Notes

1 https://gov.uk/government/speeches/pms-speech-on-big-society.
2 A warning reminder is needed at this point: given the impossibility of discriminating the nature of each of those connections in order to be able to assign them to one, and only one, of the previous categories, a decision was made to keep the same connecting lines amongst nodes. This constitutes one of the main difficulties of network analysis studies, given, on the one hand, the technical limitations imposed by two-dimensional representations, and, on the other hand, the constantly changing, multi-faceted and polygamist behavior of the actors in play. In previous and related publications (Ball 2012; Ball and Junemann 2012; Olmedo 2013; Olmedo *et al.* 2013), we have attempted to map the shape and contents of network nodes and ties by bringing together tools from Social Network Analysis (SNA) with more traditional ethnographic methods. Our approach adapts and develops further the method of network ethnography (Howard 2002) and responds to Bevir and Rhodes' (2006) call for "ethnographic analyses of governance in action."
3 Pearson Education is part of Pearson plc, one of the biggest edu-business in the growing global market of education policy. (For a more detailed account see Ball 2012.)
4 Cambridge Education, for instance, has been recently contracted to draft legislation for a new Education Act in the Maldives. The company has been hired to assess and write a new curriculum for Secondary Education in Uganda. (See: http://www.cambed.com/Experience/Casestudies/CurriculumAssessmentandExaminationReform.asp.)
5 http://teachingleaders.org.uk/who-we-are/supporters-and-partners/education-partners/.

References

ARK. (2012). ARK Annual Report. Retrieved May 19, 2015 from http://arkonline.org/media/59711/ARK%20Annual%20Report%202012%20PDF%20final.pdf.

ARK. (n.d). Retrieved May 19, 2015 from http://arkonline.org/about-us.

Arnove, R. F. (Ed.). (1980). *Philanthropy and cultural imperialism. The foundaitons at home and abroad.* Boston, MA: G. K. Hall & Co.

Ball, S. J. (2007). *Education Plc: Understanding private sector participation in public sector education.* London: Routledge.

Ball, S. J. (2012). *Global Education Inc. new policy networks and the neoliberal imaginary.* Abingdon, Oxon: Routledge.

Ball, S. J. and Junemann, C. (2012). *Networks, new governance and education.* Bristol: Policy Press.

Ball, S. J. and Olmedo, A. (2012). Global social capitalism: Using enterprise to solve the problems of the world. *Citizenship, Social and Economics Education, 10*(2 and 3), 83–90.

Besussi, E. (2006). Policy networks: Conceptual developments and their European applications. *Working Paper Series, Paper 102.* Retrieved May 19, 2015, from http://bartlett.ucl.ac.uk/casa/pdf/paper102.pdf.

Bevir, M. and Rhodes, R. A. W. (2006). *Governance Stories.* London, Routledge.

Bishop, M. and Green, M. (2010). *Philanthrocapitalim: How giving can save the world* (2nd ed.). London: Bloomsbury Publishing Plc.

Bourdieu, P. (1986). The forms of capital. In J. Richardson (Ed.), *Handbook of theory and research for the sociology of education* (pp. 241–258). New York: Greenwood.

Brooks, S., Leach, M., Lucas, H., and Millstone, E. (2009). *Silver bullets, grand challenges and the new philanthropy. STEPS Working Paper 24.* Brighton: STEPS Centre.

Chartered Management Institute (n.d.). Retrieved May 19, 2015 from http://managers.org.uk/about-us.

Dicken, P., Kelly, P. F., Olds, K., and Wai-Chung Yeung, H. (2001). Chains and networks, territories and scales: Towards a relational framework for analysing the global economy. *Global Networks, 1*(2), 89–112.

Education Endowment Foundation. (2015). Mathematics mastery: Secondary evaluation report. Retrieved May 19, 2015 from https://educationendowmentfoundation.org.uk/uploads/pdf/Mathematics_Mastery_Secondary_(Final).pdf.

Edwards, M. (2008). "Philanthrocapitalism" and its limits. *International Journal of Not-for-Profit Law, 10*(2), 22–29.

Frumkin, P. (2006). *Strategic giving: The art and science of philanthropy.* Chicago: The University of Chicago Press.

Grabher, G. (2004). Learning in projects, remembering in networks? Communality, sociality, and connectivity in project ecologies. *European Urban and Regional Studies, 11*(2), 103–123.

Gunter, H. (2011). *The state and education policy: The academies programme.* London: Continuum.

Horne, J. R. (2002). *A social laboratory for modern France: The social museum and the rise of the welfare state.* Durham, NC: Duke University Press.

Howard, P. N. (2002). Network ethnography and the hypermedia organization: New media, new organizations, new methods. *New Media Society, 4*(4), 550–574.

Jessop, B. (1998). The rise of governance and the risks of failure: The case of economic development. *International Social Science Journal, 50*(155), 29–45.

Jessop, B. (2002). *The future of the capitalist state.* Cambridge: Polity.

Junemann, C. and Ball, S. J. (2013). ARK and the revolution of state education in England. *Education Inquity*, 4(3), 423–441.

Kinsley, M. (2010). *Creative capitalism: Conversations with Bill Gates, Warren Buffet and others.* London: Pocket Books.

Knoke, D. (2011). Policy networks. In J. Scott and P. J. Carrington (Eds), *The SAGE Handbook of Social Network Analysis* (pp. 210–222). London: Sage.

Larsen, J., Axhausen, K. W., and Urry, J. (2006). Geographies of social networks: Meetings, travel and communications. *Mobilities*, 1(2), 261–283.

Lawn, M. (2006). Soft governance and the learning spaces of Europe. *Comparative European Politics*, 4(2 and 3), 272–288.

Lawn, M. and Grek, S. (2012). *Europeanizing education: Governing a new policy space.* Oxford: Symposium.

Mathematics Mastery (n.d.). Retreived May 20, 2015 from http://mathematicsmastery.org.

McCann, E. (2011). Urban policy mobilities and global circuits of knowledge: Toward a research agenda. *Annals of the Association of American Geographers*, 101(1), 107–130.

Olmedo, A. (2013). From England with love … ARK, heterarchies and global 'philanthropic governance'. *Journal of Education Policy*, 29(5), 575–597.

Olmedo, B., Patrick L., and Ball, S. J. (2013). To Infinity and beyond … Heterarchical governance, the Teach for All network in Europe and the making of profits and minds. *European Education Research Journal*, 12(4), 492–512.

Ong, A. (2007). Neoliberalism as a mobile technology. *Transactions of the Institute of British Geographers*, 32 (1), 3–8.

Ong, A. (2012). Powers of sovereignty: State, people, wealth, life. *Focaal – Journal of Global and Historical Anthropology*, 2012 (64), 24–35.

Osborne, D. and Gaebler, T. (1992). *Re-inventing Government.* Reading, MA: Addison-Wesley.

Ozga, J. and Jones, R. (2006). Travelling and embedded policy: The case of knowledge transfer. *Journal of Education Policy*, 21(1), 1–17.

Peck, J. (2003). Geography and public policy: Mapping the penal state. *Progress in Human Geography*, 27(2), 222–232.

Peck, J. and Tickell, A. (2003). Making global rules: Globalisation or neoliberalisation? In J. Peck and H. Yeung (Eds), *Remaking the Global Economy.* London: Sage.

Peterson, J. (2003). *Policy networks: Political Science Series.* Vienna: Institute for Advanced Studies.

Rhodes, R. A. W. (1996). The new governance: Governing without government. *Political Studies*, 44 (4), 652–667.

Rose, N. and Miller, P. (1992). Political power beyond the state: Problematics of government. *The British Journal of Sociology*, 43(2), 173–205.

Saltman, K. J. (2010). *The gift of education: Public education and venture philanthropy.* New York: Palgrave Macmillan.

Schultz, H. (2011). Invest in communities to advance capitalism. Retrieved May 19, 2015 from http://blogs.hbr.org/cs/2011/10/ceos_should_invest_in_communit.html.

Shamir, R. (2008). The age of responsabilization: on market-embedded morality. *Economy and Society*, 37(1), 1–19.

Sørensen, E. and Torfing, J. (2007). Governance network research: Towards a second generation. In E. Sørensen and J. Torfing (Eds), *Theories of Democratic Network Governance* (pp. 1–21). Basingstoke: Palgrave-Macmillan.

Springer, S. (2015). Postneoliberalism? *Review of Radical Political Economics*, 47 (1), 5–17.

Steiner-Khamsi, G. and Waldow, F. (Eds). (2012). *World Yearbook of Education 2012.* Abingdon, Oxon: Routledge.

Stewart, R., van Rooyen, C., Majoro, M., and de Wet, T. (2011). *Do micro-credit, micro-savings and micro- leasing serve as effective financial inclusion interventions enabling poor people, and especially women, to engage in meaningful economic opportunities in LMICs.* London: EPPI-Centre, Social Science Research Unit, University of London.

Teaching Leaders. (n.d). Retrieved May 19, 2015 from http://teachingleaders.org.uk/who-we-are/supporters-and-partners/education-partners/.

The Bellagio Initiative. (2011). Philanthropy: Current context and future outlook. Retrieved May 19, 2015 from http:/.bellagioinitiative.org/wp-content/uploads/2011/09/Philanthropy_Resource-Alliance_2011.pdf.

Tooley, J. (2007). Could for-profit private education benefit the poor? Some a priori considerations arising from case study research in India. *Journal of Education Policy, 22*(3), 321–342.

Tooley, J. (2009). Low cost private schools as part of the solution for education for all. *ATDF Journal, 5*(1 and 2), 3–9.

Verger, A. (2012). Framing and selling global education policy: The promotion of public–private partnerships for education in low-income contexts. *Journal of Education Policy, 27*(1), 109–130.

Watt, H. (2015, February 2). Massive expansion of academy programme to be announced by Prime Minister. *The Telegraph.* Retrieved May 19, 2015 from http://telegraph.co.uk/news/politics/11383017/Massive-expansion-of-academy-programme-to-be-announced-by-Prime-Minister.html.

Williams, P. (2002). The competent boundary spanner. *Public Administration, 80*(1), 103–124.

4 Private Authority or Ambiguity?

The Evolving Role of Corporations and Foundations in the Global Partnership for Education

Francine Menashy

Introduction

Private actors are unquestionably occupying increasingly prominent positions in the global education arena. Through both philanthropic endeavors and corporate social responsibility (CSR) programs, foundations and corporations have been financing, designing, and implementing education programs on a global scale. And at the same time, the private sector is now collaborating in education policy making alongside both state and non-state actors within new governance arrangements characterized as transnational public–private partnerships (PPPs).

In order to build understanding of the participation of non-state actors within these new international spaces, this chapter provides a case study of private participation at the governance level of the largest and most prominent transnational PPP in education, the Global Partnership for Education (GPE). After first contextualizing the rise in transnational public–private partnerships, this chapter introduces the notion of private authority as a conceptual approach to understanding the GPE and its inclusion of the private sector. It then introduces the GPE and traces historically the onset of private participation in its governance. It is argued that the private sector/foundations constituency is relatively disengaged and holds an ambiguous position within the GPE, rooted in a misalignment of motivations between the GPE, the private foundations, and the private companies. More specifically, this ambiguity results from inaccurate assumptions on the part of the GPE that private actors would contribute funds to the partnership, based on the mapping of health sector experiences onto GPE governance reforms. In addition, by combining companies and foundations into a single seat, internal conflict has characterized the constituency, contributing to the lack of engagement.

Through a study of the GPE's private sector/foundations constituency, this chapter aims to answer the following question: What has spurred private sector participation in the GPE, and to what degree do these private partners hold authority within the partnership? In order to answer this research question, this chapter studies the GPE through an examination of two data sources. First, an analysis has been conducted of several documents from GPE Board of Directors meetings. Documents – including minutes of meetings, final meeting reports, board presentations, and final decisions – from 14 Fast Track Initiative or GPE Board meetings held between 2009 and 2014 are included in the analysis.

The study furthermore draws from 19 in-depth interviews conducted with past and current members of GPE Board constituencies, including private sector/ foundations amongst others, and past and current GPE Secretariat staff. Via purposive sampling, interviewees were explicitly selected based on their current or past role within the GPE Board of Directors or interactions with Board members in GPE-related contexts. Interviews took place throughout 2014 and early 2015.

Contextualizing Transnational Public–Private Partnerships

The Rise of Transnational PPPs

Until very recently, the arena of international relations was characterized primarily by affairs between nation-states. Globalization has altered this environment, where an emerging global governance scenario involving non-state actors has replaced the dominance of solely intergovernmental relationships. In this current era of global governance, public policy making is now both a private and public sector shared activity (Ruggie 2004; Stone 2008). In light of this new environment, and in order to make decisions on issues that transcend nation-state boundaries, new forums have arisen that incorporate the expertise, perspectives, and funds of a range of public and private entities. These forums have been described as multi-stakeholder partnerships (Draxler 2012), or as I will use throughout this chapter, transnational PPPs. In these transnational PPPs, the public sector is often represented by governments and multilateral organizations, while the private sector includes civil society actors, private corporations, and private foundations.

Most transnational PPPs include private partners in their governance structures, as Board or Steering Committee members. Which organizations are included, however, depends upon the issue the PPP seeks to address. For example, GAVI, the Vaccine Alliance, includes representation on its Board of Directors from the for-profit pharmaceutical industry, and a seat solely dedicated to the Bill and Melinda Gates Foundation (GAVI 2014). The Global Alliance for Improved Nutrition (GAIN) includes on its Board representatives from private banks, as well as private foundations including the Children's Investment Fund Foundation and the Gates Foundation (GAIN 2014). The Consultative Group of the Cities Alliance, which tackles urban poverty, includes only the Ford Foundation as a private sector partner (Cities Alliance 2014).

Overall, the specific role a private partner takes within a transnational PPP is highly dependent on the goals of the business or foundation itself. And, as will be highlighted in this chapter, the mandates of private corporate actors are often very different from private foundations. On the one hand, private corporations who engage in international development activities and participate in transnational PPPs do so as part of a larger business objective, often within their corporate social responsibility programs. CSR activities are integral to a company's profit-oriented goals, and are often funded through a corporation's general operating budget. CSR programs promote a variety of activities, including cash contributions made to support a specific cause, in-kind contributions including, for instance, school supplies or classroom technology, or more leadership-oriented policy engagement, including participation in educational forums or playing advocacy roles concerning a particular issue (Bhanji 2008; Menashy 2013; van Fleet 2012). As argued by Utting and Zammit (2009), corporations which promote their international work under the banner of CSR do so when "management recognizes that it is in the interests of a company to ratchet up its approach, moving from the initial phases centered on denial and public relations towards new business models characterized by proactivity and heightened responsiveness to both threats and opportunities" and the inclusion of corporations within transnational PPPs are arguably a "manifestation" of such processes (Utting and Zammit 2009: 43).

On the other hand, foundations, or private philanthropies, are founded using the profits of corporate endeavors but operate independently of business interests. Such foundations consider themselves separate from their associated corporation, where oftentimes the only overlaps can be seen in name or sharing of leadership (Bhanji 2008; Menashy 2013). Some foundations function as grant-making bodies while others finance their own program activities. Most foundation funding directed towards education is spent in the United States, where philanthropists are seen as increasingly influential in public policy making (Bhanji in press; Reckhow 2013). But in the Global South, private foundations are gaining prominence, and are now members of several education-related transnational PPPs as their mandates often dovetail with the causes targeted by the PPP as a whole.

Private Authority and Transnational PPPs

According to observers, "PPPs are also seen as a logical response to structural changes in state–market–society relations that have occurred since the 1980s. Globalisation, liberalization ... have resulted in the rolling back of certain state functions and capacities, the massive growth in the number and global reach of corporations, and the emergence of new policy actors" (Utting and Zammit 2009: 43). The inclusion of the private sector in public-policy decision making via PPPs is therefore indicative of a number of recent trends, with the consequence of private actors being seen as embodying what international relations scholars have described as private authority in the global arena.

Until recently, analysts of international relations have limited their foci to the actions of individual nation-states, assuming that states are the only legitimate form of authority in the global sphere. However, in the context of new and globalized transnational arrangements, the private sector is not only widely considered to be a prominent player, but also one that embodies a new form of authority. As described by Hall and Biersteker:

> While these new actors are not states, are not state-based, and do not rely exclusively on the actions or explicit support of states in the international arena, they often convey and/or appear to have been accorded some form of legitimate authority. That is, they perform the role of authorship over some important issue or domain. They claim to be, perform as, and are recognized as legitimate

by some larger public (that often includes states themselves) as authors of policies, of practices, of rules, and of norms … What is most significant, however, is that they appear to have been accorded a form of legitimate authority.

(Hall and Biersteker 2002: 4)

The existence of transnational PPPs is therefore indicative of such a rise in private authority in global policy-making spaces, where non-state actors are not merely a presence, but ostensibly legitimate *partners*.

In education, recent literature has posited that private actors are now exercising authority in the policy-making arena via "network governance" where educational challenges are being addressed through partnerships of like-minded epistemic communities inclusive of the private sector (Ball 2010, 2012; Ball and Junemann 2012). Such networks have been argued to act as forums where "new voices and interests are represented in the policy process, and new nodes of power and influence are constructed or invigorated" (Ball 2010: 155). Policies on public education, its assessment, financing, and delivery are therefore being decided by both state and non-state actors, often within transnational public–private arrangements (Ball 2012; Ball and Junemann 2012; Rizvi and Lingard 2010). However, questions persist concerning the degree of authority that various partners hold within such public–private relationships, in particular those representing the non-state sector, a highly diverse group of organizations that, until rather recently, did not have a prominent place at the decision-making table.

The Global Partnership for Education and Private Participation in Governance

The most prominent transnational PPP in the education sector is the GPE. Its board of directors consists of 19 voting members including state and non-state representation, but only one board seat represents the private sector and foundations, which share a constituency (GPE 2012a, 2012d). Unlike many other transnational PPPs, financing is predominantly public, where the GPE Fund – a pooled fund from which disbursements are made to developing country governments – is financed primarily by Northern donor country partners of the GPE.

The GPE was initially called the Education for All Fast Track Initiative (FTI), and was launched as a trust fund of the World Bank. The FTI included a steering committee that was primarily responsible for relaying operational directions to a secretariat office, but was initially not a governing board. In 2009, the steering committee became a board of directors (Gartner 2010).

In the late 2000s, the FTI faced widespread criticism, which led to a major restructuring. In large part, the reforms responded to a 2010 external review of the organization, which cited several major shortcomings to its governance, including its over-dependence on the World Bank, and the dominance of donors on its board (Cambridge Education et al. 2010: 83). A constituency-based board model was established taking into consideration the criticism levied against the FTI, as well – as discussed below – a growing recognition of the significance of non-state actor input.

The board came to include four seats for the non-state sector, including three for civil society and one for private actors. As will be described, although a proposal was forwarded to form two separate seats, one for the foundations and another for the companies, the new constituency model would in the end include only one seat for the private sector/foundations – combining both companies and foundations. At present, the constituency includes over 20 members. The majority of members are foundations with overarching educational mandates, including such prominent organizations as the Open Society Foundation, Hewlett Foundation, Children's Investment Fund Foundation, and Mastercard Foundation. Companies represent a smaller number of members, but include large businesses such as Microsoft and Pearson Education, the latter of which is the constituency representative on the GPE Board of Directors.[1]

The Onset of Private Participation in the Restructured GPE

The participation of private sector partners in the restructured GPE was prompted and evolved rather differently for companies versus foundations. For instance, the foundations early on were seen as being important to the partnership as they held a capacity for innovation, particularly in terms of financing. One of the major criticisms of the FTI was its lack of funding to conflict-affected and fragile states, as FTI financing stipulated that countries must have a "sound education sector plan" (Cambridge Education et al. 2010; World Bank 2005: 5). Because the partnership was therefore unable to fund many countries, since, due to their fragility, they did not have strong education plans, there was a widespread "recognition that the FTI as it was, was not fit for purpose" (Private sector/foundations, interview, February 4, 2014).[2]

This acknowledgement of funding inflexibility led to a recognition that the expertise of non-state actors could inform better policies on aid to fragile states (Civil society, interview, January 22, 2014; Private sector/foundations, interview, February 4, 2014). For example, in 2007 a post-conflict country was unable to secure funding from the FTI, and was instead supported by a pooled fund which was spearheaded by the expertise of a private foundation and combined donor, multilateral, and private contributions. When the FTI began its restructuring, this pooled funding mechanism shed light on the expertise of private foundations to better support education in fragile contexts, bringing to the forefront the value that a foundation might bring to the partnership.

Foundations initially had very little engagement with the FTI:

> There was no space at all. Private foundations had not been engaged at all. Now it could be my own interpretation but I think because of the [post-conflict country] experience and how engaged we'd been, and also around that time I think the role of private foundations in global education was becoming more recognized or appreciated, I think there was a recognition that [foundations] were significant players that essentially needed to be coordinated as well.
> (Private sector/foundations, interview, February 4, 2014)

Inclusion of private foundations into the GPE was therefore in large part a result of acknowledging the limitations of the FTI, where a problematic feature of the FTI was its inflexible funding policies.

Also, at the time of the GPE restructuring, partnerships between donor governments and foundations were becoming more widespread, including various contracts and coordinated grants (Private sector/foundations, interview, January 31, 2014). And so it was a timely decision to include foundations in the discussions on the new board model. In order to develop a proposal to include foundations as a constituency, a small group of foundation representatives – each of whom had a relationship with the FTI previously – came together to gather a list of potential foundations that would consider serving as constituency members (Private sector/foundations, interview, January 31, 2014; Private sector/foundations, interview, February 4, 2014).

Concurrently, another list of potential private companies was being separately formulated, organized by a representative of the World Economic Forum (Private sector/foundations, interview, January 31, 2014; Private sector/foundations, interview, October 4, 2014). Including companies was seen as endeavoring to solidify a relationship with an increasingly important stakeholder in education. As an interviewee describes: "I think it was in anticipation of the fact that there's just a greater and greater emphasis on the role of the private sector" (Secretariat, interview, August 14, 2014).

As explained more fully below, the companies and foundations were combined into a single constituency seat. This was arguably due to a desire for keeping the board at a manageable size, but was also grounded in assumptions that actors associated with corporate entities have similar enough characteristics to be grouped together (Secretariat, interview, August 14, 2014; Secretariat, interview, September 24, 2014; Secretariat, interview, August 20, 2014). In addition, from very early on, the role of incorporating both foundations and companies into the GPE was driven by a belief that private sector actors would likely become a major financial resource in contributing to the GPE Fund. This belief was driven by a mapping of global health sector experiences onto education.

Health Sector Mapping

A key element in determining the governance structure of the GPE was the borrowing from transnational PPP models, in particular in the health sector. To advise decision making on the constituency model during the transition from the FTI to the GPE, a working group was delegated the task of producing suggestions for the board composition, to be presented at a meeting in 2010: "The working group was informed by a number of discussions and interviews with different FTI stakeholders as well as actors working with other global (mainly health) initiatives" (GPE 2010: 1). A report entitled *Strength and Weaknesses in the Governance of Selected Global Health Initiatives* was commissioned as well (Stenson 2010). Health sector experiences – informed in large part from experiences with the Global Fund to Fight AIDS, Tuberculosis and Malaria (the Global Fund) and GAVI – therefore played a fundamental role in the new GPE model.

The suggestions made from the health sector analysis included rationales for engaging the private sector, including an eagerness for foundations in particular to act as potential donors: "Foundations also represent a relatively unrestricted source of funding for special projects within FTI. If a model is chosen where foundations do not have a constituency of their own, they could possibly be included into the group of donors" (GPE 2010b: 10). However, private actors were not included as financiers in the final GPE governance model.

The mapping of health sector experiences onto the restructuring of the FTI did not go unnoticed by those involved in the process (Civil society, interview, January 13, 2014; Private sector/foundations, interview, January 31, 2014; Secretariat, interview, August 20, 2014). As one respondent describes: "there has always been a little bit of health sector envy" (Secretariat, interview, September 24, 2014), while another explains "they kept looking at what happened in health and saying 'Well, how do we get this constituency to be more non-traditional donors, actually to put money into GPE'?" although "you don't have foundations in the education sector the size of the foundations in health … We are not the health sector" (Private sector/foundations, interview, January 31, 2014; Civil society, interview, January 13, 2014).

And global education contributions made by companies and foundations indeed do not nearly match those of the health sector. For example, in its 2013 replenishment, of the over USD 12,006 million pledged to the Global Fund, 627.9 million was committed from the private sector (Global Fund 2013). As discussed below, only very recently two private foundations have pledged a contribution to the GPE Fund, yet this has been considered quite minimal. Moreover, there are far more large-scale multi-stakeholder partnerships focusing on health-related issues – including for example the Global Fund, the Global Alliance for Improved Nutrition, GAVI, the International Health Partnership and the Roll Back Malaria Partnership – which include major representation of the private sector in both policy making and financing. Private contributors to health funds often include those from the pharmaceutical and medical technology industry which has an interest in tracking the success of particular interventions (Benzanson and Isenman 2012; Hill 2011). Private participation in global education is simply not of the same size, type, or level of engagement as is seen in the health sector.

The Ambiguous Purpose of the Private Sector/Foundations Seat

Despite the fact that there were several rationales from the standpoint of the GPE that supported the involvement of the private sector, interviewees express that the purpose of the private sector/foundations constituency has persistently lacked clarity. As early as 2011, the constituency felt the need to better define their role within the context of the GPE governance. At the Copenhagen Pledging Conference in 2011, a constituency member made a "Statement from Private Sector and Private Foundations" that began with the following: "I represent one of the board's newest and most diverse constituencies: private sector and private foundations. We don't give funds directly to the GPE Fund, so you may be wondering why we're here" (GPE 2011: 1). The Statement was made in part to educate those from the constituency itself on how they could engage with the GPE even if not as funders: "it wasn't just whether you're putting money into the Fund, it was what are you doing that is contributing to these goals and objectives?" (Private sector/foundations, interview, January 31, 2014). The Statement indicates that, relatively early on within the restructured board, the private sector/foundations felt the need to clarify their involvement in the GPE, and to draw attention to their non-monetary contributions.

Yet the lack of clarity persists, and private sector/foundations board members feel they are continually questioning their role within the GPE. As one constituency member states: "What is the rationale for involving the private sector in this in the first place, and what is it that the GPE as a partnership and the Secretariat want from the private sector. You know, conversely, what does the private sector feel are the benefits and values from being involved. I don't think any of this has ever been fleshed out" (Private sector/foundations, interview, January 21, 2014). Constituency members have seen themselves as needing to respond to questions such as "Why are you contributing? Why are you at the table?" and are "constantly having to explain what the value added is … " (Private sector/foundations, interview, January 31, 2014). Interviewees describe the constituency members as "frustrated" in having to determine "ways to keep the business side interested, not just the foundation side, the business side" (Civil society, interview, March 3, 2014; Multilateral, interview, April 23, 2014). Private companies in particular, who see themselves as able to offer ideas and "solutions" to educational problems, have not been substantively supported within the GPE to take on this role (Private sector/ foundations, interview, January 21, 2014; Secretariat, interview, August 21, 2014). As another respondent summarizes: "internally and also with the GPE Secretariat they have yet to figure out how to best utilize the [private sector/foundations] constituency as a resource" (Private sector/foundations, interview, February 4, 2014).

Interviewees moreover reference a limited engagement in the GPE on the part of the private sector/foundations members, and the private sector companies in particular: "I think that the private sector has not seen the benefit of engaging the GPE, why would they do that, what's in it for them?" (Private sector/foundations, interview, February 3, 2014). Similarly, another interviewee expressed that "the GPE still struggles so much to get the private sector as fully engaged as it would like" (Secretariat, interview, September 24, 2014). A sign of this low commitment to the GPE is a limited interest in vying for leadership of the constituency, where "people aren't necessarily beating down the door" to serve as private sector/foundations board member representatives (Private sector/foundations, interview, February 4, 2014). According to a constituency member, the GPE still needs to resolve several aspects of the constituency's purpose:

> What does it mean to be, you know, part of the discussions and at the table? What does it mean to be advocating for the goals of the GPE? How does the private sector get drawn into discussions on the ground with government and others early on? And who are the representatives in all of those different pieces and how do they work together? I think all of that is really crucial.
>
> (Private sector/foundations, interview, January 21, 2014)

A Misalignment of Motivations: The GPE, the Companies, and the Foundations

GPE and Private Sector/Foundations Constituency Motivations

From an examination of past GPE board meeting documents, corroborated by the perception of interviewees, the GPE secretariat views the private sector/foundations constituency in a highly aspirational way, as potentially significant contributors to the GPE Fund. For instance, at a 2013 board meeting, the secretariat introduced a broad strategy for the GPE's future replenishment campaign, which included: "Central to the strategy for a successful replenishment was the need to focus on financing from four core target groups, namely traditional donors, developing country partners, emerging donors and *the private sector, including private foundations*" (GPE 2013b: 7; emphasis added). Interviewees concur that the secretariat seemed to be pushing for private sector contributions to the GPE Fund (Civil society, interview, January 13, 2014; Private sector/foundations, interview, January 31, 2014; Private sector/foundations, interview, February 3, 2014; Private sector/foundations, interview, February 4, 2014; Multilateral, interview, April 23, 2014). "They don't know what to talk to us about necessarily. They instinctively so often ask for money that they are getting the message now, generally, that that's not the best way we contribute" (Private sector/foundations, interview, January 21, 2014).

However, when interviewed, respondents indicated that it was improbable that the GPE Fund will ever receive substantial contributions from the private sector: "There's been some fairly unsophisticated thinking on the part of the secretariat, at least, that the private sector would, at the time at least, make financial contributions to the GPE Fund. By the way, that's incredibly unrealistic" (Civil society, interview, January 13, 2014); "I struggle to see them putting money into either the core cost of the secretariat or the big pot of money that is the GPE Fund" (Private sector/foundations, interview, February 3, 2014); "I don't think there is any chance that's going to happen" (Private sector/foundations, interview, January 21, 2014); "The private sector, these companies nor foundations, nobody is about to cut the check and put money into the GPE Fund ... It's a nice thing to talk about, but it's simply not going to happen" (Private sector/foundations, interview, February 4, 2014).

Events at the last GPE replenishment conference in June, 2014 contrast with some interviewee predictions, where two private foundations pledged a total of USD $23 million to the GPE Fund (GPE 2014). While a noteworthy commitment, it is difficult to determine if the new foundation pledges indicate a broader shift in sources of financing to the GPE. As a respondent describes, the nature of foundation funding is a "moving target" (Multilateral, interview, April 23, 2014). What is clearer is that no private companies have yet to make funding commitments, and interviewees expressed doubt, before and after the pledging conference, that this will change. Media commenters following the replenishment conference similarly stated that "GPE has failed yet again to convince businesses to pledge money to the fund" (Ravelo and Jones 2014).

Such doubt is largely rooted in the apparent priorities of the private sector, in particular the importance of tracking investments. Companies in particular "are not funding initiatives like this" but instead are seen to "invest in solutions and … expect returns on things and want to see the results" (Private sector/foundations, interview, January 21, 2014). But also, "It's hard for a foundation to say, I'm going to give a dollar into a pooled fund, unless it's for symbolic reasons, because you're accountable to your Board, and particularly with the new wave of foundations, they are in it for very specific, trackable outcomes" (Private sector/foundations, interview, January 31, 2014).

A mismatch is therefore evident between the aspirations and the reality concerning private contributions to the GPE Fund. In light of this, the attempts to parallel experiences with the health sector, where large pooled contributions are commonly made from the private sector, is simply unrealistic. And this incongruity between what is desired of the private sector/foundations constituency members and how they are in fact willing to function as partners within the GPE creates a very ambiguous situation.

Corporations' and Foundations' Motivations

A concern within the private sector/foundations constituency is what some have described as a considerable conflict within the constituency membership, between the foundations and companies. The sharing of a board seat is seen by some as problematic. Described as "strange bedfellows" and "different organizational animals," the companies are viewed as "… just a totally different kettle of fish" from the foundations (Private sector/foundations, interview, January 21, 2014; Private sector/foundations, interview, January 31, 2014). As one interviewee elaborated: "Unfortunately private foundations and the private sector [companies] in this, they come from two completely different angles" (Private sector/foundations, interview, February 4, 2014).

GPE member companies are widely seen as holding particular motivations for involvement in the GPE and in global education more generally: "The private sector is very much interested in okay how are we going to increase our profit margin? For even if it's a corporate social responsibility arm they're not there because they're just purely interested in education" (Private sector/foundations, interview, February 4, 2014). Moreover, private sector participation in the GPE is seen as embodying the "interaction of social and business issues" (Private sector/foundations, interview, January 21, 2014). Companies view themselves as "very good at solving solutions" (Secretariat, interview, August 21, 2014) and "more solutions-oriented" where they "invest in solutions and so … expect returns on things and want to see the results" (Private sector/foundations, interview, January 21, 2014).

Upon examining the rhetoric of the private companies who are members of the GPE, it is further evident that the overarching motivations of their participation in global education are inextricably tied to profit-eliciting activities, even under the banner of CSR. In a media interview, a private sector GPE member maintained that although "businesses are still seen as driven primarily by profit … there's no reason to be ashamed of that, 'we also care about outcomes and we want to invest smartly and in partnerships that are going to make a difference'" (Ravelo and Jones, 2014).

Interviewees readily contrasted the motivations and mandates of the private foundations and companies, where business actors see "profit as bottom-line, versus [foundations] where giving away is the bottom line" (Private sector/foundations, interview, January 31, 2014). Foundations are viewed primarily as grant-giving bodies, while companies seek to elevate profits whilst contributing to social causes (Private sector/foundations, interview, January 21, 2014; Private sector/foundations, interview, February 3, 2014; Private sector/foundations, interview, February 4, 2014). As one interviewee describes:

> private foundations and the business communities operate with separate mandates as certainly different cultures and in terms of the resources that they bring. Private foundations are a lot more about grants which they give to a number of partners who are on the ground, while the business community is a lot more of leveraging their expectation and using them to innovate.
> (Secretariat, interview, August 21, 2014)

As a result of these different mandates and associated motivations for involvement in the GPE, the constituency is "not a consolidated group, and they have very, very different interests" (Secretariat, August 14, 2014). As a result of such divergent objectives, there has been some past mistrust and tension within the constituency (Private sector/foundations, interview, February 4, 2014; Secretariat, interview, August 14, 2014; Secretariat, interview, August 21, 2014). One respondent made reference to "both tension and a desire for autonomy of those two combined constituencies, because they are quite different" (Civil society, interview, January 13, 2014). Others voiced that the main commonality between the companies and foundations is simplistically related to their non-state characteristic: "I think that sort of the 'private' name that links both private sector and private foundation is a bit of a red herring actually" (Private sector/foundations, interview, February 3, 2014).

This divide within the constituency led to a board proposal to split the seat between the foundations and companies (GPE 2012c: 3, 2012b). This was followed by a 2013 discussion by the GPE's Governance Working Group of potentially dividing the constituency into two (GPE 2013a: 7). Many constituency members strongly supported this proposal. As one interviewee voiced: "From [the foundation] perspective ... well that's fabulous, please have your own seat and take the rest of your private sector companies with you" (Private sector/foundations, interview, February 4, 2014).

However, the Board proposal to split the constituency did not pass. One reason cited was a practical need to keep the size of the board manageable (Civil society, interview, January 22, 2014). Other reasons, however, highlight the ambiguity around the private sector/foundation's role within the GPE. For instance, some board members expressed dissatisfaction with expanding the role of the private sector/foundations without committing resources to the GPE Fund: "They haven't had any financial contributions to GPE, and they haven't necessarily mobilized a huge amount of support for education to this day … It's not a bad thing that they have a more modest representation on the board" (Civil society, interview, January 13, 2014). In fact, some interviewees describe the private sector/foundations as too involved as board-level decision makers, and not in the role they ought to play as funders: "the private sector is hugely important in education, but they should participate through making contributions to the GPE Fund, basically … they should not be involved in setting the agenda for education on the ground" (Civil society, interview, March 7, 2014).

Another significant reason cited for the rejection of the proposal for separate board seats is the fact that the private sector/foundations had yet to influence any particular policy directions within the GPE: "We hadn't really made an impact as a joint constituency because we were so busy looking at each other and being suspicious, and what does that mean and why are these people here and … not really being as engaged and energized and mobilized as a constituency to really make an impact on the GPE. It was almost like we haven't even justified our individual seat so why would we need two seats?" (Private sector/foundations, interview, February 4, 2014). Another interviewee explains that the members of the constituency "function on paper but they really didn't come together as a very meaningful entity" (Secretariat, interview, September 24, 2014). The lack of engagement, seen as rooted in a lack of clarity as to why or how to be engaged, led to few achievements as a constituency.

According to some interviewees, there is currently less tension within the constituency than in the past, while others maintain that a separated seat would improve the governance of the GPE. It is, however, important to note that the private sector/foundations board members as well as the secretariat are actively endeavoring to better determine the constituency's purpose within the GPE through the development of a much-needed private sector engagement strategy (GPE 2012e: 2; GPE 2013b: 27). This strategy will include several dimensions of private engagement, from more effective leadership and advocacy in governance and policy, to more input in innovations within education systems. The secretariat is working in concert with the constituency to also develop more precise principles of engagement. In order to manage these new developments, the secretariat recently hired a staff member who specializes in private sector engagement. The GPE secretariat therefore recognizes the challenges concerning the involvement of private actors and is working towards improvement (GPE 2013b: 7; Secretariat, interview, August 14, 2014; Secretariat, interview, August 21, 2014; Secretariat, interview, August 20, 2014).

Conclusion

Although there is little doubt that new players are wielding authority in the current global education policy environment, including private philanthropic and business actors, this study has highlighted a case in which private participation cannot be necessarily equated with private authority.

Since the early days of the restructuring from the FTI, the role of the private partners within the GPE's governance has been poorly clarified. This is partly due to aspirational assumptions that the private actors would serve a financing function to the GPE Fund, based largely on inaccurate parallels made between the health and education sectors. The ambiguous role of the constituency has led to a relatively disengaged membership. Problematic as well has been the internal conflict between foundations and companies, who see themselves as distinct actors who aim to serve different purposes in the global education policy arena. In the absence of a common ground, the private sector/foundations constituency has yet to effectively voice a particular educational priority within the GPE.

This case therefore exposes two tensions: (1) between the GPE and private actors; and (2) between the companies and the foundations. The first tension can be described as one of conflicting goals: financing versus policy agenda-setting. The GPE's aspiration to receive funding from private actors has come in conflict with their desire to primarily inform decision making. Also, given that the private sector and foundations are restricted to only one seat on a board of 19, there is likely a limit to how much substantive policy input can come from the constituency members. However, because the vast majority of private actors still has not agreed to contribute to the pooled fund, evidently neither have the GPE nor the private sector/foundations fully achieved what they want from the relationship.

The second tension involves the relationship between two different types of organizations that must work collaboratively. According to interviews, it seems the core of this conflict rests on the mandate and modes of each – one being for-profit and entrepreneurial, the other as non-profit and grant giving. The aim of the constituency to have input into the GPE agenda has been obstructed because of this tension. And so, it seems as yet neither have the companies or the foundations benefited much from participating in the GPE. This tension moreover speaks to how the private sector as a new and growing element to international education policy making needs to be conceptualized as a very complex and dynamic group of very different actors.

Of course, the GPE is a relatively young organization, and its board was restructured only very recently. As with all organizations, the GPE is evolving. At the time of writing, the GPE Secretariat is actively working to ease the tensions described above through more clearly outlining the principles of engagement for the private sector/foundations constituency and consulting with members on how to better utilize both the companies and foundations as resources to aid in the functioning and effectiveness of the partnership. Whether and how this alters the degree to which private authority is enacted within the GPE remains to be seen.

Notes

1 Master list of private sector foundations constituency members is based on a mailing list provided directly to the author by GPE Secretariat staff.
2 Interviews are cited according to GPE Board constituency membership or as GPE Secretariat staff and date of interview.

References

Ball, S. J. (2010). New states, new governance and new education policy. In M. W. Apple, S. J. Ball, and L. A. Gandin (Eds). *The Routledge International Handbook of the Sociology of Education*. London: Routledge.

Ball, S. J. (2012). *Global education inc. New policy networks and the neo-liberal imaginary*. London: Routledge.

Ball, S. J. and Junemann, C. (2012). *Networks, new governance and education*. Bristol: The Policy Press.

Bezanson, K. A. and Isenman, P. (2012). *Governance of new global partnerships: Challenges, weaknesses, and lessons*. Washington, DC: Center for Global Development.

Bhanji, Z. (2008). Transnational corporations in education: Filling the governance gap through new social norms and market multilateralism? *Globalisation, Societies and Education, 6*(1): 55–73.

Bhanji, Z. (in press). The business case for philanthropy, profits, and policy making in education. In K. Mundy, A. Green, R. Lingard and A. Verger (Eds). *The handbook of global education policy*. West Sussex, UK: Wiley-Blackwell.

Cambridge Education, Mokoro and Oxford Policy Management. (2010). *Mid-term evaluation of the EFA Fast Track Initiative: A final synthesis*. Retrieved January 10, 2014 from http://www.mokoro.co.uk/files/13/publication/AppendixVNoteonApproachandMethods.pdf.

Cities Alliance. (2014). Our members. Retrieved December 3, 2014 from http://www.citiesalliance.org/our-members.

Draxler, A. (2012). International PPPs in education: New potential or privatizing public goods? In S. Robertson, K. Mundy, A. Verger and F. Menashy (Eds). *Public private partnerships and education: New actors and modes of governance in a globalising world*. London: Edward Elgar.

GAIN. (2014). Organization. Retrieved December 3, 2014 from http://www.gainhealth.org/organization/governance/.

Gartner, D. (2010). *Transformed governance and the Education for Al--Fast Track Initiative*. Washington, DC: The Brookings Institution.

GAVI. (2014). Board composition. Retrieved December 3, 2014 from: http://www.gavi.org/about/governance/gavi-board/composition/.

Global Fund. (2013). *Fourth voluntary Global Fund replenishment pledges*. Washington, DC: Global Fund.

GPE. (2010). *Suggestions for FTI board composition*. Retrieved March 1, 2014 from: http://www.globalpartnership.org/content/suggestions-fti-board-composition-29-april-2010.

GPE. (2011). Statement from private sector and private foundations. Statement presented at Global Partnership for Education board of directors' meeting, Copenhagen, Denmark, November 8, 2011.

GPE. (2012a). *Charter for the global partnership for education*. Washington, DC: Global Partnership for Education.

GPE. (2012b). *Constituency composition on the board of directors – Paris*. Retrieved March 1, 2014 from: http://www.globalpartnership.org/content/constituency-composition-board-directors.

GPE. (2012c). *Constituency composition and representation on the board of directors – Berlin*. Retrieved March 1, 2014 from: http://www.globalpartnership.org/content/note-constituency-composition-and-representation-board-directors.

GPE. (2012d). *Global governance manual*. Washington, DC: Global Partnership for Education.

GPE. (2012e). *Strategic plan: 2012–2015*. Washington, DC: Global Partnership for Education.

GPE. (2013a). *Report of the governance working group: Recommendations on board structure.* Retrieved March 1, 2014 from: http://www.globalpartnership.org/content/report-governance-working-group-recommendations-board-structure-annex-9-amendments-gpe-fund.

GPE. (2013b). *Report of the meeting of the board of directors – Addis Ababa.* Retrieved March 1, 2014 from: http://www.globalpartnership.org/content/report-meeting-board-directors-18-19-november-2013-addis-ababa-ethiopia.

GPE. (2014). Pledges. Accessed August 29, 2014. http://www.globalpartnership.org/replenishment/pledges.

Hall, R. B. and Biersteker, T. J. (2002). The emergence of private authority in the international system. In R. B. Hall and T. J. Biersteker (Eds). *The emergence of private authority in global governance.* Cambridge: Cambridge University Press.

Hill, P. (2011). Understanding global health governance as a complex adaptive system. *Global Public Health,* 6(6): 593–605.

Menashy, F. (2013). Private sector engagement in education worldwide: Conceptual andcritical challenges. In A. Wiseman and E. Anderson (Eds). *Annual review of comparative and international education.* Bingley, UK: Emerald Publishing.

Ravelo, J. L. and Jones, R. (2014). What the private sector wants from the GPE. Retrieved July 15, 2014 from: https://www.devex.com/news/what-the-private-sector-wants-from-the-gpe-83778.

Reckhow, S. (2013). *Follow the money: How foundation dollars change public school politics.* Oxford: Oxford University Press.

Rizvi, F. and Lingard, B. (2010). *Globalizing education policy.* New York: Routledge.

Ruggie, J. G. (2004). Reconstituting the global public domain – issues, actors, and practices. *European Journal of International Relations,* 10(4): 499–531.

Stenson, B. (2010). *Strengths and weaknesses in the governance of selected global health initiatives.* Retrieved March 1, 2014 from: http://www.globalpartnership.org/content/strengths-and-weaknesses-governance-selected-global-health-initiatives-report.

Stone, D. (2008). Global public policy, transnational policy communities and their networks. *Policy Studies Journal,* 36(10): 19–38.

Utting, P. and Zammit, A. (2009). United Nations–business partnerships: Good intentions and contradictory agendas. *Journal of Business Ethics,* 90(1): 39–56.

van Fleet, J. (2012). *Scaling up corporate social investments in education: Five strategies that work.* Washington, DC: The Brookings Institution.

World Bank. (2005). *Fast Track Initiative: Building a global compact for education.* Retrieved June 30, 2013 from: http://siteresources.worldbank.org/EDUCATION/Resources/Education-Notes/EdNotes_FastTrack.pdf.

5 Entrepreneurial Influence in Brazilian Education Policies

The Case of Todos Pela Educação[1]

Erika Moreira Martins and
Nora Rut Krawczyk

Introduction

Brazil, like many other countries, is experiencing a reconfiguration of the public policy space, in which entrepreneurs and corporations seek to alter and influence the operational capacity of the administrative apparatus, including the education system. As part of this process, private actors have become privileged interlocutors in the education policy field. In Brazil, there are a number of organizations created by the corporate sector that have become partners with government in the education arena. Among others,[2] the movement called *Todos pela Educação* (TPE – All for Education) stands out. This advocacy network represents the interests of sections of the Brazilian bourgeoisie that – with certain success, but also resistance – seek to introduce deep reforms in Brazilian public basic education.

In the last decades, basic education in Brazil has experienced important changes, particularly in its scope and coverage. Up until the 1980s, the rates of school enrollment and performance success at elementary and high school levels were embarrassingly low. After the 1990s, education policies to expand different education levels have become more evident and are tending to universalize standards at more and more levels – first at elementary level and currently at the preschool and high school levels. A growth of school enrollments and the inclusion of new social segments have been observed in the education system, yet high rates of school dropouts and school failure, as well as age/grade distortions, have persisted. Therefore, there is a clear impetus for changes in Brazilian education. However, there is no consensus about what would be the most appropriate policies for this new reality, and this raises conflicts between different sections of society. As we further explore the area in this context, corporate actors have become privileged actors in defining educational policies. However, such a privileged position does not preclude tensions, conflicts, and contradictions over the policies and their implementation in schools.

Entrepreneurial participation in education policies is not new in Brazil. On the contrary, public education has developed, from the beginning, as the result of struggles between different sectors of society, including local elites. Because of this and other sources of pressure, the Brazilian education system has evolved into a decentralized and very unequal system in different regions of the country and, for several decades, has privileged vocational training. As happened in most Latin American countries in the 1990s, the reform of the Brazilian state has altered the responsibilities and characteristics assumed by the state, the market, and society, and has introduced a new rationale for governance in the area of public education. Therefore, during the administrations of President Fernando Henrique Cardoso (1995–2002), the Brazilian Executive branch and international agencies encouraged the corporate sector to assume more responsibility for the population's welfare, especially in issues relating to education.

The slogan *responsabilidade social* (social responsibility) emerged to describe the decentralization of responsibilities and duties to the market, a process in which the *Programa Comunidade Solidária* (Community Program for Solidarity) played a leading role. Presided over by Ruth Cardoso, then Brazil's First Lady, this program promoted the effective management of a set of social programs through the participation of entrepreneurs against poverty. A range of regulatory changes contributed to the emergence of civil society actors and their penetration in the public services arena. These not-for-profit organizations, through different partnership arrangements, complemented the public budget for social services and brought other sorts of private resources into the system (Krawczyk 2008: 2014b).

Today, corporate engagement in education has entered a new stage in Brazil. It is not necessary to encourage entrepreneurs to be involved in social issues anymore, as was required in the *Comunidade Solidária* program. Now, there is constant corporate involvement at different levels of education that, collectively and/ or individually, interlaces with political actors at the federal, state, and municipal executive levels, as well as with legislative agencies. These new forms of corporate engagement, explicitly and implicitly, establish a form of co-management within the education system.

Public education is a significant market segment, constantly re-created and penetrated by private actors involved in the elaboration and commercialization of education-related materials, in training teachers, and in providing consultancy services, among other areas. However, this activity is not limited to business with the government, but also (and increasingly) is active in disseminating entrepreneurial ideology to children and young people (who are narrowly seen by the corporate sector as their future workforce). Importantly, in Brazil, the corporate sector has established itself within the advocacy coalition called TPE. In this chapter, we reveal how TPE has been aligned with the Brazilian government and what have been the main outcomes of this coalition's increasing participation in the public policy sphere.

The Creation of the "All for Education" Movement

TPE was created in 2006 by a group of entrepreneurs from several economic sectors (including finance and industry), and it represents a significant section of the Brazilian bourgeoisie. Some of the most relevant corporations that are part of the TPE are the Itaú Group, Gerdau, Pão de Açúcar, the Globo Group, and a range of institutes and foundations linked to the business world, such as the Ayrton

Senna Institute, the Group of Institutes, Foundations and Companies – GIFE, the Roberto Marinho Foundation, the Ethos Institute, and the Abril Group.

The TPE movement defines itself as a nationwide non-partisan alliance (Todos Pela Educação 2012). It represents a broad coalition of the main shareholders of companies, directors of third sector organizations, and government leaders of education sectors.[3] Important entrepreneurial groups and international organizations, such as the Inter-American Development Bank, have supported the TPE through donations.

TPE defined its plan of action on the basis of research that aimed to identify similarities between the education policies, proposals, and programs implemented by like-minded education foundations and institutes in the country:

> We are going to work on areas where everyone is aligned. This survey grid showed there were far more similarities than differences, though people were not real partners. In this grid, we included private investors, foundations, the Itaú Social Foundation, the Unibanco Institute, the Leman Foundation, the Bradesco Foundation and the Ayrton Senna Institute. We assessed the top private investors in education and realized that they had many similarities but that they rarely worked together. In 2005, there was very little alignment between the government and these institutes or civil society in general. Therefore, we *proposed an immediate piece of work: both the space and the need for an organization to articulate the different efforts towards a common objective were required. Then, we started to work on it.*
>
> (Martins 2013a: 64. Interview with TPE's executive
> director, emphasis added by authors)

A measurable, consensual, and easy-to-understand set of targets[4] was established by the TPE. On the basis of these targets, the TPE organized and disclosed public education data, identified the key problems, and promoted specific solutions and proposals through the main communication channels of the country.

The TPE movement appeared at the same time as education assumed strategic importance for Brazil's development project at the beginning of the twenty-first century. Disparate social classes that had gained representation in the government after the election of President Lula da Silva joined the cause. At that point, in addition to the universalization of basic education, it was necessary to reach international levels of competitiveness and targeted development. Governments and particular sectors of society had to be involved in basic education – in different ways – as co-responsible for improving education quality standards.

Co-Responsibility for Education Quality and Re-Organization of the Brazilian Education System

TPE actions are based on the entrepreneurial experience of their members, and are legitimatized by the idea that different segments of society need to assume co-responsibility for education in Brazil.

CO-RESPONSIBILITY FOR THE WHOLE is the ethical cornerstone of the All for Education Commitment, which consists of the convergent, complementary and synergetic actions of public policies, entrepreneurial actors and non-profit social organizations; [...] The state has the duty and obligation to be the keeper of the universal aim of assisting everyone. The entrepreneurial sector stands out for its ability to make things happen through rationalizing resources with efficiency, efficacy and effectiveness. Non-Profit Social Organizations (Third Sector) are characterized by their sensibility, creativity and spirit of struggle.

(Todos Pela Educação 2006a: 7)

TPE recognizes that there have been important improvements in public education in Brazil, but questions why governments were not able – as national and international indicators showed – to combine school enrollments with the retention of students and quality levels of education. For TPE, school failures, dropouts, and particularly the poor performance of students in international examinations, such as the Programme for International Student Assessment (PISA), are measurable signs of government inefficiency and poor quality standards of education. It concludes that "schools don't teach, students don't learn and Brazil doesn't improve" (Todos Pela Educação 2006b: 9).

TPE proposals are based on the assumption that public education is in crisis in three main areas: quality standards, responsibility, and management. To overcome these problems, the movement proposes the re-organization of public education into a nationwide program in which quality standards for public education are the real priority. For TPE, these crises are interrelated: the crisis of quality occurs because the government is incapable of administering public education and because of the lack of commitment from society to monitoring and pressing the government. That is why co-responsibility for education is one of TPE's principles.

For the Movement, co-responsibility for education must occur without contradicting the interests or leadership of entrepreneurial groups. Despite its talk of co-responsibility, the TPE itself faces some issues of representation. Although aiming to mobilize all segments of society in support of its proposals, communication with essential agents for education improvements is not only poor but also quite hierarchical. The idea of co-responsibility implies that teachers and other educationists are less important and tells them what they have to do without listening to their main concerns and proposals. TPE considers the responsibility of teachers as being restricted to mere compliance with its recommendations, despite the movement's intention to motivate all sectors of society in the education debate.

For TPE, teachers are mainly responsible for educational quality and play a central role in the education changes to come. Teachers need to be personally accountable for their students' performance and schools should provide them with support "in what they are skilled to do: teaching and assuring that pupils learn." Therefore, "teachers should have the right to feel responsible and to be accountable for their classes' performance, requiring real opportunities for improvement and professional in-service and development" (Todos Pela Educação 2006b: 26–27). Previous education reforms have not succeeded, due to a lack of consideration for teachers, which has created "strong ideological and corporate opposition among teachers concerning the plans, programs, projects and reforms proposed by political offices" (Todos Pela Educação 2006b: 25–26).

Managers should "encourage the educational inclusion and retention of all young people in order to permanently overcome the social differences in our country which are defined by educational qualifications" (Todos Pela Educação 2010: 23). To establish an efficient performance-focused mechanism for school supervision is a matter for the Department of Education. TPE also proposes that the Department of Education's management decisions should be informed by data collected from schools in real time (Todos Pela Educação 2006b: 30). TPE's inclination is toward performance-based management, entrepreneurship, excellence, and efficiency are the focus of education quality standards.

The movement also questions the role played by families in education. Parents should be "active, participative and critical regarding their children's education." Taking as an example the demand for quality in private schools, co-responsibility for education should position parents and students as consumers:

> In public, tuition-free schools, parents tend to think that they cannot claim their consumer rights as parents do in private schools. In public schools, mainly those attended by more disadvantaged and economically vulnerable segments of society, such a position could be taken as a lack of gratitude or respect for those in charge.
>
> (Todos Pela Educação 2006b: 7, 12).

There is some opposition to the movement's proposals from teachers' associations and from critical social movements. Among the claims, there are critics of the entrepreneurial focus in education, of the concept of quality linked to the achievement of goals measured by standard tests, and of TPE's modus operandi.

In the next section, we specify some of the main strategies TPE use to influence public policy making, and to advance its education policy priorities.

Action Strategies

The need for an alliance through which entrepreneurial groups, governments, and other sections of society would be committed to work toward the improvement of public school quality standards comes from the assumption that social problems are too numerous and complex for the state to handle alone. This also applies to individual corporations. Therefore, some entrepreneurs have decided to work as a coalition to influence and advance their preferred education policy solutions for the nation. The increasingly effective influence of TPE on education policies nationwide, as well as on a significant portion of Brazilian society, is based on two core strategies: network organization, and technical know-how and communication.

Inter-Organizational Network – Interrelating Subjects and Organizations

TPE members are formally and informally embedded in a broader network composed of several consultancy companies, third sector organizations, and governmental agencies. They assume positions or approach traditional agencies representing specific sectors, such as Federação das Indústrias do Estado de São Paulo (FIESP – Federation of Industries of the State of São Paulo) and Federação Brasileira de Bancos (FEBRABAN – Brazilian Federation of Banks), and act as counselors in international agencies and as state executives, representatives, or advisors. Several members of the TPE have (or used to have) important governmental positions in the education sector: as members of the National Education Council and the National Union of Municipal Directors of Education, as presidents of the Instituto Nacional de Pesquisas Educacionais (INEP - The National Institute for Educational Research), as presidential advisors in the Ministry of Education, and even as Ministers of Education.

TPE's participation is so diverse that institutions confer on it wide powers, legitimization, and influence over ideas and values such as philanthropy, voluntary actions, corporate and social commitment, collaboration, and co-responsibility. This allows the coalition to work in decision-making sectors inside the government and in society as a whole, thus contributing to the creation and consolidation of consensus around their preferred policy ideas.

It is important to emphasize, however, that TPE actions have gone beyond the goals of its founding members. The movement has worked to involve increasing sectors of society in its proposals. The high number of partners and media exposure has turned TPE into a key education reference and a nationwide movement (Martins 2013a: 105). Nonetheless, within the structure of the organization, policy positions (presidential, counseling, and coordination) are still predominately in the hands of corporate actors, who are in charge of setting the main guidelines and priorities.

According to Lima (2007), TPE is a dense and decentralized network, with a low level of fragmentation: that is, it is a coalition with a cohesive ideological orientation. Moreover, the individual actors within the TPE network, from the beginning, have been well organized. Its decisive influence in education policies shows the complexity of the TPE network and its interlacing with people and agencies. This happens because, when approaching governments, members of the movement – who are also part of other sectors and share the same ideals – sometimes act individually, or as collective actors representing the TPE itself.

The project "Lei de Responsabilidade Educacional"[5] (Education Responsibility Act) is a good example of how this mechanism of influence operates. Since 2006, the draft of this law has been under evaluation in the House of Representatives. During 2014, 49 professionals attended open meetings to discuss the law; these included secretaries of education, directors of research institutes, university professors, and researchers, among others. Twenty-one of these people were also members of the movement and shared TPE ideas. As a collective agency, TPE took part in the discussion through its executive director. In fact, it is even more important to emphasize here that a federal representative, who was a member of the TPE, proposed the basis for the draft law (Martins 2013b).

There are also partnerships set up by the TPE and governmental or private agencies – for example, the cooperation agreement established in 2014 between the TPE, INEP, and the Associação Brasileira de Avaliação Educacional (Abave – Brazilian Association for the Assessment of Education Achievement), to analyze and publicize the results of the external assessments of basic education.[6] Here, it is important to mention that both the INEP director and the director of Abave are also TPE members.

Technical Knowhow and Communication Skills

TPE is recognized as a legitimate actor in the Brazilian education field. After its constitution, it quickly achieved a high public reputation for education expertise. Part of its reputation comes from its access to the media and other communication channels, promoting disclosure of its technical know-how; in fact, TPE acts as a think tank in the education field. The TPE's Technical Committee produces and publishes documents and videos, systematizes what it considers good practice by the government and private companies, monitors and publicizes education indicators and results from state and federal evaluations, and compares the performance of the Brazilian education system with that of other countries.

The penetration of TPE in the mainstream media of the country is possible thanks to the TPE network itself (some TPE members are media entrepreneurs and communication professionals themselves), as well as through the economic power of the TPE. These resources have allowed the TPE to be part of the political debate on education and spread its proposals widely among schools, agencies, governments, and within society. To that end, TPE works primarily with opinion leaders, seeking to influence society as a whole.

Among other actions, they offer journalism training in education, collaborate in preparing interviews, and suggest topics and sources to journalists and publishers. TPE members also publish opinion articles on education in the media, disclose statistical data, and publish reports on education topics.[7] The main objective of this strategy is to generate consensus and form a single narrative on education. Through media acumen, TPE has spread its ideas, gained support and created proposals nationwide. Numerous resources are available on the TPE's homepage, and are openly accessible online.

On education targets, it is important to emphasize the alignment of the TPE and government proposals, particularly those set out in the Plano de Desenvolvimento da Educação (PDE - Education Development Plan). Not surprisingly, these targets were proposed by members of the TPE's technical committee, who are working or used to work at different levels of the Executive branch after the first administration of President Lula da Silva.

The PDE was launched in 2007, during the second term of President Lula da Silva, in the center of a series of priority programs for the development of the country. To regulate its objectives and targets, the Ministry of Education issued the decree law 6.094/2007: Plano de Metas Compromisso Todos Pela Educação (Plan of Targets, All for Education Commitment). As suggested by its name, there is a clear frame alignment between the PDE and the TPE movement:

> The main law decree signed by the then president was the Plan of Targets – an All for Education Commitment, which gathers together actions on Basic Education and is *named in recognition of the synchronicity of the 5 Targets, supported by the Movement, and the objectives of the Plan proposed by the MEC (Ministry of Education and Culture)*. Following the position supported by the 'All for Education' movement (which says that management by results would improve the quality standards of education in Brazil), the MEC introduced, among other measures, and in a non-precedented manner, a plan of targets and quality indicators as a condition for receiving state and municipal funding. It is also a nationwide program, that would not depend on a fixed-term government, therefore requiring a permanent dialogue with the whole of society, keeping its diversity of viewpoints, and different levels of public administration.
> (Todos Pela Educação 2007, emphasis added by authors)

Some researchers admitted that the alliance with the TPE allowed them to influence the definition of education policy in Brazil by incorporating (among other things) the business agenda represented by TPE in the PDE (Leher 2010). Indeed, the rising of the "Partido dos Trabalhadores" (PT – Labor Party) to the level of federal government has aligned an important faction of the party to the corporate sector, dissociating it from its original purpose. According to Saviani (2007), "this might explain why the Ministry of Education and Culture was closer to the TPE than to the teachers unions when elaborating the PDE" (Saviani 2007: 1242–3). As a result of the PDE implementation, school networks experienced an avalanche of entrepreneurial terminologies and practices: managers, targets, efficiency, total quality management systems, among others (Leher 2014), and governments evaluated the quality improvement in education through the achievement of targets and quantitative measurable rates.

The Creation of a Latin American Network – REDUCA

TPE, in partnership with the Inter-American Development Bank (IADB), organized the Latin American Meeting of Civil Society Organizations for Education, as part of a broader strategy to construct a movement for influencing Latin American public education. Held in 2011 in the city of Brasilia, the meeting was attended by 13 Latin American non-state organizations (with a similar constituency to the TPE), IADB representatives, the Ministry of Education, journalists, government representatives, and third-sector agents. REDUCA – the Latin American Network of Civil Society Organizations for Education – was created in the context of this meeting and is currently composed of 14 organizations. Apart from the TPE, these were: Proyecto EducAR 2050 (Argentina); Empresarios por la

Educación (Colombia); Fundación Educación 2020 (Chile); Fepade (El Salvador); Grupo FARO (Ecuador); Empresarios por la Educación (Guatemala); Ferema (Honduras); Mexicanos Primero (Mexico); Eduquemos (Nicaragua); Unidos por la Educación (Panama); Juntos por la Educación (Paraguay); Empresarios por la Educación (Peru); and, EDUCA (Dominican Republic).

Since its launch, REDUCA has strengthened its position in Latin America through public education action in countries where this network exists. Every year, REDUCA holds meetings with its members, attended by international organizations such as IADB, teaching professionals, and politicians. Since 2013, the European Union (EU) has supported REDUCA's implementation projects concerning school dropouts and failures, professional careers and manager training and preschool education in Latin America.

Among the organizations comprising REDUCA, TPE is perceived by the IADB and other partners in the network as the most successful case, an example to be followed because it is supported by the strong Brazilian media and because of its organization, penetration, and influence in government and in public opinion (Martins 2013a: 115). Such a success seems clear when we analyze TPE as a new source of power that, within the politics of the education landscape in Brazil, combines and advances education demands and proposals made by the government, private corporations, and other sectors of society.

Conclusions

As the TPE case shows, political–educational production has not only turned into a trading target, but also into a deeply ideological process for a segment of the Brazilian bourgeoisie. This ideological target is consolidated in public spaces around the country, with TPE being one of the most representative actors. The proactive attitude adopted by the corporate sector in education policy-making takes place in different domains of social action (meetings, media, publications, and services for education) and government realms (federal and state executive branches, legislative branches, and municipalities). Furthermore, it has the support of a state apparatus that shares its proposals and works for their implementation.

This is a process that has been prepared over decades and, with regard to education, was encouraged by national and international conditions. Among them, we find: the pseudo-democratization of education; the expansion of coverage with access for new sectors of society; the elevation of efficiency and universalization of private management (known as "entrepreneurial technology"); the encouragement – coming from international[8] and governmental organizations – for corporate sectors to influence education and the strengthening of the role that international education indicators play in shaping countries' policies in education.

The alarming narrative articulated by TPE about the poor quality of Brazilian education, which regularly penetrated different media channels, explains the impetus for quick, even magical, solutions, aligned with international policy trends, usually those of a more managerial nature. In fact, when TPE refers to the "education crisis" in Brazil, it is emphasizing the need to reorganize public education on the basis of management practices, such as those set by international bodies and advanced by the Washington and the post-Washington Consensus that, since the 1990s, have tried to alter the competencies and responsibilities of the state, the market and schools in education (Verger 2014; Fonseca 1998).

The empirical and scientific evidence used by corporate organizations in Brazil is grounded in economics due to, according to them, the capacity of this discipline for generating useful "technical knowledge" for proposing robust education policies (Krawczyk 2014a; Delvaux 2009). Evidence also comes in the form of the experience of education reform from different countries, with a focus on the United States due to its leading role in experimenting with managerial and pro-market policies, including merit-based pay, charter schools and school choice policies (Klees et al. 2012). The implementation of curriculum standards, as well as the promotion of the culture of entrepreneurship among children, adolescents, and educators are also policies from the US which Brazilian corporate actors encourage schools to emulate.

The current political–educational segment that has become hegemonic in Brazilian society, and that is represented by TPE, is the one that, as claimed by Boito, "occupies an intermediate position between the traditional national bourgeoisie, susceptible to adopting anti-imperialist practices, and an old *comprador* bourgeoisie, a mere extension of imperialism inside these countries" (Boito 2012: 67).[9] Being very heterogeneous, ranging from large industrial groups to financial firms, including retail chains and other business sectors, the internal bourgeoisie has contradictory interests. What unifies such different sectors is the commitment to international financial capital and national industry, and the necessity to be competitive with global rivals abroad. One of its main characterizing elements is its close relationship with the Brazilian government, which, according to Boito, protects their interests and supports their proposals.

With regard to education at least, this bourgeois segment of society is eager to project the image of the country they wish to have. Strengthening economic competiveness in a globalized market is the key to building the nation it imagines. Moreover, improving the development of human resources and Brazil's position in the international education rankings are essential variables to achieving this target. International indicators such as PISA are used to raise the problem of education quality in Brazil and, especially, to validate certain policy options.

Tensions, disputes, and conflicts in the governmental field are intrinsic to the democracy–capitalism relationship, since they express questions about the reproduction of power structures. In this chapter, understanding education as a political field situated to promote hegemony has allowed us to better understand the contradictions and the complex and controversial process involved in the definition of educational policies and priorities in Brazil. However, we can also assume that each phase of capitalism has a particular dynamic when it comes to building hegemony on the part of the bourgeoisie. Accordingly, it is necessary to understand and continue to analyze this dynamic, its universe of contradictions, and its counter-hegemonic forms.

Notes

1 This chapter has been developed with support from the Foundation for the State of São Paulo – FAPESP/Brazil. The chapter is based on the project *Movimento 'Todos pela Educação': um projeto de nação para a educação Brasileira* (All for Education Movement), a nationwide project for Brazilian education carried out by Erika Moreira Martins (2013), under the supervision of Professor Nora Rut Krawczyk.

2 As, for example, "*Parceiros da Educação*," Ayrton Senna Institute, Roberto Marinho Foundation, and Lemann Foundation.

3 Among TPE founder members there are some senior members of the government. For example, municipality directors of education, Secretaries of Education Councils, directors of the National Institute of Educational Studies and Research, and representatives of the Ministry of Education.

4 The TPE targets are: (1) Every child and adolescent, from 4 to 17 years of age, should attend school; (2) Every 8-year-old child should be totally able to read and write; (3) Every student should be able to keep pace with the appropriate grade level of education; (4) Every 19-year-old adolescent should be able to conclude secondary education; (5) Increase and manage well the investments in education. Investment in education should increase and be well managed.

5 Act 7.420/06 and joined related provisions (Education Responsibility Act) proposed by Raquel Teixeira, former Congresswoman from the *Partido da Social Democracia Brasileira* (PSDB – Brazilian Social Democrat Party) and founder member of the TPE.

6 http://www.todospelaeducacao.org.br/reportagens-tpe/30074/abave-assina-termo-de-cooperacao-com-todos-pela-educacao-e-inep/?pag=ultima.

7 *Notícias do Dia* newsletter is a daily informative publication and has a news clipping service on education covering the main newspapers of the country.

8 This is the case of 'Programa de Reforma Educativa para América Latina' (PREAL - Education Reform Program in Latin America)which, through its publications and meetings, promotes communication between entrepreneurs and executors of public policies in different countries of this region (Krawczyk and Grinkraut, 2014).

9 Armando Boito Jr. takes up the concept of the internal bourgeoisie, as defined by Poulantzas.

References

Boito Jr., A. (2012). Governos Lula: a nova burguesia nacional no poder. In A. Boito Jr. and A. Galvao (Eds). *Política e classes sociais no Brasil dos anos 2000* (pp. 67–103). São Paulo: Alameda.

Delvaux, B. (2009). Qual é o papel do conhecimento na ação política? *Revista Educação & Sociedade, 30*(109), 960.

Fonseca, M. (1998). O financiamento do Banco Mundial à educação brasileira: Vinte anos de cooperação internacional. In L Tommasi, M. J. Warde and S. Haddad (Eds). O Banco Mundial e as políticas educacionais. São Paulo: Editora Cortez.

Klees, S., Samoff, J. and Stromquist N. (2012). *The World Bank and education: Critiques and alternatives.* Rotterdam: Sense Publishers.

Krawczyk, N. (2014a). Conhecimento crítico e política educacional: um diálogo difícil, mas necessário. In N. Krawczyk (Ed.). *Sociologia do ensino médio*. Crítica ao economicismo na política educacional (pp. 13–32). São Paulo: Editora Cortez.

Krawczyk, N. (2014b). Ensino médio: Empresários dão as cartas na escola pública. *Educação & Sociedade, 35*(126), 21–41.

Krawczyk, N. (2008). Em busca da uma nova governabilidade na educação. In D. O. Andrade and M. F. F. Rosar (Eds). *Política e Gestão da Educação* (pp. 59–72). Belo Horizonte, Autentica.

Krawczyk, N. and Grinkraut, A. (2014). Ensino médio: um campo de disputa. Research Study Report, CNPq. *Diagnóstico e propostas dos organismos internacionais 2000–2013.* Mimeo.

Leher, R. (2014, October). Estratégia política e Plano Nacional de Educação. *Marxismo 21.* Retrieved January 10, 2015 from http://marxismo21.org/wp-content/uploads/2014/08/R-Leher-Estrat%C3%A9gia-Pol%C3%ADtica-e-Plano-Nacional-Educa%C3%A7%C3%A3o.pdf.

Leher, R. (2010). Educação no governo de Lula da Silva. In Os anos Lula. (Vv.Aa.). Contribuições para um balanço crítico 2003–2010 (pp. 369–412). Rio de Janeiro: Garamond.

Lima, J. (2007). Redes na educação: Questões políticas e conceituais. *Revista Portuguesa de Educação, 20*(2), 151–181.

Martins, E. M. (2013a). *Movimento "Todos pela Educação": Um projeto de nação para a educação Brasileira.* State University of Campinas. Education College (Master degree Dissertation).

Martins, E. M. (2013b). Responsabilidade educacional e atuação do Todos pela Educação. In L. Almeida, L., I. r. Pino, J. M. Pinto and A. B. Gouveia. IV Seminário de Educação Brasileira: PNE em foco: Políticas de responsabilização, regime de colaboração e Sistema Nacional de Educação – 1. ed. – Campinas-SP: CEDES, v.1.

Saviani, D. (2007). O plano de desenvolvimento da Educação: Análise do projeto do MEC. *Educação & Sociedade, 28*(100), 1231–1255.

Todos Pela Educação. (2012). *Todos pela educação: 5 Anos, 5 Metas, 5 Bandeiras.* São Paulo: Todos pela educação.

Todos Pela Educação. (2010). *De olho nas metas – 2010.* São Paulo: Todos pela educação.

Todos Pela Educação. (2007). *Relatório de atividades do todos pela educação 2007.* São Paulo: Todos pela educação.

Todos Pela Educação. (2006a). *Compromisso todos pela educação: Bases Éticas, Jurídicas, Pedagógicas, Gerenciais, Político-Sociais e Culturais.* São Paulo: Todos pela educação.

Todos Pela Educação. (2006b). *Todos pela educação: Rumo A 2022.* São Paulo: Todos pela educação.

Verger, A. (2014). Why do policy-makers adopt global education policy? Toward a research framework on the variegated role of ideas in educational reform. *Current Issues in Comparative Education, 16*(2), 14–29.

6 Brand Aid Funding for Educating Public Humanitarians

Lisa Ann Richey and Stefano Ponte

Private Financing of Public Education: Introduction

The existence of an escalating private education sector in developing countries is now well documented. While this trend has been received by some with enthusiasm (Tooley 2001), other scholars take a more nuanced, critical approach to the actors and institutions involved in these new forms of public–private partnership. The global education industry is "global" precisely because the fundamental debates over improving educational quality without increasing access inequality have no geographical bounds. This chapter will examine one aspect of private financing, Brand Aid (Richey and Ponte 2011), which simultaneously works at providing educational humanitarian outcomes in the South and educating local humanitarians in the North. A critical examination of two exemplary Brand Aid cases demonstrates how the problems themselves and the people who experience them are branded and marketed to consumers (through celebritized multi-media story-telling) just as effectively as the products that will "save" them (Ponte and Richey, 2014; Richey 2014).

As a conceptual reference point for international education in developing countries, we use the term "humanitarianism" as explained by Brockington (2014). This is not in the traditional distinction between "humanitarianism" (concerned primarily with dealing with the problems arising from emergencies, war, and disasters) and "development" (dealing with more mundane forms of poverty and the deeper structural causes of suffering and inequality). Rather, we underscore that while development is something that you can do to yourself or your community, humanitarianism requires a needy, often distant, other. Kapoor notes that the terms "charity," "philanthropy," and "humanitarianism" are often used interchangeably, but that "charity" carries an explicitly Christian genealogy, while "philanthropy" is used for secular, and typically corporate interventions (Kapoor 2013: 4). Littler (2008) used the term "do-gooding" to describe a particular type of response to suffering at a distance – one that "generates a lot of hype and [public relations] PR but is relatively insignificant in relation to international and governmental policy" (Littler 2008: 240). Humanitarianism has the explicit intent of helping someone else and thus is the foundation for many diverse forms of international development aid – public, private, and partnerships between the two.

Private humanitarian funding is becoming more important as conventional sources of international development aid are under stress from the ongoing economic crisis. This is reflected by shifting patterns of resource transfers from North to South. Sources of financing outside traditional aid are growing (Adelman 2009) and this is shaping the funding and agenda of non-profit organizations (NGOs) and other humanitarian agencies. As argued by Steiner-Khamsi (2008), we have seen a bifurcation of aid into two different tracks: "rule-abiding and rule-enforcing multilaterals" and "unruly, and yet very generous private funders" (Steiner-Khamsi 2008: 14). Our chapter focuses only on the "unruly" private financing. While private humanitarianism has been a more established trend in the Anglophone countries with a lengthy history of philanthropy, we can see similar tendencies emerging in continental Europe where state support for the work of humanitarian NGOs is increasingly giving way to private funders and corporate partnerships.

Within upper echelons, this has been termed "philanthrocapitalism" by *The Economist* (2006), and summarized in the subtitle by Bishop and Green (2008): *How the rich can save the world*. Exemplified by Warren Buffet's USD $30 billion donation to the Gates Foundation in 2006 (which exceeded the total amount Andrew Carnegie and John D. Rockefeller gave away in their lifetimes), the scale of philanthrocapitalism has led to immense policy influence in humanitarian sectors (McGoey 2014). As private giving becomes more important, there is more emphasis on fundraising from a wider spectrum of individuals to pay for previously public-supported goods, globally and locally.

However, the mushrooming of private humanitarian financing has sparked extensive debate. A spate of books over the past decade has examined the possibilities of whether a form of capitalism that is more creative, social-minded, and to scale can solve global problems that, historically, were subjected to political debate in democratic societies (see, *inter alia*, Bishop and Green 2008; Edwards 2008; Kinsley 2008). Criticism has come from the business side, arguing that business should focus on what it does best: providing goods and services to consumers and maximizing profits and shareholder value (Kinsley 2008). Other critics from a social justice perspective argue that forms of philanthrocapitalism are the symptoms of an unequal world, rather than being its cure (Edwards 2008). Termed "philanthrocapitalism," "creative capitalism" (by Bill Gates), "social innovation" (by US President Obama), social entrepreneurship, private philanthropy, and Brand Aid, all involve the investment by business for social returns, or "using enterprise models for social impact" (Shortall 2009). Our chapter will focus on the Brand Aid forms of financing humanitarianism, with selected cases of providing humanitarian educational outcomes in the South and educating public humanitarians in the North.

Brand aid and the Privatization of Humanitarianism

"Brand aid," encapsulating the combination of causes, branded products and celebrity, is one of the newest modalities of fundraising for humanitarianism, and accompanies this rise of private aid (Richey and Ponte 2011). Smaller in scale but larger in scope than Buffet-type philanthrocapitalism, we have private funding of humanitarian causes through Brand Aid initiatives in which consumers buy cause-marketed products and a portion of the profit is donated. Within this public sector and institutional framework, advances in technology, crowdsourcing, and marketing are being used by NGOs and their corporate collaborators to engage different audiences in innovative ways. One important aspect of the Brand Aid phenomenon is that it functions as a democratization of philanthropy in which every consumer can be "like Bill Gates" if they buy in with small amounts to support humanitarianism (Schwittay 2014).

The power of Brand Aid for shaping humanitarianism is not simply a material one, but also a symbolic one of meaning making. From a case study of Amnesty International, Vestergaard (2008) argues that humanitarian branding is becoming increasingly important as NGOs interact with business. On the basis of substantial empirical work on cause-marketing initiatives supporting the 30 most recognizable NGOs working with "international needs," scholars found that the promotional aspects of partnering with corporations were more vital than the actual financial benefits from the engagement (Hawkins 2012).

Corporations are, of course, the original actors in branding for profit, while celebrities are personified through their own brands. Examples range from Sean Penn's "bad boy," hands-on humanitarian work in Haiti (Rosamond 2015) to Angelina's global do-gooding mother (Mostafanezhad 2015). While celebrity is not the primary focus of this chapter, it remains a key component for our conceptual model for its role is signifying the communication of development causes specifically to an audience of non-specialists. As described by Brockington (2014), the increasing presence of corporate actors in relationships between NGOs and public figures or celebrities reflects the rise of private initiatives: "it is good business sense to build relationships with NGOs, particularly if it then results in associations between that business and famous faces." When celebrities become involved, we see old imaginaries woven into new subjectivities of "ironic spectatorship," which shape audience understandings of humanitarian causes (Chouliaraki 2012).

Celebrities have become increasingly visible for their roles in shaping what "we" think about the global South and poverty, and how we do this through consumption (Goodman and Barnes 2011). Trusted celebrities can create the caring, sexy brand that sells "help" (Cameron and Haanstra 2008). But the selling of a brand is not just limited to products for consumption; slowly, it is becoming recognized that humanitarian NGOs working in developing countries are also branded entities (Biccum 2007). In representations of humanitarianism, constructions of identity are co-constituted through imaginaries of "us" and "them" (Hall 2011; Crush 1995) – often with imperial (Kapoor 2013), racist (Kothari 2006; Nederveen Pieterse 1992), and religious legacies.

The increasing "privatization of helping" in both its material and symbolic forms has made engaging in humanitarianism such a desirable practice that admission can be sold to consumers as one might sell tickets to a concert or amusement park. Development outcomes themselves – such as primary education for a child – become so imbued with symbolic and ethical value that they are used to market consumer goods to Northern buyers (Ponte and Richey 2014). This brand can even be linked to virtual and interactive products and the spectacle or experience itself is the marketed commodity (see globalgaminginitiative.com). Known in the media as "gamifying charity," having fun to support a cause is today a fashionable way to raise funds for education "over there" while educating humanitarians "at home." To begin to understand the interrelationship between commodification, celebritization, and global "do-gooding," a conceptual model charting the linkages may prove useful.

Conceptual Model

In Richey and Ponte (2011), we developed the concept of "Brand Aid" to describe how branded products are sold as ethical items through their mediation by celebrities who link them to worthy causes in developing countries. Brand Aid, we argued, is "aid to brands" because it helps sell products and improve a brand's ethical profile and value. It is also "brands that provide aid" because a proportion of the profit or sales is devoted to helping others. The concept of Brand Aid was needed to describe a particular empirical example on which we conducted a book-length study – *Product (RED)*™ (Richey and Ponte 2011). Launched by Bono at Davos in 2006, Product (RED)™ is a brand created to raise awareness and money for The Global Fund to Fight AIDS, tuberculosis, and malaria by teaming up with "iconic brands" to produce RED-branded products. Typically, a percentage of the sales of these products will be donated by RED directly to the Global Fund (yet, as the model has developed to include newer partners, such as the global brand giant Coca Cola, alternative contributions have also been accepted). According to the Global Fund, "(RED) is the largest business initiative supporting the Global Fund and one of the biggest to raise money for an international humanitarian cause." In our book, we examined how Product (RED)™ reconfigures international development around aid celebrities and consumer-citizens, and we also placed RED companies against the background of the "normal functioning" of the industries in which these companies operate, and in relation to the many diverse aspects of Corporate Social Responsibility (CSR). Specifically for the case study, we examined how the corporations that are part of this initiative – American Express, Apple, Converse, Gap, Emporio Armani, Hallmark, and Motorola – use RED to build up their brand profiles, sell products, and/or portray themselves as both as "caring" and "cool." We also show that, more than simply another example of cause-related marketing (such as the pink ribbon campaign or the ubiquitous plastic wristbands), RED engages corporations in profitable "helping" while simultaneously pushing the agenda of CSR toward solving the problems of "distant others."

In this chapter, we review our conceptual model that this work generated as illustrated in Figure 6.1, where Brand Aid appears at the triple interface of branded products, celebrities, and causes. The model also shows other forms of interaction: generic cause-related marking (CRM) (the combination of branded products and causes); celebrity-driven issue campaigns (the combination of celebrities and causes – for example, George Clooney's Save Darfur campaign);

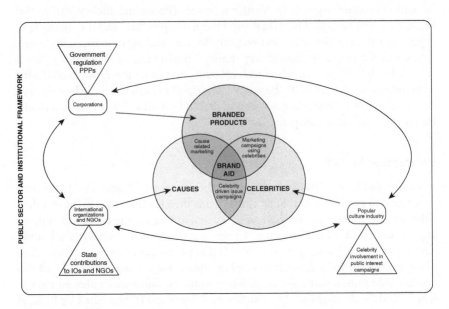

Figure 6.1 Brand aid conceptual model

Source: Richey and Ponte 2014: 70.

and marketing campaigns using celebrities (the well-established combination of celebrities and branded products). These other categories fall outside the scope of this chapter, but structured comparisons between them are part of our agenda for future research.

Each of the circles in our conceptual model represents a regime of value that contains both material and symbolic forms. Appadurai (1986) described the arrangements of meanings created by signifying images and objects within the specificity of commodity culture as "regimes of value." These regimes of value are constructs of the social imaginary, which give significance to experience through discourse. Thus, value for Appadurai refers both to economic or material value and also to the non-economic categories and understandings of particular commodity arrangements. New imaginaries of development are created, in which consumption becomes the mechanism for action and purchase creates partnership between individual consumers, corporations, nonprofits (aid organizations and NGOs), and ultimately beneficiaries in developing countries. The relationship is created, not simply documented, through the discourses, images, narratives, and truths communicated as part of "Brand Aid."

Regimes of value cannot exist outside of the institutional framework that constitutes and supports them (see actors and relations in Figure 6.1 outside the overlapping circles). Traditionally, international development is constituted through the public and private sector interactions between international organizations, NGOs, and states. However, as corporations and the popular culture industry become actors in promoting international causes, new alliances are formed.

As the regimes of value between celebrities, causes, and branded products over-lap, opportunities are created for participation in international development – including international education – by consumers. Thus, Brand Aid both forges new alliances and links new actors in the realm of humanitarian education, yet these new relationships are in need of critical scrutiny.

In our model, we are engaging with an interactive process of material exchange and conceptual engagement that links the technical and specialized activities practiced in the South by particular "experts" and "organizations" with a network and communication media of non-expert publics in the North. Our focus is on what Smith and Yanacopulos (2004) describe as the "public faces of develop-ment," or the various ways in which development organizations convey meanings and representations of the global South and the concept of development itself to a Northern public. Now, we move to the two exemplary case studies of private fundraising for public education in the North and South. The first one comes from a systematic study of Brand Aid initiatives (Ponte and Richey 2014) and focuses explicitly on linking a product purchase to the provision of an educational product – a laptop computer – with the goal of improving educational outcomes in Rwanda.

(a) "Win One Give One": Betty Crocker Fruit Flavored Snacks

The case study of "Win One Give One" (WOGO) is Brand Aid with an important twist – the beneficiaries are simultaneously American children (and their moms) and Rwandan school children. From November 15, 2011 until July 31, 2012, con-sumers who entered a UPC code from boxes of General Mills "Betty Crocker Fruit Flavored Snacks" would be registered to win an XO Laptop. Linked to this "instant win game," for every 100 UPC codes entered on the website, Betty Crocker Fruit Flavored Snacks pledged to donate one XO laptop to a child in Africa, up to 1,725 laptops. The rules for distributing the laptops in Africa are not to be found on the website; however, the rules for the American children are complicated and spelled out explicitly in the legal description of the scheme. In total, only 259 American kids will get a laptop, with a reported value of USD $220, making the total value of all prizes at only USD $56,980.[1]

These "fruit flavored snacks" for educating Africans come in 38 varieties, ranging from "Fruit-Flavored Shapes My Little Pony" to "Fruit Gushers Mood Morphers Fruit Punch," and there are snacks for religious holidays ("Fruit-Flavored Shapes Easter") and those for toys ("Fruit-Flavored Shapes Transformers").[2] Almost all of the 38 varieties are made from the same ingredients: a combination of concen-trated pears, corn syrup, modified corn starch, preservatives, and colors of red, yellow, and blue. Sugar constitutes approximately half of the total product weight, thus the products themselves are not likely to support links between better nutri-tion and better learning. The XO Laptop comes from One Laptop per Child, an international development initiative that has backing from the computer industry and works in more than 30 developing countries. It was founded in 2005 by Nicolas Negroponte, the co-founder of the Massachusetts Institute of Technology Media

Laboratory, with the idea of producing a durable laptop computer costing only USD $100 that could make technology accessible to developing country children.

What could link fruit-flavored snacks and concerned American mothers with a top-down education techno-fix and "kids in Africa"? The homepage of the initiative's "Win and Give" website centers around a portrait of a young Rwandan boy in a well-pressed school uniform in front of the Rwandan flag.[3] The child has tightly shaved hair, looks to be around eight years old, and wears an expression of alertness. He is framed with the caption, "Take a trip to Rwanda with Jean-Luc. See how XO Laptops™ are making futures brighter." You can click the bold link under the photo that reads, "Explore." To the left side of Jean-Luc is a photo of the computer with a smiling black boy on the screen, and three boxes of fruit flavored snacks. Their caption reads, "Enter a UPC code." These are linked to the words "Enter Here!" To the right side is a photograph of a Rwandan boy in the same starched school uniform, who may or may not be "Jean-Luc." His portrait is superimposed slightly behind a portrait of a smiling, supposedly American, boy in a striped casual collared shirt with pale skin and freckles, under the caption, "See the impact you can make." These boys have a link that reads, "Learn More." In small text in the right bottom corner of the page is an old-fashioned propeller airplane, pulling a banner that reads, "Hey kids, this is Advertising."

While the advertising for the fruit snacks is obvious, the more subtle, and arguably more hard-sell, approach is for an imaginary of commodity-based international development in education. One Laptop per Child (OLPC) has been controversial since its inception by the development celebrity Nicolas Negroponte. In this development scheme, the low cost laptop would result from a "tripartite perfect storm": first, sales would be only to governments and in quantities above one million; second, open-source software would bypass Microsoft and Intel's processors; and third, commodity parts would keep the price low (*The Economist* 2008). Funding was sought from education ministries on Negroponte's mantra: "It's an education project, not a technology project."

One line of criticism has been directed at the technology itself. The best thing about the OLPC computer is that it is inexpensive. However, it has yet to meet the price point of USD $100, and has remained twice that price. The physical computer was designed to prevent water and soil damage, to be readable in direct sunlight for children who school outside, and to operate on less power consumption to allow for possible solar or crank powering. A scathing technology critique in *The Economist* described how the laptop has bugs that cause occasional crashes: "a discreet message sometimes flashes when the system boots up, warning of some sort of data-check error." Additionally the "cumbersome operating system" makes it quite difficult, even in a world of abundant electricity and bandwidth, to perform basic activities, like watching a video on YouTube. While this was enough to prevent a journalist from using the computer, the kind of response from young learners new to computers and the teachers who must support them while simultaneously learning how to use computers themselves, is unclear. The technological problems in a developing country setting are likely to have various implications for achieving the OLPC mission: "to empower the world's poorest children through education" (OLPC website). It has been characterized in the press as "a high-profile deal of one man evangelizing top government officials on how he can save their poor children and in the end these politicians abandoned him" (Nussbaum 2007).

The politics of global trade and local power relations have also proved problematic for OLPC across its interventions. Countries such as Nigeria and Brazil wanted locally produced laptops. There have been questions of distribution of the computers (which are only supplied to government schools, and thus can be seen as increasing the leverage of some local leaders over others). Libya and Nigeria cancelled their informal commitments to purchase the computers when they realized that they were untried, more expensive than USD $100, and were not the only cheap laptops available[4]. Consumers in non-developing countries, many of whom still also lack computer access, wanted the possibility of buying cheap laptops as well. Other businesses such as Intel wanted to produce their own cheap laptops and, thus, OLPC came to be perceived as creating a monopoly in the market. Another line of criticism is that OLPC reflects some of the traditionally "worst practices" in international development. It is a top-down model, developed without consultation on the needs or interests of the local recipients, and it is implemented to a blueprint formula in countries that are extremely diverse.

In Rwanda, where the WOGO computers are donated, OLPC began with a specific deal reached between the country's government in 2007 and OLPC, and, by March 2012, 80,000 laptops had been donated to schools around the country. As explained by a journalist for a Rwandan newspaper, the project is working to bring electricity to the schools where computers will be used, but this is "an ongoing process." The OLPC Coordinator in the Ministry of Education, Nkubito, pointed out that the use of laptops on a daily basis in all schools was going to "drastically increase with the current deployment of servers in schools. They will enable all lessons to be covered through digital courses" (Kanyesigye 2012). However, *The Economist* concluded that "giving a child a computer does not seem to turn him or her into a future Bill Gates – indeed it does not accomplish anything in particular" (2012). An evaluation done of OLPC in Peru by the Inter-American Development Bank (IDB) found that children receiving the computers in which the government invested USD $225 million, did not show any improvement in math or reading (Cristia et al. 2012). The IDB report found no evidence that access to a laptop increased motivation or time devoted to homework or reading (Cristia et al. 2012).

Businessweek declared OLPC a failure in 2007, which it attributed to the project's rejection of the fundamental rule of product development: "design from the bottom up, not top down" (Nussbaum 2007). "Near-finished prototypes were tested out late in development, brought to village kids as a 'gift' "(Nussbaum 2007). Nonetheless, OLPC continues to operate. In spite of the criticism of the laptop's aesthetic design, awkward software and inappropriate business model for technology diffusion, and with no mention of the relatively high sugar and color content of the supposedly "healthy" fruit snacks, the links between them as part of a Brand Aid version of CRM were effective.

Whatever the impact on African children,[5] the WOGO initiative assures American mothers that "any kid can help." When you click to "Learn More," instead of information on OLPC or Rwanda, there are two links: the first is to the "Kid's Altruism Indicator." This is described as "a joint research initiative with Parenting Magazine to uncover kids' views on giving back and helping others. As a component of the partnership, The Parenting Group's MomConnection® research provided insights on how moms instill altruistic values in their kids." The questions and "findings" reported as "According to Kids: Who do you think you can help?" are interesting. Eighty three percent of children responded that they could help "Kids in another country, such as Haiti, Africa [sic], or Chile." This is only slightly less than those who reported confidence in helping "kids at my school" or "my family."[6] The second webpage link takes you to a "What's your giving style" quiz, to determine your family's giving style and "receive special tips from Dr. Michele Borba, parenting expert."[7] After you take the quiz, you can also download a coupon for "Betty Crocker Fruit Flavored Snacks." Whether the results indicate that you are a "global do-gooder," "neighborhood helper," or "project seeker," the same tips appear, including the final suggestion: "Find easy ways to help others around the world through opportunities such as the Betty Crocker Fruit Flavored Snacks 'Win and Give' campaign." And with each opportunity, large buttons on the top of the webpage encourage you to "Print a Coupon," "Share on Facebook," or "Post on Twitter," because it is not sufficient to become more empathetic, or "incorporate giving into your everyday life," but you should share your brand of heroism with others.

(b) "We Can Be Heroes": DC Comics

The second Brand Aid initiative with educational outcomes is less direct than the technology-provision of laptops in Rwandan schools of the previous example. This example is entitled "We Can Be Heroes," and its focus is on educating Northern humanitarians. DC Comics, a Warner Bros. Entertainment Company, has launched this international development fund-raising initiative based on the sale of several items carrying images of the Justice League characters, including a "We Can Be Heroes" iPhone case that reads, "One small act can make you a hero." Other products available include T-shirts, mugs, posters, and a water bottle. DC Entertainment donates 50 percent of the purchase price (USD $39.95) to their nonprofit partners – Save the Children, International Rescue Committee, and Mercy Corps – to fight hunger in Africa. This initiative also includes the possibility of directly making a donation independently from a purchase, with the funds being divided between the three campaign partners, and matched with a donation by DC Entertainment, up to a total contribution of USD $1 million. Singer Chris Daughtry provided a song entitled "Rescue Me," the net proceeds of which will go to the "We Can Be Heroes" partner organizations; the artist Jim Lee created special edition lithographs that trigger a donation of 75 percent of the purchase price; and the gaming icon Chiren Boumaaza, known as Athene, launched Op ShareCraft 2012 – Save the Children Challenge, an online fundraising campaign in which he "brought thousands of people together to fight the hunger crisis in the Horn of Africa by live streaming his own hunger strike online" (Optsharecraft website).

The initiative website is titled: "Worst hunger crisis in 60 years. Over 9 million in need of immediate assistance. The people in the Horn of Africa need you now" (We can be heroes: DC comics website). A photograph of a small forlorn-looking African girl sits above the link to donate, and another link shows the darkness and light art inspired by heroes and villains, hope and heroism. However, the centerpiece of the webpage is a powerful two-minute video clip. The video begins with an image of a white girl, who appears to be thirteen years old and from the global North (as signified by her winter jacket and the heavily trafficked street in the background). The video opens with shadowy images of the map of Africa, juxtaposed over a silhouette of Batman, and the following words fade into the screen: "In the Horn of Africa, 13 million people are suffering/through the worst hunger crisis in 60 years/They need a hero [the silhouette shifts to Wonder Woman and Superman, and Africa has faded into their background glow]/What do you do when someone needs you?" Here video close-up shots show faces of a diverse group of Northern urbanites on screen. The first to speak is an African-American man who responds to the challenge: "A time in my life when what?" followed by a young woman speaking with a British accent, "Wow, that's a really hard question." Then, there is a flash back to the African-American man, "When I was needed?" A twenty-something white man in glasses and a comical furry hat is next, "I haven't felt needed yet, so far I've been needy" he says. A Hispanic man with gold chains adds in an extremely sincere tone, "My sister. She needs me." Then two young twenty-something men are on screen, one laughs and says, "I am actually being needed right this second. Excuse me." He looks down, and then turns away to answer his mobile phone as the other young man laughs, slightly embarrassed [a tactical disruption to permit an emotional pause, after which the clip then returns to a tone of absolute sincerity].

The 13-year-old girl from the website's homepage image begins to speak in a tone of regret, "There was this kid in my class named Brady. I thought about standing up for him but I didn't want to be embarrassed so I didn't. But I should have. Yea." [She looks down remorsefully – the scene is enhanced by instrumental background piano music of profound emotion]. The initial image of the glowing African map emerges onto the screen with the written words: "You are needed/Thousands of children are struggling to stay alive/One small act can make you a hero." Here the classroom experiences of a 13-year-old are indicative of possibilities of global humanitarianism – Northern consumers are being taught that their responses are needed, appropriate, and global. The most relevant point to understand for our critique is that the necessary action in the circumstances of an American school bully or African famine is to buy the correct "helping" product.

In the "We Can Be Heroes" video, the possibility for action is shown as the camera switches back to the cameos of "normal" Northern people who begin to perform their response as the music becomes upbeat in tempo. A twenty-something-year-old woman begins: "I didn't think. I just went." Then an African-American man with short dreadlocks says, "When. Where. How. What do we need to do?" Switch back to the previous woman, "It just felt very exhilarating. I sort of had that feeling of being a hero [she shrugs]." The dreadlocked man says, "I felt like I was necessary."

An older man with a few gray hairs in a long beard, wearing a baseball cap and a hippie scarf says, "So I fell to the ground with her. And just laid right next to her. And she goes, what did you do that for? And I said, cuz, uh, someone needs to be on the ground with you. So I can help you up." The shadow image appears with seven Justice League figures and the written text "Join the Justice League to fight the hunger crisis/Give now. DC Entertainment will match it 100 percent/We Can Be Heroes/www.WeCanBeHeroes.org [with logos beneath of Save the Children, International Rescue Committee and MercyCorps and DC Entertainment]."

At 2:09 minutes, an entire imaginary of multicultural heroism is shown, in which men, women and children of all races come together to save millions of anonymous, suffering Africans. Local affective scripts for Americans of childhood bullying in school, of the 9/11 rescue by firefighters, of close family in need are juxtaposed with scripts of African suffering and Northern heroism. The only information about what "help" actually might mean in this saga is found on the partners page, which links a single, vague notion of intervention objectives with each organization. Their targets include "children of the Horn of Africa," "acutely malnourished and displaced families," and "communities" where they provide water, medical care, and food in response to lost livelihoods, drought, and hunger. If you click on the "donation" button, you can enter a credit card donation that will be divided between the 3 campaign partners and matched with a donation by DC Entertainment, up to a total contribution of USD $1 million. In this provocative example, anyone with a credit card can become an international development actor, and work in alliance with traditional development organizations in the Horn of Africa. One important aspect of the Brand Aid phenomenon is that it functions as a democratization of philanthropy and educates consumers that humanitarianism involves buying the right products.

From the previous example of how American children's altruism is wedded to better education for Rwandans through the unlikely channel of fruit-flavored snacks, "We Can Be Heroes" turns Brand Aid toward the "public faces of development" (Smith and Yanacopulos 2004) to look specifically at what kinds of humanitarians are being sold with products that are branded on helping. In the process of selling branded merchandise, this initiative is providing an explicit educational script on how consumers can be heroes through their product choices.

Conclusions

This chapter has argued that private financing of public education needs to be critically examined for its material and symbolic effects. We have presented our conceptual model of "Brand Aid" as one way to understand the financing mechanisms that link businesses with causes that are sold through mediating celebrities. Then we outlined two cases of "Brand Aid" that show different sides of the dilemma: the direct provision of education inputs in the South and the indirect education of humanitarians in the North. In the previous examples, we expand our understanding of how Brand Aid initiatives use imaginaries of development – cheap laptops to bring education to Rwanda or superheroes who defend classmates against bullies and fight famine in the Horn of Africa – to sell products to Northern consumers. These Brand Aid initiatives simultaneously engage in the work of a "story factory" – producing truths about international interventions in education, health, and development and consumer engagement that make development appear simplified, manageable, and marketable (Ponte and Richey 2014). However, in many fields, critical scholarship is beginning to scrutinize what is being "sold" under the guise of marketing these international interventions as "sexy" (Cameron and Haanstra 2008). The expansion of these "unruly" private funders who become involved in financing global humanitarianism is important for more than just the money they raise. Even if it is sometimes the case, as Steiner-Khamsi (2008) points out, that these are "generous" funders, their support comes with a price. The ideas that are being sold to Northern do-gooders (Littler 2008) about development and change must be critically interrogated together with the Brand Aid products that these ideas are meant to sell. Who are the unspecified "Africans" in the dark shadows, educating Americans about how to be good humanitarians through buying DC Comics products? What do consumers learn from these sorts of campaigns about what is expected of humanitarians at home or abroad? How are the concerns that Northern parents hold about their children's development as good altruists engaged or not, by the purchase of a cause-marketed product to donate laptops to Rwandan schools?

These are questions that focus on private consumption, corporate funding and public provision of education. We argue that Brand Aid, linking branded products to causes and celebrities, is about more than just raising private funds in a time of decreasing public investment in global humanitarianism. It is shifting the responsibilities and rights to participate in creating development outcomes themselves. International development's expansion to include new actors among the so-called "generation-net" calls for critical consideration of education, communication, and service provision, including from the perspective of those affected by it (Alhassan and Chakravartty 2011). It is important to understand how the privatization of help – replacing public donors with private philanthropy – is linked to the commodification of humanitarianism, i.e. turning people into marketable things (Ponte and Richey 2014). As businesses use Brand Aid to educate Northern publics on how to "help" educate distant others, together with providing alternative unaccountable sources of funding for education in developing countries, the underlying difficulties of such commodification become apparent across different contexts.

Notes

1 According to the rules, the American winners cede extensive publicity possibilities to the company in exchange for their USD $220 laptop. "Except where prohibited, participation in the Instant Win Game constitutes winner's consent to Sponsor's use of winner's name, likeness, photograph, voice, opinions, biographical information, hometown and state for promotional purposes in any media without further payment or consideration. For children under thirteen (13), such consent will only be to the extent allowed by COPPA [Children's Online Privacy Protection Act]" (Source: generalmills.promo.eprize.com/

winandgive/rules.html, last accessed May 8, 2012; at the time of publication, all webpages on winonegiveone.com had been removed from the General Mills website; however screenshots are available upon request from the authors).

2 http://www.generalmills.com/home/brands/baking_products/betty_crocker/brand%20product%20list%20page.aspx#{588DE128-522B-4712-9F21-ED8D2EF2CA90}

3 www.winonegiveone.com/Default.aspx; last accessed May 14, 2012; at the time of publication, all webpages on winonegiveone.com had been removed from the General Mills website; however screenshots are available upon request from the authors.

4 Since the project launched in 2005, commercial rivals have emerged: Intel's Classmate at around USD $250; Acer's laptop at USD $350; Everex PCs with Zonbu software at around USD $280; Asustek Computer's Asus Eee at under USD $400; and an Indian competitor, Novatium Solutions, which created a basic NetPC for around USD $80. The average cost per deployment, including duty, installation, maintenance, installation of the solar system, etc. has been priced at approximately USD $461 by one program in India, which seems to fall roughly along the median of estimates given in discussions among implementers of OLPC on their news website. http://www.olpcnews.com/sales_talk/price/490_per_xo_laptop_the_real_cos.html.

5 The WOGO website celebrated this success, noting: "Due to outstanding and much higher than anticipated participation from consumers, we have already reached our total donation of 1,725 laptops. In order to build on this energy and provide even more laptops to children in Africa, Betty Crocker' Fruit Flavored Snacks has decided to give away even more laptops than initially planned. From now until March 18, 2012, for every day we receive 100 UPC entries, we will donate an additional laptop to a child in Africa. So keep on entering UPC codes and together we will continue to help kids in Africa." However, the much higher conversion rate of 100 entries per day for a donation makes it difficult to estimate how many more African kids will own their own XO laptop supplied by American consumption. In fact, after the close of the initiative, the website reported that "Betty Crocker Fruit Flavored Snacks will donate even more laptops than initially planned. Great job!" (winonegiveone.com/code_entry.aspx, last accessed May 8, 2012; at the time of publication, all webpages on winonegiveone.com had been removed from the General Mills website; however screenshots are available upon request from the authors). There is no report of how many total laptops were actually donated by this scheme.

6 www.winonegiveone.com_pdf_wingive-parentingresults.pdf last accessed April 30, 2012.

7 Dr. Michele Borba is "an internationally renowned educator, award-winning author, and parenting and child adolescent expert" (as written on the product website). Among her most signaled credentials are that she has "appeared more than 100 times as a parent expert on *Today* as well as countless talk shows including *Dr. Phil, Dateline, The View Dr. Drew, FOX & Friends, The Doctors, CNN,* and *The Early Show*."

References

Adelman, C. (2009). Global philanthropy and remittances: Reinventing foreign aid. *The Brown Journal of World Affairs, 15*(2), 23–33.

Alhassan, A. and Chakravartty, P. (2011). Postcolonial media policy under the long shadow of empire. In R. Mansell and M. Raboy (Eds). *The handbook of global media and communication policy* (pp. 366–382). Chichester: Wiley Blackwell.

Appadurai, A. (1986). Commodities and the politics of value. In A. Appadurai (Ed.). *The social life of things: Commodities in cultural perspective* (pp. 3–63). Cambridge: Cambridge University Press.

Biccum, A. (2007). Marketing development: Live 8 and the production of the global citizen. *Development and Change, 38*(6), 1111–1126.

Bishop, M. and Green, M. (2008). *Philanthrocapitalism: How the rich can save the world.* New York: St. Martin's Press.

Brockington, D. (2014). *Celebrity advocacy and international development.* London: Routledge.

Cameron, J. and Haanstra, A. (2008). Development made sexy: How it happened and what it means. *Third World Quarterly, 29*(8), 1475–1489.

Chouliaraki, L. (2012). *The ironic spectator: Solidarity in the age of post-humanitarianism.* Cambridge: Polity.

Cristia, J., Ibarrarán, P., Cueto, S., Santiago, A. and Severín, E. (2012). Technology and child development: Evidence from the one laptop per child program. Washington, DC: Inter-American Development Bank.

Crush, J. (1995). *Power of development.* London: Routledge.

Economist, The. (2012, April 4). Error message: A disappointing return from an investment in computing. Retrieved May 21, 2015 from: http://www.economist.com/. node/21552202

Economist, The. (2008, January 4). One clunky laptop per child: Great idea. Shame about the mediocre computer. Retrieved May 21, 2015 from: http://www.economist.com/ node/10472304.

Economist, The. (2006, February 23). The birth of philanthrocapitaism. Retrieved June 5, 2015 from: http://www.economist.com/node/5517656.

Edwards, M. (2008). *Just another emperor? Myths and realities of philanthrocapitalism.* New York: Demos and the Young Foundation.

General Mills. (n.d.). Retrieved May 21, 2015 from: www.generalmills.com.

Global Fund. (n.d.). Retrieved May 21, 2015 from: http://www.theglobalfund.org/en/ mediacenter/newsreleases/2012-12-01_%28RED%29_reaches_record_milestone_ USD200_million_raised_to_fight_AIDS_in_Africa/.

Goodman, M. K. and Barnes, C. (2011). Star/poverty space: the making of the 'development celebrity'. *Celebrity Studies, 2*(1), 68–85.

Hall, S. (2011). The West and the rest. In S. Hall and B. Gieben, (Eds). *Formations of modernity* (pp. 275–320). Cambridge: Polity Press in association with the Open University.

Hawkins, R. (2012). Shopping to save lives: Gender and environment theories meet ethical consumption. *Geoforum, 43,* 750–759.

Kanyesigye, F. (2012, March 6). Rwanda: Project to distribute 100,000 more laptops. *The New Times.* Retrieved May 21, 2015 from: http://www.allafrica.com/stories/201203060083.html.

Kapoor, I. (2013). *Celebrity humanitarianism: Ideology of global charity.* New York: Routledge.

Kinsley, M. (2008). *Creative capitalism.* New York: Simon and Schuster.

Kothari, U. (2006). Commentary: History, time and temporality in development discourse. In C. A. Bayly, V. Rao, S. Szreter and M. Woolcock (Eds). *History, historians and development policy: A necessary dialogue* (pp. 65–70). Manchester: Manchester University Press.

Littler, J. (2008). 'I feel your pain': Cosmopolitan charity and the public fashioning of the celebrity soul. *Social Semiotics, 18*(2), 237–251.

McGoey, L. (2014). The philanthropic state: Market-state hybrids in the philanthrocapitalist turn. *Third World Quarterly, 35*(1), 109–125.

Mostafanezhad, M. (2015). Angelina Jolie and the everyday geopolitics of celebrity humanitarianism in a Thailand–Burma border town. In L. A. Richey (Ed.). *Celebrity Humanitarianism and North-South Relations: Politics, Place and Power.* London: Routledge.

Nederveen, P. J. (1992). *White on black: Images of Africa and blacks in Northern popular culture*. New Haven, CT: Yale University Press.

Nussbaum, B. (2007, September 24). It's time to call One Laptop Per Child a failure. *Businessweek*. Retrieved May 21, 2015 from: http://www.businessweek.com/innovate/NussbaumOnDesign/archives/2007/09/its_time_to_cal.html.

One Laptop per Child. (n.d.). Retrieved May 21, 2015 from: http://one.laptop.org/about/mission.

Optsharecraft. (n.d.). Retrieved April 22, 2015 from: http://www.opsharecraft.com/hungerstrike.html.

Ponte, S. and Richey, L. A. (2014). Buying into development? Brand aid forms of cause-related marketing. *Third World Quarterly*, *35*(1), 65–87.

Richey, L. A. (2014). Toward new knowledges in development: New actors and alliances. *Forum for Development Studies*, *41*(3), Routledge.

Richey, L. A. and Ponte, S. (2014). New actors and alliances in development. *Third World Quarterly*, *35*(1), 1–21.

Richey, L. A. and Ponte, S. (2011). *Brand aid: Shopping well to save the world*. Minneapolis: University of Minnesota Press.

Richey, L. A. and Ponte, S. (2008). Better (Red)™ than dead? Celebrities, consumption and international aid. *Third World Quarterly*, *29*(4), 711–729.

Rosamond, A. B. (2015). Humanitarian relief worker Sean Penn. In L. A. Richey (Ed.). *Celebrity Humanitarianism and North-South Relations: Politics, Place and Power*. London: Routledge.

Schwittay, A. (2014). *New Media and International Development: Representation and Affect in Microfinance*. London: Routledge.

Shortall, J. with Alter, K. (2009). *Introduction to understanding and accessing social investment: A brief guide for social entrepreneurs and development practitioners*. Arlington, VA: Small Enterprise Education and Promotion (SEEP) Network.

Smith, M. and Yanacopulos, H. (2004). The public faces of development: An introduction. *Journal of International Development*, *16*(5), 657–664.

Steiner-Khamsi, G. (2008). Donor logic in the era of Gates, Buffet and Soros. *Current Issues in Comparative Education*, *10*(1/2), 10–15.

Tooley, J. (2001). *The global education industry: Lessons from private education in developing countries*, (2nd ed.). Washington, DC: The International Finance Corp.

Vestergaard, A. (2008). Branding the humanitarian: The case of Amnesty International. *Journal of Language and Politics*, *7*(3), 471–493.

We Can Be Heroes: DC comics. (n.d.). Retrieved June 6, 2014: from http://www. wecanbeheroes. org/.

Part II
Selling School Improvement

7 Corporate Social Responsibility and Neo-Social Accountability in Education

The Case of Pearson plc

Anna Hogan, Sam Sellar, and Bob Lingard

Introduction

The focus of this chapter is the recent business strategy of the world's largest *edu-business*, Pearson plc. While the spotlight is on Pearson, our analysis is about a much broader phenomenon, namely the emergence of edu-businesses as aspiring public policy actors globally. We are specifically interested in how Pearson has reconstituted its mission, and we look at their new business strategy and the reframing of their educational work in terms of its efficacy. Pearson now describes itself as having a social responsibility to improve learning outcomes for its "customers," running together neo-liberal accountability and Corporate Social Responsibility (CSR) to frame education as "good business," in terms of both profit and improving people's lives.

Our analysis shows that the rapid expansion of Pearson's education work, and indeed their aim to help shape educational policy agendas globally, has been enabled by the restructuring of the state within nations. This restructuring has witnessed a move beyond New Public Management to what has been called network or "heterarchical governance" (Ball and Junemann 2012), opening up a policy space for the profit making of edu-businesses. As Koppenjan and Klijn (2004: 25) observe, today "[g]overnment is understood to be located alongside business and civil society actors in a complex game of public policy formation, decision-making and implementation." Some have seen this as the quasi-privatization of the education policy community (Mahony et al. 2004), with edu-business involvement across many aspects of the education policy cycle, from agenda setting through research for policy to text production, policy enactment, evaluation, professional development, and the provision of supporting materials. We also note how international organizations have opened up spaces for the involvement of edu-businesses such as Pearson. For example, the Organization for Economic Co-operation and Development (OECD) has employed contractors to help develop the Programme for International Student Assessment (PISA) tests, including Pearson, and more recently Pearson's former philanthropic arm, the Pearson Foundation, sponsored the dissemination of videos and reports highlighting what nations might learn from schooling systems that perform well on PISA or have used PISA to drive successful reform initiatives. Pearson abolished this Foundation in late 2014, and its functions, which can be characterized as a form of "philanthrocapitalism" (Bishop and Green 2008), have been incorporated into their main business strategy under the rubric of CSR, which is now a central defining feature of the company's new culture and *raison d'être*.

Our focus here is on Pearson's work in the nations of the Global North. However, we need to make the point that Pearson is also expanding its edu-business work in the nations of the Global South, particularly with support for low-fee, for-profit schools in sub-Saharan Africa and Asia through their *Pearson Affordable Learning Fund* project. There is some possibility that the UN post-2015 agenda will further enhance opportunities for such schools. Pearson has also expanded into China with English language schools. We must keep in mind, then, the global scope of Pearson's business strategy: there is a complementarity between their strategies in the Global North and those in the Global South, particularly in terms of framing "affordable learning" as a contribution to development goals relating to education.

Schooling systems in the Global North, as with other parts of the public sector, have experienced the shift from professional to neo-liberal modes of accountability (Ranson 2003), as part of the emergence of a broader audit culture (Power 1997). Ranson (2003) argues that neo-liberal accountability consists of four elements, namely performative accountability, consumer accountability, contract accountability, and corporate accountability. We argue that, to different degrees, all four elements are at work in Pearson's refocus of their business strategy to emphasize: the measurement of outcomes (performativity); their responsibility to consumers for the efficacy of their products; their contractual relations with governments and international organizations; and their organizational transformation to maximize the opportunities for profit for their shareholders from global educational expansion. We introduce the term "neo-social accountability" (see Rose 1999; Savage 2013; Vogelmann 2012 for a discussion of the "neo-social") to indicate how neo-liberal modes of accountability are evolving through the incorporation of demands for social responsibility within market rationalities, which Shamir (2008) describes as "market-embedded morality."

We begin by examining the reconstitution of Pearson as a global edu-business and then turn to a consideration of the mainstreaming of CSR within Pearson, in response to the closing down of the Pearson Foundation. We argue that this mainstreaming is linked to the introduction of Pearson's Efficacy Framework, a tool for monitoring the performance of its learning products and for ensuring accountability to consumers (international organizations, national and subnational schooling systems, schools, testing authorities, and so on) for the quality and effectiveness of the services it provides. Drawing on Lyotard (1984), we argue that the underpinning concept of the "good" driving accountability systems is being redefined in terms of the technical criterion of efficiency: pursuing the best possible input/output equation and keeping social systems functioning in the face of the collapse of meta-narratives. In this context, Pearson is presenting itself as a company acting for the public "good," but what counts as "good" is counted in narrow technical terms as measurable outcomes for individuals and systems. We conclude by reflecting critically on what this involvement of edu-businesses in the education policy cycle means in terms of the democratic governance of schooling today. We also reflect upon political resistance to these developments in the activities of teacher unions, particularly the global federation of teacher unions, Education International, and in the work of global civil society activist organizations such as Action Aid, the Global Campaign for Education, Results Educational Fund, and the Global Initiative for Economic, Social and Cultural Rights.

The interview data analyzed in this chapter are drawn from a research project that sought to critically analyze the work of global edu-businesses in education policy and practice more generally (Hogan 2015). These data were collected from 2012 to 2014 using a network ethnography methodology (Howard 2002; Ball and Junemann 2012), which comprised three interrelated methods: internet searches; semi-structured interviews; and the use of these two data sources to construct network diagrams (Ball and Junemann 2012). Specifically, for this chapter, we also analyzed corporate documents relating to Pearson's Efficacy Framework and the reworking of its business strategy, including a number of Pearson's annual reports. We also draw on three interviews with representatives from Pearson. These interviews were conducted during 2013, and pseudonyms, generic work titles, and no geographic locations are used when quoting passages of interview text, in order to help ensure anonymity.

The Reconstitution of Pearson as a Global Edu-business

Over the past decade, there has been a global explosion of edu-businesses seeking to capitalize on a burgeoning and highly profitable education industry (Burch 2009). According to Mayer-Schonberger and Cukier (2014), spending on education in the United States is currently estimated within the trillions, meaning that the education industry that was "termed sluggish a decade ago by Wall Street analysts is exploding through rapid influx of capital investments and public education revenue" (Burch 2009: 23). Increasingly, private sector organizations, ranging from huge multinational corporations through to smaller national operators and individual educational entrepreneurs operating locally, are beginning to diversify their businesses to take advantage of this rapidly growing and increasingly lucrative education market. Pearson, in particular, has recognized the potential value of this market and declared to its shareholders in its 2012 annual report that "we think education will be the biggest growth industry of the 21st century" (Pearson plc 2012: 8). The company has been undertaking a significant restructure over recent years, moving from an Anglo-American media holding company to a globally integrated education services company and, in the process, rebranding itself as "the world's leading education company" with the motto, "Always Learning."[1]

This organizational and strategic change has been underpinned by the general strategy of Pearson over the past decade, which has seen it engage in a series of high profile acquisitions, mergers and tradeoffs (Ball 2012; Picciano and Spring 2013). Part of this transformation included the 2013 merger of Penguin – one of Pearson's key subsidiaries – with Bertelsmann's Random House. But, as explained by one Pearson interviewee, this was only one facet of the broader transformation:

Pearson used to own *Baywatch* the TV series, distribution units, resorts ... [and] wineries in France as late as the early 2000s. The history of Pearson was that it was basically a holding company where it owned a lot of really interesting brands, with educational brands being a part of it. Then slowly it started shifting more and more toward education because it was both a good business opportunity *and also it was a social opportunity.*

We are at this point where, even last year, Pearson's biggest disposal was this company called Merger Market, a very profitable company, but wasn't really an educational product. It provides merger and acquisition data to hedge funds. Even though it was a very profitable business, we said "we're an education company now, this doesn't fit in." So we disposed it, and sold it, and used the capital to go deeper into education by acquiring a group in Brazil, which has a chain of language centers.

(Emphasis added)

This not only points to the reconstitution of Pearson as an edu-business, with elements of the company that are unrelated to education being traded for educational assets, but also highlights the ways in which Pearson is looking for and creating opportunities in the education market globally and with a stated social purpose for this investment.

While Pearson's £5.2 billion in sales during 2013 indicates that most of its education revenue comes from its business in North America, much greater growth is being seen in Pearson's international education sales. As Pearson Chief Executive Officer (CEO), John Fallon commented in the 2012 Annual Report:

Our growth prospects are also fuelled by a remarkable socio-economic trend: in this decade, the global middle class will almost double in size to more than three billion people. Nearly all of that growth will be in the developing world. That's important to many industries but especially to ours, because as consumers join the middle class and earn higher incomes, they tend to invest more in education – either to advance their careers or give their children a good start in life.

(Pearson plc 2012: 8)

As Prahalad (2004) argues, the world's fastest growing market is at the "bottom of the pyramid" where people from the developing world have untapped collective buying power that edu-businesses are able to target. Interestingly, Prahalad also makes the point that, in helping these people, businesses are not just making money, but they are helping millions of the world's poorest people escape poverty. John Fallon expresses a similar sentiment in Pearson's 2013 Annual Report:

Governments spend trillions of dollars per year on education and training; and, each year, the still rapidly growing middle class invests more of its own increasing wealth in the education of themselves and their children. And yet, the world fails to meet the learning needs of far too many of our fellow citizens ... Pearson has a unique set of advantages with which to help meet this global demand for better education and skills ... And, by being better able to meet some of the biggest challenges in global education, we can build a stronger, more profitable and faster growing company.

(Pearson plc 2013: 9)

Here we can see how Pearson's reworking of its corporate strategy is bringing together CSR and profit-making rationales for the provision of education products and services in both the Global North and Global South.

A prime example of this conflation is the Pearson Affordable Learning Fund (PALF), which makes equity investments in "education entrepreneurs who deliver high quality, for-profit education solutions for the low-income segment in the developing world" (PALF 2012). The objective of PALF is "to help millions of the poorest children in the world with a quality education, in a profitable and sustainable manner," and, moreover, "to demonstrate to governments and donors that low-cost private education can help educate low-income earners in a cost-effective way" (PALF). As Sir Michael Barber, Pearson's Chief Education Advisor and Chair of PALF explains, governments around the world need to understand that "for-profit providers of education are doing a better job; so learn from them, make them part of the system and see them as part of the solution" (PALF 2012). While the PALF initiative is currently focused on the Global South, with the restructuring of states and changing public legislation regarding education delivery, Pearson is potentially opening the door to for-profit private schools in the Global North as well, just as Pearson's involvement in testing in nations of the Global North has potential future application in the schooling systems of the Global South. Indeed, we see these moves as part of a globally integrated strategy by Pearson, and as a response to stringent criticisms and critiques of their work, particularly in the US, by opening up new markets in the Global South.

Pearson is not a traditional edu-business. Instead, we see the emergence of a new type of actor, a major international business, which, having operated across various sectors and industries, is now entering the education market with a promise to shareholders that, in the twenty-first century an "investment in education" will "pay the best interest" (Pearson plc 2012: 8). Pearson's bottom line, clearly, is the pursuit of profit for its shareholders. However, it also claims that its "commercial goals and social purpose are mutually reinforcing" (Pearson plc 2012: 34). Pearson's self-defined purpose is "to help people make progress in their lives through learning," and the company argues that it has a responsibility, as the world's leading learning company, "to support educational improvement and to actively share our experience on models that work and those that do not" (Pearson plc 2012: 38). Yet, to many education stakeholders, this presents as a contradictory tension between Pearson's profit motive and their desire to contribute to individual wellbeing and the public good. As such, Pearson's strategy presents a challenge to arguments about the necessity of high quality public schooling to a democratic society.

In fact, many social commentators, particularly in the US, where Pearson's influence is currently felt to be most pervasive, focus on this apparent contradiction. Diane Ravitch (2013), the former Assistant Secretary of Education in

President George W. Bush's administration, and now an outspoken opponent to what she calls the "Pearsonization" of US schooling, argues that the increasing corporatization of education is unquestionably linked to investor interest, rather than any altruistic aspiration to improve education globally. Indeed, many critiques levelled at corporations such as Pearson speak of their power and their lack of public accountability; they are responsible to shareholders, not to a democratic constituency. However, as Holzer (2010) points out, while the likes of Pearson may appear to be powerful, monolithic entities, it is near impossible for corporations to avoid the "goldfish bowl" of public scrutiny and they are thus forced to respond to the public's perception and evaluation of their actions and activities. Additionally, and as we will take up in the conclusion, there is concerted teacher union and civil society opposition, including activist bloggers, to these developments in the privatization of/in schooling (Ball and Youdell 2008). Shamir (2008: 3) describes this pressure as a form of "moralization of the market." Thus, Pearson's current transformation not only presents a reconstitution of its business strategy, but also a reconstitution of its image in the light of a global "politics of mutual accountability" (Nóvoa and Yariv-Mashal 2003; Ranson 2003) and in response to political critique and opposition to many of these developments. Pearson is reconstituting itself as simultaneously accountable to its shareholders and the "public," understood as the collection of individuals who engage with its products and services.

Neo-Liberal Accountability and Corporate Social Responsibility

As a public limited company, Pearson is fundamentally committed to creating shareholder value. The company's annual reports begin with a succinct statement of Pearson's financial highlights and a strategic business overview from the CEO. Since 2006, when Pearson's annual report was first made available online, these overviews have largely focused on sales, growth and profit figures, as well as a synopsis of share price performance. However, over this period of time, there has also been an increasing focus on Pearson's accountability as a socially responsible business. Kolk (2008) suggests that this is a common trend among all large corporations, which now understand that being accountable to stakeholders means being accountable to both shareholders and broader publics affected by their business. Moreover, Glac (2014) contends that the demands of shareholders have expanded over recent years to include non-financial expectations of corporate conduct and concerns for both the social and financial aspects of their investments. Comments from one Pearson interviewee reflect this changed environment for investors and consumers:

> [I]f you look at the history of capitalism and traditional large operations, it's over the last few years that there has been a lot of distress against large institutions. Consumers have lost confidence in large institutions, and what Pearson is saying is that as a large institution, to really gain back customer trust it has to be a more responsible corporation. It has to be accountable for not just the financial returns, but also the outcomes it delivers.

In this context, we are seeing the promotion of new conceptualizations of and approaches to CSR. In the past, CSR has been considered a matter of philanthropy: corporations invested some of their profits back into the community to make a positive contribution to society and as a public relations exercise for the company. Until recently, this approach to CSR was still evident in Pearson's business model; its philanthropic arm, the Pearson Foundation, worked with partners to promote "literacy, learning and great teaching" (Pearson Foundation 2014). In 2014, the Pearson Foundation announced an end to its operations and explained that,

> this follows a decision by Pearson plc to integrate all of its corporate social responsibility activities and functions into its business as a way to maximise social impact and to no longer fund the Foundation as the primary vehicle for its philanthropic and community activities.

> (Pearson Foundation 2014)

As further elaborated by a Pearson interviewee:

> In the past you see a lot of CSR initiatives which, often large corporations do a lot of bad stuff but then they have the CSR arm that does some good marketing and just donates money. What we are saying is that a responsible corporation can't function like that. CSR can't be just a sideshow, it has to be a core part of the mission of the company.

Thus, CSR has been "mainstreamed" by Pearson to enhance the broader activities of the company and, in particular, its social impact and public perception. This presents a slightly different understanding of the "new philanthropy" and "social capitalism," which Ball (2012: 66), Ball and Junemann (2012), and Olmedo (2013) have analyzed, in which the contributions of philanthropic organizations function as morally strategic components in new education policy processes. Pearson now claims that CSR is not a separate philanthropic mission and is instead being integrated into its everyday business activities. This is a phenomenon described by Bishop and Green (2008: 177) as "philanthrocapitalism," in which CSR is driven by the belief that doing good can be profitable.

As Power et al. (2009) argue, businesses now audit themselves to manage their "reputational risk," with reputation often understood in terms of customer perceptions and the construction of a particular organizational image and identity. Further, Power and colleagues suggest that, "reputational risk has grown to become a distinctive and pervasive risk category which is not merely descriptive but also reactionary and performative" (2009: 310). This is part of the shift that Power (1999) outlines in his description of the "audit society," in which there has been a systematic growth of auditing activity associated with the rise of New Public Management, increased demands for accountability and transparency and the implementation of quality assurance models of organizational control. This development is also linked, he argues, to declining trust in governments and professionals, and, as the Pearson representative above indicated, big corporations.

Thus, the importance of CSR for Pearson is at least partly a matter of managing reputational risk and engaging with relevant stakeholders to frame its new business strategy in positive ways; CSR for Pearson is about creating reputational capital. This is a neo-social construction of accountability, in which social responsibility is incorporated within market rationalities.

To this end, Pearson is seeking to communicate with external stakeholders by anticipating how its actions are being evaluated by the public and by positioning itself as accountable and responsible for the outcomes of its services and products. As Holzer (2010) observes, the company is making substantial efforts to portray itself as a good "corporate citizen." Pearson's new Efficacy Framework, which we turn to in the following section, reflects an appreciation that continuing success, or power in education policy networks, is dependent on playing by "the rules of the game," where "power is not something that can be acquired, seized or shared" (Foucault 1979: 94), but is rather something embedded in social relations – in this case, between Pearson, their shareholders and the public, who are becoming increasingly critical of Pearson's activities.

Pearson's Efficacy Framework

In November 2013, Pearson released its Efficacy Framework as part of a new commitment to ensuring that its products and services have a measurable impact. In Pearson's promotional materials, efficacy is styled as a social movement that people can advocate for in support of Pearson's agenda, which includes a commitment to report on audited learning outcome measures and targets, alongside its financial accounts, by 2018. As explained in the 2013 Annual Report:

> This new and transparent approach to efficacy is central to our purpose and also makes good business sense. We hope that by demonstrating the evidence base that supports our products we will encourage a deeper engagement with learning outcomes across the education sector and at the same time clearly demonstrate the benefits of using those products.
>
> (Pearson plc 2013: 14)

Pearson's emphasis on "efficacy" borrows from usage of the term in the pharmaceutical industry and reflects the trend toward the medicalization of education research that has been insightfully analyzed by Trohler (2015). Indeed, the promotional materials describing Pearson's efficacy agenda include an image of a researcher in a laboratory working with test tubes, conjuring an association between Pearson's evaluation of its products and the "rigor" of medical research. While we have provided a detailed discussion and critique of the Efficacy Framework elsewhere (Hogan et al. 2015), we will give a brief overview here in order to show how Pearson's reworking of its corporate strategy to focus on the measurable outcomes of its products is part of a broader "responsibilization" of the company.

Pearson's Efficacy Framework is a standardized review process, including a review tool in rubric format, which is used by the company to evaluate how well its products and services achieve desired outcomes. The Framework enables the rating of a product, program or service against criteria in the following four areas: outcomes; evidence; plans; and capacity. By giving each criterion a rating on a four-point color scale, from green to red, the *Framework* can be used to assess how well a product is achieving its objectives and how it might be improved. This is one example of the rise of data visualization as a new policy semiotic. As stated in Pearson's 2013 Annual Report, "the Framework serves to identify specific areas, which if improved, will increase our likelihood of intended impact. Teams are able [to] focus their activity on taking these steps before the product is assessed again" (Pearson plc 2013: 15). Indeed, Pearson claims that, "all new product developments will have defined and measureable student outcomes" (Pearson plc 2013: 15).

Importantly, efficacy is defined differently in relation to the different contexts of Pearson's products and services and in ways that overlap with the broad purposes of education, such as the aim for low-fee, for-profit Pearson schools in developing countries to provide students with basic standards of literacy. The notion of efficacy thus acts as a pivot between Pearson's internal performative accountability mechanisms and the public representation of its corporate mission as advancing wellbeing through learning. Achieving efficacy means that every aspect of its work should have a measurable impact and should be continually improved to provide guaranteed learning outcomes. Pearson's emphasis on efficacy reflects a concern for accountability to customers, as explained by a Pearson interviewee:

> It's not just about: Oh trust us. We're Pearson. We're an education company. It becomes very much about, well trust us, because you've got the evidence. Really, everything that we do should be evidence based, so you're actually able to demonstrate to whomever it is you're going to be working with that this is actually something that should work well for you.

This focus on efficacy is an attempt to build trust with customers through recourse to an "evidence base" that legitimizes its activities. Importantly, the notion of efficacy and the associations with medical research are used to bolster the authority of this evidence and to enhance the legitimacy of Pearson's work.

Given the dominant market position of the company and its considerable global influence (Ball 2012), including contractual arrangements with numerous governments and other organizations, one may ask why Pearson is attempting to be more publicly open and accountable, rather than just focusing on meeting its internal targets and contractual commitments? In answering this question, a Pearson interviewee highlighted an internal view that it must respond to its critics and legitimize itself as acting in the public interest in terms of getting its products "right":

> The more you do, the bigger the target becomes on your back to be honest, and you just need to be aware of that. You need to be sensitive to it, because, with that level of influence comes an awful lot of responsibility, which is, in some respects, where the Efficacy Framework comes in for us. If we're going to have this level of responsibility, then we need to get it right.

The Efficacy Framework is, at least in part, a reaction to public criticism and concerted opposition, say by the American Federation of Teachers and civil society activists, particularly but not exclusively in the US. In the wake of neoliberal globalization, financial crises and much talk of growing inequality (Piketty 2014), multinational corporations have faced increasing amounts of public criticism from various groups. Among the concerns of these groups is fear that for-profit edu-businesses may undermine the sovereignty of national education policy practices, exclude teachers from a role in policy making, contribute to a democratic deficit in public debate and public policy making and, as a result, contribute further to the undesirable consequences that can be associated with privatizing the provision of public "goods." There is also real concern that the involvement of edu-businesses such as Pearson in testing encourages the standardization of schooling.

Pearson recognizes that it has achieved an influential and powerful position within the global education market and risks being seen as "irresponsible" by critics if is not transparent and accountable in relation to the outcomes of its products and services. For example, in the US there is a tension between calls from teachers and schools to release tests constructed by Pearson for educative purposes and the company's desire to keep tests confidential in order to use them from year to year, thus reducing costs. Pearson seeks to openly embrace its responsibility for contributing to learning opportunities and outcomes that would previously have been considered the responsibility of governments, seeking to position the company as a publicly accountable policy actor and its products and services as legitimate alternatives to the public provision of education. This business strategy is indicative of Pearson's desire to become a major agent in global education policy processes; it seeks to engage with these accountability processes, not simply as an edu-business, but as an actor that is considered to be influential and responsible in ways similar to national governments and international organizations.

Performative Accountability and the Redefinition of the Educational "Good"

> Pearson is committed to measure our performance in improving people's lives through learning with the same clarity that we measure product sales and corporate profits today. *The pursuit of better learner outcomes is our responsibility and our mission.*
>
> (Pearson n.d., emphasis added)

Pearson's efficacy strategy can be understood to combine trends toward systematic performative accountability, new approaches to corporate social responsibility, and the medicalization of education research. Thrift (2005) argues that today capitalism has become a project of itself, and performative accountability has become a key mechanism through which business and government continually monitor and modulate practices through the generation of data and its continual evaluation. Performativity involves making ourselves "calculable" (Ball 2003) as we adapt to the "challenges of reporting and recording our practice" and "informational structures and performance indicators become the principle of intelligibility of social relationships" (Ball 2013: 138).

Ranson (2003) argues that, with the shift from professional to neo-liberal modes of accountability, performative, consumer, corporate and contract accountabilities have become pervasive throughout society: "since the late 1970s such regimes of public accountability have been strengthened systematically so that accountability is no longer merely an important instrument or component within the system, but constitutes the system itself" (Ranson 2003: 459).

Numbers, metrics and rankings of comparative performance are central today to the structuring of schooling systems: they constitute the system. This shift, and particularly the effects of performativity becoming a dominant means for the legitimation of knowledge (Lyotard 1984), have had a significant impact on the values that guide social practices. As Lyotard observes, "since performativity increases the ability to produce proof, it also increases the ability to be right: the technical criterion, introduced on a massive scale into scientific knowledge, cannot fail to influence the truth criterion" (Lyotard 1984: 46). Efficiency and effectiveness are the technical and truth criteria in neo-liberal accountability systems and have also become a "good" and an end in themselves, rather than a means to achieve other purposes. Ball (2013) observes that,

> performativity … is a "new" moral system that subverts and re-orients us to its truth and ends. It makes us responsible for our performance and for the performance of others. We are burdened with the responsibility to perform, and if we do not we are in danger of being seen as irresponsible.
>
> (Ball 2013: 138)

The Efficacy Framework is a performative mechanism for pursuing organizational change and effectiveness. As Broadhead and Howard (1998) point out, people and organizations do not necessarily participate in performative contexts reluctantly, but imaginatively, aggressively and competitively. Indeed, as Ball (2013: 140) observes, "performativity works best when we want for ourselves what is wanted from us."

Pearson has embraced performative accountability as a way to conjure a moral dimension to their "mission," presenting a corporation focused on a double bottom line of profitability *and* responsibility for improving people's lives through learning. This wedding of economic and social purposes reflects the rise of the "neo-social" (Vogelmann 2012), which Savage (2013: 187) describes as "a rejuvenated governmental interest in enabling healthy and positive social environments, but primarily for the sake of fostering greater economic productivity." Neo-social corporate strategy arises from a two-fold process whereby pressure is exerted on companies to embrace social responsibility and this responsibility becomes incorporated within the rationalities of market competition:

> [T]he moralization of the market thus has a critical potential in that the demand for socially responsible market actors – typically exerted through social struggles in the form of consumer boycotts and public shaming campaigns – may somewhat restrain their drive for financial gains. Yet, at another level, the moralization of markets also entails the economization of morality; a process which is compatible with the general neo-liberal drive to ground social relations in the economic rationality of markets.
>
> (Shamir 2008: 3)

This dynamic is clearly evident in the case of Pearson. The neo-social corporation recognizes that new forms of CSR are necessary for its continuing success and this recognition stems from the realization that its power and influence are susceptible to public scrutiny and pressure, in terms of consumers exercising their capacity for exit by taking business elsewhere or exerting public pressure to increase regulation. However, this is not simply a matter of bowing to external pressure, but represents a new business and political opportunity, as Pearson helps to redefine the "good" in terms of what is profitable. In the neo-social market economy, as Shamir (2008) observes, "doing good is good for business and the responsible corporation thus at once also becomes no less a moral authority" (Shamir 2008: 13).

Ranson (2003) argues that social relationships of accountability can operate according to two types of goods: external and internal. Efficiency and effectiveness are external goods that increasingly underpin relationships of accountability, orienting practices toward achieving what Lyotard (1984: 46) described as "the best possible input/output equation." In contrast, internal goods are intrinsic to the definition of what makes a given activity worthwhile and, importantly, are open to revision through processes of deliberation and debate among groups involved in and affected by the activity. In Pearson's refashioning of their business strategy, we see both kinds of goods invoked in complex and contradictory ways. For example, Pearson has defined its mission as improving people's lives through learning, but has provided a mechanism for evaluating its success in this task that is thoroughly informed by the external good of efficacy. Users of Pearson's products and services can engage in a discussion about their effectiveness, but this discussion is not one about the internal goods of education but rather the efficacy of a particular commercial product.

By invoking the internal goods of education (improving people's lives), while restructuring the company to focus on external goods, Pearson can present itself as responsive to the public interest in education, while undermining possibilities for deliberation about the values and purposes of education as a public good. In other words, we must consider the contestability or otherwise of the values and "goods" that underpin neo-liberal accountability and its use to evaluate the extent to which Pearson improves people's lives. Performative accountability assumes efficiency and effectiveness as the driving values of systems, and only the data that are collected to monitor systems and the actions that are taken to change systems are open to revision. This has implications for other modes of accountability too. As Ranson (2003) observes,

Corporate/contract accountability is inappropriate to the public sphere. The goods of effectiveness need to be subordinated to the internal goods of a service that can only be clarified through deliberation in the public sphere.

(Ranson 2003: 473)

This potential democratic deficit is compounded by the trend toward "evidence-based" policy making in education (Wiseman 2010), informed by research that increasingly follows a medical model. Evidence-based policy is redolent of a technocracy rather than a democracy, which is why we prefer the notion of evidence-informed policy. This captures the reality that in a democracy policy is constituted through evidence, politics and professional knowledge (Head 2008).

Pearson's referencing of pharmaceutical research as the model for its efficacy approach is a good example of this trend toward medicalisation of educational research. As Trohler (2015) argues,

this expertocratic and medical shift in social research led to a massive reduction in reform opportunities by depriving the reform stakeholders of professional experience, common sense, and political deliberation and by assigning policy to a new caste of so-called experts that work within the logic of bio-medical research.

(Tröhler 2015: 2)

Put simply, Pearson invokes its mission as increasing the public good by improving the lives of individuals through learning. The company has "mainstreamed" its corporate social responsibility for providing efficacious learning and is putatively willing to be held accountable for its activities in this regard. However, the accountability mechanisms that are made available for this purpose assume efficacy as a driving principle and thus exclude debate about the internal goods of education: that is, debate informed by the views of teachers, parents, students, and other publics and debate about appropriate purposes of schooling, including its democratic citizenship goals and the provision of socially just opportunity for all irrespective of social background. Lingard et al. (2014) have shown how the rearticulation of social justice and equity through such modes of accountability – a form of "policy as numbers" – has reductive effects on these broader purposes of schooling.

Discussion and Conclusion

In this chapter, we have documented the reconstitution of Pearson plc as a global learning company. While the focus has been on Pearson, this is just one exemplary manifestation of further privatization of education across the globe. This enhanced role of edu-businesses has been enabled by the restructuring of the state within nations toward network modes of governance and the creation of new roles for edu-business in the global governance work of international organizations such as the OECD.

We have shown that Pearson has an integrated global business strategy, working in both the nations of the Global North and those of the Global South. In the former, its involvement has been in respect to testing, accountability, data management, and various performance measures. In the nations of the Global South, support for low-fee, for-profit schools has been a central strategy, while in China the focus has been on English language schools. While our lens has been on Pearson's Efficacy Framework, which is currently more targeted on the Global North, we need to understand that its various strategies across the globe are symbiotically linked with potential for expanding strategies from the North to the South and vice versa. For example, Pearson is interested in promoting for-profit schools in wealthier nations of the Global North. We also note that an important component of Pearson's business strategy is to influence education policy agendas globally.

We have also documented how Pearson abolished its philanthropic arm, the Pearson Foundation, in late 2014, to place CSR at the core of its new business strategy and company culture. We referred to this as the mainstreaming of corporate social responsibility – an example of what has been called philanthrocapitalism (Bishop and Green 2008). Corporate social responsibility is now central to Pearson's *raison d'être* as a global edu-business.

Following Trohler (2015), we argue that with its Efficacy Framework Pearson is contributing to the medicalization of educational research, drawing on the example of the pharmaceuticals industry. This is research *for* policy, located within the rise of a narrowly pragmatic ("what works") technoscientific reworking of knowledge production. The Framework is an exemplification of Ranson's (2003) argument about the emergence of neo-liberal accountability, including elements of performative, consumer, contract and corporate modes of accountability. The Efficacy Framework is performative in its stress on outcome measures; the consumer focus offers a potential guarantee for "customers" (here governments and international organizations) of the efficacy of Pearson's products and services; Pearson enters into contracts with governments and international organizations; and the company seeks to ensure corporate accountability by maximising profits for their shareholders. In our analysis, we have argued that the Efficacy Framework is a mode of neo-social accountability in education, which elides the distinction between benefits for shareholders and contribution to (a reductive construction of) educational "goods." Here we see, as Shamir (2008) has argued, "a shift from deontological ethics to teleological (consequentialist) ethics that subordinate socio-moral sensibilities to the calculus of possible outcomes, to the tests of cost-benefit analyzes and to the criteria of reputational-risk management" (Shamir 2008: 14).

We are critical of the potential democratic deficit in these developments, particularly in Pearson's desire to shape global education policy agendas. This desire is evident in Pearson's attempted construction of putative policy problems in education and the proffering of solutions to the problems so constructed. We stress that Pearson has no democratic constituency; rather, it is responsible to its shareholders for profit making. In seeking to construct policy agendas and policy problems and proffering solutions to them, Pearson is seeking involvement in the policy cycle in education, both globally and within nations. What we have here then is the quasi-privatization of the education policy community, as argued by Mahony and colleagues (2004). Our research has shown that Pearson is very influential with policy makers and politicians. Their research *for* policy is much more influential than academic research *of* policy, which is aimed more at understanding. The encouragement as well of evidence-based policy fails to understand that in a democracy we can only ever have evidence-informed policy (Head 2008; Lingard 2013), as democratic politics, reflecting the will of the people, frame the broader goals of schooling, and function as meta-policy. This is recognition that, in a democratic polity, policy is the "authoritative allocation of values" (Easton 1953; Rizvi and Lingard 2010), consisting of ideology/discourses, facts/research and professional knowledge (Head 2008). The Efficacy Framework simplifies, indeed bowdlerises, the complexity of actual policy making processes in democratic polities. There is a huge professional deficit in these developments as well; indeed, there is the total exclusion of the teacher voice and teacher unions; teachers are constructed as simply the implementers or enacters of policy with no legitimate policy development interests. Professional knowledge is thus excluded from the construction of policy processes.

In our critique here, we acknowledge that Pearson has some legitimate business interests in education – for example, being contracted to construct tests or sell textbooks. However, we are deeply concerned about the Pearson Affordable Learning Fund supporting the creation of low-fee, for-profit schools in developing nations. This reflects our position that free, universal, publicly provided quality schooling is central to democratic societies and to development agendas. There is also an ethical question about profiting from some of the poorest people on the planet, those at the so-called "bottom of the pyramid." We are concerned at Pearson's attempt to gain broader involvement across the globe in policy agenda setting, policy construction, implementation, and evaluation, which raises concerns for us in respect of the democratic deficits adumbrated above and in denial of the legitimate voice of teachers in these processes. Relevant here is the level of access Pearson has to senior policy makers globally. There is also a way in which Pearson's involvement in testing encourages standardization of schooling with potential reductive effects on curriculum provision and the broader, democratically framed purposes of schooling in relation to opportunity and citizenship.

Pearson does not have it all its own ways in these developments. There is opposition to Pearson's growing influence in education within nations: for example, the American Federation of Teachers' opposition to the undemocratic, dubious, and illegitimate aspects of Pearson's work in the US. Diane Ravitch, and other activist bloggers such as Alan Singer, have also been vocal critics and others, including individual whistle-blowers, former employees, and investigative journalists across the US, have raised concerns about Pearson's operations. Education International, the international federation of teacher unions, representing more than 30 million teachers globally, has also been strategizing effectively around the issues raised in this conclusion and recognizes the need for a global response. This includes the argument that privatizations of the kind we have articulated in this chapter damage and potentially undermine public education. Global civil society organizations (Global Campaign for Education, Global Initiative for Economic, Social, and Cultural Rights, Action Aid and the Results Educational Fund) are all turning their research, political gaze, and activism on to the provision of low-fee private schools in the developing world and have had some success (see Macpherson et al. 2014). An effective political strategy will also need to work with governments, because new modes of network governance and outsourcing of educational services are part of the problem. And while we have focused on Pearson and its work in the Global North here, we suggest that any effective global strategy of resistance to the nefarious aspects of these developments in neo-social accountability in education must understand Pearson's integrated global business strategy and recognize that Pearson is only the largest player in this new phase of global education policy.

Note

1 Critics of Pearson parody this branding as "Always Earning."

References

Ball, S. J. (2003). The teacher's soul and the terrors of performativity. *Journal of Education Policy*, 18(2), 215–228.

Ball, S. J. (2012). *Global education inc. New policy networks and the neo-liberal social imaginary*. Oxon: Routledge.

Ball, S. J. (2013). *Foucault, power and education*. New York: Routledge.

Ball, S. J. and Junemann, C. (2012). *Networks, new governance and education*. Bristol: The Policy Press.

Ball, S. J. and Youdell, D. (2008). *Hidden privatisation in public education, education international*. Retrieved May 12, 2015, from: http://download.ei-ie.org/docs/IRISDocuments/Research%20Website%20Documents/2009-00034-01-E.pdf.

Bishop, M. and Green, M. (2008). *Philanthrocapitalism: How giving can save the world*. London: Black Publishers Ltd.

Broadhead, L. and Howard, S. (1998). "The art of punishing": The research assessment exercise and the ritualisation of power in higher education. *Education Policy Analysis Archives*, 6(8), 1–16.

Burch, P. (2009). *Hidden markets: The new education privatization*. Hoboken: Routledge.

Easton, D. (1953). *The political system: An inquiry into the state of political science*. New York: Alfred A. Knopf.

Foucault, M. (1979). *Discipline and punish: The birth of prison*. London: Penguin Books.

Glac, K. (2014). The influence of shareholders on corporate social responsibility. *Economics, Management and Financial Markets*, 3/2014, 34–79.

Head, B. W. (2008). Three lenses of evidence-based policy. *The Australian Journal of Public Administration*, 67(1), 1–11.

Hogan, A. (2015). *The role of edu-business in new global education policy networks*. Unpublished doctoral dissertation, University of Queensland, Queensland, Australia.

Hogan, A., Sellar, S. and Lingard, B. (2015). Network restructuring of global edu-business: The case of Pearson's Efficacy Framework. In W. Au and J. Ferrare (Eds). *Mapping corporate education reform: Power and policy networks in the neoliberal state*. New York: Routledge.

Holzer, B. (2010). *Moralizing the corporation: Transnational activism and corporate accountability*. Cheltenham: Edward Elgar Publishing.

Howard, P. N. (2002). Network ethnography and the hypermedia organization: New media, new organizations, new methods. *New Media and Society*, 4(4), 550–574.

Kolk, A. (2008). Sustainability, accountability and corporate governance: Exploring multinationals' reporting practices. *Business Strategy and the Environment*, 17(1), 1–15.

Koppenjan, J. and Klijn, E. (2004). *Managing uncertainties in networks*. London: Routledge.

Lingard, B. (2013). The impact of research on education policy in an era of evidence-based policy. *Critical Studies in Education*, 54(2), 113–131.

Lingard, B., Sellar, S. and Savage, G. C. (2014). Re-articulating social justice as equity in schooling policy: the effects of testing and data infrastructures. *British Journal of Sociology of Education*, 35(5), 710–730.

Lyotard, J. F. (1984). *The postmodern condition: A report on knowledge*. Minneapolis: University of Minnesota Press.

Macpherson, I., Robertson, S. and Walford, G. (Eds). (2014). *Education, privatisation and social justice: Case studies from Africa, South Asia and South East Asia*. Oxford: Symposium.

Mahony, P., Hextall, I. and Menter, I. (2004). 'Building dams in Jordan, assessing teachers in England': A case study in edu-business. *Globalisation, Societies and Education*, 2(2), 227–296.

Mayer-Schonberger, V. and Cukier, K. (2014). *Learning with big data: The future of education*. New York: Houghton Mifflin Harcourt Publishing.

Nóvoa, A. and Yariv-Mashal, T. (2003). Comparative research in education: A mode of governance or a historical journey? *Comparative Education*, 39(4), 423–438.

Olmedo, A. (2013). From England with love ... ARK, heterarchies and global 'philanthropic governance'. *Journal of Education Policy*, 29(5), 575–597.

PALF. (2012). *Pearson Affordable Learning Fund*. Retrieved May 15, 2015 from: http://www.affordable-learning.com/#sthash.URdRPWdX.dpbs.

Pearson Foundation. (2014). Pearson Foundation. Retrieved June 1, 2015 from: http://www.pearsonfoundation.org.

Pearson plc. (2012). Annual report and accounts 2012. Retrieved June 1, 2015 from: https://www.pearson.com/content/dam/corporate/global/pearson-dot-com/files/cosec/2013/15939_PearsonAR12.pdf.

Pearson plc. (2013). Annual report and accounts 2013. Retrieved May 13, 2015 from: https://www.pearson.com/content/dam/corporate/global/pearson-dot-com/files/annual-reports/ar2013/2013--annual-report-accounts.pdf.

Picciano, A. and Spring, J. (2013). *The great American education-industrial complex: Ideology, technology and profit*. New York: Routledge.

Piketty, T. (2014). *Capital in the twenty-first century*. Cambridge, MA: The Belknap Press of Harvard University Press.

Power, M. (1997). *The audit society: Rituals of verification*. Oxford: Oxford University Press.

Power, M. (1999). *The audit society: Rituals of verification*. 2nd ed. Oxford: Oxford University Press.

Power, M., Scheytt, T., Soin, K. and Sahlin, K. (2009). Reputational risk as a logic of organizing in later modernity. *Organizational Studies*, 30(2–3), 301–324.

Prahalad, C. K. (2004). *The fortune at the bottom of the pyramid: Eradicating poverty through profits*. Upper Saddle River, NJ: Prentice Hall.

Ranson, S. (2003). Public accountability in the age of neo-liberal governance. *Journal of Education Policy*, 18(5), 459–480.

Ravitch, D. (2013). *Reign of error: The hoax of the privatization movement and the danger to America's public schools*. New York: Vintage Books.

Rizvi, F. and Lingard, B. (2010). *Globalizing education policy*. New York: Routledge.

Rose, N. (1999). Inventiveness in politics. *Economy and society*, 28(3), 467–493.

Savage, G. C. (2013). Tailored equities in the education market: Flexible policies and practices. *Discourse: Studies in the Cultural Politics of Education*, 34(2), 185–201.

Shamir, R. (2008). The age of responsibilization: on market-embedded morality. *Economy and Society*, 37(1), 1–19.

Thrift, N. (2005). *Knowing Capitalism*. London: Sage.

Tröhler, D. (2015). The medicalization of current educational research and its effects on education policy and school reforms. *Discourse: Studies in the Cultural Politics of Education*. 36(5), 749–764.

Vogelmann, F. (2012). Neosocial market economy. *Foucault Studies*, 14(2), 115–137.

Wiseman, A. (2010). The uses of evidence for educational policymaking: Global contexts and international trends. *Review of Research in Education*, 34(1), 1–24.

8 Knowledge Production and the Rise of Consultocracy in Education Policymaking in England

Helen Gunter and Colin Mills

Introduction

The focus of this chapter is on the rapid development in consultancy services in England in the past 40 years, with a specific emphasis on the privatization of knowledge production. We locate this analysis in England as a site for how knowledge production as a global process actually takes place in local and localizing contexts. We examine the inter-relationship between the state, public policy, and knowledge, where we are concerned with how networks of knowledge actors identify, use, and mobilize particular types of knowledge and ways of knowing in the scoping, framing, and enacting of education policy. Specifically, we are concerned with the rise of the commissioning of knowledge production within, for, and by public services from business, where private interests, ideas, ideologies, as well as common sense notions about purposes and practices in education have come to dominate. England has been a laboratory for the use and normalization of neoliberal ideas, and these have been communicated and traded on a global scale through consultant and consultancy processes. Such is the influence of consultants and consultancy that scholars have suggested that a form of 'consultocracy' (Hood and Jackson 1991) is emerging, where it seems that consultants have power in the system without formal accountability through democratic channels (Saint-Martin 2004).

We begin by examining the evidence base for our analysis by drawing on a range of empirical projects with data sets from over 50 consultants, and with a specific focus on the National Literacy Strategy (NLS) in England. In doing this, we aim to demonstrate how the 'tools' of policy scholarship – a recognition of policy influences, texts, discourses, and effects (Bowe et al. 1992) – assist us in charting both the provenance and the patterns of consultants and consultancy. While clearly the focus is on England, the reach of this demand for appropriate and preferred knowledge is global in regard to commissioning researchers from outside of the UK to undertake evaluations of major evaluations (Earl et al. 2002). We bring understanding and explanations throughout the chapter by deploying Bernstein's (1971, 1996, 2000, 2001) conceptual tools to read the data, and by doing this we enable an empirical contribution through the mapping of consultants and consultancy, combined with new ways of thinking about their location within and contribution to public policy.

Positioning Our Research and Conceptual Tools

We position consultants as private knowledge producers, located in a rapidly developing consultancy industry composed of: (a) large-scale globally significant companies; (b) small to medium-sized companies of networks of consultants; and (c) lone person businesses. The expansion in their activity and importance in England is based on a rise in centralized government commissioning of research projects, policy implementation, and evaluations by large companies and individual entrepreneurial experts. In addition, local services are being changed from provision to commissioning and oversight, where changes in patterns of employment (e.g. redundancies and early retirements brought about by the dismantling of public services) are producing a pool of former state employees who are setting up their own consultancy businesses.

We have been studying this phenomenon through a range of projects: first, the Knowledge Production in Educational Leadership (KPEL) project (ESRC, RES-000-23-1192) (Gunter 2012a); second, the Consultancy and Knowledge Production in Education Project (British Academy, SG121698) (Gunter and Mills 2016); and third, the Consultancy and Literacy Project (Gunter and Mills 2016). Within this program of research, we have been studying the business of consultants and consultancy using three main methodologies: *conceptual,* using resources from social science to map and understand consultants' work (e.g. Gunter et al. 2015); *policy scholarship,* using our interest in policy cycles and texts to trace consultants' influences (e.g. Gunter et al. 2014a), and *empirical* methods, where we have examined webpages generating information about 500 consultants who work in education, conducted interviews with 50 consultants from global companies to the individual 'sole trader', and followed consultants into the field to observe them at work and to interview their clients regarding issues of options, choices, exchange, and impact (Gunter and Mills 2016).

We have found Bernstein's (1996, 2000) groundbreaking work valuable. One of Bernstein's central concepts is that of *the pedagogic device* – an ensemble of rules and processes whereby knowledge is selected, moved around, and 'translated' into knowledge that is to be taught, sequenced, and evaluated. Another concept that we draw on is that of *recontextualization.* Knowledge, once selected and sequenced, is transformed into the underpinning of policy and pedagogy ('what gets done' in schools). These policies are then subject to 'complex processes of fleshing out, being given substance, or recontextualized, by specialized agencies created by or linked to the state or who thrive by doing its business' (Fitz et al. 2006: 18). Bernstein also identified the concepts of *recontextualizing fields and agents.* The Official Recontextualizing Field (ORF) refers to the field dominated by the state and its agents. The Pedagogic Recontextualizing Field (PRF) consists of agents who interpret and translate these policies, enabling practitioners to 'enact' them (Singh et al. 2013, 2014). Methodologically, we are drawn to Bernstein's conceptual resources as they enable us to 'map' his (sometimes highly complex and structured) concepts to the fields of knowledge and policy as they are *shifting* and *changing.* Moreover, his 'toolkits' and his 'conceptual accounts' (Singh et al. 2010) enable us to develop a language so as to describe, analyse and critique what are novel and previously unexamined processes in public policy, and its enactments in schools.

Knowledge Work

Our starting point is to identity that there are three types of consultants and consultancy: first, *Business*, where people work on their own, or in association, or in a large company in order to trade knowledge; second, *Research*, where people who are employed by higher education institutions produce and trade knowledge; and third, *State*, where people are employed by public institutions at national and/or local levels to disseminate knowledge through training. In examining the work that these types of consultants do, we have used a mapping process (for antecedence see Raffo and Gunter 2008; Gunter et al. 2013, 2015) to examine the trade in knowledge and knowing by knowers, and the assertions made about what is demanded and what is provided, and why. This framework is focused on *Functional, Critical,* and *Socially Critical* approaches to consultancy.

Functionality is dominant in published accounts by professionals (e.g. Collarbone 2005) and by researchers about how they act as 'consultants' (e.g. Ainscow and Southworth 1996; Learmonth and Lowers 1998) or as 'critical friends' (e.g. MacBeath 1998) to remove the dysfunctions from within schools as organizations.

Our data show a strong commitment to functionality. There is an emphasis on providing information and skills to enable practitioners to meet the unrelenting accountability protocols which schools have to evidence:

> **Clare (pseudonym, consultant, interview 2013):** Most of the time I'm working on training and consultancy for individual schools ... In addition to that there are about three companies that I do work for, as an associate consultant.

> **Jane (pseudonym, consultant, interview 2013):** I see a large part of my job as giving schools and teachers the tools they need to raise standards and to reach the standards that OFSTED demands of them. Local Authorities are not able to provide things in the same way. Schools are seeking the help of people like me to keep them above water.

There is a strong emphasis on enabling the reform process to work; their disposition is to enable functional efficiencies:

> **Olive (pseudonym, consultant, interview 2013):** the main piece of work is with Teaching Schools, Federation Partnerships, Initial Teacher Training.

> **Geoffrey (pseudonym, consultant, interview 2013):** at the moment I am the Executive Principal of [name] Academy.

> **Henry (pseudonym, consultant, interview 2013):** I do quite a bit of work acting as Director of Human Resources and Governance in a Multi-Academy trust.

> **Suzannah (pseudonym, consultant, interview 2013):** I am there to provide solutions that match the outcomes they're seeking.

There is demand for this 'functional' approach to solving the problems that practitioners encounter in an educational arena that is focused on performance, competitiveness and on 'finding solutions.' Mills (2012) reports on an interview with 'Dave', a primary school head teacher, discussing the decisions he has to make when engaging and 'employing' consultants to assist him:

> **Dave (pseudonym, consultant, interview 2010)**: I really have to be concerned with 'getting the best deal'. I get dozens of adverts, people selling their services each week now. I now have to buy in what the NLS and the local authorities used to provide. So I constantly have to balance priorities. Do I think about the kinds of knowledge and refreshment that my teachers need to invigorate their practice? Or do I keep my eye on the test scores, which are now 'high stakes'? Which of the consultants is going to help me hit the kinds of targets I have set for me in reading and writing?

Dave's account represents the kinds of functional tone that sees heads having to become 'entrepreneurial' themselves in selecting the kinds of expertise that is marketed by the consultants.

Critical analyses of such functionality bring new insights where researchers such as Cameron (2010) have revealed the realities of professional work and how consultants shape and engage with this. Our data also adds to this, where the case studies that Mills (2011a) has documented show clear evidence of diverse patterns of 'hiring', contracting, sub-contracting, and complex 'third party' agents. In one primary school, a local authority in the North West of England had 'bought in' the services of a large private company to boost standards and test scores in many of their 'underperforming' schools. Following Bernstein, we deploy the concept of 'recontextualizing agents' to demonstrate how the consultants at work in the school act as (using Bernstein's terms) shapers, steerers and marketers, and work both in the fields of 'symbolic control' (developing teachers' knowledge and awareness of particular kinds of literacy) as well as in the field of 'economic control' (they were also marketing and selling knowledge about policy 'solutions' for the school) (Bernstein 2000).

Socially critical research is increasingly evident in published accounts where the relationship between consultancy and capitalism is explored. Investigative projects (e.g. Beckett 2007; Coffield 2012; Gunter 2012b) illuminate the relationships between knowledge production, marketization, and profit. Mapping is taking place regarding the inter-connections between knowledge actors (e.g. Ball and Junemann 2012; Grek et al. 2009; Gunter 2012a, 2012b) where networks are sites for knowledge exchange and corporate intervention in policy processes. Mills's (2011a, 2011b, 2012) study of the NLS (DfEE 1998) not only charts how the state mimics the corporate world through the creation of 'state-appointed consultants', but also how businesses have corporatized public services: first, the contracting out of the NLS to CfBT (Centre for British Teachers) and then to Capita; second, the role of major publishers such as Richard Jolly, of *Jolly Phonics*, and Debbie Hepplewhite, of *Phonics International*, not least as policy advisers and members of influential committees.

Knowledge Practices

This mapping illuminates how the self-reported work of consultants tends to be functional, but how research into that work can bring critical perspectives. To take this further we draw on policy scholarship in order to provide examples of both consultancy's development and its interconnections with other forces within and outside of schooling, not least the links between consultancy and the marketization of knowledge.

Successive UK governments have produced policy documents for education in England that make clear statements about a situation, usually a crisis, with planned reforms. There is a demand for functional knowledge, delivery processes and a disposition to work for efficiency and effectiveness. Moss's (2009) forensic study of the NLS's origins draws attention to the fact that key foundations of the strategy, and its extended reach into pedagogy, were the perceived failure of a number of London state schools in teaching children to read (OFSTED 1996). 'Insider' accounts (e.g. Stannard and Huxford 2007) and other studies (e.g. Barkham 2010) describe and analyse the NLS's origins in terms of its knowledge bases. There were key kinds of selections and recontextualizations of knowledge and pedagogy that characterized the NLS that were relevant in terms of the positions of 'important' knowledge and knowers. First, the knowledge that was seen to be important was (for the first time in English policy arenas) *inscribed in key policy texts,* including a document called a *Framework for Teaching,* consisting of a list of 808 teaching objectives, distributed in a term-by-term progression, along with definitions of 'successful teaching', lesson plans, related resources and details of a highly structured Literacy Hour, with 'recommendations' for its organization. Certain kinds of pedagogy and teaching styles were recommended: examples of 'visible pedagogies' that can be 'characterized by explicit hierarchies' (Bernstein 1975: 119). The knowledge was, again drawing on Bernstein's account, 'vertical' knowledge, taking the form of a 'coherent, explicit, systematically principled structure, hierarchically organised' (Bernstein 1996: 170–171).

There are two aspects of the NLS that connect the above features of its policy influences, texts and 'technologies' to the emergence of consultocracy. First, in the drive towards 'improvement' and 'effectiveness' in literacy teaching, key 'agents' were incorporated into policy-making communities and this gave them status, position and knowledge. Several were seconded from higher education institutions, several from high-performing school leadership roles. It is significant in the scope of this chapter that many moved from these quasi-governmental and regulative roles (with the ORF) into the setting up of consultancy businesses and entrepreneurial careers. Much of the knowledge that they had produced in the public sphere became 'privatized', economized and marketable (Clark 2014). The 'vertical' nature of the knowledge and the 'visible' nature of the pedagogies made them more marketable and able to be packaged and sold (Lambirth 2011).

Second, the 'technologies' of the NLS included a business-focused view of knowledge production, delocation and relocation. Centrally organized and monitored within the highest levels of government, the NLS was 'overseen' by Michael Barber, the head of the Standards and Effectiveness Unit within the New Labour government (Barber 2007). The NLS had regional directors, who monitored the work of local consultants (many moved from local authorities). Local 'consultants' closely monitored the work of school leaders and literacy consultants. Overlooked in the policy makers' accounts of Stannard and Huxford (2007) and of Barber (2007), but drawn attention to in more critical accounts (e.g. Bourne 2000; Moss 2007, 2009; Lambirth 2011), these modes of organization and 'policy technologies' inscribed particular patterns of authority, status and control. The NLS also facilitated career mobility and changes in identity as former local authority advisers assumed power-driven relationships with schools (Cameron 2010). Importantly, for the purposes of the main arguments of this chapter, the NLS developed and inscribed in primary school practices modalities of 'advice', control, and authority. The study of the career moves of several NLS agents shows how they became 'freelance' consultants, marketing the knowledge and pedagogies that they had developed as government-focused employees. One of the claims within that work was that easily commodified versions of literacy are easier to 'sell' (Gunter and Mills 2016). The blurring between policy and marketization resonates with those proposed by Burch (2009) in her studies of the effects and influences of the market-driven *No Child Left Behind* versions of literacy that proliferated in US schools at the same time.

The NLS is a clear example of a reform initiative that involved the selection and recontextualization of certain kinds of knowledge, and of the empowering of particular kinds of agents. Mapping the NLS on to the other kinds of studies that we (and our colleagues) have carried out into periods of rapid reform (e.g. Gunter et al. 2014a), it is clear that, although its main focus was on literacy, it also revealed a commitment to organizational effectiveness and improvement which impacted on a great deal of the scoping, design and delivery of major reforms regarding the purposes and structure of public education in England. The various reforms that have delivered these changes are complex, and not always coherent. But what is emerging is a privatized system of educational services that is shifting from a state-provided universal public system to a state-regulated business model (Ball 2007; Chapman and Gunter 2009; Gunter 2011). Our examination of the policies that have produced such changes demonstrates that the emphasis is on the functionality of delivery from policy codification in London to enactment in 24,000 schools, with high compliance secured through training, alongside monitoring and evaluation through inspection (Barber 2007). Integral to this is the emphasis on data design and delivery in order to quantify performance. This is made explicit in targets and value-added analysis for each student, performance related pay for staff, and investment decisions based on schools identified and then located in different categories as failing through to excellent. Educational professionals are exhorted to remove failure (Courtney and Gunter 2015), and to make interventions into practice in order to bring about improvements in student outcome data (e.g. DfES 2004).

Our key argument is that the acceptance, use, and promotion of a hybridized edu-business model is now located in the regime of knowledge production within public institutions. This location was brought about in four important 'moves' in policy and in practice. First, the model was attractive to ministers and civil servants who had strong beliefs in functionality, and who sought modernization through the adoption of organizational effectiveness and improvement business models. Second, researchers were located in the production and development of such models, and sought to generate income streams from providing ministers and civil servants with evidence and solutions. Third, professionals from schools and local authorities who accepted such models (and some who allied with the researchers) took up roles within institutions (e.g. the NLS; National College for School Leadership from 2000) and, since 2010, many have lost their jobs and are working on the reform agenda and delivery in the private sector, e.g. the literacy consultants (Gunter and Mills 2016). Fourth, private sector businesses have promoted such models and worked on the integration of business and research through various projects. For example, Mills's research (2012) investigated the work of two of the largest providers of services in literacy, both 'insiders' on NLS development and dissemination. Such 'exchange relationships', real and symbolic, are important factors in the growth of consultancy's influence and are worth fuller discussion.

Knowledge Exchanges

Integral to our argument so far is that consultants doing consultancy are mainly focused on the functionality of education, and in doing so can be (a) brought into a public organization such as a school or even central government to inform policy with techniques and strategies; (b) bought in by government to replace public servants to deliver policy; and (c) contracted to work in delivery units where educational professionals, researchers, and private consultants have secured, disseminated, and enacted government policy that previously would have been undertaken through local partnerships between the profession, local government and higher education. However, our critical work on the realities of this, and our socially critical work on the power structures which construct and enable this, suggest there is a need to examine exchange relationships regarding knowledge, knowing and know how. Furthermore, our sample case of the NLS illustrates how functionality has generated opportunities for knowledge recontextualization that are based on what is offered, what is taken, and what is used.

Exchange relationships take place through formal encounters, such as the tendering process for projects, through to informal networked relationships based on knowing and trusting like-minded people. This is visible through the award and reporting of commissioned research (e.g. DfES/PwC 2007), and to the appointment of people to employment and governance roles (Gunter 2012a). Consultants do consultancy in the form of having knowledge about a situation that can be *substantive* (e.g. former local authority advisors who have been made redundant and are now selling their knowledge of effectiveness and improvement); and can be *process* (e.g. business consultants who have knowledge through the use of a 'template' about performance related pay or the removal of underperforming staff that can be interpreted and transferred into education). In addition, they have forms of knowing that are valued. These can be forms of knowledge about the provision of research evidence, or forms of 'know how' that are regarded as relevant and legitimate. This generates knowledgeability whereby the person, background, track record, and general dispositions are seen as valid and worth paying for. Hence UK governments have focused on the need for change, and the particular changes it wanted, but also relied on these various types of consultants and forms of knowledge to help them to shape and define the reforms.

What our data show is that trustworthiness is linked to claims about *relevance*. The consultants' knowledge needs to be seen to be relevant to how something should be done. The consultant needs to be trusted to understand what it means to do the job that is being consulted about. Hence, having previously done the job of your client, or having worked with the client in another role such as a local government advisor, is seen as being both substantially and symbolically important. Many of the profiles of consultants show hybridization, whereby biographical research enables the 'shape shifting' from insider to consultant (Newman and Clarke 2009) to be evidenced. An example of a 'recontextualizing agent' who has moved between these different kinds of activity is Ruth Miskin. Recently awarded an Order of the British Empire (OBE) for services to literacy teaching, Miskin has worked within *business consultancy*, as managing director of Read Write Inc, one of the largest providers of training and publication, and *state consultancy*, as one of the earliest advisers to the NLS and, more recently, under the 2010 Conservative-led Coalition government, as an adviser to both the Bew Committee in assessment in primary schooling from 2011–2013, and as a member of the advisory group on the revised national curriculum for primary schools, chaired by Professor Andrew Pollard. Miskin's connections with New Labour and with the coalition governments are illustrated in research (Clark 2014) and journalist accounts (e.g. Private Eye 2012; Wilby 2008).

This growth of consultants and consultancy and exchange relationships within and for public services has been subject to academic research (Saint-Martin 1998, 2004), investigative journalism and commentary (Toynbee 2011), and Parliamentary scrutiny (House of Commons Committee of Public Accounts 2007). A key theme running through this analysis is the operation of accountability and responsibility in regard to the relationship between policy and knowledge. In the UK constitution, a government has a mandate based on the number of seats in the House of Commons won in a general election (Parliament is bi-cameral with the second chamber, the House of Lords, not elected), where the leader of the largest party is asked to form a government by the monarch. That leader becomes the Prime Minister, and, in forming the government, portfolios linked to offices of state, such as education, are allocated and teams of Ministers with civil servants begin their work implementing their reform agenda. Accountability and responsibility operate through Ministers to Parliament, not least through Select Committees, and to the wider public through the media and ongoing election cycles. Usually elections produce majority governments, though sometimes, and not least in 2010, a coalition is produced. At local level there are systems of local government based on elections to town/city and regional councils, with responsibilities for services from education to transport to cemeteries. Local government raises taxation for local services, but is also funded from central government, and so publicly funded state schools are controlled from Whitehall in London and the Town Hall in their locality.

Governments at national and local levels draw on knowledge and produce knowledge in order to support policies, with a system of bureaucracy focused on providing advice from career civil servants/officials through to political advisors linked to the party, and from experts in particular fields (e.g. engineers for transport, and medics for health). Major changes are underway regarding this, not least in local government where education provision has been reduced through the introduction of private providers at local government and individual school levels. What we raise here is how a form of depoliticization is taking place, and by this we mean that services and debates about services that were politicized through public systems of governance have been relocated (Flinders and Wood 2014). In other words, publicly funded education was politicized through a national system of schools that were locally administered, with regulation of the profession, curriculum and purposes, and this is being depolitcized through the corporatization of exchange relationships.

Such depoliticization operates beyond the particular people, systems, and structures involved, but permeates the identities of those with whom they exchange, and so headteachers may be in a local authority school but they access knowledge and support from private consultants who are either provided under state schemes such as the NLS or who are bought in using school budgets because the local authority advisors have been made redundant and replaced, although they often re-emerge as local consultants. In addition, the types of knowledge used and the methodologies by which they claim to know have permeated the system beyond their particular work or contract location, and this is evident in the dominance of data design, collection, and analysis as a key feature of school leadership and management, through to the adoption of particular language and ways of thinking about education in regard to 'best practice', 'improvement' and 'effectiveness'.

Thinking Theory

In order to bring perspective to this account, and to conceptualize our work in ways that might assist future researchers, we would like to join the concepts we have utilized from Bernstein's work with the insights from public administration, where Hood and Jackson (1991) have coined the label 'consultocracy' for the integrated relationship between consultants and public administration/services.

From 'consultocracy' we draw the following insights. The removal of salaried and publicly accountable professionals from central and local government, and the relocation of their work and their employment to private exchange relationships, means that public service is only of value if it is economized and traded. The challenge, as Saint-Martin (2004) has identified, is that

> once politics is out of public administration … it should no longer be difficult to import into the bureaucracy management ideas and techniques from the private sector because the presence of politics is the only thing that made public sector organizations different from businesses.
>
> (Saint-Martin 2004: 21)

Essentially, what this means is that, as politicians are increasingly busy with the complexities of public services, the reality of accountability and responsibility becomes muddied, where policy design and delivery by others who are at a distance from the minister or outside of the system of governance through outsourcing and privatization means that they have a privileged position without direct answerability to the public. Furthermore, the solutions offered to major issues can marginalize or even silence debates that are integral to public services.

For example, workforce reform in education with regard to composition and training can be resolved through people qualified in particular skills (e.g. premises and site management, human resources management, business strategy) in a way which allows educational professionals to focus on education, but it also enables non-qualified people to take on roles that educational professionals might be expected to do, such as curriculum design, teaching and assessment (Butt and Gunter 2007). In the field of literacy, for example, decisions about 'what counts' as school literacy, about what it means to be fluent and powerful readers and writers is (we would claim) being debated, not in educational communities, nor in political circles, but in the marketplace. The merging of 'the market' with the framing of policy, evidenced in, for example, incorporation of 'sellers' of policy into the 'shaping' of policy, brings with it significant (and unacknowledged) changes in the ways that policy is being formulated, shaped, and disseminated in schools. This has been widely recognized in US-based critical policy study (e.g. Burch 2009; Goodman et al. 2014), but, while important work is taking place in England (e.g. Ball 2007, 2012), it is less acknowledged in the busy territory that is policy change.

Bringing such changes into the public arena is challenging. That is where the insights we draw from work such as that of Saint-Martin (2004) are critically important. He notes how consultants are concerned about the position they can find themselves in. Investigative journalism has raised questions about how the failure to deliver a project does not necessarily cut costs or result in contract termination (e.g. Toynbee 2011), and where Parliamentary scrutiny has raised questions about the deployment and management of consultants (House of Commons Committee of Public Accounts 2007). We agree that the situation is complex, and that the idea of 'consultocracy' should not be over played (Saint-Martin 1998). It does seem to us that there are important trends and patterns to the work of consultants and we would like to acknowledge that the removal of political debates with options and choices in favour of consultancy solutions is a challenging trend, not least through the replacement of local debates through the market-trusted networked consultants who can help professionals deliver changes which the locality can no longer comment on or influence.

Thinking with Bernstein provides tools that enable the investigation in ways that focus attention on the kinds of knowledge and knowing that are located in work, practices and exchange relationships. We have been able to probe the structure and the forms of that knowledge, and to look at knowledge's modalities and its movements from one location to another. One of the particular challenges (and part of the value) of Bernstein's (2000) methodological accounts is that he gives 'blueprints' for the mapping of his conceptual framework on to new data. Power (2010) expresses well the potential of Bernstein's concepts in 'interrogating' the kinds of 'new' empirical patterns that we uncovered in our research. The task, she suggests, is not in discovering whether the (sometimes complex) concepts such as 'the pedagogic device' or 'recontextualizing fields and agents' are 'right'. The task is more to 'explore how we can develop a more productive relationship between Bernstein's work and empirical research' (Power 2010: 246). In another recent account of the potential of Bernstein's thinking in investigating new patterns of knowledge exchange in education, Moore (2013) emphasizes that the power of Bernstein's conceptual tools is that they can be applied to new 'landscapes' of knowledge and practice to enable us to see what has changed, and what remains the same.

Applying this precept to our work on literacy (for example) we can see that policy is still produced (to a greater or lesser extent) by the Official Recontextualizing Field (ORF), by governments. For example, in England there is at present a drive towards systematic synthetic phonics as the key method for teaching children to read. But where is that knowledge drawn from? Not from published research and from academic circles, but from 'pressure groups' such as the Reading Reform Foundation (a group sponsored by large publishing houses). Moreover, knowledge is mediated (or translated into the then Pedagogic Recontextualizing Field (PRF)), not through training courses for teachers, nor through peer-reviewed journal articles reporting research, but from the marketizations and promotions of consultants (Clark 2014). As Moore (2013) phrases it, the 'rules' are still the same, but the players, and those who have power, are different (Moore 2013: 41).

Another gain from thinking with Bernstein is that he allows us to locate our work within the critical and socially critical accounts outlined above. Charting consultants' work as new kinds of delocations and relocations of knowledge, within arenas of power and control, enables us to locate our inquiries within Bernstein's (1990) larger project of uncovering cultural reproduction and the processes of symbolic control, defined by him as 'the means whereby consciousness is given a specialized form and distributed through forms of communication which relay a given distribution of power and dominant cultural categories' (Bernstein 1990: 134). He acknowledged that his theorizations shared concerns with other social theorists (including Bourdieu), viewing schools and schooling as reproductive of class relations; they legitimated, reflected and reproduced hierarchically arranged bodies of knowledge, which usually – and this is crucial for our analysis here – *reinforced the interests of dominant social groups*. He argued for empirical descriptions of the ways in which 'specific agencies of cultural reproduction' do their work, in ways that (we would claim) give his concepts a particular potency for our current work.

Bernstein's formulations and concepts are often criticized for being over-deterministic, structural, and rigid in form and framing (e.g. Atkinson 1985). Bernstein tended to formulate his descriptions in terms of 'rules'. However, we have found his concepts productive in examining the case studies of eight consultants who were 'bought in' by schools to help them develop knowledge and to adapt pedagogy to enhance their practice in reading, writing, speaking and listening (Gunter and Mills 2016). For example, Lynn (pseudonym, consultant, interview 2010) tended to draw on her training and interactions with practitioners on strongly classified, vertical knowledge (about children's writing) and on very visible pedagogies:

> I aim to give teachers the tools to do their job. My approach to writing is straightforward and explicit. I give them a range of resources and techniques. The structures are all in place ... the processes are all in my materials.
>
> (Lynn: pseudonym, consultant, interview 2010)

Mike's account was a contrast, in that his knowledge appeared to be more weakly classified and horizontal. The pedagogies he promoted to teachers in their own teaching (and those he demonstrated in his own training) were more invisible.

> I essentially want to give teachers a set of choices and options. I take them through my thinking on writing. I draw on all sorts of things for that. After all that, I listen to their anxieties. But I want to get them thinking.
>
> (Mike: pseudonym, consultant, interview 2010)

These different approaches to the forms of knowledge and to the modes of pedagogy have prompted theorizing through questions: what happens when there is a mismatch between the views and the requirements relating to knowledge and to pedagogy between consultants and those who are 'purchasing' their services?

Two extracts from our data illustrate this. Zoe (pseudonym, consultant, interview 2010) was a deputy head teacher of a school who had hired Lyn's services to assist them in their teaching of writing. She experienced a lack of agency, and an over-prescriptiveness in the use of techniques: 'I appreciate Lynn's knowledge and experience but I didn't feel I had much space. There seems to be just one way to do things'. In contrast, Pete (a class teacher in a school who had employed Mike) experienced difficulties in Mike's less classified, less visible approaches to knowledge and pedagogy about writing:

> I wonder if Mike really appreciates the pressure we are under. He was almost saying follow your nose and do what is best for the kids you teach. The messages we got from Inspectors were different. We were 'done' for not doing things in particular ways. I guess I need to think about how to put those two things together ...
>
> (Pete: pseudonym, consultant, interview 2010)

We wish to continue the interplay of theory and data by returning to another of Bernstein's key concepts, that of pedagogic discourse, as a 'principle for appropriating other discourses and bringing them into special relation with each other for the purposes of their selective transmission and acquisition' (Bernstein 1990: 181). He argued that the concept had the facility to enable an examination of how the reproduction of culture actually takes place through knowledge becoming shaped in specific ways in pedagogic practices. In our terms here, the concept's value is in mapping how certain kinds of knowledge get moved into schools. Bearing in mind that our particular focuses in our empirical work to date have been knowledge/s about leadership and administration and knowledge/s about literacy, we are concerned with mapping whose knowledge is seen as being important (and marketable?).

Key to our linking of Bernstein to the work we describe in this chapter is our understanding that, in the exchange of knowledge, issues of power and ideology are always at play. Apple (2000) catches this well in his reading of Bernstein:

> When knowledge and discourse from the field of production is pulled within the recontextualizing field, it is subject to ideological transformations due to various specialized and/or political interests whose conflicts structure the recontextualizing field.
>
> (Apple 2000: 250)

We would encourage other researchers to acknowledge these issues of 'power' and 'conflicts' when investigating consultants, consultancy and consultocracy. Marsh (2007) reminds us that the recontextualizing process is always one 'shaped by ideologies' and that 'in the creation of pedagogic discourses, different groups of people will focus on and prioritize different areas of their ideological frameworks' (Marsh 2007: 270). Our claim is that these arguments about pedagogic discourse, and the rule of recontextualization, which, 'selectively appropriates, relocates, refocuses and relates other discourses to constitute its own order and orderings' (Bernstein 1990: 184), assist us in investigating consultants and consultancy. First, we make the (perhaps obvious) point that consultancy is not neutral functional work but is always ideological, in that consultants make selections about what kinds of work they wish to do and which kinds of knowledge they wish to promote. Second, the kinds of de-locations, re-locations and recontextualizations they make need careful and sensitive investigation.

Conclusion

We have presented evidence of how consultants do consultancy within education policy in England, and in doing so we have examined the emphasis on functionality and the dynamics of exchange relationships. In doing this, we note the location within the particular nation state that is itself located in a globalizing economic system, where corporatization within and across borders shapes national policy and is shaped by it. Our contribution to analyses of such developments is twofold:

first, we have provided empirical evidence of how the people who are the objects of change and who make change work provide rationalities and narratives about this, and we have been able to make visible the consultancy practices; second, we have related the functionality of knowledge production to wider demands within and for exchange relationships within policy-making processes, where global solutions to the global demand for a literate workforce have been adopted as fit for purpose. Public sector trained and accredited professionals are increasingly relocated (whether they like it or not) into the private sector. By focusing on these rapid shifts, on the ways in which individuals and networks have responded, we have been able to bring descriptive and explanatory perspectives. Thinking theoretically in productive and novel ways through deploying Bernstein's analytical tools and the concept of a consultocracy have helped us to think about power processes, about knowledge and its location, and the nature of the exchange relationships that are at work – often unrecognized – in our schools.

Acknowledgements

We would like to thank the ESRC and the British Academy for the funding to undertake this work, and to our respondents who allowed us to enter and produce accounts of their working lives.

References

Ainscow, M. and Southworth, G. (1996). School improvement: A study of the roles of leaders and external consultants. *School Effectiveness and School Improvement: An International Journal of Research, Policy and Practice, 7*(3), 229–251.
Apple, M. W. (2000). Mathematics reform through conservative modernization: Standards, markets and inequality in education. In J. Boaler. (Ed.). *Multiple perspectives in mathematics teaching* (pp. 243–260). Westport, CT: Greenwood.
Atkinson, P. (1985). *Language, structure and reproduction.* London: Methuen.
Ball, S. J. (2007). *Education plc.* London: Routledge.
Ball, S. J. (2012). *Global education inc: New policy networks and the neoliberal imaginary.* London: Routledge.
Ball, S. J. and Junemann, C. (2012). *Networks, new governance and education.* Bristol: Policy Press.
Barber, M. (2007). *Instruction to deliver.* London: Politico's Publishing.
Barkham, J. (2010). *Bridging the gap: Personal and policy trajectories of the national literacy strategy.* Unpublished Ph.D. thesis. University of the West of England.
Beckett, F. (2007). *The great city academy fraud.* London: Continuum.
Bernstein, B. (1971). *Class, codes and control: Volume 1. Theoretical studies towards a sociology of language.* London: Routledge and Kegan Paul.
Bernstein, B. (1975). *Class, codes and control: Volume 3. Towards a theory of educational transmissions.* London: Routledge and Kegan Paul.
Bernstein, B. (1990). *Class, codes and control: Volume 4. The structuring of pedagogic discourse.* London: Routledge.
Bernstein, B. (1996). *Pedagogy, symbolic control and identity: Theory, research, critique.* (1st ed.). London: Taylor and Francis.

Bernstein, B. (2000). *Pedagogy, symbolic control and identity: Theory, research, critique,* (rev edn). Oxford: Rowman and Littlefield.

Bernstein, B. (2001). Symbolic control: Issues of empirical description of agencies and agents. *International Journal of Social Research Methodology, 4*(1), 21–33.

Bourne, J. (2000). New imaginings of reading for a new moral order: A review of the production, transmission and acquisition of a new pedagogic culture in the UK. *Linguistics and Education, 11*(1), 31–45.

Bowe, R., Ball, S. J., and Gold, A. (1992). *Reforming education and changing schools.* London: Routledge.

Burch, P. (2009). *Hidden markets.* New York: Routledge.

Butt, G. and Gunter, H. M. (Eds). (2007). *Modernizing schools: People, learning and organizations.* London: Continuum.

Cameron, D. H. (2010). Implementing a large-scale reform in secondary schools: The role of the consultant within England's Secondary National Strategy. *Journal of Education Policy, 25*(5), 605–624.

Chapman, C. and Gunter, H. M. (Eds). (2009). *Radical reforms: Public policy and a decade of educational reform.* London: Routledge.

Clark, M. M. (2014). Whose knowledge counts in government literacy policies and at what cost? *Education Journal, 186,* 13–16.

Coffield, F. (2012). Why the McKinsey reports will not improve school systems. *Journal of Education Policy, 27*(1), 131–149.

Collarbone, P. (2005). Touching tomorrow: Remodelling in English Schools. *The Australian Economic Review, 38*(1), 75–82.

Courtney, S. J. and Gunter, H. M. (2015). 'Get off my bus!' School leaders, vision work and the elimination of teachers. *International Journal of Leadership in Education, 18*(4), 395–417.

DfEE. (1998). *The national literacy strategy: Framework for teaching.* London: DfEE.

DfES. (2004). Smoking out underachievement: Guidance and advice to help secondary schools use value added approaches with data. London: DfES.

DfES and PricewaterhouseCoopers. (2007). *Independent study into school leadership.* London: DfES.

Earl, L., Watson, N., Levin, B., Leithwood, K., Fullan, M., and Torrance, N. (2002). *Final report of the external evaluation of England's national literacy and numeracy strategies.* London: DfES.

Fitz, J., Davies, B., and Evans, J. (2006). *Education policy and social reproduction: Class inscription and symbolic control.* London: Routledge.

Flinders, M. and Wood, M. (2014). Depoliticisation, governance and the state. *Policy and Politics, 42*(2), 135–311.

Goodman, K. S., Calfee, R. C., and Goodman, Y. M. (2014). *Whose knowledge counts in government literacy policies: Why expertise matters.* Abingdon: Routledge.

Grek, S., Lawn, M., Lingard, B., Ozga, J., Rinne, R., Segerholm, C., and Simola, H. (2009). National policy brokering and the construction of the European Education Space in England, Sweden, Finland and Scotland. *Comparative Education, 45*(1), 5–21.

Gunter, H. M. (Ed.). (2011). *The state and education policy: The academies programme.* London: Continuum.

Gunter, H. M. (2012a). *Leadership and the reform of education.* Bristol: The Policy Press.

Gunter, H. M. (2012b). Intellectual work and knowledge production. In Fitzgerald, T., White, J., and Gunter, H. M. *Hard labour? Academic work and the changing landscape of higher education* (pp. 23–40). Bingley: Emerald.

Gunter, H. M. and Mills, C. (2016). *Consultants and consultancy: The case of education.* Cham, Switzerland: Springer.

Gunter, H. M., Hall, D., and Bragg, J. (2013). Distributed leadership: A study in knowledge production. *Educational Leadership, Management and Administration, 41*(5), 556–581.

Gunter, H. M., Hall, D., and Mills, C. (2014a). *Education policy research: Design and practice at a time of rapid reform.* London: Bloomsbury.

Gunter, H. M., Hall, D., and Mills, C. (2015). Consultants, consultancy and consultocracy in education policymaking in England. *Journal of Education Policy, 30*(4), 518–539.

Hood, C. and Jackson, M. (1991). *Administrative argument.* Aldershot: Dartmouth Publishing Company Limited.

House of Commons Committee of Public Accounts. (2007). Central government's use of consultants. *Thirty-first Report of Session 2006–2007.* London: The Stationary Office Ltd.

Lambirth, A. (2011). *Literacy on the left: Reform and revolution.* London: Continuum.

Learmonth, J. and Lowers, K. (1998). 'A trouble-shooter calls': the role of the independent consultant. In L. Stoll and K. Myers. (Eds), *No quick fixes: Perspectives on schools in difficulty* (pp. 133–143). London: The Falmer Press.

MacBeath, J. (1998). 'I didn't know he was ill': the role and value of the critical friend. In L. Stoll and K. Myers. (Eds). *No quick fixes: Perspectives on schools in difficulty* (pp. 118–132). London: The Falmer Press.

Marsh, J. (2007). New literacies and old pedagogies: Recontextualizing rules and practices. *International Journal of Inclusive Education, 11*(3), 267–281.

Mills, C. (2011a). Framing literacy policy: Power and policy drivers in primary schools, *Literacy, 45*(3), 103–110.

Mills, C. (2011b). *Primary literacy for sale: Investigating new assemblages and influences in policy formation and enactment.* Paper presented at the annual conference of the British Educational Research Association, London, September.

Mills, C. (2012). *Shaping and selling policy: A critical study of policy entrepreneurs in English elementary school literacy.* Paper presented at the annual conference of the American Educational Research Association, Vancouver, April.

Moore, R. (2013). *Basil Bernstein: the thinker and the field.* Abingdon: Routledge.

Moss, G. (2007). *Literacy and gender: Researching texts, contexts and readers.* London: Routledge.

Moss, G. (2009). The politics of literacy in the context of large-scale educational reform. *Research Papers in Education, 24*(2), 155–174.

Newman, J. and Clarke, J. (2009). *Publics, politics and power: Remaking the public in public services.* London: Sage.

OFSTED (1996). *The teaching of reading in 45 inner London primary schools: a report by Her Majesty's Inspectors in collaboration with the LEAs of Islington, Southwark and Tower Hamlets.* London: Ofsted.

Power, S. (2010). Bernstein and empirical research. In P. Singh, A. R. Sadnovik and S. F. Semel. (Eds). *Toolkits, translation devices and conceptual accounts: Essays on Basil Bernstein's sociology of knowledge* (pp. 239–248). New York: Peter Lang.

Private Eye. (2012). Phonics a friend. *Private Eye, 1317*(12).

Raffo, C. and Gunter, H. M. (2008). Leading schools to promote social inclusion: Developing a conceptual framework for analysing research, policy and practice. *Journal of Education Policy, 23*(4), 363–380.

Saint-Martin, D. (1998). The new managerialism and the policy influence of consultants in government: An historical-institutionalist analysis of Britain, Canada and France. *Governance: An International Journal of Policy and Administration, 11*(3), 319–356.

Saint-Martin, D. (2004). *Building the new managerialist state.* Oxford: Oxford University Press.

Singh, P., Heimans, S., and Glasswell, K. (2014). Policy enactment, context and performativity: Ontological politics and researching Australian National Partnership policies. *Journal of Education Policy, 29*(6), 826–844.

Singh, P., Sadnovik, A. R., and Semel, S. F. (Eds). (2010). *Toolkits, translation devices and conceptual accounts: Essays on Bernstein's sociology of knowledge.* New York: Peter Lang.

Singh, P., Thomas, S., and Harris, J. (2013). Recontextualising policy discourses: A Bernsteinian perspective on policy interpretation, translation, enactment. *Journal of Education Policy, 28*(4), 465–480.

Stannard, J. and Huxford, L. (2007). *The literacy game: The story of the national literacy strategy.* Abingdon: Routledge.

Toynbee, P. (2011, April 5). This benefit bonanza is more big Serco than big society. *The Guardian.* Retrieved May 22, 2015 from: http://www.theguardian.com/commentisfree/2011/apr/04/benefits-bonanza-big-serco-welfare.

Wilby, P. (2008, April 1). A tonic for the phonics queen. *The Guardian.* Retrieved May 22, 2015 from: http://www.theguardian.com/education/2008/apr/01/schools.uk2.

9 Donors, Private Actors, and Contracts

Recasting the Making and Ownership of Education Policy in Pakistan

Shailaja Fennell and Rabea Malik

Introduction

Multi-and bi-lateral donors have a long history of involvement in Pakistan's social sectors, particularly in the educational sector. This involvement has taken place largely through interventions in the realm of policy as well as through funding of various modalities such as project aid and budget support. These funding modalities that have been donor-facilitated, or donor-led, have supported the emergence of the Educational Public Private Partnerships (ePPPs) through education reform policies that have been promoted at the provincial level in Pakistan. The consequence has been a growing presence of private providers, contracted to provide services in the educational sector and as a better alternative to the existing but faltering state educational system.

This chapter argues that there are three new educational policy spaces that have seen an increase in private actors: service delivery, where the emergence of low-fee private actors has been particularly noticeable; policy, traditionally inhabited by multi- and bi-lateral donors, and where the emergence of the international development consultancies (IDCs) is becoming evident; and public–private-partnerships, that have seen the rise of contracts between the state and both national and international business actors to provide, deliver, and manage education.

This chapter examines the role of new non-state actors in these three educational spaces, through the analysis of secondary documents, research and policy reports, and interviews conducted with key stakeholders in the education sector. The aim of the chapter is to investigate the relationship between the new private sector actors, the policy orientation of donors, and the new forms of contracts that are being introduced in the educational sector. The intention is to understand how the new contracts between donors, the provincial governments and the new private actors are changing the political economy of education policy making in Pakistan. We argue that the growing presence of new global and domestic players, new contractual obligations in the provision of education by donors, and the tacit agreement by the Pakistani state, has resulted in an unregulated environment for the provision of education. This recasting of the provision of education could have inimical consequences for the future ownership of educational policy in Pakistan.

Conceptual Framing of the Educational Market

The global discussion of the changing nature of the educational market in Pakistan hinged on the weaknesses of the state in providing education, and the consequent need to bring in PPPs to improve the delivery of educational services (Ginsburg 2012). The emphasis in this exchange has been on the ability of PPPs to bring about cooperation between the government and business to share risks and responsibilities through the pooling of resources and competences (Draxler 2012).

The ways in which global analyses understand the need for partnerships is to emphasize the additional value that they bring to the education system through two types of contribution. The first type of contribution is that of the "gap filler," where the private sector is seen as having the management competencies to reach "difficult to access" populations. The presumption here is that the state has provided mass education but some sub-groups are excluded from education due to physical or social distances.[1] The typical bodies for providing improved access are NGOs who have local knowledge, as in the case of reaching girls in communities that have a gender gap in education (Fennell 2008). There was no initial consideration in these arrangements, which predominated in the 1990s, that the state had in fact been a failure in providing education for the majority of children. This argument is more evident in the discussions within international agencies in the last decade, which came to regard the entire state education system as a failure (Barrera-Osorio et al. 2009).

The second type of contribution emerges from the argument that a mass schooling system provided by the state suffers from poor quality due to the lack of competition in the education sector. The problem of "inferior quality or second best" identified in public provision[2] is supposed to be resolved through the introduction of ePPPs. The rationale for introducing ePPPs is that it is a direct response to the unmet demand of the parents who would like to send their children to private schools (Tooley and Dixon 2007). This type of argument emphasizes that private schools are necessary for improving the quality of education provision in state schools. A more extreme variant of the argument is that state schools have been deteriorating and private schools should replace them. The implication is that the state has been guilty of a dereliction of duty with regard to the provision of educational services and that these should consequently be transferred to the private sector. In recent years, both the "gap filler" and "second best" arguments have been applied, the first to criticize the ability of the state to deliver services and the second to suggest the inability of the state to govern the education system.

In this changing educational market, there has been an associated shift in the manner in which development assistance, which includes funding and technical assistance, has been provided for education. The move from government funding to a channeling of resources to non-governmental organizations (NGOs) and non-state providers, and the increasing emphasis on ePPPs and associated changes in funding appear to be driven by donor agendas (Brady 2012). The theory of new public management has now become part and parcel of the thinking about effective governance and has come to regard the government as a poorer and lesser form of provider that should be replaced by private provision, whenever and wherever possible. It is within this changing global political economy that has moved away from regarding education as a public good in the first instance to regarding the market as the primary method of delivering education that we situate the new modalities of international assistance for education. This recasting of education as a good that is more effectively produced and purchased through the market is gaining the upper hand in policies, and, in a national context where a mass education system has still not been fully rolled out (Fennell and Malik 2012), it could become a trigger for consistently choosing private actors over the state.

The role of international agencies in the design and implementation of educational policies is directly related to the magnitude and destination of their funds. The strong directional impact of donor agencies on the educational policy of poor countries appears to be the latest means by which policy texts become the base on which educational realities are constructed (Lingard and Ali 2009). The increasing importance of donor agencies in devising and formulating policy in low-income countries based on policy text conceived and written up in the Global North has potentially negative implications for the sovereignty of the nation state with regard to educational provision.

Educational Delivery and Policy Space in Pakistan Today

The Service Delivery Space

Official estimates in Pakistan register a growth in private sector enrollments from 15 percent to 35 percent (primary level) between 1990 and 2005. In Punjab, 43 percent of total enrollments are in private schools, and 44 percent of all schools are private (Government of Pakistan 2011–12).[3] Close to 30 percent of total primary enrollments in Sindh are in private schools (Government of Pakistan 2011–12). A particular feature of these trends is that a significant proportion of the growth has been in low-fee private schools (LFPSs). While enrollment shares have increased across the wide spectrum of private providers, the rise of LFPSs has most significantly changed the educational landscape in the country, by expanding the reach of the fee-charging sector to middle- and low-income households, and into rural areas (Andrabi et al. 2007). The growth rate of private schools is reported to be higher than that for public schools: in the period between 2000 and 2008, the number of private schools grew by 69 percent and government schools by 8 percent (Humanyun et al. 2013). The Annual Status of Education Report (ASER) survey 2013–14 reports a 7 percent increase in enrollments in private schools from the year prior.

The state sector, particularly at the primary level, has suffered from declining quality of service provision, which is a result of governance failures such as misaligned incentives for public servants, lack of sufficient resources in schools and a shortage of schools and teachers. It is within this context that the LFPS sector has grown to fill the gap and to meet the demands of parents for better schooling. Growth in private sector schools, particularly LFPSs, has given rise to an active and expanding marketplace for education. This LFPS sector is a segmented marketplace, and there is a wide range of private schools located at specific locations on the fee and quality spectrum. At the top end are the high-fee elite private schools catering to high income households, charging upwards of Rs.18,000[4] (USD $180) a month in fees (5th or 6th grade). At the other end of the spectrum are schools charging on average Rs.1000 (USD $10). The middle tier schools charge between Rs. 2000 (USD $20) and Rs. 5000 (USD $50).[5] In the context of very slow expansion of public sector facilities for education, the private sector is arguably providing access to schools for a significant proportion of children who would otherwise be out of school.

Private schools have been a part of the educational landscape since independence.[6] In 1972, all private schools were nationalized, and a ban was put on the establishment of new private schools.[7] This move was later recognized by the government as having contributed to worsening the fiscal burden of education provision, compromising expansion and quality of service delivery (GoP 1983). The ban was lifted in 1979, as the government realized that it had capacity and resource limitations as the primary provider of education and in the sixth five-year plan "announced its intention to motivate and encourage private education through grants-in-aid" (Jimenez and Tan, 1987: 178).[8]

Successive education policies have recognized the role of the private sector as a partner, and as a source of additional resources. However, there is no specific reform policy that clearly states the government's position on the opening up of the educational sphere to the private sector. There are contradictions in the current legislation and policy documentation, with the constitution now promising free education as a basic human right (Article 25A), while the government is neither regulating nor checking the growth of the fee-charging sector, nor putting in place financing mechanisms that would subsidize private provision for parents.

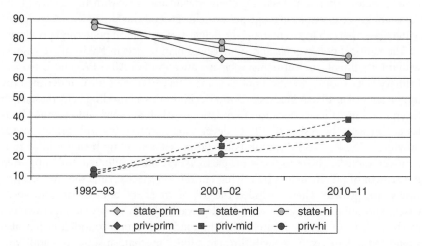

Figure 9.1 Trends in state and private school enrollment shares 1992–2011 (percentages)

Source: Government of Pakistan 1993, 2002, 2011.

There are also conflicting impulses evident in the opening up of the education service delivery space to private actors that has been conceded by the government and encouraged by donors. Official policy documents recognize the inability of the government to achieve goals of universal access on its own, and recognize the private sector as a partner with a role to play in expanding access. At the same time, the state accepts the responsibility of remaining the primary provider, and the necessity of retaining its regulatory role. Yet there is no concerted attempt toward the regulation of private schools. Further, provincial and federal education foundations, which semi-autonomous bodies set up with a mix of government and donor funding, have been mandated to develop and expand public–private partnerships in the service delivery space.[9] After two decades of operations, the foundations have largely focused their financing efforts on generating mechanisms that promote the establishment and expansion of private sector providers rather than encouraging forms of ePPPs.

The Policy Space[10]

The private school growth that has occurred over these two decades might appear at first glance to have happened more by default than by design. Demand-side factors have contributed to the spread of private schooling, while the state has been ambivalent at best as regards its policy towards these schools. The NEPs in 1999 and onwards explicitly recognize the role of the low-fee private sector and state that the government lacks the capacity to ensure that the enrollment targets set in relation to the objective of meeting the Millennium Development Goals (MDGs) are achieved. The policy notes that it remains the state's responsibility to fund and regulate education service delivery. In the early 1990s, the federal government mandated education foundations to be set up to develop partnerships with the private sector. There has been a growing disillusionment with the ability of the Pakistani government to manage policy delivery, and this is particularly palpable with regard to its ability to manage the delivery of education policy and provision.

The national policy goals and subnational plan targets in Pakistan are aligned with international commitments, such as Education For All (EFA) and Universal Primary Education. Education policies since the early 1990s have underlined the importance of ePPPs in Pakistan. Donor facilitation and funding helped establish federal and provincial education foundations, which are semi-autonomous bodies tasked with the responsibility of developing partnerships with private sector providers. The Punjab Education Foundation, led and set up by a group of eminent economists, chose to focus on partnerships that facilitated and supported the growth of private actors by relying entirely on mechanisms that funded private sector growth. These included the use of vouchers, both merit- and need-based, and the promotion of subsidized private schools for providing education to children from poorer households. The Sindh education foundation has also supported private sector growth through similar mechanisms, but has additionally developed partnerships for building the state's capacity for service delivery. The difference in provincial government responses to the directive to improve educational policy indicates that there are differing provincial perceptions regarding the nature of contracting services from the private sector.

The admission in policy documents of the inability of the government to finance education does make the case for new actors, but what is noteworthy is that the state has not yet developed a policy for accrediting or regulating the new private actors, despite having already opened up the educational space for private sector provision to the point of no return. The inability of the state to stem the decline in quality of service provision in state-run schools has resulted in private providers that were brought in to fulfill a "gap filler" intervention becoming the preferred option to address the "second best" problem. The shrinking policy space in the Pakistani state is evident in its inability to devise and implement a strategic plan for private sector involvement, with a well-structured regulatory framework for private actors. The ineffective paltry manner in which the state has driven the policy agenda to deal with the failing state education system does not bode well for ensuring that those in the "last mile" are able to access education and improve their educational outcomes.

The political economy of the broader changing policy reform environment within which the state is struggling to make a difference is also reflected in legislative changes. The eighteenth amendment, which was set out to create decentralization and make provincial and local governance more effective, failed to provide the provinces with equal ability to ensure service delivery, nor was it able to assist more economically backward provinces to improve their capacity to raise resources (Adeney 2012). While recent initiatives to develop regulatory frameworks for private schools in some provinces and regions have gotten underway, such as the North West Frontier Province Registration and Functions of Private Education Institutions Ordinance (2002), the Sindh Education Institutions (Regulation and Control) Ordinance (2001) and Amended Act (2003), and the Islamabad Capital Territory Education Institution (Regulation and Promotion) Ordinance XII (2006), the focus of educational policy at provincial level has not been on devising a regulatory framework for education, but solely on setting up private educational institutions (Humanyun et al. 2013: 184). The narrow fire-fighting approach that is evident on the ground, while possibly necessary to bring about short-term increases in educational provision, has the potential to bring about an uneven, even motley, group of private schools with the result that "the diversity and complexity of [private schools] has posed serious challenges for the government in terms of articulating a coherent response to regulation that can balance concerns of equity and the public good" (Humanyun et al. 2013: 183).[11]

The absence of a set of regulations that would lay out the criteria that must be met by all educational institutions, whether state, ePPPs, or private providers, has proved to be a big lacuna. The consequent lack of guidance on requirements regarding salary scales for teachers, the teacher–student ratio, and the necessary physical characteristics to be deemed a registered school has meant that there are almost no entry restrictions on new providers. On the other hand, if stringent limitations on the new providers were to be introduced at this juncture, then there would be an adverse impact on the LFPSs. As LFPS schools owe their ability to operate to their paying very low wages to their teachers and having minimal teaching resources in their establishments, the introduction of standards would almost inevitably force them out of business.[12] If the LFPSs were to try to meet minimum standards imposed by regulation, it would drive up their fees, price out the poorer parents in an area and push them back into the government school system, without ensuring any improvement in the teaching quality in government schools.

International Non-State Actors in the Education Policy Space in Pakistan

International donors, of both the multi-lateral and bi-lateral kind, have had a long history of involvement in the education space in Pakistan, providing financial and technical assistance to support education sector reform efforts that extend back to the early 1990s. The nature and modalities of the assistance have been recast in the past two decades, and this section uses evidence from interviews that were conducted in 2008 with representatives of multi-lateral and bi-lateral donors to examine the causes and implications of these changes for future developments in the educational sector in Pakistan.

The contribution of overseas aid to the education sector has accounted for 5 percent of total government expenditure on education between 1990 and 2005, with individual year variations having a high of 7.4 percent in 1994 and a low of 2 percent in 2004 (Malik and Naveed 2012).[13] In recent years, the funding channeled to the education sector in Pakistan has seen marked increases, and today Pakistan's education sector accounts for one of the biggest aid programs undertaken by multi-lateral and bi-lateral donors. The modality of financing has seen a series of rather puzzling shifts; over the years, it first shifted from program support to budgetary support and then went back to project support (King and Malik 2005).

The policy reform interventions by donor agencies such as the Social Action Program (SAP) provide useful milestones to mark out changes in direction that have been brought about by agendas set by international institutions. The SAP was the largest coordinated donor effort in the early 1990s and it formalized the Pakistani government's financial commitment to providing services through a borrowing agreement with the IMF.

> The "social" sectors, or sectors covered by SAP include education, health, family planning and rural water supply and sanitation. Of these education received around half of the "development" budget, and over three-quarters of the recurrent budget. The early phase of SAP (up to 1996) was, to a great extent, focused on raising literacy through raising primary school enrolments. The interventions included the establishment of new primary schools, the upgrading of existing ones, and projects for non-governmental and non-formal initiatives in basic education, and specific interventions for girls' schooling.
> (Gazdar 1999: 6)

The SAP was largely considered to have failed to achieve its objectives and the program seemed to falter on multiple counts.[14] A big "take-away" that the donors accepted at the end of the 1990s was that pushing money through the government would not be sufficient in itself to improve outcomes if the government did not have capacity to deliver.

In contrast to the focus in the 1990s on programs that emphasized bricks and mortar, there was a shift in the 2000s to encourage the use of technical assistance from the donor in the form of monitoring and assessment systems. The government received revised and improved technical support from the British Council and the World Bank at the provincial levels.[15] This shift followed on the heels of the Local Bodies Ordinance of 2001 that heralded the decentralization of education policy development and gave implementation authority to the provinces.

Interviews with donor officials emphasized key aspects of the differences in international donor policy during the two periods of the 1990s and the 2000s with regard to donor operations and modalities in the educational sector. The *first* modality shift was that in the 1990s the donors were focused on working with the national government to build capacity, while, in the 2000s, there was a shift from supporting the federal level of the state to working with the provincial level. The *second* modality shift was a greater emphasis on meeting targets and priorities in educational policy in the 2000s. This was primarily directed at achieving the MDG and EFA goals that had been signed up to by international agencies. As the Pakistani government had signed international conventions, the donors saw it as their task to help the government move toward achieving EFA targets. An interview with the Asian Development Bank representative revealed that, in the 2000s, there was also a *third* shift in donor modalities that occurred with regard to financing mechanisms. The assumption made in the 1990s by donor agencies that money provided for macro level policy in Pakistan would make an impact at the micro level, such as being translated from an educational budget to improvement in individual classrooms, was no longer held in the 2000s.

While all donors continue to work with governments at the provincial level, the shift away from funding governments directly to overcoming the problem of tracking the use of donor funds to identified objectives remains a challenge. The evidence of dissatisfaction with the state's capacity for delivery is found most clearly articulated in the UK Department for Intertnational Development (DfID)'s *Business Case for the Sindh Education Fund*:

> The lack of political will to reform education in Sindh is troubling. The education sector has suffered extremely high levels of political interference and corruption over the years, and attempts to improve government schools have been, at best, slow and often thwarted. A number of binding constraints to change remain, in particular around the use of teacher posts for personal and political ends, with teachers, principals and district authorities frequently opposed to reform. Governance and institutional capacity remain substantial risks to any education investment in Sindh.
>
> (UKAID Sindh Business Case, 2012: 13)

The evidence provided by the Sindh business case document is indicative of the new thinking among donors with regard to how business initiatives could improve educational provision by entering the educational market in Pakistan. Market mechanisms such as third party testing of teachers and teaching, the devolution of school budgets to the schools themselves, and the merger of schools so as to provide a management takeover of non-performing schools are identified as means by which donors could create a new policy framework to improve the provision of education in Pakistan.

The result of such a line of thinking among key donors, such as DfID and the World Bank, shows that the lessons learnt by the donors regarding the inadequacy of government capacity in Pakistan have propelled them to draw on ideas currently circulating in the global policy sphere that the private sector could be a new solution to solving the problems of the educational sector.

The donor disillusionment with the ability of the Pakistani state to deliver agreed objectives needs to be recognized as an important trigger for the agenda of privatization in service delivery in Pakistan. The case of the World Bank's commissioned study on the low-fee private schooling sector in Pakistan in the mid 2000s, which assessed the role of the sector in service delivery, is noteworthy in this regard. This study, entitled *Learning and Educational Achievements in Punjab Schools* (LEAPS), was a review of the relative effectiveness of state and private schools. Though the study was the first attempt to compare learning outcomes in private and state schools and was based only on a sample of schools in the province of Punjab, it has been used in the global field of educational policy as a robust and comprehensive evidence base for making the case for the rise and spread of the low-fee private sector in the country. The comparisons between state and private schools that were provided by this study have come to be regarded in Pakistan as indisputable evidence that private schools produce higher learning outcomes than public schools.

There is resistance in global policy circles to comparing the data and results of the LEAPS study with that provided by other studies on ePPPs and showing that the difference between state and private schools is not necessarily large in all cases (Malik 2013). The reason for the strong institutional interest in pushing these data is to show that the reason for the better performance of private schools has to do with the explicit agreement by donor institutions that engaging with the state is not a viable alternative. It is for this operational reason that the donors continue to emphasize the positive impact of private players in the educational field. This donor perspective needs to be understood in the context of the global agenda of the last decade, which has emphasized that the private sector institutions should be invited through ePPPs to enter the educational sector (Draxler 2013) so that they could realize their potential by contributing to improving enrollments and meeting learning outcome targets through better management practice.

The case of Pakistan is quite remarkable with regard to the extent to which donor modalities have shifted away from state engagement and moved to development financing through direct funding of the private sector. Pakistan is one of only seven countries, within the very large set of countries that the World Bank funds in the sphere of education, where the expansion of private providers is undertaken directly through the use of market instruments such as the provision of vouchers, subsidies and other partnership mechanisms (Bano 2008).

Donor Shifts and the Rationale for the Rise of Private Actors

The importance of Pakistan in donor education budgets in recent years has resulted in new demands for meeting aid objectives, which have replaced the demand for technical assistance with the demand for much stronger measures of proven financial ability. The professional skills required to manage large disbursements of funds far exceed those that are ordinarily associated with the teaching profession. The global agenda that promotes a management approach to education has used this very argument of new and far more complex technical requirements as the *raison d' être* for bringing large management consultancy companies into the educational market. The need for a set of technical skills, such as the understanding of complex financial bidding protocols and legal understanding of contractual obligations, which are de rigueur in international consultancies, are part of the new requirements imposed by donors to improve the tracking of these much larger financial outlays that are currently allocated to educational delivery in Pakistan. That these corporate skills reside only in global consultancy companies with a wide range of very highly qualified experts has triggered a very new set of global consortia-based private educational providers in the new millennium.

The donor space has also revised its understanding of the technical expertise required from assistance to the Pakistani state to encouraging provincial governments to work with these international consultancies to ensure that the Pakistani state meets its international educational obligations. The consequences of bringing in this new type of private entity is evident in the following ways:[16]

- multi-lateral and bi-lateral donors working with provincial government through new local intermediaries in the form of aid disbursement agencies. These agencies are subordinate to the government and are responsible for the actual transfer of funds to the project and for ensuring the everyday aspects of project management.
- the rise of a group of powerful global intermediaries, termed international development consultancies (IDCs). These are more often players in the consultancy world such as Development Alternatives International, the Adam Smith Institute, and McKinsey.
- an inflow of other technical facilities that encourage measurement and calibration of outcomes.

Aid disbursement agencies and IDCs have emerged to meet the new requirements of donors' programs that have much larger financial outlays than ever before. The role of global and local intermediaries is to interact with the domestic stakeholders, such as the state, NGOs, and civil society organizations. They now play the same role as the donors used to undertake themselves, in the period prior to the 2000s. Both sets of intermediaries receive funds from the donors to undertake their activities and have been introduced to ensure ease of monitoring by the donors.

The interactions and contracts between international non-governmental organizations and local NGOs currently involved with delivering services is another new area where non-state actors have entered the educational sector. The rise of contractual responsibilities to deliver teacher training as well as to grow and promote educational entrepreneurship are explicitly recognized in donor documents and conversations.[17]

The traditional technical assistance that was designed with the help and expertise of management professionals is being replaced by an explicitly contractual form, where new private players are working through contractual obligations for the donors. The rise of intermediary levels of local and international experts in the implementation of education policy, often with the assistance of new ways of evaluating educational outcomes, has led to a greater role for legal and managerial expertise to ensure that large financial outlays are project managed effectively through complex contracts.

The technical assistance provided within the new funding modalities, which has created the intermediaries of the IDCs, are based on the management expertise of business analysts and on financial procurement criteria, rather than on expertise related to the educational sector. The contracts are based on a business mentality that emphasizes problem-solving skills to create outcome-based solutions and thereby restructure and improve the efficiency with which Pakistan can deliver services. The donors do not regard the entry of the IDCs as heralding a new emphasis on technical assistance; rather, they see it as a scaling up of the requirement for existing technical assistance in the total donor budget. They point out that the increase in size has been the reason why bids for technical assistance are now automatically put out to international tendering rather than being sourced within the country.[18]

The donor agencies interviewed agreed that the current technical expertise model was preferable to the earlier one, as the move to the use of business consultants with management skills and away from the professional expertise of academics has resulted in the creation of a strategic partnership to replace the earlier advisory service. In the case of DfID, this has resulted in a move from collecting educational statistics to building a new and results-oriented development management agenda. The World Bank is also moving its global practice in this direction.

The difficulty of tracing financial flows in Pakistan continues to be a central reason for the recent international donor demand requiring the involvement of specialist development corporations for the disbursement of aid. The introduction of an increasingly technical dimension to service delivery ensures that monies provided by donors will now be disbursed through contractual obligations. The contract provides the possibility of ensuring a basic level of financial accountability in a national context in which the donors do not regard it as possible to meet their objectives using existing channels of engagement with the state. It is in this recasting of the donor modality that ePPPs are regarded as a preferred form of engagement with the private sector. The reason provided is that explicit contractual obligations will be helpful in tracking both the aid delivery and the policy implementation that are currently required for successful budget support to the Pakistani government.

The international donors have also now developed an explicit argument for why ePPPs have become a central plank for ensuring that the Pakistani government is able to meet its international mandate to ensure education delivery. The reason is that ePPPs are undertaken through contracts with global intermediation by IDCs, to ensure the best delivery of educational services possible in the current political environment of Pakistan. At the local level, the donor agencies regard this as a route by which they are able to bypass the inability of the government to ensure a comprehensive reform of the education sector. They see the possibility of working with local intermediaries as the most efficient way to ensure that the routine aspects of project management are overseen adequately. The particular aspect of IDCs that is appealing to the donors is their ability to devise cost-effective solutions, while the local intermediaries work to advance the entrepreneurial spirit of private school provision on the ground.

The strategic partnership that international donors are designing and operationalizing with provincial governments is geared to supporting the private sector. In the case of Punjab, there is an emphasis on market instruments such as voucher schemes and foundation-assisted schools, while in Sindh there is work with BRAC to set up a not-for-profit company to manage the educational fund. The role of the intermediary IDCs is dependent on the program modality set out by the donor and the procurement protocol for bidding for the program delivery and management. As the increased size of the technical assistance requirements have triggered the need for internationally established management consultancies that have greater experience on procurement regulations, donors are increasingly turning to consultancies that can ensure metrics for value for money and accountability for taxpayers' monies.[19]

Another reason for the growing concern with tracking finances appears to be the fallout of the financial crisis in the Northern economies. As donors face close to zero growth rates in their own economies, this has reduced the share of international aid in their national budgets, with a greater emphasis on value for money and the need for accountability to domestic taxpayers in the North. It has now become more important for donors to be able to convince their domestic constituencies of the legitimacy of international aid budgets. In Pakistan, this has led to donors supporting demand-side campaigns, such as the advocacy campaign for education *Alif Ailan*, promoting civil society engagement campaigns, and supporting voice and accountability funds, all of which can be transmitted back to domestic constituencies in the North as evidence of meeting the mandate accepted and approved by the taxpayer.

Conclusions

There has been a recasting of the provision of education in Pakistan as a consequence of changes witnessed in education service delivery, educational policy and public–private partnership spaces in recent years. These changes have been created by the crossfire between national-level donor discussions on the inability of the Pakistani state to provide education and international discussions about the importance of bringing in the private sector to improve management practices and entrepreneurship in the provision of public services.

The unequivocal donor position is that (a) the changes in forms of service delivery, (b) the reorganization of donor assistance from capacity building to technical assistance, and (c) the new demand for the entry of international consultancy companies to ensure financial and legal accountability are consequent on the impossibility of working with the state. The current position, of donors working with provincial governments through new local and global intermediaries, is also regarded as part of these three necessary modality changes. It is explained that, at a time when the donor budget for education allocated to Pakistan has grown rapidly, the contract-based system between donors and new private actors is necessary to achieve the educational objectives they are required to meet.

The international donors have unanimously expressed the view that they have been disillusioned with the Pakistani government since the 2000s, and this is evident from donor documents and interviews with key stakeholders in the educational sphere and the donor community. The recognition of the inadequacy of government capacity coincided with a global normative shift, consisting of the private sector being conceived as an appropriate contractual partner for improving enrollments and meeting learning outcome targets (Lingard and Ali 2009).

This has resulted in a conscious change in the donor space, with a shift from focusing on working with the federal government on improving state capacity to deliver education, to an engagement with the provincial-level government, and, more recently, with district-level government to increase the role of private actors. The new instrument of technical expertise that replaces the older form of technical assistance also emphasizes the importance of the private sector, in this case global consultancies that have the expertise to introduce monitoring and assessment systems. This emphasis on newer and more managerial forms of expertise has been an important driver for the bringing in of large corporates to the global provision of educational services (Draxler 2012).

In the light of the failure of the government education system, the donors in Pakistan have come to regard private schools as the way forward to expand access and to act as a "gap filler" and also to provide choice through quality improvement, overcoming the problem of the "quality improvement or second best." Donors have put forth the argument that private sector involvement has helped to focus attention and efforts toward meeting important service delivery goals agreed upon by the Pakistani state. It is also asserted that the need to ensure that donor funding was being effectively used to deliver educational services was the reason for supporting ePPPs and expanding the role of private entrepreneurs, using market instruments such as vouchers. It follows that, while ePPPs might be considered to be a vehicle for privatization in many quarters, the donors regard Pakistani ePPPs as having provided opportunities to promote access to good quality education.

The implications of the shifting modalities of donor involvement in education in Pakistan, and the associated rationale for expanding the role played by non-state actors in the education delivery space, have not been universally beneficial. The encouragement given by donors to new forms of private provision without any corresponding engagement with the federal state has allowed the state to abdicate its responsibility to be the primary provider and regulator of educational provision. The wide variety of private providers has thrown up a range of schooling, from high end to LFPS, in the absence of regulation. Any regulatory standards that might be considered at this stage run the risk of being particularly inimical to the educational outcomes of poorer households who have chosen the private sector over the state education system.

The new global and local intermediaries that have emerged from the latest modality of technical expertise and contractual obligations demanded by international donors are also not without their own set of stumbling blocks for the making and ownership of educational policy in Pakistan. The entry of IDCs to support donor programs is argued to be based on the need to have access to the best corporate skills in financial and legal accounting, and on competitive contracting. This presumes a strong set of global applicants, yet the world of corporate consultancy is based on a highly oligopolistic market. This market configuration does not generate competition, and the Pakistani state could end up with consultants who are contracting with provincial and local governments, but do not add new skills to the existing competencies of domestic players in Pakistan. The non-competitive and low-quality domestic environment within which the IDCs operate is further exacerbated by the very poorly developed regulatory framework in Pakistan, which does not even set minimum conditions for private educational providers. Given this condition of very limited recognition of legal responsibility in the county, it would be difficult to prosecute local or global players for malpractice. In the current context of the poor capacity of the Pakistani state to deliver, it does seem incongruous that the donor community should regard it as an easy proposition for global consultancies to be able to be external drivers to instill the principles of law and regulation in an educational environment that does not even approximate to a fully functional educational market.

It would appear that the demands of international donor agencies over the past two decades, using the language of the Washington and post-Washington consensus, have provided a global policy context that is nigh impossible in the Pakistani institutional environment, where private schools are not regulated and remain low cost, but low quality, providers of education. In fact, the idea of public–private partnerships and of privatisation in education that emerged in Pakistan during the 1990s, particularly under the influence of donor agencies' sponsored projects (Farah and Rizvi 2007), has remained a rather underwhelming alternative to the state sector. The current educational reforms in Pakistan appear to be a consequence of international agendas and do not seem to feed into national concerns or meet the demands and needs of the last mile or most disadvantaged sections of Pakistani society.

Partnerships in education can prove to be useful policy tools for ensuring sustainable improvements. However, in a context of weak state ownership, unchecked expansion of private actors can have very negative consequences. Menashy et al. (2014: 245) write: "Pakistan has been a poster child for international donor interventions in many ways," and this begs the question of whether the Pakistani state has any opportunity or desire to demand ownership of the aid outcomes. The case of Pakistan is clear evidence of an exercise in policy intervention that was not led by national directives, but by the interest of donors in promoting the private sector involvement to fund education foundations to replace the existing school system. Furthermore, the inability of the government to take any clear stance on the criteria for these new schools and instead to limit its role to a willing acceptance of the donor guidance (Menashy et al. 2014) makes this a rather exceptional case of state negligence.

The changing modalities of donors in Pakistan appear to be led by a mixture of concerns, and, while they have emphasized the limitations of the national environment in the country, they have shied away from highlighting their own limitations in responding to domestic constituencies in the North as well as global pressures from international corporate agendas. The relationship between the new private sector actors, the policy orientation of donors, and the new forms of contracts indicate that increasing use of IDCs and contractual obligations have been touted as a game changer as they usher in entrepreneurial skills to the educational sector. On the other hand, it might result in a less than competitive environment due to the very low legal and financial ability in the country and a very poor history of state regulation. The end result could very well be a new modality that is unable to ensure provision of education by donors through the new intermediaries. It is likely that the changes are not so much recasting the making of educational policy, but shifting the ownership of policy making from national to international institutions. The combination of an increasing level of donor finance for education provision, associated with recalcitrance on the part of the Pakistani state to actively design and implement regulation of either the new educational providers or the new intermediaries, indicates that recasting of the future ownership of educational policy is already underway.

Notes

1 This is often termed as the "last mile" problem in the management literature, and often heard in relation to management of new markets in consultancy literature such as McKinsey reports.

2 The problem of the "second best" is a central proposition in economics that makes the case that a poorer (less efficient) form of provision is accepted because the most efficient production method is not feasible. In the case of education this translates into state provision of education taking place, because educational markets do not exist.

3 Estimates from non-governmental sources put private sector enrollments in the province at 40 percent (Barber 2013).

4 The conversion rate is currently Rs. 100 = $1. World Bank statistics for 2014 calculate that just over 20 percent of Pakistanis are living on below $1 a day.

5 Schools that charge up to Rs. 2000 ($20) are categorized as low-fee, though the majority in Pakistan charges less than Rs. 1000 ($10).The middle tier schools are a combination of individual enterprises and franchises of larger organizations. Some run both a middle tier and a lower tier school, others have a top tier and a middle tier, such as Beacon House and The Educators.

6 Lack of data on private schools prevents mapping/representation of historic trends in market shares and patterns of enrollment. The earliest figures cited are from 1968 when private schools accounted for over half of the enrollments (Jimenez and Tan 1987).

7 This policy however remains an anomaly and occurred under Bhutto's regime. He was a socialist leader, and the policy was in line with his economy-wide nationalization policies. When private institutions were nationalized, their properties and assets were stripped without any compensation being paid to their owners. This was tantamount to destroying an existing infrastructure rather than a gradual and systematic rollback of private sector involvement. It was a shock to the system with far-reaching consequences.

8 The authors link the growth in private sector schools since 1983 to liberalization policies, and argue that gains in fiscal savings and enrollments made lifting the ban a popular and useful policy.

9 The Punjab Education Foundation was established in 1992, and the Sindh Education Foundation was established in 1991. The KP and Baluchistan foundations are more recent.

10 The data in this section is based on interviews conducted with key educational policy experts in Pakistan, with further substantiation based on a review policy documents and the grey literature between 2008 and 2014.

11 There is no documented policy analysis work exploring the efficacy of these frameworks and impact on private schools, and the market for education. Research in the context of regulation in education in the country is severely limited, apart from the study mentioned: Analysis of the one operational regulatory framework that does exist in the Islamabad Capital Territory reflects a lack of clarity in objectives of the policy and gaps in implementation. The regulatory authority is tasked with both promoting and holding the sector accountable, pointing to a fundamental contradiction in the very objectives of the framework. Furthermore, the authority has not yet taken effective action to provide service standards, or to ensure consistent policy regarding curricula, teaching staff, service conditions and academic standards and evaluations (Humanyun et al. 2013).

12 In our interviews, educational policy experts in Pakistan indicated that they were concerned that the introduction of regulation would result in accreditation only for the new higher-end private schools that can meet the financial and physical requirements to be deemed a school. It would push out the LFPS schools that are preferred by the poorer households that cannot afford the higher-end schools but still regard the private sector as preferable to the state schools. This would put policy makers in a quandary, as introducing regulation would queer the pitch for poorer households who want to choose private schools, but lack of regulation would perpetuate the motley collection of schools that operate without any thought to abiding by the current requirements for state educational institutions.

13 These numbers are based on official Economic Affairs Division (EAD) and World Development Indicator (WDI) estimates. Aid flows have also fluctuated considerably by year over this time period.

14 The size of the program was too large, and the objectives and targets much too ambitious. As it was a multi-donor effort, it required both oversight and coordination between individual donor agencies and this feature was never fully achieved.

15 Interview with international educational policy advisor to an international donor.

16 Interviews with international donor officials.

17 The Sindh Business case provides detailed description of the need for increased entrepreneurship in the provision of education.

18 While donor officials emphasized that the older and newer forms of technical assistance were merely different because of the growth in financial budgets, the donor documents indicate that there is a shift in modalities.

19 Our major programs are therefore implemented at provincial level and are tailored to the context in each province, and to the opportunities for and obstacles to achieving impact for funds invested by the UK taxpayer (UKAID Sindh Business Case 2012: 15).

References

Adeney, K. (2012). A step towards inclusive federalism in Pakistan? The politics of the 18th Amendment, Publius. *The Journal of Federalism*, 42 (4), 539–565.

Andrabi, T., Das, J., Khawaja, A., Vishwanath, T. and Zajonc. T. (2007). *Learning and educational achievement in Punjab schools: Insights to inform the education policy debate.* Retrieved June 2, 2015 from http://leapsproject.org/assets/publications/LEAPS_report.pdf.

Bano, M. (2008). *Public Private Partnerships (PPPs) as an 'anchor' of educational reforms: Lessons from Pakistan.* Background paper prepared for the Education for All Global Monitoring Report 2009.

Barber, M. (2013). The good news from Pakistan. London: Reform.

Barrera-Osario, F., Patrinos, H.-A. and Wodon, Q. (2009). *Emerging evidence on vouchers and faith-based providers in education.* Washington, DC: The World Bank.

Brady, K. (2012). Under what conditions can MSPEs be successful? Public private partnerships and the global reform of education in less wealthy countries – a moderated discussion. *Comparative Education Review*, 56 (1), 155–175.

Draxler, A. (2012). Global public private partnerships for education: New strategies or skillful rebranding? Public private partnerships and the global reform of education in less wealthy countries – a moderated discussion. *Comparative Education Review*, 56 (1), 155–175.

Draxler, A. (2013). International PPPs in education: New potential or privatizing public goods. In S. Robertson, K. Mundy, A. Verger and F. Menashy (Eds). *Public Private Partnerships in education: New actors and modes of governance in a globalizing world.* Cheltenham: Edward Elgar.

Farah, I. and Rizvi, S. (2007). Public–private partnerships: Implications for primary schooling in Pakistan. *Social Policy and Administration*, 41 (4), 339–354.

Fennell, S. (2008). Contested gender frameworks: Economic models and provider perspectives on education. In S. Fennell and M. Arnot. *Gender education and equality in a global context: Conceptual frameworks and policy perspectives.* London: Routledge.

Fennell, S. and Malik, R. (2012). Between a rock and a hard place: the emerging educational market for the poor in Pakistan. *Comparative Education*, 48 (2), 249–261.

Gazdar, H. (1999). *Policy failure, political constraints and political resources: Basic education in Pakistan. Working Paper No. 5.* London: Asia Research Centre. London School of Economics.

Ginsburg, M. (2012). Public private partnerships and the global reform of education in less wealthy countries – a moderated discussion. *Comparative Education Review*, 56 (1), 155–175.

Government of Pakistan. (1983). *Pakistan education statistics 1982–83.* Academy of Educational Planning and Management. Islamabad: Ministry of Education.

Government of Pakistan. (1993). *Pakistan education statistics 1992–93.* Academy of Educational Planning and Management. Islamabad: Ministry of Education.

Government of Pakistan. (2002). *Pakistan education statistics 2001–02.* Academy of Educational Planning and Management. Islamabad: Ministry of Education.

Government of Pakistan. (2011). *Pakistan education statistics 2010–11.* Academy of Educational Planning and Management. Islamabad: Ministry of Education.

Government of Pakistan. (2012). *Pakistan education statistics 2011-12.* Academy of Educational Planning and Management. Islamabad: Ministry of Education.

Humanyun, S., Shahzad, R. and Cunningham, R. (2013). Regulating low-fee private schools in Islamabad: A study in policy and practice. In Praachi Srivastava (Ed.). *Low-fee private schooling aggravating equity or mitigating disadvantage?* Oxford: Symposium Books.

Jiminez, E. and Tan, J. (1987). Decentralized and private education: The case of Pakistan. Discussion Paper EDT67. Washington, DC: The World Bank.

King, K. and Malik, R. (2005). *Donor coordination in an uncoordinated development environment? The case of education in Pakistan.* Retrieved on June 2, 2015 from: http://ceid.educ.cam.ac.uk/publications/KingMalik_Donor_coordination_Pakistan_16_3_08.pdf.

Lingard, R. and Ali, S. (2009). Contextualising education in Pakistan: global/national articulations of in educational policy. *Globalisation, Societies and Education,* 7 (3), 237–256.

Malik, R. (2013). *Exits, voices and social inequalities: A mixed methods study of school choice and parental participation in Pakistan.* Ph.D. thesis. Cambridge: University of Cambridge.

Malik, R. and Naveed, A. (2012). Financing education in Pakistan: The impact of public expenditure and aid on educational outcomes. *RECOUP Working Paper Series No. 42.*

Menashy, F., Mundy, K. and Afridi, M. (2014). The Role of the World Bank in the Private Provision of Schooling. In I. Macpherson, S. Robertson and G. Walford (Eds). *Education Privatisation and Social Justice.* Providence, RI: Symposium Books.

Tooley, J. and Dixon, P. (2007). Public private partnerships and the global reform of education in less wealthy countries – a moderated discussion. *Comparative Education Review,* 56 (1), 155–175.

UKAID. (2012). Education fund for Sindh pilot programme 2012/13 – 2014/15: Business Case.

10 Teach for All, Public–Private Partnerships, and the Erosion of the Public in Education[1]

Daniel Friedrich

Introduction

In one of the most influential documents on public–private partnerships (PPPs) in education from the past decade, Patrinos, Barrera Osorio, and Guáqueta begin their argument with the assumption that, while "the public sector remains an important player in providing education services ... making high-quality education accessible for all in developing countries requires innovative programs and initiatives in addition to public resources and leadership" (Patrinos et al. 2009: 1), implying a commonsensical need for the State to partner with the private sector. The main goal of these partnerships, thus, is "to maximize the potential for expanding equitable access to schooling and for improving education outcomes, especially for marginalized groups" (Patrinos et al. 2009: 9). In order to understand the role and efficacy of PPPs in education, the World Bank review proposes to examine "PPPs in which the government guides policy and provides financing while the private sector delivers education services to students" (Patrinos et al. 2009: 1).

This chapter will compare the ways in which Enseña Chile and Enseñá por Argentina (two programs that are part of the Teach For All movement) navigate their respective relationship to the State, and the consequences – for good or for ill – that this has both for the organizations and for the field of teacher education. Through this comparison, I will question whether equitable partnerships are even possible between the public and private sectors in (teacher) education. Instead of taking for granted Patrinos et al.'s foundational assumptions, my chapter wonders: Can the State truly guide policy and provide partial financing, while the private sector delivers education services? If so, what sort of State and what kinds of services would those be? What are the costs of such partnerships for the notion of education as a public good?

The chapter is born out of a deep concern about the direction of the conversation about public education currently taking place in most of the Western world. The economization of the social sphere brought about by neoliberal political economy produced a shift toward understanding education as one more commodity, an investment in human capital in which the "audit State" (Ranson 2003) both decoupled itself from the responsibility of guaranteeing a right to the whole population, and assumed the role of accountability keeper for a service provided by any interested party. In this context, PPPs in education become not only possible, but commonsensically necessary. And while the effects of neoliberal policies in education has been widely studied from a critical perspective (e.g. Ball 2012; Olssen 2009; Peters 2011), the assumption of a need for the State to partner with the private sector in providing education has remained relatively untroubled (with the notable exception of Verger 2012, among a few others).

A few characteristics of this paper and the argument being put forth are worth mentioning in advance. First, while the dispute this piece opens up is anchored in the case of Teach For All, this is, for the most part, a chapter that explores ideas and different understandings of the changing role of the State in education. That is to say, the core of the text is not to be located in empirical data and methods of analysis, but in questioning the philosophical and political underpinnings of PPPs in education. Second, obviously PPPs are not proposed only as a solution to society's ills in the field of education. However, even though many of the points I will raise could be mobilized to think about other areas, my argument is bound to the right to education and the specificity it entails. Finally, this piece should not be read as a defense of any particular administration, or an attack on others. States are complex and contradictory bureaucracies that should not be read as harmonious wholes.

The Public, the Private, and the Democratic Dissensus

While the question of the role of the State has been debated along the continuum of modern Western political thought, the political philosophy of Jacques Rancière brings a novel twist to the discussions, not by finding common ground or a middle point, but by shifting the locus of the main questions. Rancière's core concern with equality leads him to re-define the very notion of democracy, as "the equality already there at the core of inequality ... the wrench of equality jammed into the gears of domination, it's what keeps politics from simply turning into law enforcement" (Rancière 2011: 78–79). Democracy, as the power of those who have no qualifications for exercising power (Rancière 2004), rests on the notion of the common as a space in which the equality of all gets continuously verified in the face of the unequal conditions of living that constitute the wrong of this tension. Democracy (or politics, which Rancière uses interchangeably) is opposed to policing, understood as "an order of bodies that defines the allocation of ways of doing, ways of being, and ways of saying, and sees that those bodies are assigned by name to a particular place and task" (Rancière 1999: 29). If the *police* order is constituted by the consensus about who belongs where doing what,[2] democracy is the dissensus enacted in the challenge of that order that forces a re-ordering of the parts in the name of equality.

While Rancière is quite clear in stating that democracy cannot be institutionalized, but is a fleeting moment in which equality disrupts the *police* order and forces a new partition of the sensible, the privileged space for that to happen is in the common space of the public.[3] Returning to the main question guiding this chapter – Is it even possible to have equitable PPPs in education? – Rancière's scholarship invites us to think about the "public" aspect of that partnership in different terms. If the public is a site of dispute, of verification of equality by interrogating who counts as a speaking subject (and whose voice is merely noise), initiated by anyone, then how can the public sector partner with a private sector that, by definition, is exclusionary? In other words, the private sector has inherently already settled the dispute of who and what is visible, who and what counts as something or someone worth noticing. The private sector is precisely private because it has delimited who gets to participate in the conversation.

Teach For All and Global Efforts to Reform Teacher Education

Teach For All is a global network

> of independent social enterprises that are working to expand educational opportunity in their nations by enlisting their most promising future leaders in the effort. [It] aspire[s] to the vision that one day, all children will have the opportunity to attain an excellent education.
>
> (Teach For All 2012)

Founded in 2007 at the Clinton Global Initiative, Teach For All seeks to support local social entrepreneurs as they bring the model pioneered by Teach For America in the US in the 1990s and Teach First in the UK in the 2000s to each country. By May 2015, Teach For All included programs in 36 countries in 6 continents, each year incorporating more programs in the network.

Although the specificities of each local program need to be studied in relation to their context – including but not limited to the histories of schooling and teacher education, the policy arenas, the pedagogical practices, and labor organizations in each location – some common aspects of all Teach For All programs should be highlighted:

- **Program development**: It is important to note that TFAll does not literally export programs, but instead, individuals – social entrepreneurs – apply to the organization, submitting a set of forms and plans before they are allowed to open a program within the network. In other words, these people need to convince TFAll of the existence of a "need" and how this specific model will address it.
- **Recruitment**: One of TFAll's grounding assumptions is that the teacher is the most important factor in determining students' success in school, thus the importance of recruiting the best of the best for this difficult and fundamental task in social reconstruction. TFAll's programs take pride in conducting rigorous recruitment processes, looking for high achievers who graduated from college with impressive records. Candidates that pass this first bar then write essays and are interviewed before being admitted into the programs.
- **Targeted action**: In principle, TFAll is concerned with education inequities. Therefore, it aims at placing most of the corps members in high-needs

schools. Though this may not always be possible due to local circumstances, the programs are designed to place recruits as full-time teachers for two years in schools where students are underperforming and good teachers tend not to stay for long.

- **Funding**: While the funding scheme varies from program to program in terms of presence or absence of public monies, all programs are at least partially funded by private corporations and donors. Some companies are global partners, such as DHL, while others fund only specific programs. Funding is used to run the programs but not to pay salaries to corps members, as that falls under the jurisdiction of schools and local education authorities.

- **Teacher training**: The model to *train*[4] teachers used by TFAll is relatively constant around the globe. Before getting into the classroom, corps members undergo an intensive five to six week institute, aimed at providing individuals with the basic skills needed to plan lessons, manage classrooms, and assess learning progress. Whereas some programs continue providing professional development for corps members in partnering universities during the two years of the contract, this is not the case for all programs.

- **Pedagogical model**: Borrowing another page from the Teach For America book, programs within the TFAll network share the pedagogical model termed Teaching as Leadership.[5] This model, which adapts a managerial discourse to classroom practice, breaks down teaching into discrete components that can later be assessed by an external observer and rated using a comprehensive rubric. This allows program managers to categorize corps members as "pre-novice," "novice," "beginning proficiency," "advanced proficiency," and "exemplary," and act accordingly. It also facilitates comparisons among programs and sharing of "best practices."

- **Student assessment**: Finally, all programs in the network share a concern with tracking student performance by using quantifiable indicators as proxy for learning. Assessment and tracking techniques are taught at the institute and teacher effectiveness is equated with growth in student performance as measured by these assessments.

Teach For All programs present themselves as potentially revolutionary partners for the State: they promise to deliver teacher education in a cost-effective manner (public monies cover only a portion, if any, of the service), providing high-needs schools with quality educators in a matter of weeks. The risk for the State is minimal: if Teach For All programs do not deliver a high-quality product in an efficient manner, there will be no demand for them, and they will be forced to close (as was the case with the Brazilian *Ensina!*). As opposed to State-provided teacher education, Teach For All follows the market logic of supply and demand to manage growth, contraction and closure. In exchange for providing this service, the *only* thing Teach For All seems to be asking of the State is a seat at the table where educational policy is decided. The analysis of the policy network supporting Teach For America provided by Kretchmar, Sondel, and Ferrare illustrates this point clearly.[6] The authors cite a speech given by Kaya Henderson, interim chancellor of

Washington, DC and Teach For America alumnus, at the twentieth anniversary of the organization:

> Twenty years ago, Wendy Kopp started an organization, and that organization became a call to action, and that call to action became a movement, and that movement is changing this country ... We need you in our charter schools, our superintendents office, writing our policies, and the list goes on ... This is the revolution we've been waiting for.
>
> (Henderson as cited by Kretchmar et al. 2014: 743)

The authors continue by affirming that "[Teach For America] claims to be an apolitical organization, yet they are explicit in their desire to drive systemic change through neoliberal educational policies" (Kretchmar et al. 2014: 743). When asking about why this exchange between providing teacher education and participating in policy discussions matters when thinking about the current and future state of the global education industry, it is central to understand neoliberalism as a set of governing principles that shape a particular common sense and worldview, and not simply as a way of allocating resources. Teach For All can definitely be understood as a Transnational Advocacy Network (Keck and Sikkink 1998) that seeks to reduce the role of the State and unions in educating teachers, deregulate the field by introducing market-based principles of supply and demand, and, perhaps even more importantly, attribute a moral dimension to these changes in the image of the social entrepreneur as agent of change and salvation. As such, Teach For All is enmeshed in neoliberal systems of thought that make the market possible.

The effectiveness of these programs in terms of raising student scores in standardized tests is a contested issue (Darling-Hammond et al. 2005; McConnney et al. 2012), not only around the question of whether they do it or not, but also on whether student scores are the most appropriate way of measuring educational success (Laczko-Kerr and Berliner 2002). Given the recent emergence of Teach For All on the global stage, most studies and critiques have been directed at Teach For America and, to a lesser degree, Teach First (UK). Some of these criticisms relate to the simplistic view of solving education inequities through teacher training (Cochran-Smith 2005), the ways in which Teach For America has been used as a union-busting tool (Labaree 2010), the disregard the organization has shown for knowledge and theory in teacher education (Friedrich 2014c), their role in policy networks that advocate for neoliberal education reform (Kretchmar et al. 2014), and the cultural impact and assumptions they bring to low-income communities (Popkewitz 1998), among others. Some have praised the effort for mobilizing youth (Guazzone di Passalacqua and Soule 2014) and bringing an innovative entrepreneurial mentality to a field seen as lagging behind and resistant to change (Hess 2008).

Enseña Chile, Enseñá por Argentina, and a Divergent Story

The neighboring countries of Argentina and Chile present a fascinating opportunity to compare the conditions and interactions between programs within the

Teach For All network and two different kinds of State configurations. At a distance, many historical characteristics of these two nations would point to a convergence of sorts: becoming independent from Spain around the same time in the first quarter of the 1800s; economies largely based on exploitation of natural resources that put them in similar positions within the global economic order; more recently, coming out of brutal dictatorships that further fragmented the economic class-based hierarchies. Yet behind these broad strokes lie profound differences, especially in regards to the role that the State has played in the past four decades. These differences will be the basis for the comparison between Enseña Chile and Enseñá por Argentina.

Enseña Chile was among the first cohort of Teach For All programs to open its doors. Founded in 2008 by a group of professionals pursuing graduate studies in the US, it started training and deploying corps members a year later.[7] As of 2014, the organization boasts of having received over 6,000 applications, and having 161 alumni and 148 corps members in classrooms across the country.[8] Enseña Chile is one of the programs within Teach For All that is funded by a combination of public monies (27 percent), a non-profit organization (12 percent), and private donations (61 percent),[9] describing itself as a PPP.

Enseñá por Argentina, on the other hand, is funded almost exclusively by private sector donations. In fact, from the moment it was funded in early 2010, to mid-2012, it received no governmental support. The next year, 5 percent of its operational costs were covered by public monies.[10] In a country with about 2.5 times the population of Chile, the program has about 40 alumni and 57 corps members working in schools.[11]

Perhaps the biggest difference between these two programs in relation to their partnership with the public sector lies in the ways in which the programs have been received by the education authorities. In Chile, the same year Enseña Chile was founded, a law was passed making it easier for college graduates without teaching licenses to teach at the secondary level (given that teachers unions are not major players in Chile – one of the many legacies of Pinochet's dictatorship that remains untouched – there was little resistance to this reform). Tomás Recart, the program's Chief Executive Officer (CEO), has been invited to participate in policy conversations and panels, to present Enseña Chile's achievements in Congress, and has met the country's president on several occasions, being lauded as a social innovator and educational revolutionary (Chileno fue premiado como emprendedor social del año por el Foro Económico Mundial, 2011). Meanwhile, Enseñá por Argentina's relationship with the State has not been so productive. In Argentina, in order to get a full-time teaching position within a public school, teachers have to participate in a public examination [concurso] in which they are assigned points for seniority, as well as for the amount and quality of education and professional development received. As vacancies appear, teachers seeking a teaching position sign up for the examination. The person with the highest score gets the job. This regulation is highly supported by the teachers' unions, as it allows for a powerful gatekeeping mechanism. So far, the State has not allowed Enseñá por Argentina's corps members to bypass this regulatory system, effectively removing the possibility of them entering public schools if they do not hold a previous teaching license.[12] This situation has posed a problem for the growth of the organization, relegating them to the only other kind of schools serving disadvantaged population: religious schools (Friedrich 2014b). These schools are mostly funded by the State, yet they are run as private schools with complete hiring freedom. The lack of a partnership with the State has also meant that Enseñá por Argentina has not had a voice in discussing educational policy at any meaningful level. While the reasons for each State's involvement with these initiatives (or lack thereof) are multiple and complex – and may relate to factors such as the connections that the CEOs and main players within the organizations have with public sector employees and political figures – the different histories and configurations of the State in Argentina and Chile are central to the argument I am posing.

Chile as the Perfect Partner

Chile has been described as the neoliberal experiment par excellence (e.g. Silva 2012; Valdes 2008), one of the first playgrounds for the "Chicago Boys" to implement economic policies aimed at contracting the State's capability of providing services, privatizing most of them, and emphasizing the State's role as an accountability checker for the free flow of market forces, as an integral part of Pinochet's dictatorial regime (1973–1990). As Espinoza and González explain:

> The foundations of neoliberal policy were deeply intertwined with the country's economic development model fostered by the military dictatorship, aimed at uprooting any vestige of a welfare State. The economic and social transformation carried out in Chile since 1980 was supported by ad hoc legislation passed by Pinochet's regime and strengthened by the support provided by international agencies such as the World Bank, the Inter-American Development Bank, the International Monetary Fund, and other academic and economic organizations prone to this ideological stance. The change's roots are so solid that its influence persists today, even when in the last few years it has been subjected to numerous critiques.
> (Espinoza and González 2014: 55, author's own translation)

The neoliberal experiment in Chile has had deep consequences in the field of education. Following a yearly decline in the percentage of public schools out of the total of educational institutions, by 2013 only 44.8 percent of schools were publicly run and funded.[13] Almost half of all schools are privately run and partially or fully funded by public monies. Since the late 1970s, "privatization, freedom of education and competitiveness were the discursive and political keys of [the neoliberal] strategy, which was promoted as the way of developing equality in education" (Cabalin 2012: 221). As a result, "Chile has the most segregated educational system among the countries that form [OECD]" (OECD 2011, as cited in Cabalin 2012: 222). Whereas Chile ranks above all other Latin American countries in the latest Programme for International Student Assessment (PISA) test, studies measuring equality of opportunities in the region tend to point to Chile as the "unfairest" country (Gamboa and Waltenberg 2012).

Under these conditions, the soil is fertile for PPPs in (teacher) education. This statement can be understood as attending to several layers:

- **A deregulated profession**: The historical, social, and legal groundwork set in motion by Pinochet's regime has left the teaching profession almost completely deregulated, first in terms of teacher education, then in terms of the marginalization of unions, and finally in terms of not requiring teaching licenses in order to teach.

- **A contracted, yet powerful audit State**: After decades of shedding most vestiges of welfare, the Chilean State has been reconfigured into an audit agent, focusing more on assessing the outputs of schooling and teacher education,[14] and less on providing those services. This emphasis on outputs might be seen as a particular way of driving policy, while the private sector delivers services, although, as I will argue below, the question of who is driving what remains open.

- **A call for change "from below"**: The erosion of the State is accompanied by distrust in its ability to produce meaningful social change. The State, like all large bureaucracies, is seen as too sluggish, inefficient, and rigid. Concurrently, a new assemblage emerges as the locus of change: the social enterprise, channeling the redemptive narratives of non-governmental organizations (Appadurai 2000), led by social entrepreneurs (Friedrich 2014b), and connected to policy networks through global policy entrepreneurs (Ball 2012).

- **An already dominant private sector**: By 2008, 73.6 percent of all pre-service teacher education was provided by private institutions, following the shutdown of public normal schools in 1974, the defunding of public universities since the Pinochet regime, and the above-mentioned deregulation of higher education (Inzunza et al. 2011).

- **A State willing to partner and share the risks**: Between 2006 and 2010, public expenditure in higher education doubled in real terms, going from 2.1 percent to 3.4 percent of gross domestic product (GDP). In 2006, 59 percent of public investment went directly to the institutions (funding supply), while the rest went to students (funding demand). By 2010, these numbers were almost inverted, with 34 percent going to universities and other tertiary institutions and 66 percent to students. By law, state monies directed to higher education institutions cannot differentiate between public and private entities, and most of it goes to the institutions admitting the top scorers in the national university entrance examination (Rodríguez et al. 2010).

Teach For All is by no means a pioneer in the provision of teacher education by a private party, yet it appears as both a perfect partner – once again, it provides a path for individuals to become teachers that is cost-effective and requires little to no State resources, it is conceived as "audit-friendly" in its emphasis on quantifiable outcomes, and it emerged from the efforts of specific individuals concerned with social change "from below" – and as a bridge between the for-profit private sector (investors and donors) and schools. Taken at face value, the initial question of this chapter about the very possibility of establishing PPPs in education can then be answered positively, with Teach For All (and specifically, Enseña Chile) as an exemplary model. Yet the question begs a deeper look, especially when bringing back the notion of the common proposed by Rancière.

Enseña Chile's partnership with the Chilean State, and the State's role as mere auditor in the provision of education and teachers, presents the State with the pre-determined solution to a consensualized problem. But consensus, Ranciére reminds us,

> means much more than the reasonable idea and practice of settling political conflicts by forms of negotiation and agreement, and by allotting to each party the best share compatible with the interests of other parties. It is a means to get rid of politics by ousting the surplus subjects and replacing them with real partners, social groups, identity groups, and so on. Correspondingly, conflicts are turned into problems that have to be sorted out by learned expertise and a negotiated adjustment of interests.
>
> (Rancière 2004: 306)

Since the private sector is brought in to PPPs to solve the public sector's problems, the problems need to be sorted out in advance, and so do the solutions. In this kind of partnership, stating that the State "guides policy and provides financing while the private sector delivers education services to students" (Patrinos et al. 2009: 1), misses the point that, if one is concerned with equality, the public "sector" is not of the same kind as the private sector, and thus cannot *guide* policy delivered by anyone else, but it has to remain open as a *common* space of contestation. The consensus needed for the PPP to be possible is a way of getting rid of politics, of turning real conflicts (What is a quality education? What does it mean to understand education as a right and not a privilege? Who counts as a quality educator?) into problems to be sorted out by the technical expertise of social entrepreneurs,[15] and the negotiation of interests between a private sector with specific sets of goals and a State weakened by neoliberal policies.

Enseñá por Argentina and a Difficult Relationship

In some ways similarly to Chile, the past military dictatorship in Argentina (1976–1983) also relied on neoliberal tenets to dismantle the welfare State and squash political resistance through deregulation, market-based reform, deindustrialization, and a widening wealth gap (Cooney 2007). This political and economic model was deepened by Carlos Menem's administration (1989–1999), expanding the privatization of the remaining public services, and, perhaps more importantly, reshaping the public imaginary about the role and possibilities of the State in addressing any meaningful issue, and replacing it with the notion of the free market (Grimson and Kessler 2014). However, and departing from the Chilean parallel, the neoliberal model became harshly questioned after the social, economic, and political collapse of 2001–2002 (on the crisis, see e.g. Teubal 2004). The crisis exposed the consequences of decades of growing wealth disparities, lack of social planning, political corruption, and economic laissez-faire. Unexpectedly, and after almost two years of a transitional regime, the crisis also led to a political shift towards the "left" (for a nuanced discussion of the left turn, see Arditi 2008) and toward a different relationship between the State and a large portion of the population.

Under the administrations of Néstor Kirchner (2003–2007) and Cristina Fernández de Kirchner (2007–present), the country experienced a shift towards a growing role of the State in the economy and other aspects of social life. The State re-appropriated several services and strategic industries that had been privatized during Menem's administration, such as the national oil company, the national airline, mail, drinking water, and others. In terms of educational expenditures, the country went from spending 3.54 percent of its GDP in 2003, to 6.26 percent in 2011 (Chile went from 3.85 percent to 4.54 percent in the same period).[16] At the primary level, 83.3 percent of schools are public, whereas at the secondary level, 72 percent are (Dirección Nacional de Información y Evaluación de la Calidad Educativa 2013). It is worth noting, though, that paradoxically, enrollment in private schooling grew at twice the rate of enrollment in public schooling between 1994 and 2010 and public subsidies to the private sector tripled in the same period (Narodowski and Moschetti 2015), indicating once again the contradictions and tensions within State configurations, as well as the disconnect between policy, political rhetoric, and families' choices.

Yet the growth in expenditure in public schooling, which included a significant increase in public school teachers' salaries, reconfigured the relationship between the State and the teacher unions. The unions had been a constant thorn in the side of Menem's presidency, striking often and making visible in dramatic ways the consequences of the defunding of public education embraced by neoliberal policies. A central issue in the strikes was the Federal Education Law passed in 1994, criticized for not being explicit about the State's responsibility for educating the population, privileging families choices instead. The passing of a new National Education Law in 2006 that replaced the Federal Education Law, and opened with an unambiguous statement of the State's duty to provide free education for all was seen as a symbol of the changing times in education (Friedrich 2014a).

Within this political/pedagogical arena, the appearance of Enseñá por Argentina was marked mainly by utter indifference. Despite the organization's efforts at advertising their work in mass media, Enseñá por Argentina's CEO has remained low profile, and the program has not grown nearly as fast as its Chilean counterpart. The tight regulations governing the teaching profession have not been "loosened" to allow corps members to work in public schools serving the populations Teach For All is aimed at. As importantly, the Kirchners' administrations revived the belief in traditional political structures and bureaucracies (if not in "old" politicians) as locus for meaningful social change among a large percentage of Argentine youth (Kriger and Bruno 2013). This is not to say that this is not contested, given the political fragmentation and high partisanship currently present in Argentine society. This is also not a judgment on whether that trust is misplaced or not, but a reflection on the effects of the turn against neoliberal discourses (at least at the rhetorical level) that attempted to reduce the role of the State to that of mere oversight, partnering with the private sector in the delivery of services.

Within a State configuration in which the State is understood to hold the responsibility to guarantee the right to education for all citizens, partnerships such as the one sought by Enseñá por Argentina are seen, not as superfluous, but as threatening to the State's ethical and political duties. Allowing third parties to deliver core educational services guided by the State's policies could then be seen as always binding the State's potential to actually guide in ways that address the best interest of society as a whole. This is not to say that the same State does not engage in some of these practices by subsidizing a large portion of private schools, yet retaining control over the education of teachers points to the centrality of this mission.

Concluding Thoughts

In this chapter, I have interrogated the possibility of establishing public–private partnerships in the field of education by questioning some of the fundamental assumptions embedded in the way of thinking that makes them possible. The argument I am exploring has its own set of assumptions, the main one being the understanding of education as a right that the State needs to guarantee for the entire population. Without this anchor, the entire argument becomes moot.

Furthermore, the argument presented here requires a more nuanced intervention. First of all, current State configurations make it hard to establish clear-cut distinctions between the public and the private. Neoliberalism is exposed here not only as a set of policies, but also as a common sense that has shaped the ways in which we understand governance and the commons. The naturalness with which PPPs are proposed as solution to social issues are indicative of the difficulty of seeing where the boundaries lie. The capitalist State has always been implicated in the production of the conditions needed for the market to exist, and, as such, has always had a foot in the "private." Yet, for the sake of the argument, I still consider the distinction, as problematic as it may be, to be useful in thinking about what happens to the State when it steps back to be *just a partner* in the provision of education. Finally, a comparison of the kind I embarked on here almost necessarily implies caricaturizing the two models to emphasize the contrast. Yet both Argentina and Chile have complex histories and present blurry relations between the State and the private sector, even in the narrow field of teacher education.

Nevertheless, an analysis of the cases of Enseña Chile and Enseñá por Argentina and the different relations they hold with the respective States opens the door for questioning the neoliberal common sense. In Chile, the neoliberal experiment dictates that the State has very few inherent mandates. As an auditor in charge of making sure that certain basic rules are followed, its responsibilities are related to listening to what the market demands, and partnering with other stakeholders capable of delivering the supply. The notion of justice here is two-fold: to provide consumers with transparent information, and to control outputs in order to guarantee some basic quality levels. For this State, PPPs in education are an unquestioned aspect of proper functioning. The State is, at its peak, an efficient machine that uses technical expertise to contribute to the functioning of the market. In this environment, a cost-effective, "evidence-based," and highly demanded program for supplying teachers such as Enseña Chile thrives, even at the cost of limiting the spaces for teacher education and the teaching profession to participate in public discussions about the common good.

The Argentine State's reluctance to partnering with Enseñá por Argentina has its costs. Many of those potential teachers would not be entering the profession if not for this opportunity, and probably several of them could eventually become quality educators. Second, it is clearly more economical to partner with an organization willing to bear the costs of teacher training than to use only public monies for this purpose. Third, delegating these sorts of responsibilities to the private sector brings a flexibility that the State could never have. If a specific effort is seen as not working, it becomes a matter of "switching dance partners" for a different experiment. Not having to deal with public deliberation does certainly allow more nimbleness for action.

Yet the costs of engaging in PPPs in education with organizations such as Enseñá por Argentina are, as I hope to have successfully argued above, even more dangerous to a democratic society. The public sphere is the privileged site for contestation, for staging scenes of dissensus about who has a right to be heard and considered part of the common (Rancière 1999), and as a constitutive site for politics to take place. The private sector, in its understanding of political problems as technical problems – in which it is possible to have a State "guiding" while the private sector merely delivers – has already *resolved* the issues at the core of politics. In Rancière's terms, they have already established a consensus that gets rid of politics, and replaces it with problems to be solved by technical expertise (Rancière 2004), removing them from the commons. This is no partnership, as the very association changes the terms of the problem. And this is, without a doubt, too high a price to pay.

Notes

1 I would like to extend my gratitude to my research assistant, Christopher Ongaro, for his invaluable help in reviewing literature for this chapter.
2 "The essence of the police is to be a partition of the sensible characterized by the absence of a void or a supplement: society consists of groups dedicated to specific modes of action, in places where these occupations are exercised, in modes of being corresponding to these occupations and these places. In this fittingness of functions, places, and ways of being, there is no place for a void. It is this exclusion of what 'there is not' that is the police-principle at the heart of statist practices" (Rancière 2001).
3 While the actual democratic disruption can happen everywhere (even in the private sphere, such as in the work place, or in private schools), the dispute that is opened in the verification of equality *makes* the space public, by anchoring the question about who is included in the count on the equality of *all*.
4 I consciously use the term train instead of educate here to point to the difference between a focus on techniques to be learned and mastered versus a set of conversations to be opened and assumptions to be questioned.

5 www.teachingasleadership.org.
6 For Teach For All's policy network in Europe, see Olmedo et al. (2013).
7 http://www.ensenachile.cl/quienes-somos/historia-ech/.
8 http://www.ensenachile.cl/lo-que-nos-mueve/impacto-ech/.
9 http://www.ensenachile.cl/comunidad/socios/.
10 http://www.helpargentina.org/en/ensenaxargentina.
11 http://ensenaporargentina.org/nosotros.html.
12 As of November 2014, a new partnership has been announced between Enseñá por Argentina and the government of Salta, one of Argentina's poorest provinces. It is unclear yet what the partnership entails, how it will unfold, and where corps members will be working.
13 http://centroestudios.mineduc.cl/index.php?t=96&i=2&cc=2036&tm=2.
14 In 2014 the Chilean government instituted the "Inicia" evaluation for all teachers seeking jobs in public or State-funded schools (http://www.mineduc.cl/index2.php?id_contenido=26726&id_portal=79&id_seccion=4226).
15 This point is reinforced by Rambla and Verger's (2009) argument that, in Chile, education inequality is still mainly seen as a technical problem, in need of better technical solutions.
16 http://datos.bancomundial.org/indicador/SE.XPD.TOTL.GD.ZS.

References

Appadurai, A. (2000). Grassroots globalization and the research imagination. *Public Culture, 12*(1), 1–19.

Arditi, B. (2008). Arguments about the left turns in Latin America: A post-liberal politics? *Latin American Research Review, 43*(3), 59–81.

Ball, S. J. (2012). *Global education inc. New policy networks and the neoliberal imaginary* (1st ed.). London: Routledge.

Cabalin, C. (2012). Neoliberal education and student movements in Chile: Inequalities and malaise. *Policy Futures in Education, 10*(2), 219–228.

Chileno fue premiado como emprendedor social del año por el Foro Económico Mundial. *Emol.* Retrieved April 28, 2011 from: http://www.emol.com/noticias/economia/2011/04/28/478524/chileno-fue-premiado-como-emprendedor-social-del-ano-por-el-foro-economico-mundial.html.

Cochran-Smith, M. (2005). The new teacher education: For better or for worse? *Educational Researcher, 34*(7), 3–17.

Cooney, P. (2007). Argentina's quarter century experiment with neoliberalism: From dictatorship to depression. *Revista de Economia Contemporânea, 11*(1), 7–37.

Darling-Hammond, L., Holtzman, D. J., Gatlin, S. J. and Heilig, J. V. (2005). Does teacher preparation matter? Evidence about teacher certification, Teach for America, and teacher effectiveness. *Education Policy Analysis Archives, 13*(42), 1–51.

Dirección Nacional de Información y Evaluación de la Calidad Educativa. (2013). *La educación argentina en cifras.* Ministerio de Educación de la Nación. Retrieved May 31, 2015 from: http://repositorio.educacion.gov.ar:8080/dspace/bitstream/handle/ 123456789/110007/2013%20Educaci%C3%B3n%20Cifras%20WEB%2031-3-14.pdf.

Espinoza, O. and González, L. E. (2014). El impacto de las políticas neo liberales en el sistema de educación superior chileno. *Revista Latinoamericana de Políticas Y Administración de La Educación, 1*(1), 55–74.

Friedrich, D. (2014a). *Democratic education as a curricular problem: Historical consciousness and the moralizing limits of the present.* London: Routledge.

Friedrich, D. (2014b). Global micro-lending in education reform: Enseñá por Argentina and the neoliberalization of the grassroots. *Comparative Education Review, 58*(2), 296–321.

Friedrich, D. (2014c). "We brought it upon ourselves": University-based teacher education and the emergence of boot-camp-style routes to teacher certification. *Education Policy Analysis Archives, 22*(2), 1–21. Retrieved May 31, 2015 from: http://epaa.asu.edu/ojs/article/view/1193.

Gamboa, L. F. and Waltenberg, F. D. (2012). Inequality of opportunity for educational achievement in Latin America: Evidence from PISA 2006–2009. *Economics of Education Review, 31*(5), 694–708.

Grimson, A. and Kessler, G. (2014). *On Argentina and the Southern Cone: Neoliberalism and national imaginations.* London: Routledge.

Guazzone di Passalacqua, V. and Soule, F. (2014). *El cambio empieza en el aula: El compromiso de Enseñá por Argentina.* Buenos Aires: Boutique de contenidos.

Hess, F. M. (2008). The future of educational entrepreneurship. Retrieved December 12, 2014 from: http://www.frederickhess.org/5135/the-future-of-educational-entrepreneurship.

Inzunza H., J., Assaél, J. and Scherping, G. (2011). Formación docente inicial y en servicio en Chile: Tensiones de un modelo neoliberal. *Revista Mexicana de Investigación Educativa, 16*(48), 267–292.

Keck, M. E. and Sikkink, K. (1998). *Activists beyond borders: Advocacy networks in international politics.* Ithaca, NY: Cornell University Press.

Kretchmar, K., Sondel, B. and Ferrare, J. J. (2014). Mapping the terrain: Teach For America, charter school reform, and corporate sponsorship. *Journal of Education Policy, 29*(6), 742–759.

Kriger, M. and Bruno, D. (2013). Youth and politics in the Argentine context: Belief, assessment, disposition, and political practice among young students (2010–12). *Les Cahiers Psychologie Politique, 22.* Retrieved December 12, 2014: from http://lodel.irevues.inist.fr/cahierspsychologiepolitique/index.php?id=2365.

Labaree, D. (2010). Teach for America and teacher ed: Heads they win, tails we lose. *Journal of Teacher Education, 61*(1/2), 48–55.

Laczko-Kerr, I. and Berliner, D. C. (2002). The effectiveness of "Teach for America" and other under-certified teachers. *Education Policy Analysis Archives, 10*, 37.

McConney, A., Woods-McConney, A. and Price, A. (2012). Fast track teacher education: A review of the research literature on Teach For All schemes. Murdoch University: Centre for Learning, Change and Development. Retrieved May 31, 2015 from: http://researchrepository.murdoch.edu.au/10228/.

Narodowski, M. and Moschetti, M. (2015). The growth of private education in Argentina: Evidence and explanations. *Compare: A Journal of Comparative and International Education, 45*(1), 47–69.

Olmedo, A., Bailey, P. and Ball, S. J. (2013). To infinity and beyond … Heterarchical governance, the Teach for All network in Europe and the making of profits and minds. *European Educational Research Journal, 12*(4), 492–512.

Olssen, M. (2009). Neoliberalism, education and the rise of a global common good. In M. Simons, M. Olssen, and M. A. Peters (Eds). *Re-reading education policies: A handbook studying the policy agenda of the 21st century.* Dordrecht: Sense Publishers.

Patrinos, H. A., Barrera Osorio, F. and Guáqueta, J. (2009). *The role and impact of public–private partnerships in education.* Washington, DC: World Bank.

Peters, M. A. (2011). *Neoliberalism and after? Education, social policy, and the crisis of western capitalism.* New York: Peter Lang Publishing.

Popkewitz, T. S. (1998). *Struggling for the soul: The politics of schooling and the construction of the teacher*. New York: Teachers College Press.

Rambla, X. and Verger, A. (2009). Pedagogising poverty alleviation: A discourse analysis of educational and social policies in Argentina and Chile. *British Journal of Sociology of Education*, *30*(4), 463–477.

Rancière, J. (1999). *Dis-agreement: Politics and philosophy*. Minneapolis, MI: University of Minnesota Press.

Rancière, J. (2001). Ten theses on politics. *Theory & Event*, *5*(3). Retrieved May 31, 2015 from: http://muse.jhu.edu/journals/theory_and_event/v005/5.3ranciere.html.

Rancière, J. (2004). Who is the subject of the rights of man? *South Atlantic Quarterly*, *103*(2/3), 297–310.

Rancière, J. (2011). Democracies against democracy. In G. Agamben (Ed.). *Democracy in what state?* (pp. 76–81). New York: Columbia University Press.

Ranson, S. (2003). Public accountability in the age of neo-liberal governance. *Journal of Education Policy*, *18*(5), 459–480.

Rodríguez, J. C., Flores, L. S., Sugg, D. H. and Hernández, T. J. (2010, February). Inversión pública en educación superior en Chile: Avances 2006–2010 y desafíos. Dirección de Presupuestos del Ministerio de Hacienda. Retrieved May 31, 2015 from: http://www.dipres.gob.cl/594/articles-60597_doc_pdf.

Silva, P. (2012). *In the name of reason: Technocrats and politics in Chile*. University Park: Penn State University Press.

Teach For All. (2012). Teach For All. Retrieved July 12, 2012 from: www.teachforall.org.

Teubal, M. (2004). Rise and collapse of neoliberalism in Argentina: The role of economic groups. *Journal of Developing Societies*, *20*(3/4), 173–188.

Valdes, J. G. (2008). *Pinochet's economists: The Chicago School of Economics in Chile* (1st ed.). Cambridge: Cambridge University Press.

Verger, A. (2012). Framing and selling global education policy: the promotion of public–private partnerships for education in low-income contexts. *Journal of Education Policy*, *27*(1), 109–130.

11 Professional Consultancy and Global Higher Education

The Case of Branding of Academia

Gili S. Drori

Introduction

A new and, by definition, visible feature of global higher education is the branding of universities and colleges worldwide. In efforts often appended to strategic planning exercises, universities and colleges worldwide labor to develop coherent "brand identities," and they subsequently launch branding campaigns, redesign their emblems and often originate logos, and many also register their logos as proprietary trademarks. Such branding action is justified as consolidating institutional character and thus building reputation among prospective students, corporate partners, donors and alumni. Yet still, within academia, branding is met with much suspicion: academics are often dismissive, if not disparaging, of any branding initiative taken by their universities and regard branding as one among the new managerial fads that infringe on the essence of their institutions. Out of this contempt, the once guild-like Republic of Scholars, which still prides itself on peer-review culture and self-generating standards for excellence, is delegating brand management decisions to professional public relations (PR) and marketing experts. In this way, the ethos of the profession of academia drives it to allow endogenous, or hidden, privatization of this once aloof ivory tower.

Drawing on two empirical studies on the branding in academia – an international study of the emblems of over 1,000 universities (Drori et al. 2013; Delmestri et al. 2015) and a national case study on branding of academic institutions in Israel – in this work I highlight the role of professionalization in accounting for the current wave of worldwide branding of academia. I argue that several professionalization paths – within academia and of the branding sector outside it – combine to further the socialization of science (Drori et al. 2003). And, I argue, such contemporary socialization of science perforates the boundaries of academia, making it particularly susceptible to marketization and mediatization and transforming the university into a "promotional university" (Hearn 2010). With that, academia is now thoroughly immersed and actively engaged in "brand society." This means that, for academia, like other sectors, brands became a "new way of organizing production *and* managing consumption" (Kornberger 2010: xiii, italics in original) and an intra-university organizing principle (Kornberger 2010: 12) masked as a mere marketing tool. Overall, I argue, the authority of professionals and the legitimacy of expert knowledge, here of branding consultants and branding know-how, construct higher education as a commodity, academia as a quasi-market, and universities as modern organizations.

Worldwide Branding of Academia: A Review

Given that modern branding[1] emerged in the 1950s, powered by the advent of media and the springing of consumerism, the branding of academia is a very recent phenomenon, traced to the turn of the millennium. For the branding of academia to emerge, there needed to be a realization that academia, and specifically education and scientific knowledge, are marketable commodities. Therefore, the conceptual roots of the branding of academia are commodification and marketization of higher education (Etzkowitz et al. 1998; Bok 2003; Willmott 2003; Slaughter and Rhoades 2004; Wedlin 2008; Rhoten and Powell 2010) and the transformation of its prime organizational form into the "entrepreneurial" (Clark 1998) or "third generation" (Wissema 2009) university. Once such conceptual foundations solidified, branding of academia sprouted in the US and now blooms worldwide.

Campaigns and Prescribed Practices

Branding was institutionalized as a prescribed set of practices related to the marketability of the object, here of academia. Prime practice in this set is the redesign of the organization's insignia and the development of an "aesthetic language" that presumably conveys the organization's identity. A common redesign is to transform emblems into logos, which aesthetically means a turn from content-rich symbols to simplified ideograms (Drori et al. 2013). This change in the aesthetics of the university's identity is intended to promote instant recognition, much like the recognition of other consumer items. Additional prescribed practices of the branding of academia include adding redesigned logo-style symbols to specific activities or university units. In this way, these universities reserve their traditional insignia for official uses (such as diplomas) while relying on stylish and media-suitable logos to deliver their images as cutting-edge and accessible institutions. This multiplicity of identity markers reflects the tension in universities between capitalizing on their heritage and the legacy of the institution, on the one hand, and projecting contemporary relevance on the other hand. Branding consultants approach this tension as a strategic choice, requiring universities to develop a plan for their identity vis-à-vis their various constituents.

Initiatives such as these, to redesign a university's insignia into a branded logo, commonly include the production of a brand book, trademarking, media campaigns, and press releases, all of which are based on market research strategies. Depending how comprehensive the branding "package" is, a single branding initiative can cost some USD $200,000 and the initial stage of research and graphic design can last about a year. And still such branding campaigns are further wrapped within broader identity exercises, which also formulate core values and compose mission- and vision statements. In these ways, branding campaigns are comprehensive initiatives, highly prescribed and formally set to create a favorable organizational image.

Social Context and Meaning

Branding initiatives in academia are heavy with "brandspeak," meaning with terminology that quickly developed as the acumen of marketing and PR schemes designed for higher education (Müller 2010). Most importantly, this branding terminology reframes academic practices anew, infusing them with marketized and mediatized meanings. Principally, the underlying theme of a branding initiative is the logic that drives them: competition. The justification given to branding of academia is competition over students, faculty and financial resources (Marginson 2002, 2006; Hasse and Krücken 2013). The context for this sense of urgency is the coupling of the knowledge economy, where education is an important resource and commodity, with the age of media, where recruitment is carried visually and pithily. Therefore, branding consultants pitch branding to university officials by building a strong link with marketing and service logics: they speak of (product) differentiation, market (field) position and visibility and exposure (Müller 2010; Zwick and Cayla 2011). This talk of competition is fueled by the triumph of ranking culture: as argued by Martin Kornberger (2015), branding, including of academia, is accelerated by the advent of professionalized evaluation devices, especially by rankings. Moreover, the global scope of ranking of academia drives the branding of academia worldwide. Therefore, branding initiatives, similar in theme and procedure, are sprouting in countries as diverse as Malaysia (Osman 2008), Germany (Kosmütski 2012), Norway (Wæraas and Solbakk 2009), Finland (Aspara et al. 2014; Aula et al. 2015), the UK (Melewar and Akel 2005; Chapleo 2011), Singapore and Hong Kong (Gray et al. 2003), Sweden (Holmberg and Strannegård 2015) and elsewhere (Delmestri et al. 2015).

Similarly, branding acumen restates numerous academic and organizational phenomena. For example, the dramatic expansion and differentiation of academic fields of knowledge and also of university structures is redefined as a branding matter. Consequently, the proliferation of institutes and centers outside the traditional bounds of the disciplinary departments and faculties is understood in terms of proliferating brand images. Indeed, while in most universities each faculty and center develops a unique logo affecting certain disciplines more acutely than others (see Engwall 2008b regarding business education), this is not analyzed as a matter of institutional coordination or of academization of lay knowledge, but rather this trend is interpreted as a branding challenge. In branding terms, such definition of this tension is a matter of "identity cohesion" and professionalized strategies to resolve the problem of fragmentation within the institution by creating a "coherent brand identity."

Overall, the branding trends in academia reflect the borrowing of management models from the business sector. Academic institutions came to be considered complex organizations and, as such, to require those management techniques that have been proven successful in the business world. As a result, the once gaping divide between these "cathedrals of learning" and the corporate "cathedrals of earning" (Engwall 2008a: 9; also Serrano-Velarde and Krücken 2012) has been narrowed dramatically. Challenging the prevailing explanations that the emulation of business models by academia is a result of corporate pressure and of academic dependence (Slaughter and Rhoades 2004; Press and Washbrun 2000; Hearn 2015), I here advance an institutional explanation that highlights the role of professional authority. I argue that the authority of professionals and the legitimacy of expert knowledge, here of branding consultants and branding know-how, construct higher education as a commodity, academia as a quasi-market and universities as modern organizations. In this way, professional brand consultants, within academia and outside it, power and guide the embeddedness of academia in the Western, now global, society and its culture of rationalized agency and diffuse authority (Meyer et al. 1997; Meyer 2010).

Professionals in Brand Society

The branding profession and professionals, like other knowledge-based occupations, hold high legitimacy to offer solutions for organizational challenges and to drive institutional change. Drawing upon their professionalized knowledge, which is highly rationalized, standardized and thus prescribed, they are given the authority to create new organizational forms, as well as to advocate and then prescribe organizational reform (Ernst and Kieser 2002; Zald and Lounsbury 2010; Suddaby and Viale 2011). Whereas much of the attention given to professions and professionals in sociological, and organizational studies literature is directed at the pathways to professionalization, I draw attention to the power of the branding profession to traverse the boundaries of the university. Specifically, in the following section I describe how branding consultancy operates through service-sector firms as well as by university branding or PR administrators and I argue that their echoing of each other magnifies the penetrative impact of branding on academia.

Branding Consultancies for Academia: Exogenous Expertise

Today, hundreds of service firms worldwide specialize in branding and – seeing that they are organized around knowledge intensity, low capital intensity and a professionalized workforce (Von Nordenflycht 2010) – together they define a new professional service sector. Whereas most are small workshops or offer limited services (e.g. offering only trademark or domain name services), dozens of branding firms are international in scope. The comprehensive and international branding consultancies offer a range of services: from identity exercises to domain and trademark registration to design and graphics to media campaigns.

The consolidation of branding as a differentiated sector among the creative industries was bolstered also by the development of professional rituals specific to this sub-specialty. Among them are awards, such as the Graphis Award for logo design, posters, or advertising. The sector is further consolidated by ranking:

when industry specialists construct comparative scales for performance and success, firms within the branding sector align with the norms that underlie these scales of excellence. For example, the reputable Famous Logos portal and Tony Spaeth's "World's Top Ten Identity Firms," which rank the most prestigious international branding consultancies, overlap and professional discussions of these lists include little contestation. This broad unanimity about what is valued in branding is amplified by the international reach of most large branding firms. Only one of Spaeth's top ten branding firms does not have company offices outside its home country, and most pride themselves on having over five international offices. Among them, the San Francisco-headquartered Landor Associates boasts having "26 offices in 20 countries." In connecting their many intra-firm offices and in offering their branding services to clients worldwide, branding consultancies form a global network of knowledge diffusion. And, such a network – within a global firm or across the wide field of branding consultancy – delivers the standards and scripts of branding, creating global assemblages of branding knowledge and, in general, of creative imagination (Prince 2014; Schultz et al. 2000). In this way, aesthetic codes such as branding style and criteria for brand value diffuse worldwide through the work of these branding consultancies.

Numerous consultancy firms within this global sector now specialize in delivering branding services to the academic sector. All of the largest 25 international branding consultancies showcase at least three academic institutions among their clients. Still, their specialization in academia draws upon their prescribed ideas of identity formation in general: they bring their branding know-how, which was created for the corporate, product-based and sales-driven sector, to the academic sector and to its research and teaching missions. Indeed, those successful branding consultancies that serve the academic sector also serve a diverse portfolio of other clients, from a variety of industries and service businesses. Also, these consultancies serve a wide variety of academic institutions, from various countries and of various academic foci. For example, the renowned Chermayeff, Geismar and Haviv agency trumpets its long list of successful and celebrated clients in the ten-minute video titled *Logomotion*. The video proudly parades the trademarked logos of public agencies (The American Film Institute, The Smithsonian, US Bicentennial), firms (Merck, PanAm, Mobil), aquaria (Lisbon, Boston, Tennessee, Baltimore), libraries (JFK Presidential Library, Library of Congress), international clients (United Nations Development Programme, Conservation Trust of Puerto Rico and the Turkish firm Koç Holding), as well as New York University and The New School University. Similarly, the renowned international branding consultancy Interbrand lists among its clients such diverse academic institutions as Hanyang University (Korea), Boston University's School of Management (US), Royal College of Art (UK), and Ryukoku University (Japan). The coupling of global reach and diversity of audiences with consolidated professional scripts for branding results in the "flattening" of branding campaigns for academia. In other words, the abstraction or theorization of branding into a so-called "best practice" is driving the implementation of this all-purpose, non-specific model across sectors and across countries.

The prescribing of the branding of academia is further amplified by the recent springing of prêt-à-porter and do-it-yourself branding services. These services are websites and software that offer logo design, for a nominal fee, based on an online questionnaire regarding company characteristics. This new form of branding consultancy is an outcome of the institutionalization of professional branding and is explained as an expression of "sector segmentation" or "differentiation" in a maturing service sector. In this case, alongside the established global branding consultancies springs this "low end," "production line" sort of branding industry. In sociological terms, the importance of this new form of branding consultancy comes from the extreme form of prescribing and modeling that it configures under the guise of customization: online services, such as GraphicSprings, and software, such as The Logo Creator, bring an extreme form of standardization by offering logo features per categorical designation. Specifically, when identifying the client organization as an educational institution, these do-it-yourself branding services commonly suggest logos that display images of a book, a red apple, a laboratory or scientific instrument, a tree, a check mark, or images referring to children. In this way, these branding services "typecast" academia, configuring categorical standardization while offering a proprietary and unique logo for each academic institution. This, as will be discussed in the concluding section of this chapter, is an expression of what sociologist Roland Robertson terms "the universalism of particularism" (1994, 2014).

Academic institutions are increasingly dependent on these various consultancies for branding services. The impulse to launch branding campaigns, which has been sweeping academia in the past couple of decades, requires more than a university administration can deliver. Also, the faith in professional instruction drives even universities that have PR units or in-house graphic designers to rely on the services of outside branding consultancies. Therefore, while media, advertising or marketing units in universities have been expanding rapidly in the past few years, branding campaigns in academia are almost exclusively led by contracted branding consultancies. The challenge of branding from the outside, where exogenous professionals are to capture the "soul" of the university they are to brand, is mitigated through professional tools: the campaigns customarily begin with extensive surveys of the university's constituencies, focus groups of stakeholders and interviews with key personnel, all in the name of inclusion and representation, on the one hand, and of professionalism and tailoring, on the other hand.

In summary, since the turn of the millennium, academia has joined the branding frenzy, and the field of branding consultancies has evolved to also include branding consultancies that specialize in the higher education sector. The transition is made when a "critical mass" of academic clients allows these consultancies to market themselves as specialists. Indicating that such a transition has already occurred, dozens of consultancies worldwide describe themselves as specializing in servicing academia and becoming the external arm of the advertising, marketing, and spokesperson's units of universities.

Branding Professionals within Universities

Along with the expansion of university administration and the rise of a managerialist culture in academia worldwide (March et al. 2000; Logue 2010, 2014; Krücken
et al. 2013), the administrative arm responsible for media and marketing expanded
dramatically. For a while now, universities have had administrative units charged
with addressing external audiences – from student registration to donor relations
to a spokesperson's office – reflecting academia's publicness, or responsiveness to
its constituents (Feeney and Welch 2012). Still, it is only in the past decade or so that
we have witnessed the founding of units explicitly charged with media and reputation management. And, most importantly, this administrative expansion and the
managerialist turn are accompanied by professionalization: more and more of the
personnel of these university units are PR, marketing and media professionals who
made their careers in these fields prior to joining university administration. With
that, they serve as the link with the outside world of professional branding consultancy: they are attuned to branding methodologies, maintain personal contacts
with branding peers and bring "brandspeak" into academic discussions. Branding
professionals within universities are, therefore, the brokers between two networks:
professional branding consultancy and academia. And, as such, they serve as a critical node for the transfer of branding models.

These intra-university branding units are oriented toward the media world,
rather than toward their home institution. This is demonstrated in the unit titles:
the titles of most new administrative units include such terms as "media," "branding," or "marketing," and universities that already had a spokesperson's office now
differentiate this function from the branding and marketing function. With this
discursive move, branding is defined as a marketing-oriented identity function and
thus distinct from the spokesperson's role as the voice of the university's leadership.

Intra-university branding also brims over the administrative units that
are charged with its strategy. Most clearly, the university's academic leadership "brandspeaks," using the terminology and logic of brand experts. As one
among countless examples, Professor Jeremy Myerson, who serves as Director
of Innovation at the Royal College of Arts in London, is quoted on the website of
RCA's branding consultancy InterBrand as speaking of brand valuation:

> Until now, we have had no way of putting a monetary value on the very many
> intangible benefits that accrue to the college due to its international reputa-
> tion. This valuation has been a robust financial exercise that shows how the
> RCA's brand gives the college an economic leverage.
>
> (cited in Spellman 2011: 183)

Through such proclamations by university leaders, professionalized branding permeates academic life: academics reframe the life of research and teaching in terms
of organizational strategy, effectiveness, and value. By assimilating management
terminology and modes of thinking, academics too redefine academia as a modern, marketized, and mediatized organization.

Illustration: The Professionalization of Branding in
Israeli Academia

The global wave of branding of universities reaches the shores of Israel, too, and the 69 academic institutions in Israel are also involved, to varying degrees, in branding campaigns. Several processes combined to spur the branding of academia in Israel. First, seeing that most academic institutions in Israel were founded after the 1995 regulatory reform[2] (Volansky 2005; Menahem 2008; Davidovitch and Iram 2011), they were born into the era of mediatization, marketization, and managerialism in academia and were imprinted by this atmosphere. Second, the privatization and diversification that accompanied the expansion of the higher education field in Israel (Menahem et al. 2008; Gaziel 2012; Davidovitch and Iram 2014) constituted a sense of competition among academic institutions over undergraduates and funding. Finally, the internationalization of Israeli higher education (Zehavi and Zer 2012) means that Israeli universities are concerned with their international rank and engage in recruitment of international students. Together, these trends heighten the sense of competition and, seeing that branding is conceived as a tool for PR and marketing, they stimulate PR, marketing, and branding campaigns.

As a result, all seven Israeli research universities, as well as the recently accredited Ariel University in the West Bank, led branding campaigns in the past decade or are currently wrestling with branding dilemmas. Seeing that 54 of Israel's academic institutions are categorized as public, drawing over 65 percent of their budgets on average from the governmental Planning and Budgeting Committee of the Council of Higher Education (EC 2012), the adoption of private sector practices such as marketing to public sector institutions of higher education builds inherent tensions into any branding campaign (see Serrano-Velarde and Krücken 2012). Indeed, while overall both Israeli faculty and university administrators are increasingly market oriented and are therefore concerned with student satisfaction (Hemsley-Brown and Oplatka 2010), tensions are mounting when plans for marketing and branding campaigns come before university leaders, especially when discussed in faculty committees or the university senate. These tensions are somewhat moderated by professionalism: branding consultancies and in-house branding experts accompany the process and provide rationale, plan details, and legitimacy.

Several Israeli branding consultancies service educational institutions and specialize in leading branding campaigns in universities and colleges. Much like their international counterparts, Israeli branding consultancies speak in terms of providing "marketing excellence for academic excellence," as the tagline of one such Israeli branding consultancy goes. Also, much like their international counterparts, Israeli branding consultancies deliver their clients a branding "package" that includes everything from logo design to market research to media campaign to fundraising strategy.

It is difficult to assert how many Israeli branding consultancies specialize in education and academia. It is clear, however, that all Israeli academic institutions have used some form of professional assistance for branding purposes: some small colleges hired graphic designers to draft their logos, while others had full market research, identity strategy and marketing campaigns led by hired branding consultants. Indeed, even Israel's first academic institutions – the Technion and The Hebrew University of Jerusalem, which opened their doors in the mid-1920s and were spurred to create stylized emblems for their twenty-fifth anniversaries in the 1950s – relied on professional graphic designers. Still, the transition from emblem to logo, which is an aesthetic transformation that captures the professional turn from graphic design to branding consulting, is a recent shift in Israel, as it is worldwide (Drori et al. 2013). Today, of the 69 accredited academic institutions in Israel, 60 could be categorized as displaying logos, either ideogram or logotype. Seeing that the first academic emblems were designed in the mid-1950s, it is not surprising that all emblems of all academic institutions in Israel are modernistic in style. Still, some display more literal, rather than abstract, rendering of symbolic elements. For example, the Technion's primary symbol displays a cogwheel and a plume of smoke, thus referencing the industrial horizon for this primarily engineering university. Still, the Technion's recent rebranding initiative, driven by the institution's internationalization, seeks to redesign this symbol into a more abstract logo-style icon: the general outlines of a triangle and a circle remain, but they do not recall the cogwheel or drafting tools that are included in the original emblem. As to be expected, this rebranding campaign was led by branding consultants within the Technion's new Marketing Division with the aid of contracted branding consultancy firms.

The professionalization of the branding of academia in Israel is also evident in the structuration of branding within academia. Of Israel's 69 accredited academic institutions, 22 have an administrative unit dedicated to marketing and PR and charged also with the branding of the institution; most others have such functions enveloped in a spokesperson's office, and a very few, mostly very small, colleges place the public affairs of the institution solely in the President's care. Also, the units charged with branding almost exclusively include "marketing" in their formal title, and often also PR; the titles of a few also include the terms "registration" (two institutions), "media" (one) or "image" (one). Such differentiation of media, PR, marketing, and branding functions from the spokesperson's role, as well as the bundling of media, PR, marketing, and branding into a single operational unit, speak to professionalization: whereas a spokesperson is tasked with delivering the word of leadership, branding is conceived as publicizing the character of the academic institution.

The personnel of the university administrative units charged with marketing, PR, and branding are all professionals in these fields. The heads of most of these units spent their careers in advertising agencies, management consultancies, or media firms. Some led branding campaigns in smaller colleges, either as unit heads in these colleges or as their contracted branding consultants, before moving on to head units in the research universities. Obviously, this "revolving door" of professionals opens the bounds of academia to professional codes and management strategies that were, until recently, antithetical to the spirit of academia.

Institutional Outcomes

Professional expertise is a prized source of legitimacy (Ernst and Kieser 2002; Zald and Lounsbury 2010; Suddaby and Viale 2011). Therefore, branding professionals are authorized to speak for organizational identity, here of academia. The influence of branding professionals – inside universities and as exogenous consultancy – signals the "socialization of science" (Drori et al. 2003), namely the penetration of society-wide practices and modes of thinking into academia. Specifically, it signals the penetration of "brand society" (Kornberger 2010) into academia, where "the product turns out to be nothing but the material extension of the brand" (Aaskegaard 2006: 100 in Kornberger 2010: 18). In this context, branding concerns legitimately intervene also with core academic considerations: the university's branded image as a "world class" institution or as a "science and engineering" institution guides decisions on such principal matters as course offerings and budget allocation. In this way branding became the metaphorical dog's tail that "wags" the university it purports to serve.

Further challenging the autonomy and authority of academia, the boundary-spanning character of professional branding services, which allows for branding professionals and expert knowledge to flow and traverses the formal boundaries of the particular university, confirms that the modern university is a "partial organization" (Ahrne and Brunsson 2011). Whereas academia has always been structured as a network of universities, with much of its life occurring in the "invisible college" of collegial relations (Crane 1972), in the case of branding of academia in the current era, the bonds of the professional character of the organization are opened. Professional business consultancies link universities to organizations outside academia, thus reifying the definition of the university as an organization like any other.

Professionalized branding acts in complex ways to affirm the institution of the university and to construct the particular university it is charged with. On the one hand, branding expertise de-contextualizes the university: professional branding neutralizes the institution through abstraction and "best practice" routines. On the other hand, branding expertise simultaneously re-contextualizes the university by requiring that branding accentuates the particular and unique characteristics of the specific university and distinguishes it from all other universities and all other organizations. With that, branding professionalism means that uniqueness is defined in standardized tools, akin to Roland Robertson's notion of the "universalism of particularism" and to Michel Foucault's notion of "omnes et singulatim" (totalizing and individualizing).

Concluding Comments

Worldwide and in Israel, the privatization of higher education was accompanied by intensifying administrative governance, and these brought about the reign of managerialism over academia. Managerialism weakens the once guild-like autonomy of faculty in universities and of academia as a whole. In the context of a loosely coupled system that is coordinated and managed by administrators even if formally governed by faculty, the door is open to "organization," namely a modern, rationalized, professionalized, and agentic entity (Drori et al. 2006). And the transformation of the university into a modern organization (Krücken and Meier 2006; Ramirez 2010) that is increasingly governed by a regulation-based administrative regime (Ramirez and Christensen 2013) is fraught with institutional barriers to policy implementation and reform. Shoham and Perry (2009) detail the challenges facing Israeli universities in implementing technological changes, and the challenges are far greater when identity conflicts are stirred by branding campaigns.

The rise of managerialism in universities is not merely a response to the evolution of the university, but it is mainly a normative shift in the social role of higher education: from a public institution of study and research to a "knowledge corporation" which operates in a global marketplace of knowledge and education (Scott 2012: 11). Putting this change in historical perspective, Sir Peter Scott adds that "the days when Clark Kerr could describe, even in jest, the university as a set of 'faculty entrepreneurs held together by a common grievance over car-parking' are long gone" (Scott 2012: 11), replaced by a new form where "universities are crossing, or have crossed, boundaries in their governance and (especially) management – and there is no way back to the old ways, despite the quiet despair of many senior professors" (Scott 2012: 11). Professionalization is the spirit of managerialism in universities: professionalization of university administration and the professionalization of the service economy to which many of the administrative tasks are outsourced.

The profession of branding consultancy acts as an epistemic community for strategic identity work in organizations in general, and lately in universities and colleges. In this manner, professional knowledge is a prime ordering mechanism, introducing a rationalized and standardized order to organizations and, with that, mitigating the complexity of markets or uncertainty. Branding consultancies, even those that specialize in academia, equate universities to any other organization, thus confirming the recasting of the university as a modern organization (Krücken and Meier 2006; Ramirez 2010). With professionalization as a powerful driver for modern organization in general (Drori et al. 2006, 2009), the professionalization of the branding of academia drives the notion of the university as a modern organization that, in recent years, has opened itself up to marketized and mediatized managerial models and to commercial interests.

Notes

1 As distinguished from ancient branding, which focused solely on the marking of proprietary ownership, modern branding has 3 main distinctions: (1) a strong link between branding and marketing; (2) the conflation of branding with identity, culture, and image; and (3) the professionalization of branding services.

2 Amendment 10 to the Council of Higher Education Law, 1995.

References

Ahrne, G. and Brunsson, N. (2011). Organization outside organizations: The significance of partial organization. *Organization*, 18(1): 83–104.

Aspara, J., Aula, H. M., Tienari, J. and Tikkanen, H. (2014). Struggles in organizational attempts to adopt new branding logics: The case of a marketizing university. *Consumption Markets and Culture*, 17(6): 522–552.

Aula, H. M., Tienari, J. and Wæraas, A. (2015). The university branding game: Players, interests, and politics. *International Studies of Management and Organization*, 45(2): 164–179.

Bok, D. (2003). *Universities in the marketplace: The commercialization of higher education.* Princeton, NJ: Princeton University Press.

Chapleo, C. (2011). Exploring rationales for branding a university: Should we be seeking to measure branding in UK universities? *Journal of Brand Management*, 18(6): 411–422.

Clark, B. R. (1998). *Creating entrepreneurial universities: Organizational pathways of transformation.* Oxford: Pergamon and IAU Press.

Crane, D. (1972). *Invisible colleges: Diffusion of knowledge in scientific communities.* Chicago: University of Chicago Press.

Davidovitch, N. and Iram, Y. (2011). Globalization and higher education reforms: Legislation, policy, and market forces in Israel. *Educational Practice and Theory*, 33(2): 43–62.

Davidovitch, N. and Iram Y. (2014). Regulation, globalization and privatization of higher education: The struggle to establish a university in Israel. *Journal of International Education Research*, 10(3): 201–218.

Delmestri, G., Oberg A. and Drori, G. S. (2015). The unbearable lightness of university branding: Cross-national patterns. *International Studies of Management and Organization*, 45(2): 121–136.

Drori, G. S., Delmestri G. and Oberg, A. (2013). Branding the university: Relational strategy of identity construction in a competitive field. In Engwall, L. and Scott, P. (Eds), *Trust in higher education institutions.* (pp. 134–147). London: Portland Press.

Drori, G. S., Meyer J. W. and Hokyu Hwang (Eds) (2006). *Globalization and organization: World society and organizational change.* Oxford: Oxford University Press.

Drori, G. S., Meyer, J. W. and Hokyu Hwang. (2009). Global organization: Rationalization and actorhood as dominant scripts. In Meyer, R., Sahlin, K., Ventresca, M. and Walgenbach, P. (Eds). *Research in the sociology of organizations: Ideology and institutions,* 27: 17–43.

Drori, G. S., Meyer, J. W., Ramirez, F. O. and Schofer, E. (2003). *Science in the modern world polity: Institutionalization and globalization.* Redwood City, CA: Stanford University Press.

Engwall, L. (2008a). The university: a multinational corporation? In Engwall, L. and Weaire, D., (Eds), *The university in the market.* (pp. 9–21). London: Portland Press.

Engwall, L. (2008b). Minerva and the media: Universities protecting and promoting themselves. In Mazza, C., Quanttrone, P. and Riccaboni, A. (Eds), *European universities in transition: Issues, models and causes.* (pp. 32–48). Cheltenham: Edward Elgar.

Ernst, B. and Kieser, A. (2002). In search of explanations for the consulting explosion. In Sahlin-Andersson, K. and Engwall, L., (Eds), *The expansion of management knowledge: Carriers, flows, and sources.* (pp. 47–73). Redwood City, CA: Stanford University Press.

Etzkowitz, H., Webster, A. and Healey, P. (Eds) (1998). *Capitalizing knowledge: New intersections of industry and academia.* Albany, NY: SUNY Press.

European Commission. (2012). *Higher education in Israel.* A Tempus study, No. 9. Brussels: EACEA.

Feeney, M. K. and Welch, E. W. (2012). Realized publicness at public and private research universities. *Public Administration Review,* 72(2): 272–284.

Gaziel, H. H. (2012). Privatisation by the back door: The case of the higher education policy in Israel. *European Journal of Education,* 47(2): 290–298.

Gray, B. J., Shyan Fam, K. and Llanes, V. A. (2003). Branding universities in Asian markets. *Journal of Product and Brand Management,* 12(2): 108–120.

Hasse, R. and Krücken, G. (2013). Competition and actorhood: A further expansion of the neo-institutional agenda. *Sociologica Internationalis,* 51(2): 181–205.

Hearn, A. (2010). 'Through the looking glass': The promotional university 2.0. In Aronczyk, M. and Powers, D. (Eds), *Blowing up the brand: Critical perspectives on promotional culture.* (pp. 197–219). New York: Peter Lang.

Hearn, A. (2015). The politics of branding in the new university of circulation. *International Studies of Management and Organization,* 45(2): 114–120.

Hemsley-Brown, J. and Oplatka, I. (2010). Market orientation in universities: A comparative study of two national higher education systems. *International Journal of Educational Management,* 24(3): 204–220.

Holmberg, I. and Strannegård, L. (2015). Students' self-branding in a Swedish business school. *International Studies of Management and Organization,* 45(2): 180–192.

Kornberger, M. (2010). *The brand society: How brands transform management and lifestyle.* Cambridge: Cambridge University Press.

Kornberger, M. (2015). Think different: On studying the brand as an organizing device. *International Studies of Management and Organization,* 45(2): 105–113.

Kosmütski, A. (2012). Between mission and market position: Empirical findings on mission statements of German higher education institutions. *Tertiary Education and Management,* 18(1): 57–77.

Krücken, G. and Meier, F. (2006). Turning the university into an organizational actor. In Drori, G. S., Meyer, J. W. and Hwang, H., (Eds), *Globalization and organization: World society and organizational change.* (pp. 241–257). Oxford: Oxford University Press.

Krücken, G., Albrecht B. and Kloke, K. (2013). The managerial turn in higher education? On the interplay of organizational and occupational change in German academia. *Minerva,* 51(4): 417–442.

Logue, D. M. (2010). *The diffusion of management innovations: Understanding 90 years of global organisational change in universities.* Doctoral dissertation. Oxford University.

Logue, D. M. (2014). Adoption and abandonment: Global diffusion and local variation in university top management teams. In Drori, G. S., Höllerer, M. A. and Walgenbach, P. (Eds), *Global themes and local variations in organization and management: Perspectives on glocalization.* (pp. 175–188). London: Routledge.

March, J. G., Schulz, M. and Zhou, X. (2000). *The dynamics of rules: Change in written organizational codes.* Redwood City, CA: Stanford University Press.

Marginson, S. (2002). Competition and markets in higher education: A 'glonacal' analysis. *Policy Futures in Education,* 2(2): 175–244.

Marginson, S. (2006). Dynamics of national and global competition in higher education. *Higher Education,* 52(1): 1–39.

Melewar, T. C. and Akel, S. (2005). The role of corporate identity in the higher education sector: A case study. *Corporate Communications: An International Journal,* 10(1): 41–57.

Menahem, G. (2008). The transformation of higher education in Israel since the 1990s: The role of ideas and policy paradigms. *Governance,* 21(4): 499–526.

Menahem, G., Tamir, E. and Shavit, Y. (2008). Changes in Israel's higher education system in the 1990s. In Yogev, A., (Ed.), *Spread of Higher Education in Israel.* (pp. 25–54). Tel Aviv: Ramot.

Meyer, J. W. (2010). World society, institutional theories, and the actor. *Annual Review of Sociology*, 36: 1–20.

Meyer, J. W., Boli, J., Thomas G. M. and Ramirez, F. O. (1997). World society and the nation-state. *American Journal of Sociology*, 103(1): 144–181.

Müller, M. (2010). *Brandspeak: The homogeni-euphemization of language and meaning and the idea of internal branding.* Paper presented at the 2010 European Group for Organizational Studies Conference.

Osman, H. (2008). Re-branding academic institutions with corporate advertising: A genre perspective. *Discourse and Communication*, 2(1): 57–77.

Press, E. and Washburn, J. (2000). The kept university. *Atlantic Monthly*, 285(3): 39–54.

Prince, R. (2014). Consultants and the global assemblage of culture and creativity. *Transactions of the Institute of British Geographers*, 39(1): 90–101.

Ramirez, F. O. (2010). Accounting for excellence: Transforming universities into organizational actors. In Rust, V., Portnoi, L. and Bagely, S. (Eds), *Higher education, policy, and the global competition phenomenon.* (pp. 54–75). London: Palgrave.

Ramirez, F. O. and Christensen, T. (2013). The formalization of the university: Rules, roots, and routes. *Higher Education*, 65(6): 695–708.

Rhoten, D. R. and Powell, W. W. (2010). Public research universities: From land grant to federal grant to patent grant institutions. In Rhoten, D. and Calhoun, C., (Eds), *Knowledge Matters.* (pp. 319–345). New York: Columbia University Press.

Robertson, R. (1994). Globalisation or glocalisation? *Journal of International Communication*, 1(1): 33–52.

Robertson, R. (2014). Situating glocalization: A relatively autobiographical intervention. In Drori, G. S., Höllerer, M. A., and Walgenbach, P. (Eds), *Global themes and local variations in organization and management: Perspectives on glocalization.* (pp. 25–35). London: Routledge.

Schultz, M., Hatch, M. J. and Larsen, M. H. (Eds) (2000). *The expressive organization: Linking identity, reputation, and the corporate brand.* Oxford: Oxford University Press.

Scott, P. (2012). Crossing boundaries: Mass higher education in multiple perspectives. *Higher Education in Review*, 9: 1–14.

Serrano-Velarde, K. and Krücken, G. (2012). Private sector consultants and public universities: The challenges of cross-sectoral knowledge transfers. *European Journal of Education*, 47(2): 277–289.

Shoham, S. and Perry, M. (2009). Knowledge management as a mechanism for technological and organizational change management in Israeli universities. *Higher Education*, 57(2): 227–246.

Slaughter, S. and Rhoades, G. (2004). *Academic capitalism and the new economy: Markets, state, and higher education.* Baltimore, MD: Johns Hopkins University Press.

Spellman, R. (2011). *Managers and leaders who can: How you survive and succeed in the new economy.* Chichester, UK: John Wiley & Sons.

Suddaby, R. and Viale, T. (2011). Professionals and field-level change: Institutional work and the professional project. *Current Sociology*, 59(4): 423–442.

Volansky, A. (2005). *Academia in a changing Environment: Higher education policy in Israel 1952–2004.* Hakibbutz Hameuchad Publishing.

Von Nordenflycht, A. (2010). What is a professional service firm? Toward a theory and taxonomy of knowledge-intensive firms. *Academy of Management Review*, 35(1): 155–174.

Wæraas, A. and Solbakk, M. N. (2009). Defining the essence of a university: Lessons from higher education branding. *Higher Education*, 57(4): 449–462.

Wedlin, L. (2008). University marketization: the process and its limits. In Engwall, L. and Weaire, D. (Eds), *The university in the market*, Wenner-Gren International Series 84. (pp. 143–153). London: Portland Press.

Willmott, H. (2003). Commercializing higher education in the UK: The state, industry and peer review. *Studies in Higher Education*, 28(2): 129–141.

Wissema, J. G. (2009). *Towards the third generation university: Managing the university in transition*. Cheltenham: Edward Elgar.

Zald, M. N. and Lounsbury, M. (2010). The Wizards of Oz: Towards an institutional approach to elites, expertise and command posts. *Organization Studies*, 31(7): 963–996.

Zehavi, A. and Zer, N. (2013) A public road to globalization: Public services and customer internationalization in Israel. *Administration and Society*, 45(2): 187–212.

Zwick, D. and Cayla, J. (Eds) (2011). *Inside marketing: Practices, ideologies, devices*. Oxford: Oxford University Press.

Part III
New Market Niches

12 Financial Markets and Investment in Education

Diego Santori, Stephen J. Ball, and Carolina Junemann

Private sector involvement in education is not something new. In our previous work we have sought to map and categorize the participation of business in public sector education at a national level (Ball 2007) and the increasing role of business, social enterprise, and philanthropy in education service delivery and education policy at a global level (Ball 2012). In this chapter, we revisit the *financescape* of global *edu-business*, with particular attention to the role of venture capital and private equity investment, in order to account for its relation to educational opportunities and education policy. In order to illustrate the changing nature of investment in education, we map the emergence of specialized players in the education investment sector. We then focus our analysis on the Pearson Affordable Learning Fund (PALF) as a case in point of developmental investment in the sector, drawing upon secondary sources as well as data from interviews conducted as part of a Leverhulme Trust-funded study on new philanthropy, education policy and governance.[1]

According to the *ICEF Monitor*, a dedicated market intelligence resource for the international education industry, '2013 was bookended by major investment transactions that drew headlines around the world and called attention to the fact that investors are taking a greater interest in key education sectors.' Ed-Tech is a paradigmatic illustration of this exponential growth in business interest in education as an investment opportunity characterised by a dramatic increase in the *volume* and *speed* of transactions. The US represents the largest Ed-Tech market in the world. According to CB Insights (2014), a venture capital and angel investment database, while the reported overall Ed-Tech investment remained below USD $100 million in the first quarter of 2012, it surpassed half a million dollars in the first quarter of 2014 via 103 transactions, attracting more venture capital and angel investors than ever before. Indeed, *Education Week* notes that:

> Venture capital is flowing into the sector at a torrential pace, fuelled by the belief that start-ups can use new digital tools to transform education – and generate profits. At the same time, established companies are changing the way they do business, shifting from print to digital resources and materials, and merging with or acquiring other companies to help them make that transition.
>
> (Education Week 2014: 1)

Notably, based on customer metrics from Strategy Analytics, a US-based market research and consultancy firm, the McKinsey–GSMA (2012) report highlights:

> 25 million education-linked apps were downloaded in 2009 and 270 million in 2011 – a more than tenfold increase. The growth in free education apps has been significantly higher than the overall market growth. Paid education apps have also grown to 36 million downloads in 2011, representing a total revenue of USD $120 million – a sharp rise over the 4.5 million paid downloads in 2009 worth USD $15 million.
>
> (McKinsey–GSMA 2012: 12)

Many of these Ed-Tech products have turned into significant business deals, such as Providence Equity Partners acquiring BlackBoard Inc. (an education software company that developed BlackBoard Learn, a virtual learning environment and course management system) in 2011 for around USD $1.64 billion; the sale of a 90 percent stake in Wireless Generation (mobile assessment software) to News Corporation in 2010 for approximately USD $360 million; and Research in Motion's acquisition of Chalk Media (the developer of Mobile chalkboard, a software to create, manage, and track mobile content including courses and training materials) in 2008 in an all-cash deal of USD $18.7 million (Education Week 2014: 24; McKinsey–GSMA 2012). Overall, these changes in the volume and speed of business transactions have modified the *topography* of the education sector globally, bringing new players into education service delivery, of different kinds, and altering the network of interactions between investors and providers.

A Changing Ecosystem

Education has moved from being a rather marginal area of investment with focus on private institutions and publishing, to become a central node with unprecedented capacity to attract funding from investors. This is a shift from the periphery of the investment scene to the center of private equity firms' portfolios. Indeed, GSV Advisors (2012c) claim that Tier 1 venture firms such as ACCEL Partners, Benchmark Venture Partners, Bessemer Venture Partners, Greylock Partners, Highland Capital, Kleiner Perkins Caufield and Byers, and Sequoia Capital have all entered the education market. Consonant with these developments, companies such as peerTransfer, Groockit, UniversityNow, 2Tor, Edmodo, BetterLesson, Atilus Ed, Chegg, and Piazza have raised capital from at least three private equity firms (see Appendix 1).

This relatively recent centrality of education as a space for profitmaking within financial markets is apparent in the emergence of specialized *eduspace* players. First has been the emergence of *specialized non-profit investment ventures,* which aim to transform particular sectors of education by investing in high-potential initiatives. New Schools Venture Fund raises capital from individual and institutional investors to fund teacher training (Learning to Teach Fund), charter schools and charter districts (DC Fund, Boston Fund, Oakland Fund), and education technology start-ups (Seed Fund). There are also segment-specific non-profit investment ventures such as the US-based Charter School Growth Fund, with a focus on 'select investments in charter school management organizations that deliver outstanding academic results, while achieving sustainability on public revenues' (CSGF).[2]

A second group of new players in the eduspace is *specialized financial advisors*. One illustration of this is GSV Advisors, an education-sector-focused investment bank based in Chicago. GSV Advisors provide merger and advisory and private placement services with a focus on Ed-Tech. With over 20 years in the market, GSV claims to have completed 283 transactions totaling over USD \$41.2 billion. For instance, GSV was the exclusive financial advisor for the sale of Lexia to Rosetta Stone in August 2013 for USD \$22.5 million, advisor for the sale of Campuslabs to Higher One in August 2012 for USD \$85.4 million, and advisor for the sale of The Learning Company in 1999 for USD \$3.3 billion (GSV Advisors 2012a).

GSV stands for 'Global Silicon Valley', suggesting that 'Silicon Valley is no longer just a physical place, but also a mindset that has gone viral' (GSV Advisors 2012a). As part of their interest in creating the condition of possibility investment and leverage, GSV Advisors have published two white papers that are full of images, famous quotes, and figures. Both reports are structured around a fundamental challenge that threatens the collective possibilities of existence of a given community, a challenge to be confronted by a group of risk-takers that are willing to go beyond the limits of imagination. With the image of Berliners celebrating the fall of the wall on the front cover, GSV's white paper titled *Fall of the Wall: Capital Flows to Education Innovation* (GSV Advisors 2012b) claims that 'The "wall" of opposition to investing in education has come down, for now, bringing in a welcome flood of financial and entrepreneurial capital'. Under the title *Revolution 2.0: How Education Innovation is Going to Revitalize America and Transform the US Economy* (GSV Advisors 2012c), Ed-Tech is portrayed as a 'tidal wave' that can bring innovation to unimagined horizons. In addition, GSV Advisors, together with Arizona State University (ASU), run the *Education Innovation Summit*, which they refer to as 'the Knowledge Economy's Mecca of conversation and activism devoted to accelerating learning innovation around the world' (GSV Media 2014). The 2014 edition was sponsored by 50 companies and organizations including the Bill and Melinda Gates Foundation, Pearson, Microsoft, Dell, AT&T, and McGraw Hill Education. The summit included keynote speeches from Netflix Chief Executive Officer (CEO) Reed Hastings and even celebrities such as National Basketball Association legend and global social entrepreneur Earvin Magic Johnson, interviews with major figures such as the US Secretary of Commerce Penny Pritzker, speeches from former Governor of Florida Jeb Bush, Donald Graham (founder of Graham Holdings, lead director of Facebook, and former Chairman and CEO of the Washington Post Company), and presentations from 190 other influential speakers from the 'global Ed-Tech ecosystem'.

Another example of specialized financial services is Education Growth Advisors (EGA n.d.), a Boston-based firm that provides strategic consulting, investment banking, and financial advisory services to companies and investors that 'span the

Global Pre-K–12, postsecondary, corporate and lifelong learning sectors'. They claim to have participated and closed on more than USD $3.5 billion in education and media transactions over the past 15 years. Interestingly, EGA differentiate themselves from other wide-ranging financial advisors by their sector-specific knowledge: 'our investment banking solutions enable companies, institutions, and investors to better navigate the constantly evolving education landscape and to help identify where specific risks and growth opportunities may reside'.

The third new group of players is *specialized education private equity investors*. A landscape survey by Leventhal and Tang (2013) has identified 266 US private equity firms, which have made significant investments in education-related companies. While most private equity firms in their study have a multi-industry approach, they have identified 12 education-exclusive ones:

> Education Growth Partners
> Epic Partners
> Hart Capital
> Imagine K–12
> Kaplan Ventures
> Learn Capital
> Leeds Equity Partners
> Macmillan New Ventures
> Quad Ventures
> Renovus Capital
> Rethink Education
> University Ventures

'The Twelve', as Leventhal and Tang call them, have diverse investment parameters, that range from a focus on early stage companies (Kaplan Ventures with investments from USD $200,000 to USD $5 million) to a focus on more established companies (Education Growth Partners, Hart Capital, and Renovus Capital with investments over USD $5 million).

Fourth, *specialized incubators and accelerators* have also emerged. Imagine K–12 is a start-up accelerator focused exclusively on companies that work to improve K–12 educational outcomes. Start-ups like ClassDojo, a student behaviour management tool, and Educreations, a platform to create and share video lessons, are among its most successful incubations. Interestingly, large education companies have also launched their own incubators. ICEF Monitor notes that 'big for-profit education companies have noticed the baby start-ups creeping into their space. In response, instead of trying to squish them fee-fi-fo-fum style, these companies have introduced accelerators to work with them' (ICEF 2014).[3] First, Kaplan has introduced an Ed-Tech accelerator in partnership with Techstars, a mentorship-driven start-up boot camp. The program offers selected companies a USD $20,000 equity investment from Techstars and an optional USD $150,000 convertible note from Kaplan, as well as mentorship from top entrepreneurs, access to decision makers such as US school districts and university partners, and office space provided by Kaplan in New York. Second, Pearson has launched the Catalyst accelerator program, in partnership with 1776, an incubator platform based in Washington, DC, and aims to 'match start-ups with Pearson brands to deliver pilot programs' (Pearson).[4] Pearson Catalyst sets ten challenges each year and start-ups are selected based on their ability to address one of them. Funded start-ups include Actively Learn, an online literacy platform, Learnmetrics, a data analytics tool for schools, and Mathspace, a cloud-based application for students and teachers. Finally, McGraw-Hill is investing in the Education Design Studio, Inc., a start-up incubator program and seed fund, in partnership with the University of Pennsylvania's Graduate School of Education and venture capitalists and investors.[5]

Finally, *specialized funds*. The development of funds to tackle some of the world's most challenging issues is currently a shared practice in international development. Multilateral agencies such as the World Bank Group, (with a USD $150 million equity stake in Laureate Education, Inc. through the International Finance Corporation), bilateral agencies such as DfID (with investments in Bridge International Academies through Novastar Ventures), and philanthropic organisations such as the Acumen Fund and Children's Investment Fund are examples of this trend. However, education-focused private equity funds are new to the ecosystem. Private equity funds are collective investment schemes (typically structured as limited partnerships) used for making long-term investments in companies (Fevurly 2013; Robertson 2009). These investment pools benefit from the inherent advantages of economies of scale, such as lower management and transaction costs. For example, Kaizen is India's first private equity fund focused on the education sector, with plans to invest USD $75 million by 2019. They have already invested USD $3.6 million in corporate day care and preschool and afterschool service provider Your Kids R Our Kids, and participated in Series B in 2013 with the online education platform WizIQ. The Pearson Affordable Learning Fund is 'a for-profit venture fund, in response to the vital market opportunity and government need for low-cost private education in the developing world'.[6] With USD $15 million of initial Pearson capital, the Affordable Learning Fund was launched in July 2012 with the aim to help improve access to quality education for low-income families. In the following section we provide a brief overview of the evolution of the Pearson business and its rebranding as an education/learning company to frame our subsequent analysis of PALF's origins, aims, strategies, and portfolio.

A History of Acquisitions, Mergers, and Sales

Founded by Samuel Pearson in 1844 as S. Pearson and Son, and initially concerned with building and engineering services, Pearson is now the world's largest education company and book publisher. Its early acquisitions include the *Financial Times* (1957), Longman (1968), and Penguin (1970), just one year after going public on the London Stock Exchange. More recent transactions in the education market evidence three main areas of investment.

Testing and assessment is a growing area of investment, as evidenced by key acquisitions such as the US-based educational testing and data management company National Computer Systems (NCS) in 2000 for USD $2.4 billion; the British examination awarding body Edexcel in 2003 for £75 million; the acquisition of Harcourt Assessment and Harcourt Education International from Reed Elsevier in 2007 for USD $950 million in cash; and the recent success in a competitive tender by the Organisation for Economic Co-operation and Development (OECD) to develop the Frameworks for the Programme for International Student Assessment (PISA) 2018.

English language is another major area of investment for Pearson, particularly in fast-growing economies. Examples of this are the acquisition of Wall Street English, a chain of English language learning centers, in 2009 for USD $145 million; the acquisition of a controlling stake in TutorVista, an Indian network of English language coaching centers and classroom ed-tech provider, in 2010 for USD $127 million; the purchase of the Chinese English-language test preparation provider Global Education and Technology Group (GETG) in 2011, in a deal worth USD $294 million, and the acquisition of Brazil's largest private network of English language schools Grupo Multi in 2013 for £500 million.

Finally, software and online learning solutions have been the focus of recent transactions, with significant investments such as the acquisition of the value-added postsecondary and K–12 education information service eCollege in 2007 for USD $477 million; the acquisition of the instructional improvement education software company Schoolnet in 2011 for USD $230 million; the acquisition of Connections Education, an online public school for students in grades K–12 available in many states in the US in 2011 for USD $400 million; and the acquisition of the online learning services provider EmbanetCompass in 2012 for USD $650 million.

Interestingly, Pearson has gradually disinvested in non-education business,[7] as evidenced by the selling off of a 61 percent stake in the financial market information and analytics provider Interactive Data Corporation in 2010 to private-equity firms Warburg Pincus and Silver Lake Partners for USD $2 billion; the sale of FTSE International Limited, a global leader in indexing, to the London Stock Exchange Group plc. in 2011 for USD $450 million; and the sale of the Mergermarket Group, a media company specializing in corporate financial news and analysis, to funds advised by BC Partners in 2013 for £382 million.

Pearson has re-invented itself as an education, or 'learning' company. Pearson's self-defined purpose is 'to help more people make progress in their lives through learning' (Pearson) and it argues that it has a responsibility as the world's leading learning company 'to support educational improvement and to actively share our experience on models that work and those that do not' (Pearson plc 2012: 7).

This has, at least, two aspects to it. One is a relationship to governments and policy through testing and the management of 'big data' – its wholesale business in a sense. The other is 'retail' business and has two aspects to it. One is the provision of standardized services and materials (curricula, pedagogy, assessment, finance and management) for running educational institutions; the other is the development of personalized 'learning solutions' for individual consumers, evidenced by Pearson's partnership with the Knewton Adaptive Learning PlatformTM, a recommendation engine for learning (Pearson).

The Need for Affordable Solutions to Global Challenges in Education

As part of its re-working as a 'social purpose' company, Pearson also sees itself having a responsibility to contribute solutions to the world's educational problems: 'Our responsibility as a company is to play our full part in informing, shaping and making learning effective for people of all ages, abilities and locations. This focus on learning outcomes is a critical part of our responsibility vision' (Pearson plc 2012: 6).

Drawing upon data from United Nations Educational, Scientific and Cultural Organization (UNESCO), PALF's website highlights that access and achievement still represent a major challenge for education systems in developing countries:

> Despite USD $75 billion of aid dedicated to education over the last seven years, 57 million children remain out of school. Even more challenging is the issue of achievement: in sub-Saharan Africa, after five years of education, a child still has a 40 percent chance of being illiterate.
>
> (UNESCO)[8]

This global crisis, PALF argues, cannot be tackled by public systems alone, but demands a joint effort from both governments and the public sector. Indeed, PALF claims that the private sector is already contributing to increasing access, since, for instance, the ratio of low-cost private schools enrollment amounts to 70 percent in Delhi, 64 percent in Accra, 70 percent in Lagos, and 67 percent in Punjab (Pakistan).[9] Taken together, the scale of the problem and its urgency, in the light of the Millennium Development goal for universal primary schooling, are presented as the grounds for private intervention. These views set the scene for Pearson's interest in the design of products and services for high-growth emerging markets as part of their long-term strategy. Accordingly, John Fallon, Pearson CEO, notes:

> All around the world parents want their children to be educated, and their children want to go to school. But for those living in poverty there is often not much choice of school or much access to a good one that can teach those children effectively. Sometimes charity provides those choices, but charity cannot by its nature be reliable, nor does it give the parents the dignity and privilege of providing their children's education. We believe that a free-enterprise model of low-cost schools – schools affordable for many of the poorest – may be the best chance to provide both benefits.[10]

As Sir Michael Barber explained in interview:

> So we've set up this fund, the Pearson Affordable Learning Fund, which I
> chair, and it's – we've got fifteen million dollars, which is not a huge sum of
> money in the scale of things but … but we think it's enough to …. What we
> want to demonstrate is that with an injection of capital and the governance
> that goes with it – and we will take minority stakes in businesses that are
> developing, either chains of schools or providers of support services to chains
> of schools – we can demonstrate that you could improve the quality of that
> sector and you could build the sector.
>
> (Sir Michael Barber, interview, 7 August, 2012)

The Pearson Affordable Learning Fund (PALF)

In creating PALF, Pearson was interested in moving away from its traditional position as mid-market and high-end operator in education. As Katelyn Donnelly, the
managing director of PALF, explained:

> Pearson traditionally has been a US–UK company that has been a book pub-
> lisher; how do we actually think about how does Pearson approach emerging
> markets in developing countries and can it provide low-cost education for
> the mass market? And that's when we decided to set up this venture fund to
> see if it's possible.
>
> (Katelyn Donnelly, interview, 23 November, 2014)

This expansion towards the lower income market was influenced by C. K. Prahalad,
the author of the well-known article and book *The Fortune at the Bottom of the
Pyramid* (2002), who used to sit on the Pearson board. Ravi Patel, business development manager at PALF, noted that Scardino and Prahalad 'had a joint vision to say
how Pearson can impact low-income communities across the world with educational products and services' (Ravi Patel, interview, 17 September, 2013). Scardino
recruited Sir Michael Barber from McKinsey and Company in 2011, who founded
PALF a year later. Barber's framing of the problem conveys a sense of urgency
towards incorporating available policy solutions that can be easily scaled up:

> The question every education leader needs to answer is: 'How do we get every
> child in this district, city, state, province or country a good education as soon
> as possible?'. Low-cost private education is becoming an increasingly impor-
> tant part of the answer, in almost every country in the developing world.[11]

However, PALF acknowledges that, given most schools are small standalone
schools run by local proprietors with access to a limited array of teaching and
learning practices, only investment in best practices towards efficacy and scale can
meet the demands of investors and the need for social impact. According to Patel,
Barber and other senior executives mapped the low-cost education space globally

over a six-month period[12] and 'realised that low-cost private schools exist but no one is really investing in them in an institutionalized manner' (Ravi Patel, interview, 17 September, 2013). These fieldtrips resulted in case studies that informed the design of the fund, 'how they were going to invest, in what areas, what stage of investments, and what they were looking for in business models' (Ravi Patel, interview, 17 September, 2013). The scope of the sector included school chain case studies in India (BRAC, Gyan Shala, M.A. Ideal, Pudami, and Takshashila), Kenya (Bridge International Academies), Ghana (Omega Schools), and Uganda (PEAS), as well as service provider case studies in India (ARK and Gray Matters Capital) and Colombia (Escuela Nueva), with particular attention to school, growth, and business models of each company. These chains of schools are based 'in markets where Pearson wants to have a bigger footprint going forward', and hence the creation of a for-profit fund is aimed to 'ensure that the schools or the Ed-tech you invest in are scalable, and can generate revenue, and through generating revenue you will naturally have an impact' (Ravi Patel, interview, 17 September, 2013).

While PALF works under the premise that 'governments are unable to take the risks needed to produce the innovation required to change education systems',[13] governments are not excluded from their business approach. Quite the contrary, they envisage governments as key partners in the long run:

> So if we can work with governments through our investments, whether it's Omega Schools in Ghana, for example, and say to the government, hey, look at this school chain, you should fund this in three years' time once it's grown to a big enough size, you should partner with us for vouchers or public–private partnerships. That's the long-term view of the investments we make.
> (Ravi Patel, interview, 17 September, 2013)

A Global Portfolio

With a focus on high quality, for-profit education solutions for the low-income segment in the developing world, PALF's investment approach encompasses:

- an investment horizon of 5–10 years, with competitive market returns generated over the investment lifecycle;
- minority to significant minority equity stake investments, with strategic input and board representation;
- investment in proven models and credible management teams (seed stage, Series A and beyond).

One significant sector of investment for PALF is low-fee private school chains.

Bridge International Academies (BIA) is a for-profit chain of low-cost nursery and primary schools in Kenya. Founded in 2009 by Jay Kimmelman, Shannon May, and Phil Frei, BIA received initial funding from Deutsche Bank America's Foundation, Gray Ghost Ventures, and the Kellogg Foundation through the

Clinton Global Initiative (see Junemann 2015). In 2009 BIA got off the ground with a further USD $1.8 million investment from the Omidyar Network, which led its Series A investment round and participated equity in a second and third rounds of funding in 2010 and 2012 (Series B and C).

Before the creation of PALF in 2012, Pearson had already invested in the LFPS sector, leading BIA's Series B investment round, through the Learn Capital fund, an education venture capital firm that concentrates on education technology start-ups, in which Pearson is the biggest limited partner (Learning Capital n.d.). The first formal investment in the sector since the creation of the Affordable Learning Fund was Omega Schools, a chain of LFPS founded by Ken Donkoh and James Tooley in 2009, with the aim of scaling up the service. A central feature of this chain is the 'Pay as You Learn' system, which is an all-inclusive daily fee designed to meet the needs of households living on daily wages.

More recent investments in the LFPS sector include Affordable Private Education Centers in 2014, a chain of low-cost secondary schools in the Philippines. This is a joint venture with the Ayala Corporation, the largest conglomerate in the country.[14] Another investment in the LFPS sector is eAdvance, which runs a South African school chain called SPARK Schools. SPARK schools incorporate a blended learning model with adaptive software. PALF invested in SPARK during a Series A round in 2014 to support the expansion of the school network over the next three years.

Ed-tech is another key area of investment for PALF, with a recent focus in India. Avanti Learning Centers received seed investment from PALF in 2013 of less than £500,000, with two angel investors. The start-up education company operates stand-alone and in-school centers across India, providing college exam preparation for low-income students. Another illustration of PALF's interest in the sector is Zaya Labs, a school service provider delivering blended learning experiences for schools serving students from low-income families, as noted by the recent announcement (May 2014) of a minority equity investment by PALF with an additional angel investor. Zaya Labs flagship product is the LabKit, which comprises 'low-cost tablets, a projector, curated digital content and ClassCloud, an adaptive learning platform that can store and deliver digital content in both online and offline environments' (Business Standard 2014).

Finally, like other big edu-corporations, Pearson is investing in education start-ups through another incubator business program called Edupreneurs. The program, as a partnership between PALF and Village Capital, is focused on enterprises that can achieve 15–25 percent internal rate of return over five years, with plans to raise more than USD $500,000 within the next two years, and consists of 'three activity-based, modular workshops, each 4 days long, over 12 weeks, supplemented with regular webinars and online communication with program staff and mentors.[15] Starting with a focus on understanding the strengths and weaknesses of each individual project, the workshops are designed to help participants refine their scope and objectives (the value proposition and demonstrating customer validation and traction) as well as financial support, including methods of calculating valuation, setting reasonable projections and negotiating term sheets;

'an insight into their own enterprises through the lens of the investor'.[16] A significant feature of the program is that the participants themselves choose the ventures that receive funding through a peer ranking process based upon six central criteria: (1) Team, (2) Product, (3) Customer validation, (4) Financials, (5) Scale and impact, and (6) Return of capital. Since rankings are public, participants have to defend their assessment to the whole cohort. Edupreneurs' first cohort was launched in India in 2013, where 14 participants received training and mentorship from PALF and VilCap. The winners of the 2013 edition were Experifun, which offers low-cost interactive science learning products aimed at improving science learning at the 6–10 grade level, and Sudiska, a chain of low-fee pre-schools across Andhra Pradesh and Hyderabad. Both start-ups received seed investment of USD \$50,000.

The second Edupreneur workshop series ran in South Africa in 2014–2015, which we attended as part of our research work. Out of around 120 applicants, 13 start-ups from 5 African countries were selected to participate, focused on providing for-profit solutions to the 'challenges plaguing the educational ecosystem in Africa'[17] as identified by PALF and VilCap, that is, access to quality affordable education, including pedagogy and curriculum relevance. Not surprisingly, technology innovation was a significant focus of activity among the selected participants (online platforms for digital learning content and mobile applications), related to PALF's and VilCap's belief that technology 'carries the power to open up access to communities living below the poverty line or off the grid'.[18] A low-fee private secondary school start up in Nigeria was also part of the cohort. At the time of writing this chapter, the third and final peer-ranking had not yet taken place, but it was specified that the two top ranking companies would be eligible to receive up to USD \$75,000 each (drawn from USD \$100,000 and USD \$50,000 of capital committed by Pearson and Village Capital, respectively). PALF's incubator programs rest on the idea that the participating edupreneurs would benefit not just from the potential financial investment but also from a broader set of social and intellectual capitals. As Yiming Ma, PALF's senior business development lead – African Markets, noted, 'Many education entrepreneurs have transformational ideas, but lack the business background or industry relationships to successfully operationalize their novel concepts' so the workshops aim to instill in them 'superior business acumen and [provide access to] a network of mentors and industry relationships' (Ma 2014).

Overall, PALF's investments are clearly not one-off transactions but represent a wider interest in building the low-fee school sector. As Ember Melcher, the Edupreneurs program manager, explained in an interview:

> We are an ecosystem player at the same time as being an investor. I think that's also one of the reasons why we started the Edupreneurs incubator. And so even though I find a lot of companies that can't directly benefit us, it's still a great working environment because we understand that it's in our best interests to have as many entrepreneurs succeed as possible in this sector, because it proves that it is possible.
>
> (Ember Melcher, interview 5 May, 2013)

That is to say, Pearson's strategy for growth is not simply based on the accumulation of assets but on the development of an ecosystem, incorporating new players and producing regulatory frameworks to shape their interactions.

> I wouldn't rule out a Pearson chain but that's not – we're not thinking about that at the moment. We're not systematically thinking about that. We're looking to take minority stakes and learn what works and demonstrate it and demonstrate that bringing in private capital could make a big contribution to solving the problems of the developing world.
>
> (Sir Michael Barber, interview, 7 August, 2012)

Conclusion: Investment Beyond Investment

In this chapter, we have discussed some of the ways in which the increase in the volume and speed of equity investment in edu-business is significantly transforming the dynamics of the sector. Furthermore, we noted the entry of new players in the education ecosystem, such as specialized equity investors and advisors, as well as impact funds, accelerators, and incubators, extending the scope and breadth of the private sector. But perhaps more importantly, our analysis also suggests the emergence of a more subjective form of investment, an investment in discourse. This new kind of investment is manifested in three main forms and courses of action. The first one is investment in creating the conditions of possibility for the proliferation and leverage of for-profit education 'solutions', that is, investment in the development and growth of a for-profit education service ecosystem. Through comprehensive overviews of the sector, such as landscape reports, as well as more informal channels such as blogs or tweets, this type of investment aims to convey a sense of ubiquity, inevitability and magnitude, as noted by the metaphors and symbols deployed. As noted above, GSV reports and PALF's website illustrate this point.

The second type of investment is investment in the development of an entrepreneurial culture, evidenced by the increasing investments from large edu-corporations in the development of Dragons' Den-like incubators and accelerator programs such as those recently announced by Pearson, Kaplan, and McGraw-Hill and the work of PALF as an incubator, investor, and site of the discourse of enterprise. This operates in both specific and general ways. Specifically, through workshop activities PALF inducts its participants into modes of business thinking. Generally, by pumping investment funds into local educational economies it gives impetus to and creates spaces in which for profit 'solutions', outside or over and against state provisions, are given possibility and legitimacy.

A final form of investment relates to the production and diffusion of forms of rationality that delineate and to some extent govern intelligibility. Again, Pearson's 'efficacy framework' (Hogan et al. 2015) and GSV's Return on Education suggest that these frameworks can also be understood in terms of assets with potential capital appreciation for the due diligence of future investments. This rests on Pearson's re-focus on learning outcomes (in some kind of relation to financial ones) and the use/sale of data to support policy decisions (both in-house and by governments) and to identify 'what works' in education.

Taken together, these changes in the volume and speed of investment in edu-business and the extension of the for-profit business model, with its emphasis on efficiency, as a frame of legitimation seem to displace or maybe silence the questions of equity that these 'disruptive innovations' may pose. There is a felicitous concomitance here between corporate investment in educational services and the displacement of public by private provision and individual investment in education for self-improvement and future returns.

Notes

1 This research looks at global policy networks through a focus on Low-Fee Private Schools (LFPS) in sub-Saharan Africa.
2 http://www.bloomberg.com/research/stocks/private/snapshot.asp?privcapId=102233672.
3 http://monitor.icef.com/2014/02/money-talks-major-private-investments-in-educa tion-reflect-expectations-for-further-growth-ahead/.
4 http://catalyst.pearson.com/about/.
5 http://blogs.edweek.org/edweek/marketplacek12/2013/10/mcgrawhill_other_companies_ invest_in_penn_startup_venture.html.
6 https://www.affordable-learning.com/about/vision.html.
7 with the exception of the acquisition of the premier macro policy intelligence provider to investment banks Medley Global Advisors in 2010 for an undisclosed sum.
8 https://www.affordable-learning.com/resources/what-is-affordable-learning.html.
9 PALF references the data for Pakistan as based on the findings of a DfID-commissioned Nielsen household survey carried out in 2011 (not publically available for scrutiny). However, estimating enrollment rates in the low fee private school sector is fraught with methodological difficulties (see for example Walford 2013) and a DFID-commissioned systematic review of the evidence on the sector concludes that there is a critical gap in the evidence in relation to the true extent and diverse nature of private schools (Day Ashley et al. 2014).
10 https://www.affordable-learning.com/about/pearson.html.
11 http://www.affordable-learning.com/what-is-affordable-learning/Whyafund. html#sthash.ITJQUsdv.dpbs.
12 See PALF's Notes from the field, available at http://www.affordable-learning.com/news-views/notes-from-the-field.html#sthash.ehJRb5bV.dpbs.
13 http://www.affordable-learning.com/what-is-affordable-learning/Whyafund. html#sthash.ICQV124q.dpbs.
14 http://www.affordable-learning.com/what-is-affordable-learning/Whyafund. html#sthash.ICQV124q.dpbs.
15 https://www.affordable-learning.com/edupreneurs/further-details.html.
16 https://www.affordable-learning.com/edupreneurs/further-details.html.
17 https://www.affordable-learning.com/blog-and-news/blog/06-11-12-workshop1.html.
18 https://www.affordable-learning.com/blog-and-news/blog/06-11-12-workshop1.html.

References

Ball, S. J. (2007). *Education plc: Understanding private sector participation in public sector education.* London: Routledge.
Ball, S. J. (2012). *Global education inc. New policy networks and the neo-liberal imaginary.* London: Routledge.

Business Standard. (2014, 20 May). Pearson makes minority investment in Zaya Labs. Retrieved 15 April, 2015 from: http://www.affordable-learning.com/news-views/viewpoints_blog.html#sthash.4Im4LxTP.dpbs.

CB Insights. (2014, 5 April). Global edtech financing hits record in Q1 2014. Retrieved 23 April, 2015 from: https://www.cbinsights.com/blog/ed-tech-venture-capital-record/.

Day Ashley, L., Mcloughlin, C., Aslam, M., Engel, J., Wales, J., Rawal, S., Batley, R., Kingdon, G., Nicolai, S., and Rose, P. (2014). *The role and impact of private schools in developing countries: A rigorous review of the evidence*. London: Department for International Development.

Education Growth Advisors. (n.d.). *Website*. Retrived 24 April, 2015 from: http://edgrowthadvisors.com/services/strategic-consulting/.

Education Week. (2014). Navigating the Ed-Tech marketplace. *Special report on K–12 educational technology*. Retrieved 29 July, 2014 from: http://ew.edweek.org/nxtbooks/epe/ew_06112014_v2/index.php#/0.

Fevurly, K. (2013). Private equity funds. In *The Handbook of Professionally Managed Assets*. (pp. 209-228). New York: Apress.

GSV Advisors. (2012a). Retrieved 22 July, 2014 from: http://gsvadvisors.com/.

GSV Advisors. (2012b). Fall of the wall: Capital flows to education innovation Retrieved 23 July, 2014 from: http://gsvadvisors.com/wordpress/wp-content/themes/gsvadvisors/GSV%20Advisors_Fall%20of%20the%20Wall_2012-06-28.pdf.

GSV Advisors. (2012c). Revolution 2.0: How education innovation is going to revitalize America and transform the U.S. economy. Retrieved 24 July, 2014 from: http://gsvadvisors.com/wordpress/wp-content/themes/gsvadvisors/American%20Revolution%202.0.pdf.

GSV Media. (2014). ASU+GSV Summit. Retrieved 18 July, 2014 from: http://asugsvsummit.com/.

Hogan, A., Sellar, S., and Lingard, B. (2015). Network restructuring of global edu-business: the case of Pearson's efficacy framework. In W. Au and J. J. Ferrare (Eds), *Mapping corporate education reform: power and policy networks in the neoliberal state*. New York: Routledge.

ICEF Monitor. (2014, 12 February). Money talks: Major private investments in education reflect expectations for further growth ahead. Retrieved 14 April, 2015 from: http://monitor.icef.com/2014/02/money-talks-major-private-investments-in-education-reflect-expectations-for-further-growth-ahead/.

Junemann, C., Ball, S.J. and Santori, D. (2015). Joined-up Policy: network connectivity and global education policy. In K. Mundy, A. Green, R Lingard and T. Verger, *Handbook of Global Policy and Policy-Making in Education*. New Jersey, Wiley-Blackwell.

Learning Capital. (n.d.). Retrieved 21 April, 2015 from: http://www.learncapital.com/.

Leventhal, M. and Tang, I. (2013, 3 September). Specialized Eduspace investors: 'the twelve'. Retrieved 23 April, 2015 from: https://equityforeducation.wordpress.com/2013/09/03/specialized-eduspace-investors-the-twelve/.

Ma, Y. (2014, May 5). Starting a new relationship in education. *Stanford Social Innovation Review*, Retrieved 15 April, 2015 from: http://www.ssireview.org/blog/entry/starting_a_new_relationship_in_education.

McKinsey–GSMA. (2012). Transforming learning through mEducation. Retrieved 31 July, 2014 from: http://www.gsma.com/connectedliving/wp-content/uploads/2012/04/gsmamckinseytransforminglearningthroughmeducation.pdf.

Pearson plc. (2012). Our impact on society. Retrieved 14 January, 2015 from: http://cr2012.pearson.com/assets/downloads/Pearson_Summary_Corporate_responsibility_report_2012.pdf.

Pearson. (n.d.). *Website.* Retrieved 25 April, 2015 from: http://catalyst.pearson.com/about/.

Prahalad, C. K. and Hart, S. L. (2002, 10 January). The fortune at the bottom of the pyramid. Retrieved 22 April, 2015 from: http://www.strategy-business.com/article/11518.

Robertson, J. (2009). Private equity funds. *New Political Economy, 14*(4), 545–555. doi: 10.1080/13563460903288270.

Walford, G. (2013). Low-fee private schools: A methodological and political debate. In P. Srivastava (Ed.), *Low-fee private schooling: Aggravating equity or mitigating disadvantage?* (pp. 199–213). Oxford: Symposium Books.

Appendix 12.1 Top tier VCs, Super Angels and growth investors have re-entered the market

Investors	Year	Investment
ACCEL	2011	Fidelis College
	2008–2010	Knewton
	2010–2011	LearnVest, Inc.
	2011	peerTransfer
Atlas Venture	2009	EnglishCentral
	2010–2011	Grockit
	2009	Simpletuition
Andreessen Horowitz	2011	Hyperink
	2009	Kono
	2011	Science Exchange
Bessemer Venture Partners	2009–2012	2Tor
	2007–2009	Cornerstone OnDemand
	2010	FlatWorld
	2010	LearnBoost
	2012	Piazza
	2009–2011	Knewton
BrainCapital Ventures	2010	MyEdu
Benchmark	2007–2011	Grockit
	2011	Edmodo
	2012	The Minerva Project
Charles River Ventures	2010	Altius Ed
	2011	CampusLive
	2010	LearnBoost
	2012	Udacity
Foundation Capital	2011	Airy Labs
	2008	Chegg
	2008–2011	Tree House Education
GSV	2011	Altuition
	2009	Altius Ed
	2011	Apangea Learning
	2012	Avenues: The World School
	2003	Capella Education
	2011	Chegg
	2012	CorpU
	2011	Dreambox Learning
	2011	Fingerprint Play
	2012	Fullbridge
	2012	Global Education Learning
	2009	GoingOn
	2011	Grockit
	2010	HotChalk
	2011	Kno
	2012	Maven

	2010	MyLanguage 360
	2011	rSmart
	2011	Stormwind Studio
Greylock Partners	2011	Edmodo
	2011–2012	Treehouse
	2012	UniversityNow
Highland Capital Partners	2010–2012	2Tor
	2011	BetterLesson
	2011	CampusLive
Kapor Capital	2011	Desmos
	2011	EduLender
	2010–2011	Inkling
	2011	Magoosh
	2011	MindSnacks
	2011	Motion Math
	2012	Piazza
	2012	SendHub
	2010–2012	UniversityNow, Inc.
KPCB	2010	Callaway Digital
	2008–2012	Chegg
	2012	Codeacademy
	2012	Coursera
	2008	StudyPlaces
Learn Capital	2012	Acceptly
	2011	Desmos
	2010–2011	Edmodo
	2011	Formative Learning
	2012	LearnZillion
	2011	MasteryConnect
	2012	OneSchool
	2011	ShowMe
	2012	Verbling
Maveron	2009–2010	Altius Ed
	2011	General Assembly
	2010–20011	KidZui
	2010	Latimer
	2009–2011	LiveMocha
	2011	peerTransfer
Menlo Ventures	2011	Lumos Labs
New Markets Venture Partners	2011	Apangea
	2011	BetterLesson
	2010–2011	Moodlerooms
New Schools Venture Fund	2009	BetterLesson
	2010	Beyond12

(continued)

Investors	Year	Investment
	2011	ClassDojo
	2012	Educreations
	2012	Education Elements
	2012	EdSurge
	2012	Engrade
	2012	eSpark
	2012	GoalBook
	1999	GreatSchools
	2011	Grockit
	2011	Junyo
	2011	LearnZillion
	2011	Mastery Connect
	2012	Mytonomy
	2011	Presence Learning
NEA	2012	Coursera
	2010	EverFi
Novak Biddle Venture Partners	2009–2012	2Tor
	2009–2010	Capital Schools
	2011–2012	Parchment
	2011	Fidelis College
	2011–2012	PlaySay, Inc.
	2008	Spectrum K12
	2010–2012	UniversityNow, Inc.
Norwest Venture Partners	2010–2011	BookRenter
	2011	iProf
	2011	Lumos Labs
Redpoint Ventures	2009–2012	2Tor
Shasta Ventures	2011	Coursekit
Sequoia Capital	2010–2011	Inkling
	2011	Piazza
	2006–2008	TutorVista
	2011	Tutorspree
Spark Capital	2009–2010	8D World
	2010–2011	Academia.edu
	2009–2010	Altius Ed
	2010–2011	peerTransfer
	2011	Skillshare
University Ventures	2011	Ameritas
	2001	EDEX
	2011	Synergis Education
	2012	UNnow
Warburg Pincus	2008	iParadigms

Source: GSV Advisors. (2012c).

13 Unbundling the University and Making Higher Education Markets

Susan Robertson and Janja Komljenovic

Introduction

Markets do not simply appear as a result of policymaker diktat or policy fiat. And nor do markets – once made – exist in a space which sits outside, or beyond, a society and its complex of institutions and practices. Rather, markets are both made and remade, as new products and services, frontiers and spaces, are imagined, invented, implemented, inventoried, vetted and vetoed. Yet as Berndt and Boeckler argue, despite the ubiquity of markets, "the market is rarely treated as a process, to be taken seriously in its own right" and that "for all their force and spatial relevance" many researchers working on markets have "steered clear of attempts to achieve a better understanding of how markets are assembled and put to work" (Berndt and Boeckler 2012: 203). We agree with them. This, in the case of higher education, means examining the processes involved in unbundling existing institutionalised higher education practices which constitute the non-market university sector, *and* bringing into view "societal transformations and the investment necessary to make markets work" (Berndt and Boeckler 2012: 205).

It follows that, in order to understand the making of higher education markets, we need to focus our attention on what we call "moments" in the making of higher markets. These include those moments when policymakers, politicians, investment advisors, education firms, and universities begin to imagine higher education as a "new," "emerging," or "mature" market to be opened up and exploited; the governance frameworks which shape a sector (including the role universities play as market actors and profit-making centers), are challenged, repurposed, and transformed; and when the nuts and bolts of making diverse higher education products and services that are exchanged in a range of marketplaces – from identifying suppliers to developing a sustainable "customer" base, creating niche opportunities, pricing of products and services, providing a means for accessing credit, developing a means for settling disputes over contracts, use of legal tools and advice, and so on – are bought together and put to work. What we have called different moments might also be referred to as macro, meso, and micro processes involved in making higher education markets.

Our wider purpose in this chapter is to show the complexity of these processes so as to open up what has become something of a black box, at worst, and a flat canvas at best. Politically this is important in that, if higher education markets require work, by opening up and revealing this activity, we not only see power and interests at play, but the basis on which these processes and outcomes might be challenged and changed.

Our chapter is developed in the following ways. We begin by locating our approach to studying higher education markets (Komljenovic and Robertson 2015; Robertson and Komljenovic 2015). We then introduce four cases that we work through using this approach – showing that market-making takes a great deal of *ongoing* political, economic, and cultural work by a range of actors, institutions, technologies, instruments, and the strategic deployment of space, time, and sociality. We conclude by reflecting on the epistemic gains of this approach and what it reveals regarding the unbundling of the university and its remaking in terms of market processes and relations.

Studying Higher Education Markets – Approaches and Entry Points

We start with a reminder that, in mainstream economic theory, markets are understood to be governed by impersonal laws, where arms-length relations between disembodied economic agents prevail. Agents are in this sense reduced to those with calculative competencies who respond to price signals (Callon and Muniesa 2005; Peck and Theodore 2007). In line with this logic, the construction of a market is dependent on the disentangling and framing of agents and goods so that calculations can take place (Garcia 1986). Yet as sociologists remind us – most notably Polanyi (1944) and Granovetter (1972) – markets are not impersonal but are instead instituted and embedded in society, a point we will return to shortly.

Looking at the literature on markets in higher education, the focus has tended to be on market ideology, as represented in those policy discourses aimed at reforming higher education (Brown 2011a; Jessop et al. 2008), or on the extent to which those discourses reflect a perfect "free market" (Brown 2011b; de Boer and Jongbloed 2012; Jongbloed 2003; Marginson 2013, 2014). While making an important contribution to policy analysis and ideology critique, this approach falls short on revealing *how* markets get made from non-market activity – the key question we are grappling with here.

More recent work on networks in the study of creating education service industries (Ball 2007, 2012; Hogan et al. 2015) do make visible the actors and their relations with each other. But what is missing for us are the micro-processes at work – such as framing goods and services in such a way that they are amenable to exchange, the design and maintenance of markets, pricing, and so on.

With our interest in *processes of market making*, we have found the work of Karl Polanyi (1944) useful as a starting point. Polanyi argued that markets have to be produced through social institutions, and legal and political strategies and processes – in what he called "institutedness" (see Slater and Tonkiss 2001). But in order to make a link between broader social transformations that make market making thinkable and possible (macro), to the actors and techniques that deliver the detail of the "who" and "how" (meso and micro) of market making, we have also drawn on the work of Berndt and Boeckler (2009, 2012) and that of Çalışkan and Callon (2009, 2010). In this way we link together different macro, meso, and micro processes to make visible the complex moments in the work of market making.

As Berndt and Boeckler (2012: 205) also point out, market making takes "investment" – that is ongoing effort is expended in "framing markets" through the development and deployment of policies, technologies, instruments, and other "formatting devices." For example, trade departments in various countries develop calculations of the value of higher education trade to the economy, and represent this in terms of gross domestic product (GDP). Similarly, in framing higher education as a services sector consistent with the trade in goods, the World Trade Organization has used the same kind of language found in the *General Agreement on Trade in Goods* (Robertson et al. 2002) – such as "commercial presence," "presence of natural persons" – to frame education in the *General Agreement on Trade in Services* as part of an education services market. Investment means exerting effort – such as enrolling those who might ease the way, side-stepping or confronting head on regulatory difficulties, advancing operations in spaces where the regulations are more lax, or being imaginative about new ideas, products and services and how to get these into the marketplace.

This takes us to the importance of micro-processes, or the micro-foundations of market making. Çalışkan and Callon's (2009, 2010) work is a useful starting point in that they develop a conceptual grammar though which to undertake that task. They elaborate five processes at the micro level that they call "framings" of markets: pacifying goods; marketizing agencies; market encounters; price setting; and market design and maintenance. In the different cases that we present in the second part of this chapter, we show these different elements at work.

Pacifying goods refers to those dynamics in which things (that range from material things, services, to human beings or human relations, and other intangibles) are disentangled, made passive and stable, and invested in. Disentanglement or unbundling of intangibles is a process of representing things and services as "packages" that are describable and predictable. Passivity in this respect refers to stability, predictability, and having fixed qualities to which value and price can be attached. This is why investment in standardization, stabilization, and domestication of such new things in the market context is crucial (Çalışkan and Callon 2010). This might mean framing a higher education institution as an object that can be bought or invested in; a student experience as a thing to be bought with clear distinctive elements that are part of the package; or information about the higher education sector as intelligence worth buying to guide strategic decision making. These processes are sometimes difficult to frame as objects for market exchange, especially because of cultural and political notions of higher education as a non-market sector. Consequently the process of pacifying goods is in constant dynamic with perpetually changing managing entities.

Marketizing agencies set in train a complex of dynamics whereby many actors compete in defining what is a good or service, and in valuing them. This process takes place in socio-technical *agencements* – that is, arrangements of people, technology, tools, laws, calculations, and so on. A competitive university, for example, is likely to depend upon a range of socio-technical arrangements so as to create an efficient market actor. This might include the creation of new positions – such as the market analyst. It might also involve other processes, such as increasing the number of staff in the marketing department; building new market intelligence computer software; creating techniques to determine strategic markets from which to recruit students; or engaging private companies to help with specific tasks (such as Internet marketing in Nigeria or alumni engagement in the Middle East) (see Drori's chapter in this volume).

Market encounters refer to the need for market agencies (such as students, academics, administrators, investors, regulators) and pacified goods to meet one another. Such encounters are multiple, and part of overlapping calculations (Çalışkan and Callon 2010). In our four cases there are a huge number of market encounters, some coincidental, but most created – higher education fairs, industry conferences, invitational seminars. Market encounters are also virtual, material, social, and technological arrangements, using the Internet, social media, or web pages. Market encounters are invested in, and thus cost money, labor, and time.

Çalışkan and Callon (2010) argue that marketization theory is successful if it manages to present the above three processes; however, it is incomplete without two more micro-foundations: the study of *price setting* and *market design and maintenance*. In terms of price setting, Çalışkan and Callon (2010) argue that this is where valuations and calculations emerge – as prices, but establishing a price is a struggle between different agencies. Our cases reveal a range of ways in which prices are created – such as using other prices (for example, existing fees for public universities) to create prices (fees for online student enrollment), or determining how much to "sell" specific services for to the university. But it is not only the seller who determines price; we have shown that the university also decides on the prices it is willing to pay when acting as a buyer by comparing offers in the market (Komljenovic and Robertson 2015).

The last framing is *market design and maintenance* (Çalışkan and Callon 2010: 19). As implied, the design and maintenance dimensions help bring into being, as well as reproduce, those elements that enable more efficient use of resources, the extraction of profits, the legitimation of the activity as a commodity, and ongoing stability. But the ways in which markets are conceived and shaped are diverse. Those involved in design and maintenance might create working groups and advisory committees to which they invite representatives from universities to reflect on new products and strategies. They might finance conferences, host marketing retreats, or award honors to particular individuals, so as to buy the support of well-placed individuals, and thus ensure market maintenance. An important part of design and maintenance is the creation of relations of trust, which in turn help to lubricate markets, but building trust requires investment.

Imagining and Making Higher Education Markets – Encountering Cases, Generating Insights

It is now time to introduce the four cases drawn from a much larger piece of empirical work we are undertaking on making higher education markets, which is funded by a European Commission grant.[1] Data includes interviews, documents (annual reports, websites, financial statements), newspaper reports, and other secondary data sources such as statistical databases. All four cases are framed inside wider macro-level social transformations (Jessop et al. 2008; Leys 2003; Marginson and Considine 2000; Robertson 2010; Slaughter and Rhoades 2004).

Reformatting and Lubricating International Student Recruitment Flows and Markets

INTO University Partnerships Ltd (INTO) is a private limited company based in the UK, founded by Andrew Colin (who is still the chairman), and incorporated in 2005. Its initial focus was on recruiting international students into foundation programs that the joint venture between INTO and universities would deliver – and from there to place the students into an undergraduate program. INTO builds on the macro-level transformations of higher education aimed at making the (public) education sector into an industry, contributing to national economic development measured in terms of GDP. In this respect universities are diversifying their financial incomes by tapping into the "international student market." In doing so universities also become marketizing agencies.

INTO first created two joint ventures in 2006 with the University of East Anglia and the University of Exeter. By 2015 it had expanded to 22 joint ventures in the UK, USA and China. So far the financial success of INTO and its centers/ventures is huge and growing. Data show that, in 2013, 7,000 students were enrolled in its joint ventures (INTO 2014). INTO, as a parent company with its shares in joint ventures (that is excluding financial data about the entirety of INTO and its joint ventures operations), had a turnover of £70 million in 2012 and £86.5 million in 2013 (INTO 2014). INTO reported its profit in terms of EBITDA (profit adjusted to add back depreciation, amortization, and exceptional items) as £9 million in 2012 and £6 million in 2013. In 2013, INTO had an equity investment from Leeds Equity Partners (New York), selling a 25 percent stake of its business for £66 million.

INTO centers and ventures continue to provide education for students entering UK or US universities; that is, undergraduate and graduate pathway courses, English language training, and diploma courses. Diploma courses act as the first year of undergraduate education if successfully completed, and are consequently innovative alternate ways to enter the second year of studies at public British and US universities. These programs are interesting also, in the sense that they act as an alternative route for students, and new revenue streams for the university. To students, INTO promises an excellent education, world class premises, study and pastoral support, and guaranteed progression to UK universities in case of successful completion of the pathway or diploma programs. INTO manages to guarantee enrollment after completion by helping its graduates to get places in their initial center, other universities in partnerships, or universities that do not have partnerships but are looking for foreign students.

Here we see an interesting example of pacifying goods as a way of market framing (Çalışkan and Callon 2010); the service that the student from another country is paying for has very clear elements and promises. In addition, INTO puts a lot of work into marketing "evidence," such as promoting student success rates, which are above 90 percent for practically all INTO centers. In order to sell student experience at a specific joint venture, INTO has to play strategically – disentangle it in just the right way from the attached university, but still keep the connection in order to create association to the established reputation of a pre-existing university. Moreover, it has to strike the acceptable way on how to present the things it sells and package them so that it is not foreign to the higher education sector and other actors in it.

Discursively, INTO legitimates its activities in the following ways. First, it argues that there is high demand for higher education from a growing body of students who cannot be accommodated in their home countries. Second, it argues that internationalization of higher education is crucial for the quality of study, and for the economic development of nations in the knowledge economy. Third, it argues that INTO partnerships "deliver" promised results – in terms of student numbers and student satisfaction, and also in terms of financial returns to partner universities and economic development to the countries they are located in. Thus making a profit and creating jobs are entangled together and conveyed in parallel with excellent education provision. Finally, INTO promotes itself as being able to guarantee such results.

This set of processes, and the quality of its operations, have also been legitimated by industry recognition. In 2011, INTO received the Exporting Excellence award from the magazine *Education Investor*, which recognizes the contribution education providers make to the UK economy – in INTO's case through the recruitment of international students and widening of access to the UK. It also won the title of the Higher Education Provider of the Year (INTO 2011).

INTO's market locations are further instituted through the creation of organizational structures within national legal systems, and by being in line with particular university decisions. For example, in the US, they take the form of university departments, since, legally, public universities cannot have this kind of cooperation with a private company. In the UK, INTO have instituted their market relations through joint ventures – new private companies owned half by INTO and half by the partner university – or new centers owned by INTO. This fits well with the wider regulatory environment in the UK which has promoted Public–Private Partnerships as the preferred governance model for public sectors (Robertson et al. 2012). INTO also guarantees contracts with selected British universities who are not partners in the sense of joint ventures, but engage in enrolling students who complete programs in INTO centers. These contracts enable INTO to find and guarantee study places for all students completing their programs. This is yet another example of Çalışkan and Callon's (2010) market framing by a marketizing agency. INTO invests in the process of the valuation of the services it delivers and their price. It actively promotes financial profits and education quality in order to establish new partnerships with universities. Participating universities consequently also become active agents in the process of market creation and expansion. Yet instituting these markets has not gone unchallenged. There are occasions when news is reported that university staff have protested about the university being approached by INTO to partner (Newman 2008). In 2007, there was a dispute between INTO and The University and College Union (a labor union from the UK) which publicly challenged INTO approaches, and published a briefing on its web page called "Into the unknown." INTO reacted with a threat to sue the union for defamation, after which the union removed the document from the Internet (Lipsett 2008).

In the different INTO partnerships, there are different arrangements as to how to organize labor and the INTO infrastructure. In some cases, staff from the university are recruited to teach also at the INTO centers; in other cases, new staff are recruited, mostly on fixed-term contracts. In some cases, the international office of the university works for the venture, or at least does some work; in other cases, the venture does it on its own. The criteria for staff recruitment and student recruitment is determined by the university and by the specific center/venture, but, in order to stay competitive and attractive, they are often lower than criteria for the universities in question. This dynamic is part of the changing relations within the higher education sector as a result of marketizing.

INTO promotes itself as offering world-class, purpose-built spaces and markets the millions of pounds of investments that it has put into new buildings. These centers offer study spaces and infrastructure and student dormitories. INTO helps universities access capital for these financial investments, which are often on the campus of partner universities. These new models of joint ventures and spaces for studying are based on the long-term partnership; in the case of one university, this is a 35-year period to which both parties commit and share the financial profits or losses, regardless of the circumstance. If specific ventures do not enroll students to cover costs (e.g. the government decides to restrict the migration of international students), the university would have to cover their part of any financial losses.

INTO is also experimenting with variety: some INTO centers will start to provide online courses as well as developing Massive Open Online Courses (MOOCs). While the markets around the primary activity of the company and its centers are about providing education leading to a university place, it is engaging in other markets too. One market is international student recruitment more generally; a two-decade-old "industry" populated by recruitment agents around the world, Internet recruiters, marketing companies, language schools, representation offices of universities in other countries, other companies with similar services like INTO, and national agencies such as the British Council. All of these actors use multiple technologies, ranging through soft diplomacy at the political level, visits to schools, attending fairs, advertising, social media, partnering with foreign universities or schools and so on. INTO's marketing budget is significant; it reports investing USD \$45 million per annum on marketing (INTO 2015 webpages). INTO is thus one of a growing number of similar actors positioning themselves as a legitimate and powerful player within the higher education sector (others include NAVITAS and StudyGroup).

INTO is a fascinating case of market making. Not only does it help lubricate the recruitment process of international students for universities, but its joint venture model enables the university to outsource what might have been more expensive activity for the university while benefitting from the efficiencies that INTO adds when they not only bring students to the campus, but make students "learning ready."

Financing New Higher Education Frontiers

Our second case is Laureate Education, now one of the largest global for-profit education companies in the world. In terms of macro and meso market-framing processes, for-profit firms have been encouraged, and selectively enabled, to operate in the higher education sector as providers of university credentials. The overarching political projects include neoliberalism, and knowledge economy strategies. Laureate Education is therefore only one of a growing number of for-profit universities who operate around the globe; what makes Laureate interesting is its financing model.

The Laureate footprint outside of the US tops that of any US higher education institution; 80 percent of its revenues come from outside of the US (Redden and Fain 2012). In 2015, it enrolled 950,000 students spread across 29 countries and over 75 campuses around the globe (Fain 2014a, 2014b) employing 70,000 employees, faculty, and staff (Laureate 2015 webpages). Students study mostly in low cost programs, such as education, health sciences, business education, engineering, and hospitality management.

Tracing through the history of Laureate Education helps illustrate the model of expansion: private equity investment; buying up highly indebted institutions; operating in those parts of the world where the regulatory environment is more conducive; a strong marketing department; most recently investment from the World Bank's private investment arm – the International Finance Corporation; and legitimacy through courting the rich and famous. These elements combine to make a particular kind of global higher education market.

Laureate Education began life under a different name and company – Sylvan Learning Systems, a public company, established Sylvan International Universities in 1998, and headquartered in Baltimore, Maryland in the US. Rapid expansion through global acquisitions is part of Laureate Education's DNA. In 1999, Sylvan Learning Systems acquired a 54 percent share of Universidad de Europea de Madrid for USD $51 million. In 2000, it added a hotel management school located in Switzerland, along with the Universidad de Las Américas, Chile, and the Universidad del Valle de México. In 2003, the company made the decision to focus exclusively on post-secondary education. It sold its interests in schools to Educate Inc., (formed by Apollo Management). By 2004, it had changed its name to Laureate Education Incorporated.

In 2007, Laureate Education was acquired by an investor group led by Doug Becker – and went private in a deal worth USD $3.8 billion (sized at 240,000 students located in 15 countries). Financial analysts said that going private enabled

Laureate to pursue a more aggressive strategy at a time when Wall Street was both skeptical of potential growth and emerging anxieties about investments more generally (Lederman 2007). The investor group included some of the biggest names in global finance: Henry Kravis (KKR), George Soros (Soros Fund Management), Steve Cohen (SAC Capital Advisors), and Paul Allen (Vulcan Capital). Kravis's firm, KKR, was reported to have taken a USD $487.5 stake (Kimes and Smith 2014) in Laureate Education. By 2010, KKR had increased its value to USD $710.8 million. And while Laureate Education's annual revenue is USD $4 billion, those in the industry worry about its very high level of indebtedness. In 2014, Moody's, the credit rating agency, downgraded the credit outlook for Laureate Education to "negative" from "stable," citing concerns about Laureate's increasingly leveraged position following its purchase of the Brazilian university – Centro Universitário das Faculdades Metropolitanas Unidas (FMU) for USD $500 million – bringing the total debt to USD $6 billion. This level of debt is more than Laureate's annual revenue (Fain 2014b).

Laureate Education's acquisition and investment model is fascinating and illustrates the development of strategies to pacify goods, and the refining over time of its market design (Çalışkan and Callon 2010). In his role as Chief Executive Officer of Laureate – Becker has to convince investors that Laureate is worth investing in, in persuading universities to sell a share to this private equity-backed business, and students to pay. Laureate's promise to students is that Laureate's close links to industry will enable them to secure a job in the future because of the social capital Laureate can mobilize.

Laureate has also pursued a rapid growth strategy, not so much in the US, though that is where the company's headquarters are, but in those countries with an emerging middle class, historically low levels of investment in higher education, and a regulatory environment more open to for-profit or private investments in education: for instance, Brazil, Chile, Mexico, Turkey, and South Africa. Laureate pulled out of plans to invest in India, in the face of uncertainty about whether higher education institutions could continue operating a for-profit model (Kinser 2010: 159). Its operational model is to build efficiencies through economies of scale the Laureate network brings (Kinser 2010: 159).

Laureate invests a great deal in marketing; its budget is around USD $200 million, and telemarketers are new kinds of agents who have scripts and recruitment targets (Çalışkan and Callon 2010). Those turning in a good sales performance are promised bonuses (Kimes and Smith 2014). This level of spending means there need to be cost savings elsewhere; in comparison to a more conventional university, Laureate has most of its academic teaching staff on part-time contracts, and contracts which do not involve and value research.

Laureate's investment strategy has changed over time. In an interview with Paul Fain reported in InsideHigherEd in 2014, Becker stated that, in the early days of Laureate, we would

> go around the world to identify countries that were experiencing the most severe imbalance of supply and demand – who would really benefit from our assistance and support – and find a partner in each country. And we would

typically invest in the university as a financial partner and an operating partner with the local entrepreneur.

(Fain 2014a)

More recently, Laureate has also partnered with non-profit and high ranked institutions, such as Monash University to deliver Monash's investments in South Africa, and the University of Liverpool in the UK. For instance, Laureate provides the platform for Liverpool's online degrees; Laureate students are able to study in Liverpool summer school programs, and Laureate provided the £1 million bond and financial backing for Liverpool to operate its joint venture in China – X'ian Jiaotong Liverpool University, near Shanghai (Ball 2012: 132).

In 2013, the International Finance Corporation, a member of the World Bank Group, made a USD \$150 million equity investment in Laureate, to expand access to quality higher education in "emerging markets." In the same year, Coursera, a major provider of Massive Open Online Courses, announced that it had raised USD \$43 million in funds from an investment group that included Laureate Education.

Laureate has also courted the politically rich and famous which helps both in terms of marketing and in market maintenance (Çalışkan and Callon 2010). Two examples are worth noting. In 2010, former US President Bill Clinton was made an Honorary Chancellor for Laureate. Other members of Clinton's administration also have roles in key executive and board positions. As Honorary Chancellor, President Clinton is reported to provide advice on matters such as social responsibility, youth leadership, and increasing access to higher education. On Laureate's website, Clinton states:

> These private universities exemplify the same principles of innovation and social responsibility in education that we worked to advance during my presidency and now through my foundation, and I am pleased to support their mission to expand access to higher education, particularly in the developing world.
>
> (Laureate Education 2015 website)

In Turkey, Laureate acquired an ailing Bilgi University in Istanbul. In 2010, Laureate's Universidad de Europea de Madrid awarded Turkish Prime Minister Erdogan an honorary doctorate.

This does not mean that Laureate has always managed to convince the regulators as to the probity of its investments. In 2013, Laureate tried to set up a joint venture with the US Arizona-based Thunderbird School of Global Management. However the accreditor for Thunderbird, the Higher Learning Commission, raised a series of questions about standards – a move that can be understood against a wider set of concerns in the US around for-profit provision. The Apollo Education Group, with significant investments in the US under its flagship University of Phoenix, have found themselves financially under-performing as a result of "a series of lawsuits, tight governmental scrutiny, above average costs, and below industry-standard quality" (Zimmerman et al. 2015).

Infrastructures and Data Markets

Universities use many services and products for which they do not necessarily pay, and thus there is no immediate monetary compensation (e.g. social media). In this respect, using such services might not be interpreted as market activity if we were to follow economic theory. However, universities are feeding into the opportunities of companies to operate in other markets, or are transforming themselves to take advantage of new market possibilities. Transformations at the macro level are tied to new digital technology developments. These are characterised by speed, immediate information dissemination, low (re)production costs, and immense innovation opportunities. Higher education does not stay intact and market innovations successfully penetrate education institutions and individuals through particular solutions at the meso level, which are in turn designing new markets.

LinkedIn is a fascinating case in this regard. LinkedIn is a corporation (public company) based in the US and created in 2003, an Internet platform specializing in professional networking. It relies on people creating their professional profiles around their education, career, skills, work experience and so on, and then connecting to people they know. It allows people and organizations to use basic services for free (in the sense of not paying to have a profile), or to pay a premium subscription to use additional features of the platform, such as checking who has viewed their profile, connecting to people they do not know, sending messages to them, and so on. These subscriptions are one out of three income streams for LinkedIn, the other two being "talent solutions" and "marketing solutions."

Based on the last available annual report (LinkedIn 2014) LinkedIn had 277 million members in 2013 and showed substantial growth in memberships, Internet visitors to its platform, and usage of services. It reported intensive service development in 2012 and 2013 that resulted in new ways of showcasing members' profiles, new services, and more people signing up. The year 2013 was a record in the company's history, as 75 million subscribers signed up. For 2013, revenue was USD $1.53 billion. The fastest growing income stream for LinkedIn of the three mentioned above is "talent solutions," that is, subscriptions employers (or anybody else) can pay to LinkedIn to use LinkedIn data for searching for new employees or people's profiles in more detail.

LinkedIn has developed a variety of services and products that draw data from people's profiles and their networking, and are targeted to different audiences. Such services include: creating one's own profile as a brand, networking, and connecting to known and unknown people; writing stories, news, and opinions; browsing peoples' profiles; getting information about companies; university rankings; employers' rankings; social selling; participating in groups; using alumni tools; and so on. It has also developed services and products specific to higher education that target individuals and universities. LinkedIn says 24,000 universities are represented on the LinkedIn platform worldwide. In both cases, people are motivated to keep their profiles as populated as possible with up-to-date information about skills, education, experience, endorsements and volunteer work, and to add projects, videos, and documents. Besides individuals, LinkedIn promotes

222 S. Robertson and J. Komljenovic

the benefits of rich profile data to universities and advises them to motivate their own students, alumni, and staff to upload all relevant and attractive information. Universities and organizations are motivated to create their own profiles too and form virtual social groups with students, alumni, or other interest groups to communicate and connect. It recently developed a set of university rankings based on employment and careers which is for now reserved for specific disciplines and countries, and which has the potential to become widespread.

Data provided by individuals, universities, companies and other organizations are then analyzed and repackaged by LinkedIn and offered back to different audiences, some for free and some for fees/rents. In this respect, it is crucial for LinkedIn to have as many users as possible with up to date information. Based on this data it can offer attractive products to anybody: for example, individuals, governments, universities, employers.

There is a pattern emerging here; the laboring is done by the individuals and universities who populate parts of the LinkedIn pages they use but who are not financially compensated. The company then uses the information produced by such laboring for other products and services through which it earns profits. In this sense LinkedIn's market framing – of creation, expansion, and maintenance (Çalışkan and Callon 2010), is dependent on how successful it is in attracting individuals and organizations to do such free labor, on the one hand, and how successfully it infiltrates the operations of different organizations or lives of individuals, on the other. The more useful it becomes for different actors, the more LinkedIn can reframe such use-values into commodities (exchange-values).

We also note an attempt by LinkedIn to gain a monopoly in what it does, which is why they visit universities and other actors in different countries, consulting on which services might best be developed into the future. This is an interesting development. On the one hand, it is co-creating such services as they become use-values for them (by participating in discussions on what would be created in the future); on the other hand it is populating data and using services, and later using them or paying for them as they become a new product. Moreover, if the LinkedIn rankings gain in impact, it will contribute to building a reputation and brand management of universities across the globe. If universities aim to improve their LinkedIn ranking, it will also be in their interest to motivate its own successful alumni to create their LinkedIn profiles by keeping them up to date, and by being active in discussions and other LinkedIn services in order to influence the ranking algorithm. This has the potential in the future of becoming a self-reinforcing forward-moving dynamic growth.

These peculiar markets do not need specific regulatory changes, but do get materialized as universities became dependent on them, at least in their relations with alumni, career services, and the like. Our research at British universities revealed that universities use LinkedIn exclusively for those activities. In this sense, LinkedIn is a clear marketizing agency with its strategy of constant (re)framing between "free" services and payable commodities. It is dependent on the cooperation of each university; without universities' engagement, their motivating of students and alumni and free laboring, LinkedIn would not have a big enough scale of data to create its envisaged commodities/pacified things to sell. It is no surprise that LinkedIn invests in creating market encounters with universities (which is yet another market framing) by sending its staff to tour universities around the world, visit or organize events, create meeting encounters on the Internet, and so on. What potential all this big data has for higher education in the future still remains to be seen, but penetration in governing the sector (for now through rankings) and knowledge dissemination (through sharing news, opinions, projects and so on) is clearly visible.

Higher Education Reputation Markets

The development of globally competitive knowledge-based economies is used to frame and make possible new forms of global governance and the presence of new actors and technologies in the education sector (Berndt and Boeckler 2012). Universities in this respect have learned that managing their reputation and brand is not just a way to attract students, but to prove that they take their "new" societal roles responsibly.

Quacquarelli Symonds Limited (QS), a university ranker, is based in the UK. It was created in the 1990s by Nunzio Quacquarelli, a student with an idea and entrepreneurial determination. QS was officially established in 1993 as Printsale Limited; it has subsequently changed its name twice, though Nunzio Quacquarelli has continued as Director. Initially, QS started with the publication of an MBA career guide; this was extended to educational publications looking at opportunities for business and postgraduate education. Quacquarelli also began organizing events on MBA education, and was pivotal in making QS a global company. He also wanted his media company to be an information and data company, and in 2002 started a project on rankings with colleague John O'Leary, editor of the *Times Higher Education*, UK. This resulted in the QS–THE ranking being launched in 2004 (University of Pennsylvania Wharton 2014), which later separated into two different rankings.

QS quickly evolved and now is a diverse collage of services and products. There are several existing companies connected to QS, which makes it hard to track its financial situation. From the last available financial report, QS showed an annual turnover in 2013 of above £17 million, a gross profit of £14 million and retained some profit for the group to carry forward £0.7 million (QS 2014). In 2015, QS had 250 employees and offices in five countries other than the UK, including Singapore and the US.

Besides rankings, QS has developed the following products aimed at students, academics, universities, governments, media, and other audiences: Information Technology solutions; online search engines with services such as search tools for the public and advertising and branding for institutions; publications such as guides for study courses or publications for universities; a variety of rankings; a variety of intelligence; fairs and events; conferences; and advice on student recruitment.

QS rankings are an example of how an initial product grows in space, scale and variety. Initial global rankings of universities are still prepared every year, but now there are also: subject rankings in 30 disciplines; regional rankings (in Asia,

Latin America, and Brazil, Russia, India, and China (BRICs)); best student city rankings; and rankings of "50 under 50," catering to universities established less than 50 years ago. QS has launched a service called "stars," which evaluates universities based on indicators it has developed and which awards stars to institutions, and services like QS Top global 200 Business Schools, based on employers' choice.

QS does not charge universities to be included in their global rankings. However, it has a full range of services for sale on how to improve university or country positions. It has an intelligence unit that does research, and helps institutions improve their ranking. One of our QS interviewees stated that rankings are more of a public relations event for QS since they draw a lot of attention. It is many times a starting point for QS to engage in other relationships with universities and governments, which is where QS then makes profit. In this respect, QS uses detailed data, which is freely given to it by universities for the purpose of rankings. But it then also uses this data to turn it into research and consultancy services, which it sells to those who want to improve their reputational status. In this respect, the framing of things to sell is in constant motion, as the company works to expand its markets. How things are packaged strategically varies based on the buyers' profiles, locations, and aims. In sum, QS specializes in trade in reputation; as a marketizing agency, it has managed to frame reputation as a sellable commodity. Universities and countries that not only buy these services but engage with this sort of framing become marketizing agencies as well. QS also provides advice services to universities on a range of other topics – how to internationalize, prepare the strategy, brand itself, and so on. Efficiency is very important to the QS brand; there is a policy in the company that each enquiry needs to be answered within 24 hours, as it wants to be responsive and transparent about its work.

It invests a lot in educating students to use its services, which is an important factor for the business strategy. The more widely QS search engines and rankings are used by students and the general public, the more likely institutions are to want to improve their status and pay for QS consultancy. As in the case of LinkedIn, this is an example of a market where some services are provided "for free" to different users, but those who are actually using it for free are laboring for the company to then repackage this labor and sell it in other ways and to other buyers.

The means through which QS comes to new clients and services is by networking and keeping a strong relationship with as many actors as possible. The key here is attending many events so as to build strong ties. This includes higher education conferences and fairs. Its employees present papers and mingle with other conference participants. QS lubricates its relationships with potential clients by hosting "must go to" receptions and parties – in turn building loyalty through congeniality, personality, and personalization. The dynamic is opposite to the impersonal market relations envisaged by economic theory. In fact, QS works hard to create long-standing social relations and turn them into strong ties with the aim to occupy the position of one of the central nodes in its market structure. Financial transactions for exchanges of commodities are, in this respect, just moments in the otherwise long lasting social relations and not the focal point of meetings between QS as a seller and other actors as buyers.

Unbundling the University and Making Higher Education Markets: Final Thoughts

There is nothing inevitable about creating the conditions for the unbundling of existing university structures, and the creation of the new market-making practices that are in turn instituted. Through the cases we have developed, we have shown that making markets requires a considerable amount of work, both to bring markets into being, and to maintain them. Yet, we argued that much of the literature on higher education markets tends to assume markets exist, as something of a fait accompli. Our contribution, we hope, is to show what more can be seen in the making of higher education markets when we draw on the conceptual resources that researchers such as Berndt and Boeckler (2012) and Çalışkan and Callon (2010) have developed. By bringing together these different macro–meso and micro-framing moments, we can see market making is dynamic, diverse, changes with time and in space, and can also fail. They require investment – not just agents, but also financial resources, institution building, loyalty and legitimacy. Loyalty and legitimacy seem to be crucial in enrolling potential market actors in the laboring to do with production and consumption – especially in the making of higher education markets – something we need to understand better. Perhaps this is because they are "markets in the making" with meanings yet to be fixed, stabilized, and made common sense or, as Çalışkan and Callon (2010: 6) would say, the "domestication of novelty." Profit and education, for the moment at least, continue to remain uneasy bedfellows.

Note

1 European Commission FP7 People program: Marie Curie Initial Training Network UNIKE (Universities in Knowledge Economies) under Grant Agreement number 317452.

References

Ball, S. J. (2007). *Education PLC: Understanding private sector participation in public sector education*. London: Routledge.
Ball, S. J. (2012). *Global education inc. New policy networks and the neo-liberal imaginary*. London: Routledge.
Berndt, C. and Boeckler, M. (2009). Geographies of circulation and exchange: constructions of markets. *Progress in Human Geography*, 33(4), 535–551.
Berndt, C. and Boeckler, M. (2012). Geographies of marketization. In T. J. Barnes, J. Peck, and E. Sheppard (Eds), *The Wiley-Blackwell companion to economic geography*. (pp. 199–212). Chichester: Blackwell Publishing Ltd.
Brown, R. (2011a). *Higher education and the market*. New York: Routledge.
Brown, R. (2011b). The March of the market. In M. Molesworth, R. Scullion, and E. Nixon (Eds), *The marketisation of higher education and the student as consumer*. (pp. 11–24). London: Routledge.
Çalışkan, K. and Callon, M. (2009). Economization, part 1: Shifting attention from the economy towards processes of economization. *Economy and Society*, 38(3), 369–398.

Çalışkan, K. and Callon, M. (2010). Economization, part 2: A research programme for the study of markets. *Economy and Society, 39*(1), 1–32.

Callon, M. and Muniesa, F. (2005). Peripheral vision: Economic markets as calculative collective devices. *Organization Studies, 26*(8), 1229–1250.

De Boer, H. and Jongbloed, B. (2012). A cross-national comparison of higher education markets in Western Europe. In A. Curaj, P. Scott, L. Vlasceanu and L. Wilson (Eds), *European higher education at the crossroads: Between the Bologna process and national reforms.* (pp. 553–571). Heidelberg: Springer.

Fain, P. (2014a, May 20). Laureate looks forward. *Inside Higher Ed.* Retrieved on May 17, 2015 from: https://www.insidehighered.com/news/2014/05/20/ceo-global-profit-its-expansion-accreditation-and-profit-debate.

Fain, P. (2014b, June 2). Moody's downgrades Laureate's credit outlook. *Inside Higher Ed.* Retrieved on May 17, 2015 from: https://www.insidehighered.com/quicktakes/2014/06/02/moodys-downgrades-laureates-credit-outlook.

Garcia, M.-F. (1986). La construction sociale d'un marché parfait: Le marché au cadran de Fontaines-en-Sologne. *Actes de La Recherche En Sciences Sociales, 65*(1), 2–13.

Hogan, A., Sellar, S. and Lingard, R. (2015). *Commercialising comparison: Pearson, edu-business, and new policy spaces in education.* Paper presented at the annual conference of the Compartive and International Education Society, Washington DC, March.

INTO. (2011). Press Releases: University Partnerships is Higher Education Provider of the Year. Retrieved on May 17, 2015 from: http://www.into-corporate.com/news-and-views/press-releases/2011/11/into-university-partnerships-is-higher-education-provider-of-the-year.aspx.

INTO. (2014). INTO university partnerships limited Directors' report and consolidated financial statements for the year ended 31 July 2013. Companies House.

INTO. (2015). INTO Webpages. Retrieved on May 17, 2015 from: http://www.into-corporate.com/into-performance.aspx.

Jessop, B., Fairclough, N. and Wodak, R. (Eds). (2008). *Education and the knowledge-based economy in Europe.* Rotterdam: Sense.

Jongbloed, B. (2003). Marketisation in higher education, Clark's triangle and the essential ingredients of markets. *Higher Education Quarterly, 57*(2), 110–135.

Kimes, M. and Smith, M. (2014). Laureate, a for-profit education firm, finds international success (with a Clinton's help). *Washington Post.* Retrieved on May 17, 2015 from: http://www.washingtonpost.com/business/laureate-a-for-profit-education-firm-finds-international-success-with-a-clintons-help/2014/01/16/13f8adde-7ca6-11e3-9556-4a4bf7bcbd84_story.html.

Kinser, K. (2010). A global perspective on for-profit higher education. In G. Henschke, V. V. Lechuga, and W. Tierney (Eds), *For Profit Colleges and Universities.* Stirling, VA: Stylus.

Komljenovic, J. and Robertson, S. L. (2015). "Market-making" and the university: a processual and relational account. Article under review at the Journal of Education Policy.

Laureate Education. (2010). President Bill Clinton accepts role as honorary chancellor of Laureate International Universities, 26 April, [see http://www.laureate.net/News Room/PressReleases/2010/04/PresidentClintonHonoraryLaureateChancellor.aspx], last accessed 15 September, 2015].

Lederman, D. (2007, January 30). Another move from public to private. *Inside Higher Ed.* Retrieved on May 17, 2015 from: https://www.insidehighered.com/news/2007/01/30/laureate.

Leys, C. (2003). *Market-driven politics: Neoliberal democracy and the public interest.* New York: Verso.

LinkedIn. (2014). United States Securities Exchange Commission annual report pursuant to section 13 ir 15(d) of the Securities Exchange Act of 1934. LinkedIn Corporation. Retrieved on May 17, 2015 from: http://investors.linkedin.com/secfiling.cfm?filingID=1445305-14-439.

Lipsett, A. (2008, July 30). Language trainer INTO threatens to sue university union. *The Guardian*. Retrieved on May 17, 2015 from: http://www.theguardian.com/education/2008/jul/30/foreign.students.

Marginson, S. (2013). The impossibility of capitalist markets in higher education. *Journal of Education Policy, 28*(3), 353–370.

Marginson, S. (2014). Public lecture on April 16, 2014 at the University of Bath. Capitalist markets in higher education: Utopias or possibilities. Organized by Society for Research into Higher Education.

Marginson, S. and Considine, M. (2000). *The enterprise university: Power, governance and reinvention in Australia*. Cambridge: Cambridge University Press.

Newman, M. (2008, May 1). INTO founder says his private capital supports public work. *Times Higher Education*. Retrieved on May 17, 2015 from: http://www.timeshigheredu cation.co.uk/401674.article.

Peck, J. and Theodore, N. (2007). Variegated capitalism. *Progress in Human Geography, 31*(6), 731–772.

Polanyi, K. (1944). *The great transformation*. Boston: Beacon Press.

QS Quacquarelli Symonds Limited. (2014). Group strategic report, director's report and audited consolidated financial statements for the year ended 31 December 2013 for QS Quacquarelli Symonds Limited. Companies House.

Redden, E. and Fain, P. (2012, October 10). Going global. *Inside Higher Ed*. Retrieved on May 17, 2015 from: https://www.insidehighered.com/news/2013/10/10/laureates-growing-global-network-institutions.

Robertson, S. (2010). Globalising UK higher education. London: LLAKES.

Robertson, S., Bonal, X. and Dale, R. (2002). GATS and the education service industry: The politics of scale and global reterritorialization. *Comparative Education Review, 46*(4), 472–495.

Robertson, S. L. and Komljenovic, J. (2015). Unbundling higher education: When all that is solid melts into … profit! Paper presented at the annual conference of the Compartive and International Education Society, Washington DC, March.

Robertson, S., Mundy, K., Verger, A. and Menashy, F. (2012). *Public private partnerships in education: New actors and modes of governance in a globalizing world*. Cheltenham: Edward Elgar.

Slater, D. and Tonkiss, F. (2001). *Market society: Markets and modern social theory*. Chichester: Wiley.

Slaughter, S. and Rhoades, G. (2004). *Academic capitalism and the new economy: Markets, state, and higher education*. Baltimore, MD: Johns Hopkins University Press.

University of Pennsylvania Wharton. (2014). How disruption is creating opportunity in higher education. Interview with Nunzio Quacquarelli. University of Pensylvania, Wharton. Retrieved on May 17, 2015 from: http://knowledge.wharton.upenn.edu/article/how-disruption-is-creating-opportunity-in-higher-education/.

Zimmerman, A., Orjuela, J. L. R. and Caucas, J. A. (2015). In-depth analysis of for-profit education industry and the future of the Apollo Education Group: *The Economist* Case Competition 2015. New York: *The Economist*.

14 Education Outside the Public Limelight

The "Parallel Universe" of ICT Certifiers[1]

Eva Hartmann

Introduction

This chapter seeks to deepen our understanding of the privatization of post-secondary education by studying training and certification in the area of information and communication technology (ICT). This is a major emerging market, but has not yet attracted much attention from educational researchers. The study of this sector will not only broaden our empirical understanding of the privatization of education, but will also bring to the fore the need for a more sophisticated account of privatization.

The chapter is divided into three parts. First, I outline major characteristics of the emerging ICT certifiers, bringing this area back into the public limelight. Second, I outline in more detail an analytical framework that interrelates studies of changes of the public–private nexus in education with studies of private authority. I argue that privatization should not be reduced to simply opening up the public sector to the private sector. We can also observe a change in the self-organization of the private sector, and I engage with the broader sociological literature studying this change. Finally, an emerging body of literature points out the implications of this change for private authority, which is about to gain a strong international dimension. Third, I further develop this account of transnational private authority and point out the empirical insights we obtain by studying ICT certifiers and the enabling conditions that underpin their authority.

The Certification Market

There are over 100 providers operating more than 1,300 individual certification products (CEN 2009: 10–11). In light of the growing importance of this sector, Clifford Adelman calls it "the parallel universe of postsecondary credentials" (Adelman 2000). However, the exact size of this universe is difficult to determine due to a lack of reliable data. Many providers, including the market leaders, have stopped reporting their market share, since they regard this information as too sensitive to be published. Furthermore, many studies have been funded by certification providers who have a vested interest in the findings.[2] Other studies have been carried out by for-profit research companies and can only be purchased at a considerable price.[3] This shortcoming in publicly available data indicates the degree to which this type of education is still outside the public limelight. This lacuna is even more of a concern in light of recent political efforts to introduce some regulations into the field, to which I turn in the last part of the chapter. This contribution must therefore content itself with pointing out some major features of the parallel universe of ICT certifiers, which need to be examined in more detail with further research. The study draws on a wide range of publicly accessible secondary sources, ranging from academic studies, to information provided by certifiers themselves, to newspapers and magazine articles for ICT professions.

The studies available, as well as the information provided by some certifiers, indicate a major growth of the market despite the 2008 financial crisis, which hit the sector significantly. The sector grows around 25 percent per annum, on top of the nearly four-fold growth from the year 2000 to 2007 (CEN 2009: 4; Weiss and Povalej 2007). Along these lines, the research company IDC estimated in 2009 the overall volume of all ICT education services at USD $24 billion and predicted further growth, though at a lower rate compared to before the crisis (cited in O'Sullivan et al. 2011: 17). A recent survey focusing on European Union (EU) countries estimated up to 50 percent of the 6.67 million members of the ICT workforce to have at least one ICT certification (Korte et al. 2013: 49; Gareis et al. 2014). Notably, the demand for certifications in encryption technology, such as secure socket layer (SSL), has increased in recent years as a result of the importance of online transactions and secure transfer lines. In 2011, SSL certificate revenue was estimated to have reached USD $628.6 million, with 2.5 million certificates issued (Sullivan 2013). The future growth rates for revenue and certificates are expected to be 18.5 percent and 17.8 percent, respectively, according to a forecast of the research company Frost and Sullivan (Frost and Sullivan 2013). The number of issued certificates is just the tip of the iceberg, indicating a major growth in training in this sector. Although the pass rate is usually a guarded secret, studies estimate it to be between 30 percent and 50 percent (CEN 2009: 12). Furthermore, not all learners of such training courses eventually take the exam, due to a lack of interest by their employers or to save the costs of the exam. Accordingly, the number of people attending ICT training courses might be 10 times higher than the number of certificates issued.

What Gets Certified?

ICT training and certification reinforces non-formal types of education in order to secure a timely and substantial supply of skills. There are a plethora of certifications, creating a rather fragmented and confusing landscape containing both key and niche players. Some certifications are related to specific platforms and products, while others focus more on skills, techniques, and knowledge. Accordingly, ICT training can include qualifications in rather narrowly defined technical fields. Some cover the proper, effective, and efficient handling of ICT tools, reflecting state-of-the-art software developments and the integration of computers in the overall production process. However, other certifications test soft skills such as organization, ethics, diplomacy, attentiveness, or self-reliance, and test personal attributes such as motivation.[4] Cisco Networking Academy, for instance, provides, in partnership with schools and organizations around the world, training in health information networking. Its training comprises learning modules not only about technical skills but also about healthcare policies. The default healthcare system the training introduces is the US one, but modularisation makes it possible to adapt this country-specific information to the country where the training takes place.

In many cases, registration for an exam requires previous professional experiences that then become documented through certification. Accordingly, experts praise certification as a model for validating informal learning acquired through work experience (Summerfield 2007). In other words, ICT training and certification has become vital in strengthening further education established with the aim of overcoming major ICT-skills shortages in high-income countries. A study of the Australian government showed that employers seeking ICT professionals only filled 84 percent of surveyed vacancies in 2014 (Australian Government 2014). In Europe, the shortage is estimated to be between 372,000 and 864,000 in 2015, according to recent forecasts (Korte et al. 2013: 6; Gareis, et al. 2014).

Acceleration in Knowledge-Based Societies

The rapid growth of ICT training and certification needs to be seen in the context of broader economic changes. One of its vital characteristics is what we could call an acceleration of time. The historian Reinhart Koselleck has brilliantly pointed out in his theory of historical time how ever shorter temporal cycles have been gaining ground and challenge the temporal horizon of modernity (Koselleck 2002; see also Rosa 2013). The acceleration can be partly related to the "post-industrial society" (Bell 1973), in which the delivery of services supersedes the production of goods. At the core of this transformation is a "perpetual innovation economy" (Morris-Suzuki 1984, cited in Schiller 2000: 157) that relies on a continuous stream of scientific and technical knowledge, which now increasingly focuses on information technology and networks. Notably, Manuel Castells pointed out in his seminal study that this technology enables new social structures and activities organized through electronically processed information networks (Castells 1999). Information has become key for the productivity of the economy, and a major driving force for capitalist development. It also makes new modes of organization possible, and undermines vertical bureaucracies in favor of horizontal cooperation.

However, we should refrain from generalizing this trend too hastily. The network society is gaining a global scale; however, it does so without including the world in its totality. Global cities that are better connected to each other than to their hinterland illustrate well this fragmentation (Sassen 2006). If we take the Internet as an indicator of the spread of the network society, then only 39 percent of the world's population had been included in 2014 (ITU 2014). Furthermore, the network society is characterized by major hierarchies and a struggle that aims to situate the knowledge-intensive economy at the upper end of the global value chain, while fiercely defending its privileged position against the lower end, where strong competition and Tayloristic mass production heavily squeeze profit margins. This struggle over profits translates into an ever-shorter life cycle of knowledge, which in turn further increases the challenges high-income countries are already confronted with due to demographic changes.

These changes in the economy and the global value chain have a major impact on education, since the service economy relies on a constantly evolving stream of specialized skills. Lifelong learning has become the buzzword of the new education strategy in the knowledge-based economy (cf. European Parliament and Council 2008). This new strategy is part of a reconfiguration of the relationship between informal, non-formal, and formal education.[5] Together with a further academization of skills requirements, this trend increasingly blurs the distinction between higher education (HE), technical and vocational training (TVET), and career and technical education (<A>). It is in this broader context that we need to situate the fast-growing market of ICT training and certification, providing a skill that is the basis of the network society. However, educational studies have thus far paid little attention to how knowledge about ICT is produced and taught. In the next two sections I will outline a framework for analyzing this sector in more detail.

The Williamsonian Turn

In order to study ICT certifiers in the context of privatization, we need to go beyond a notion of privatization that merely focuses on the opening up of public education to private, for-profit providers. Stephan Ball and Deborah Youdell refer to this type of privatization as *exogenous* privatization (Ball and Youdell 2007). Privatization can also include what Ball and Youdell label *endogenous* privatization, which reorganizes the public sector as if it were a market. This "great transformation of the public sector" (Krajewski 2011: 239) introduces concepts such as "choice," "accountability," "school improvement," "devolution," "contestability," or "effectiveness," without handing over the design and provision of public services to private actors. This great transformation is vital for putting public and private providers on equal footing in terms of output and efficiency, while abstracting from the specificity of their mission, the working conditions they offer, and the types of students they teach. In the name of equal treatment, the transformation thus might discriminate in favour of educational providers that take in more difficult students and pay better wages to teachers.[6]

In this contribution I would like to put forward the argument that the current wave of privatization also includes a major reorganization of the private sector. This transformation of the private sector tends to be ignored by privatization studies. The German sociologist Wolfgang Streeck provides some interesting insights into the institutional dimension of this change. His study of the reform of capitalism highlights a move from a "Durkheimian" to a "Williamsonian" type of institutional organization of the private sector (Streeck 2009: 157). The Durkheimian type is characterized by a strong neo-corporatist arrangement in which the government defers major self-regulatory competences to social partners and professions. In the vein of literature on varieties of capitalism, we can call this type of institutional setting "coordinated market economy" (Hall and Soskice 2001). Streeck contrasts this type of institution with an emerging Williamsonian type, which is more decentralized, fragmented, and diversified in nature, and part of an institutional environment in which competition has become intensified. He derives the second notion from Oliver Williamson's economics of institutions, in which the emerging institutions appear to be "shaped by individual choice and local conditions instead of public–political design representing collective values and objectives" (Streeck 2009: 157). Core features of this change are the weakening of the collective articulation of interests to the detriment of trade unions and professions, the transformation of corporate governance, as well as the weakening of networks among firms (Streeck 2009: 22).

This turn has major consequences for TVET and CTE, notably in organized market economies where trade unions and professions used to have a say. However, the change is not so much characterized simply by a weakening of TVET per se, but rather by a change of its governance. Kathleen Thelen and Marius R. Busemeyer studied the transformation along four dimensions: changes in the determination of content and degree of standardization; changes of who has the license to train and to certify skills; changes in the mode of provision; and, last but not least, changes in the control of quality (Thelen and Busemeyer 2012). Their empirical study points out a move from collectivism to segmentalism (Thelen and Busemeyer 2012: 87; see also Baethge 1999). Segmentalism, which first emerged in the Japanese training system after World War II, aims at stabilizing the labor market (see also Sako 1995). In this regard, it differs from the hire-and-fire approach of managerial unilateralism that prevails in liberal market economies. However, it also differs from collectivism and its way of stabilizing the market, since it assigns large firms an important organizational role. These firms stabilize the labor market by establishing their own internal labor market with internal career ladders, seniority wages, and company-based training (Thelen 2001: 77). Part of this company-based qualification strategy is the modularization of training, which favors a narrower notion of skills that contrasts with the holistic principle of (regulated) occupation (Berufsprinzip) established in collectivist organized markets (Thelen 2004: 172–173).

International Private Authority

The analyses of Streeck, Thelen, and Busemeyer provide interesting insights into the changes to the private sector and its consequences for VET and CTE. However, some major flaws in their analyses, notably in their conceptual reasoning, hinder the authors from fully coming to terms with the nature of the change. They essentially ignore the transformation of private authority introduced by the Williamsonian mode of coordination, which is at the core of an emerging body of literature on private authority (Cutler et al. 1999; Biersteker and Hall 2002; Graz and Nölke 2008; Hansen and Salskov-Iversen 2008). Notably, Claire Cutler's analysis of the role of coordination service firms provides a helpful notion for analyzing the change in private authority in the field of post-secondary education (Cutler 2002: 28). These firms, Cutler points out, play a vital role in enabling inter-firm cooperation. The examples Cutler lists are law, accounting, management, and insurance firms, as well as credit-rating agencies or financial clearinghouses. In many cases, these firms take over a similar coordination role to the one that cartels and business associations used to play, and thus stand for an important change in private authority and what Cutler calls "private international regimes" (Cutler 2002: 29). They enable the setting of informal industry norms and practices, and assist in the establishment of production alliances and subcontractor relations. In this chapter, I suggest considering ICT certifiers as another type of coordination service firm since they provides ICT skills that are vital for organizing the emerging network society.

The literature on private authority, which is heavily influenced by Max Weber, also provides us with a more complex understanding of the relationship between power and authority. Authority has a formal, as well as a substantial, dimension. Weber more precisely distinguishes between "legal rationality" and "substantial rationality" (Weber 1978: 656–657). An entity – be it a person, an organization, or an office – can be *in* authority: that is, have the right to command. It is, however, only *an* authority when it has the credibility and legitimacy to command. Legal rationality is rule-based, and risks becoming an iron cage without the second type of rationality. This second type makes the wall of the iron cage more porous, relating the rules to a broader context by introducing ethical impera-tives and expediential and precautionary rules, Weber argues. Together, these two rationalities ensure compliance to rules established by an authority without applying coercion.

Drawing on Weber's notion of authority entails, however, some conceptual challenges that not all scholars of private authority seem to be aware of. Weber's notion of authority has a strong public bias. In other words, his model of authority is the public bureaucracy. A too-strong equalization of public and private author-ity risks overlooking the specificity of each type, notably when it comes to coer-cion and legitimation. A government has a different enforcement capacity due to its monopoly on coercion, which is vital for law enforcement. However, demo-cratic states, at least, are also confronted with major legitimacy requirements if the ruling parties want to be re-elected. In contrast, private companies do not have to justify their rules and actions to the broad public as governments do. However, they also lack the coercive means to impose their rules and norms. Hence, the enabling conditions for their authorities differ.

I suggest further developing the notion of private authority along the lines of Weber's analysis of social closure. Closure defines who has access to certain market privileges, and who is excluded. Weber notably refers to guilds, profes-sions, and other status groups whose market-restricting power used to be broadly accepted (and still is, in many cases) (Weber 1978; Saks 2010). Due to his public bias, Weber essentially assumes that these social closures will fade away with the generalization of the market economy, for he tends to relate the closure to a feu-dal or a corporate (*ständisch*-patrimonial) system (Weber 1978: 306). Raymond

Murphy criticizes this assumption for underestimating the emergence of new social closures replacing the old ones (Murphy 1984: 551). Along these lines, I suggest interrelating private authority with social closure. Private authority *has* the authority to introduce social closure. It needs, however, to *be* an authority to make this social closure widely acceptable and thus legitimate. This double requirement is even more vital for coordination service firms who can only profit from their services if the services are broadly accepted, so that their service can have a coordination effect. However, we do not yet know on what grounds their authority stands if they no longer draw on a feudal or corporate tradition. The remainder of the chapter will analyze the enabling conditions of the private authority of ICT certifiers in more detail.

The Private Authority of Certifiers

How can we understand the provision of certifications in educational terms? Certification provides information by formally assessing how the performance of an individual meets pre-defined skill and competence criteria. The glossary of the European Centre for the Development of Vocational Training (Cedefop) defines certification in more general terms as "[t]he process of formally validating knowledge, know-how and/or skills and competencies acquired by an individual, following a standard assessment procedure. Certificates or diplomas are issued by accredited awarding bodies" (Tissot 2004: 40).

Certification is thus related to a body that has the competence to award certificates and the privileges related to them. In the vein of Weber, we can describe the body's social function in terms of social closure, which underpins the segmentation of the (labor) market (Weber 1978: 44; see also Saks 2010). Certifying bodies usually require authorization thorough accreditation, which Cedefop defines as a process by which "an institution of vocational education or training, a program of study, or a service, show[s] it has been approved by the relevant legislative and professional authorities by having met predetermined standards" (Tissot 2004: 18).

Hence, the social closure takes place at two levels: the individual, and the institutional. In its definition, Cedefop assigns the state and professions final authority in the selection process. However, in line with Streeck we could ask whether this definition is overly informed by a Durkheimian notion of institutions and does not reflect the specificity of the ICT certification sector, to which I will turn in the remaining part of the chapter.

We can distinguish three (ideal) types of certifiers: *formal post-secondary education providers, vendor-specific certifiers,* and *vendor-independents.*[7] Each type is positioned differently on a continuum of authority, with a strong market-orientation on one side and a strong state-orientation on the other. However, since they are based on voluntary standards, all certificates lack regulatory authority in a legal sense. They provide a "right-to-title" but no "right-to-practice" in the sense of a mandatory licence in regulated professions. Still, one would be mistaken to underestimate their impact on the labor market and its social closure. Studies indicate a positive correlation between most certificates and wage level (see Foote

Partners 2015; Dolton and Pelkonen 2008). In the following sections, I will outline how each type of certifier builds on different mechanisms, thereby assuring the legitimacy of its social closure.

Vendor-Specific Certifiers

The programs of vendor-specific certifiers are directly linked to a particular product, and thus to a distinct company (Adelman 2000; CEDEFOP 2006). Cisco, for example, offers programs for network tasks with three levels of certification. Other vendors that offer similar services related to a product, platform, tool, or console include Microsoft, IBM, SAP, Novell, Oracle, and Red Hat, to name but a few.[8] We can understand the move of software companies into the training market as part of their overall strategy to expand the service component of their businesses. They not only sell software and proprietary knowledge, but also verification of the appropriate competence to use this knowledge. The majority of certifiers have outsourced the training to recognized partners, while retaining the certification as their core business in this field. Accordingly, they keep the final authority to decide which provider is certified to provide the training and to test the trainees' skills and knowledge. It is in this regard that they assume an important coordination role.

Each certifier's accreditation authority is approved neither by a legislative body nor a profession; it is rather related to the company's software and technology. As the producer of software and technology, ICT certifiers have a clear knowledge advantage, which in turn gives them a privileged position within the certification market. Furthermore, their coordination role benefits from the almost monopolistic structure of the software market. The bigger the market share, the more likely employers are to know the certification, which, in turn, increases the certification's value (Tyler 2004). In the light of global migration, widely known certifications also benefit from the attractiveness of the labor market of the certifiers' home country. IT professionals from low-income countries may take an exam offered by an internationally known certifier with the intent of improving their access to high-income labor markets. Some immigration authorities have indeed started to use this type of certification alongside formal qualifications in assigning work permits (see Whitney 2007: 23). Certifiers also benefit from the international activities of other service providers, as multinational companies setting up new affiliates abroad may prefer employees with certifications from their country of origin that they are familiar with. Internationally known certifications also play an important organizational role in the field of sub-contracting. They may come to be seen as indicators of the subcontracters' quality, notably when these companies are situated in countries with a formal education system that is substantially different from that of the outsourcing companies' country of origin. These comparative advantages in the training and certification market based on an economy of scale explain why these types of certifiers pulled ahead of vendor-independent certifiers in the 1980s, and dominate the market today (CompTIA 2004: 19). These advantages provide vendor-specific certifiers with an important coordination capacity, not only regarding the stabilizing of the emerging international labor market, but also in the context of outsourcing and the organization of global value chains in more general terms.

However, the market dominance of vendor-specific certifiers raises a number of major issues, notably with regard to proprietary knowledge. The content they teach is not a public good, and thus differs from most other forms of education and training (Lambert 2014). The new dependence it risks establishing becomes particularly evident where certificates are limited by temporal validity, and thus require costly re-certification. In other words, the knowledge people acquire through ICT training never fully belongs to them. Continuing education translates here into a continuing revenue stream for ICT certifiers. However, the strength of vendor-specific certifiers is also their weakness. This oligopolistic market power risks undermining the legitimacy of vendor-dependent certifiers as coordination service providers. Vendor certifications have attracted major criticism in recent years for being too biased towards their own solutions and technology, and are seen as only being interested in building a pool of trusted individuals who know how to implement and support their product (French 2010). It is feared that such a bias could easily lead to incorrect resource allocations. This criticism, put forward by consumers and ICT professional associations, highlights the limits of a vendor-specific ICT certifier to assume a widely accepted coordinating role.

We can see the increasing philanthropic activities of ICT companies in the light of these limits. Many multinational companies have started to donate to non-profit organizations and schools as part of their social responsibility program.[9] Cisco, for instance, supports a number of non-governmental organizations active in the fields of development, health, and education, such as the American Red Cross (Cisco 2014). Critical voices are surely correct when they point out that companies have become engaged in this type of activity with the intent to extend their market share and increase sales (Draxler 2012; Ginsburg 2012). However, we can also expect companies to engage in these social activities in order to strengthen the legitimacy of their social closure and their organizational role in competition, not only with the coordinating authority of the state, but also with one of the less oligopolistic vendor-independent certifiers.

Vendor-Independent Certifiers

Vendor-neutral providers focus on issues, techniques, skills, and knowledge independent of a specific ICT product, and are thus often more generic in their orientation. Initially, vendor-independent certifications, which were developed by professional associations as a form of self-regulation, played the leading role in ensuring standards and competences were met in the computing profession. However, none of these certifications gained broad recognition by the industry (CompTIA 2004: 19). The birth of networked computing and the growth of the ICT industry in the late 1980s tilted the certification landscape in favor of the vendor certifiers (Whitney 2007). Vendor-independent certifiers include professional associations and trade associations. The most well known is the Computing Technology Industry Association (CompTIA), whose CompTIA A+ certification had been awarded to one million certified IT professionals from its creation in 1993 to 2014. CompTIA, which is headquartered in Chicago, is particularly well established in Commonwealth Nations, with offices in India, South Africa, and the United Kingdom. Like many other vendor-independent providers, it does not certify directly, but by way of centres that it authorizes (ComTIA 2004).

A more Europe-oriented consortium is Career Space, which includes 11 major ICT companies, and the European Information and Communication Technology Industry Association, which represents 39 national digital technology consumer associations from 27 European countries. Career Space aims to develop a framework for generic skills and competences required by the ICT industry in Europe. Both CompTIA and Career Space illustrate well that this second type of certifier may be independent of a particular ICT product. However, they are not independent of the overall interests of the ICT industry and do not necessarily represent the interest of the public.

Also European, though more closely related to the ICT profession, is the European Certification of Informatics Professionals, as well as the European/International Computer Driving Licence certification program. Both programs were set up by the Council of European Professional Informatics Societies (CEPIS), which was established in 1989 by nine European informatics societies and whose membership comprises, to date, over 450,000 ICT and informatics professionals in 32 European countries.[10]

A third type of vendor-independent certifier is essentially the result of the outsourcing strategy of vendor-specific certifiers, and hence only relatively independent. A good example is Certiport, which has become one of the biggest ICT testing firms, with 15 million exams conducted worldwide in 2015, in 148 countries and in 27 languages. Most of its testing is related to Microsoft and Adobe software.[11] The fact that Certiport was bought by Pearson VUE – the computer-based testing arm of Pearson – in May 2012, indicates a complex interdependence and convergence between the media, ICT, and education industries (see Chapter 7 in this volume).[12]

The "online authority" (Hoyle 2010: 48) for this type of certifier thus builds on their multi-stakeholder inclusion and their consultation mechanisms before establishing specific programs that provide them with a direct coordination role. However, the nature of these consultations varies significantly. Some certifiers focus only on the industry, while others also include professional organizations, the academic community, or governments. Only a few, however, take trade unions into account.[13]

These second types of certifiers are thus more inclusive and less profit-driven in their standard setting, which underpins their coordination role. However, they face a dilemma that puts them at a disadvantage compared to vendor certifiers. Their efforts to differentiate their offers from others in a proliferating market has resulted in a highly fragmented and confusing landscape of vendor-independent certifications, which often lack transparency and comparability (CEDEFOP 2006).

The growing confusion makes it difficult for prospective trainees and employers to assess the quality of these programs, which risks undermining their authority and the organizational effect of their certification (Tittel 2006).

Formal Post-Secondary Education System

The third group of certifiers is part of the formal education system. Providers may be public entities or non-governmental bodies with delegated authority, and are often HE institutions. Accordingly, their authority is derived from the general authority of the state and its coordinating role. For 30 years, this type of education was the main sphere for qualifying ICT professionals (Hoyle 2010; Brookshear 2014). However, such programs experienced major pressure in the 1980s, when the demand for developers and programmers substantially increased, opening the door for individuals with qualifications outside of the electrical engineering discipline.[14]

The increasing influence of the parallel universe not only reflects the increase in demand for ICT skills, but also the time horizon of a perpetual innovation economy where a timely, reliable, and constant renewal of skills has become instrumental. While post-secondary education institutions still have formal authority, they often lack the reputation to be able to respond quickly to such requirements, due in part to their bureaucratic structure and efforts to build their curriculum on a broader societal consensus (Haimson and VanNoy 2004). Thus, they may still be in authority in the field of ICT training. However, they have lost much of their authority. As a consequence, many HE institutions have outsourced part of their IT training and testing to private ICT certifiers, which benefit from the general assumption that they know how to make the best use of the technology (Adelman 2000; Randall and Zirkle 2005). Some HE institutions have even agreed to waive some of their general entrance requirements for holders of ICT certifications (Schiller 2000: 143–202).

This public–private partnership (PPP) has created new markets for private ICT trainers and certifiers (for an excellent introduction in PPP, see Robertson et al. 2012). Cisco Networking Academy is just one example of close collaboration between vendor-specific certifiers and public universities. It includes 9,000 academies in 170 countries that deliver courses by certified instructors in partnership with schools, community colleges, universities, and other organizations.[15] More than 500 Academy Support Centers and Instructor Training Centers supervise the delivery, and ensure that the trainers are sufficiently qualified to guarantee the quality of the course (Cisco 2014: E6). The authority that has final say on the provisions of the program is thus of a hybrid nature: it includes both the public authority of schools, and the private authority of Cisco and its support and training centers.

Other PPPs go beyond individual HE and VET institutions, as is the case of the Digital Media and ICT Vendor Alliance (DIVA), which was established in 2003 as a collaboration between the Scottish Qualifications Authority, which authorizes all Scottish vocational qualifications, the Scottish education sector, and the

ICT industry. This PPP includes 14 companies, such as Microsoft, Adobe, and Oracle, but also the vendor-independent provider CompTIA, and aims to provide "learners with industry-enriched ICT vocational qualifications and certifications aligned to the needs of the workplace" (SQA 2007: 37). Like a number of other initiatives, DIVA aims to offer vocational programs by developing assessments and credentials for jobs that do not require a four-year college degree (Haimson and VanNoy 2004).

The European Dimension

Notably, the European Commission has also started to become active in this sphere of ICT standard setting, mostly in close collaboration with vendor-independent multi-stakeholder associations. It has mandated, for instance, CEPIS with carrying out forecasting analyses in the field of e-skills, which in turn inform the EU e-skill initiatives.[16] Since 2003, CEPIS has been the chair of the ICT Skills Workshop of the European Committee for Standardization (CEN), which comprises a multi-stakeholder group including professional associations, universities, and companies such as Airbus, Deutsche Telekom, Cisco Systems, and Microsoft. This initiative has launched an ambitious project to establish a European e-competence framework (e-CF).[17] The fact that this initiative also involves workers' representatives distinguishes it from other multi-stakeholder projects in which trade unions are rarely included.

Major efforts have been undertaken in recent years to integrate the European e-CF into the overarching European Qualifications Framework, which the EU has developed in an attempt to coordinate the education policy of its member states in more general terms, and to facilitate mutual recognition of qualifications (Sherry et al. 2013; European Parliament and Council 2008). This integration will further strengthen the European e-CF since it will become part of a formal educational framework underpinned by public authority and its stronger enforcement power.

We can consider these different European initiatives, to a certain extent, to be a European answer to the international dominance of vendor-specific certifiers, which are in most cases headquartered in the US. The European standard-setting initiatives do not exclude big US ICT companies such as Microsoft or Cisco, but mediate their influence by embedding them in a framework with a broad range of public and private actors.

International Dimension

The International Organisation for Standardization (ISO) became involved in the field of standards for ICT skills, drawing heavily on European standards developed by CEN. Over the last few years, the organization has developed a wide range of standards for e-learning that are also relevant for ICT training, although most of these standards focus on narrow technical specifications related to ICT training.[18] However, an increasing number of standards address broader issues that aim to assure the quality of providers, notably in the sphere of non-formal education.[19]

More recent standards address the issue of mutual recognition of ICT qualifications. ISO/IEC 20006-1:2014, for instance, sets standards for the exchange of information about competence in the sphere of ICT education and training.[20] The multi-stakeholder nature of standard-setting activities underpins the authority and legitimacy of the final product. The standards, however, also benefit from the already well-established reputation of ISO as a global standard-setting body, and thus have an advantage that other multi-stakeholder certifiers do not.

The United Nations Educational, Scientific and Cultural Organization (UNESCO) has only recently entered the field of international standard setting. Its standards focus, in particular, on the training of teachers through its ICT Competency Framework for Teachers, which was launched in 2008. This framework outlines the competencies that teachers should have in order to make best use of ICT in their professional practice. Interestingly enough, this UNESCO initiative builds little on the standards developed by multi-stakeholder initiatives. In publicly available documents, ICDL is only mentioned briefly. The core partners are Microsoft, Cisco, and Intel. The use of ICT-CFT standards is regulated through an "open license," that allows for sharing and copying the standards. However, Microsoft holds the copyright of the recently integrated Appendix 2, whose use it has only released to UNESCO through a legal agreement.[21] The US ambassador to UNESCO David Killion praised this UNESCO initiative on the occasion of its launch as "[b]ringing American businesses to work with UNESCO in areas like science, education, communications and culture" (Killion 2011). This can be taken as an indication that vendor-specific certifiers are using UNESCO with the intention of strengthening their position against vendor-independent certifiers that have become increasingly global in their reach, not least as a result of financial support from the EU. This competition between different standard-setting platforms brings the geopolitical dimension of the internationalization of ICT skill standards to the fore. The fact that ICT companies have decided to side with UNESCO, an organization that used to play an important role in the 1970s in challenging the US supremacy and its media industry in the name of a new global information order, just adds to the tragedy of this organization (for a detailed study see Hartmann 2010).

Conclusions

This chapter has argued that the emerging parallel universe of post-secondary education needs to be seen in the context of a major socio-economic transformation that paves the way for a knowledge-based economy. This type of economy requires perpetual innovation to remain at the upper end of the global value chain and therefore relies heavily on continuing adjustment of ICT skills in response to new innovation. As a consequence, the learning has become characterized by an ever-shorter temporal rhythm. This has major consequences for the public–private nexus, as well as for the self-organization of the private sector. I have further developed this analysis in the vein of Streeck's (2009) study of the reform of capitalism, which points out a major transformation of the self-organization of the economy, moving from a Durkheimian type to a Williamsonian type. The institutions of the latter type are more decentralized, fragmented, diversified, and private in nature, and part of an intensification of competition at the global level. The move transforms corporate governance, and weakens networks among firms, as well as the role of trade unions, notably in countries where trade unions once had a say in the design of TVET and CTE. Thelen and Busemeyer (2012) describe this change in the context of TVET as a move from collectivism to segmentalism, where major firms have become decisive in determining the context of TVET. I outlined how these studies have overlooked the change in private authority. Further developing the emerging literature on private authority, I focused particularly on the role of coordination service firms, which have taken over parts of coordination of the public and, notably, the private sectors. However, these companies require broad acceptance of their coordinating role in order to be effective. Hence, they need to have both *the* authority to coordinate and to select, as well as being *an* authority, and thus legitimate. I have argued that we can consider ICT certifiers to function as coordination service firms, since they contribute to coordinating vital dimensions of the emerging network society by introducing standards for ICT skills. More specifically, they help to stabilize the labor market as they facilitate inter-firm cooperation in more general terms.

The empirical study has explored in more detail the enabling conditions of their private authority, and has identified two main types that compete with each other. The authority and coordination capacity of vendor-specific certifiers is closely related to their software and technology. They benefit not only from the reputation of knowing best how to use their software and technology, but also from their economy of scale and oligopolistic market position. They directly compete with vendor-independent certifiers whose standard setting and coordination authority is grounded in more inclusive consultation mechanisms, but often suffer from a lack of scale. However, the range of actors this second type of certifiers involves can fundamentally differ, as the study has highlighted. Some certifiers represent the interest of the overall ICT industry, while others go beyond by including, predominantly, ICT professions. However, only a few vendor-independent certifiers are constituted by a broader range of stakeholders such as members of the academic community and trade unions. These two types of provider notably compete with each other on establishing partnerships with public educational institutions with the intent not only to extend their market share, but also their coordination capacity by including public authority.

Furthermore, the study has highlighted how these two types of transnational private authority intend to gain public support for their international standard-setting activities. Notably, the EU supports standard setting by vendor-independent certifiers through the European standard-setting organization CEN, and through ISO, whose standards are accepted worldwide. The case study has also highlighted how UNESCO has become involved in international ICT standard setting. The empirical findings indicate that oligopolistic US-based ICT companies are particularly keen on using UNESCO to fortify their authority in global standard setting, notably in the area of teacher training. This competition at the global level highlights the geopolitical dimension of ICT training and certification, and its coordinating function for the emerging global network society. However, much more research is needed to bring this emerging sphere of post-secondary education further into the public limelight. For too long, this sphere has managed to hide itself behind the idea that ICT training merely provides technical skills that are framed in terms of consumer knowledge.

Notes

1 I wish to thank Gita Steiner-Khamsi for her comments on a previous version. The usual disclaimers apply. This article has been developed with support from the European Research Council within the project "Institutional Transformation in European Political Economy – A Socio-legal Approach" (ITEPE-312331).

2 This is particularly obvious for studies that outline a positive link between certifications and wage level. (For a critical review of the 2014 IT Skills and Salary Report, see Tittel 2014).

3 IDC is one of the few research companies that offers an annual global survey of education and certification Services. An IDC report costs about USD $4,500 (see www.idc.com).

4 Market observers underline the increasing importance of additional business skills (see Lisican 2008; Povalej and Weiss 2007: 38).

5 For the analytical framework distinguishing formal, informal, and non-formal education, see Coombs 1968; Coombs and Ahmed 1974. For a current overview of these types of education in the EU Member States, see Colardyn and Bjornavold 2004; Council of the European Union 2012.

6 I have elsewhere developed a theoretical framework aimed at better understanding the dissociation that such an equalization requires, and the violence of this abstraction, which masks the relations of power (Hartmann 2014).

7 This is a simplified typology derived from Povalej and Weiss (2007: 8).

8 For a comprehensive overview of vender-specific certifiers, see CEDEFOP (2006: 102–111).

9 However, the philanthropic records of some ICT companies are not particularly good. Bill Gates was long criticized as a greedy monopolist, before he and his wife set up the Bill and Melinda Gates Foundation (*The Independent* 2006). There is no public record that Steve Jobs, the co-founder of Apple, ever donated to charity. He even closed Apple's philanthropic programs on his return to the company in 1997 (Sorkin 2011).

10 http://www.eucip.com.

11 http://www.certiport.com/PORTAL/desktopdefault.aspx?tabid=684&roleid=101.

12 http://www.certiport.com/PORTAL/desktopdefault.aspx?tabid=684&roleid=101.

13 KIBNET was such an exception. This German joint project was funded until the end of 2008 by the Federal Ministry for Education and Research, and involved the trade union IG Metall and the German Association for Information Technology, Telecommunications, and New Media. See www.kibnet.org.

14 Though a closer look at the wage structure in the ICT labor market indicates that formal qualification continues to be decisive at the upper end of the qualification level. The parallel universe has predominantly gained momentum at bachelor's and master's degree levels, where ICT certificates – not degrees – are more likely to determine wage level, according to a number of studies (Tegan et al. 2006; Bartlett et al. 2005). This is less likely to be the case for ICT professionals with a PhD.

15 https://www.netacad.com/web/about-us/about-networking-academy.

16 https://www.cepis.org/index.jsp?p=636&n=637.

17 See "Education for all," *ISO Focus,* November 2007; CEN, "A common European framework for ICT Professionals in all industry sectors European e-Competence Framework 1.0." (Brussels 2008; European Committee for Standardization, European Commission). See also http://www.ecompetences.eu.

18 ISO/IEC 24751-2:2008 focuses, for instance, on the individualized adaptability and accessibility in e-learning, education, and training. ISO/IEC 19778-1:2008 establishes norms for collaborative technology in this sphere.

19 ISO/IEC 17024:2003, for instance, established standards for the certification of persons; for more information see also IAF, "IAF Guidance on the Application of ISO/IEC 17024:2003 Conformity assessment – General Requirements for Bodies operating Certification of Person," Cherrybrook, International Accreditation Forum 2004, and CEDEFOP 2006, 24. ISO/IEC 23988:2007 provides recommendations on the use of ICT to deliver assessments to candidates and to record and score their responses. ISO/IEC 19796-1:2005 establishes a description scheme for quality management and describes a process model, defining the basic processes to be considered when managing quality in the field of ICT training. As such, it provides generic quality standards for certifications that have to be taken into account by the certifiers if they want to become ISO-certified. See Pawlowski, J. M. (2007), "The quality adaptation model: Adaptation and adoption of the quality standard ISO/IEC 19796-1 for learning, education, and training," ISO, *ISO Focus* (November/December, 2009, Geneva, International Standard Organization), pp. 31–34. *Educational Technology and Society* 10(2), 3–16. ISO 29990:2010 provides standards for non-formal education and training developed by the ISO technical committee on "Learning services for non-formal education and training." Most ICT training-related standards are, however, developed by the technical committee ISO/IEC JTC 1, and are still rather technical in focus.

20 See https://www.iso.org/obp/ui/#iso:std:iso-iec:20006:-1:ed-1:v1:en.

21 UNESCO (n.d.). *What is the ICT CFT?* Retrieved June 20, 2015: from: http://www.unesco.org/new/en/communication-and-information/access-to-knowledge/unesco-ict-competency-framework-for-teachers/what-is-the-ict-cft/.

References

Adeleman, C. (2000). A parallel universe – trend toward replacing academic degrees with information technology certificates. *Change,* 32(3), 20–29.

Australian Government. (2014). Labour market research – Information and Telecommunications (ICT) professions Australia. http://docs.employment.gov.au/system/files/doc/other/ictclusterreportaus.pdf.

Baethge, M. (1999). Glanz und Elend des deutschen Korporatismus in der Berufsbildung. *WSI MITTEILUNGEN,* 52(8), 489–497.

Ball, S. J. and Youdell, D. (2007). *Hidden privatisation in public education.* Preliminary Report Institute of Education, University of London, Education International 5th World Congress. July 2007. Retrieved May 27, 2015 from: www.researchgate.net/profile/Deborah_Youdell/publication/228394301_Hidden_privatisation_in_public_education/links/0a85e539232ed78325000000.pdf.

Bartlett, K. R., Horwitz, S. K., Ipe, M., and Liu, Y. (2005). The perceived influence of industry-sponsored credentials on the recruitment process in the information technology industry: Employer and employee perspective. *Journal of Career and Technical Education,* 21(2), 51–64.

Bell, D. (1973). *Coming of post-industrial society: A venture in social forecasting.* New York: Basic Books.

Biersteker, T. J. and Hall, R. B. (2002). *The emergence of private authority in global governance.* Cambridge: University of Cambridge.

Brookshear, J. G. (2014). *Computer science: An overview (12th ed.).* Upper Saddle River, NJ: Prentice Hall.

Castells, M. (1999). *The rise of the network society.* Cambridge: Blackwell.

CEDEFOP. (2006). ICT skills certification in Europe. European Centre of the Development of Vocational Training, Thessaloniki. www.cedefop.europa.eu/files/6013_en.pdf

CEN. (2009). Workshop agreement 16052:2009: ICT Certification in Europe. European Committee for Standardization, Brussels. www.ict-certification-in-europe.eu.

Cisco. (2014). Corporate social responsibility report. Retrieved March 2, 2015 from: http://www.cisco.com/assets/csr/pdf/CSR_Report_2014.pdf.

Colardyn, D. and Bjornavold, J. (2004). Validation of formal, non-formal and informal learning: Policy and practices in EU member states. *European Journal of Education* 39(1), 69–89.

CompTIA. (2004). *The situation and the role of e-skills industry certification in Europe.* The Computing Technology Industry Association, European E-skills. Conference 2004. Thessaloniki, Greece.

Coombs, P. H. (1968). *World educational crisis: A systems approach.* New York: Oxford University Press.

Coombs, P. H. and Ahmed, M. (1974). *Attacking rural poverty: How non-formal education can help.* Baltimore, MD: Johns Hopkins University Press.

Council of the European Union. (2012). *Council recommendation on the validation of non-formal and informal learning,* of 20 December 2012. (2012/C 398/01). http://eur-lex.europa.eu/LexUriServ/LexUriServ.do?uri=OJ:C:2012:398:0001:0005:EN:PDF.

Cutler, A. C. (2002). Private international regimes and interfirm cooperation. In R. B. Hall and T. J. Biersteker (Eds). *The emergence of private authority in global governance.* (pp. 23–40). Cambridge: Cambridge University Press.

Cutler, A. C., Haufler, V., and Porter, T. (1999). Private authority and international affairs. In A. C. Cutler, V. Haufler, and T. Porter. (Eds). *Private Authority and International Affairs* (pp. 3–28). Albany, NY: SUNY Press.

Dolton, P. and Pelkonen, P. (2008). The wage effects of computer use: Evidence from WERS 2004. *British Journal of Industrial Relations,* 46(4), 587–630.

Draxler, A. (2012). International PPPs in education: New potential or privatizing public goods? In S. Robertson, K. Mundy, A Verger and F. Menashy (Eds). *Public Private Partnerships and education: New actors and modes of governance in a globalising world.* (pp. 43–62). Cheltenham: Edward Elgar Publishing Ltd.

European Parliament, and Council. (2008). Recommendation of the European Parliament and the Council on the establishment of the European Qualifications Framework for lifelong learning, January 29, 2008, PE-CONS 3662/07. http://eur-lex.europa.eu/legal-content/EN/ALL/?uri=CELEX:32008H0506(01).

Foote Partners, LLC. (2015). 2015 IT skills demand and pay trends report. Retrieved May 25, 2015 from: http://www.footepartners.com.

French, M. (2010, April 6). Why IT certification matters. *TechCentral.* Retrieved May 24, 2015 from: http://www.techcentral.co.za/why-it-certification-matters/13743/.

Frost and Sullivan. (2013). Analysis of the global SSL certificate market. The growing need for value-added solutions. Retrieved May 25, 2015 from: http://www.frost.com/sublib/display-report.do?id=NC0A-01-00-00-00.

Gareis, K., Husing, T., Birov, S., Bludova, I., Schulz, C., and Korte, W. B. (2014). *E-skills for jobs in Europe – measuring progress and voving ahead*. Final report. Accessed May 24, 2015 from: http://www.openeducationeuropa.eu/en/news/e-skills-jobs-europe-measuring-progress-and-moving-ahead-report.

Ginsburg, M. (2012). Public private partnerships, neoliberal globalization and democratization. In S. Robertson, K. Mundy, A Verger and F. Menashy (Eds). *Public Private Partnerships and education: New actors and modes of governance in a globalising world*. (pp. 63–79). Cheltenham: Edward Elgar Publishing Ltd.

Graz, J. C. and Nölke, A. (Eds). (2008). *Transnational private governance and its limits*. London: Routledge.

Haimson, J. and VanNoy, M. (2004). *Developing the IT workforce: Certification programs, participants and outcomes in high schools and two-year colleges*. Mathematica Policy Research Reports, Mathematica Policy Research, Inc. Retreived May 4, 2015 from: www.mathematica-mpr.com/~/media/publications/pdfs/itworkforce.pdf.

Hall, P. A. and Soskice, D. (2001). *Varieties of capitalism: The institutional foundations of comparative advantage*. Oxford: Oxford University Press.

Hansen, K. and Salskov-Inversen, D. (2008). *Critical perspectives on private authority in global politics*. New York: Palgrave Macmillan.

Hartmann, E. (2010). The United Nations Educational, Scientific and Cultural Organisation: Pawn or global player? *Globalisation, Societies and Education*, 8(2): 307–318.

Hartmann, E. (2014). The fetish of global competition. *Capital and Class*, 38(1), 184–196.

Hoyle, T. (2010). Credentials for success. An evolution in the IT Industry. *T+D*. 64(7), 48–51.

Independent, The. (2006, June 27). Bill Gates: Where are his billions going? *The Independent*. Retrieved May 25, 2015 from http://www.independent.co.uk/news/world/americas/bill-gates-where-are-his-billions-going-405626.html.

Jones, T., Margolis, D., Summerfield, B., Whitney, K., and Stone Wunder, S. (2006). CertMag's 2006 salary survey. *Certification Magazine*, December.

Killion, D. (2011). Ambassador Killion's remarks at the ICT CFT launch. Retrieved March 2, 2015 from: http://unesco.usmission.gov/ambassador-remarks-ict-cft.html.

Korte, W. B., Husing, T., Hendriks, L., and Dirkx, J. (2013). Towards a European quality label for ICT industry training and certification. Retrieved May 24, 2015 from: http://ec.europa.eu/digital-agenda/en/news/towards-european-quality-label-ict-industry-training-and-certifications.

Koselleck, R. (2002). *The practice of conceptual history: Timing history, spacing concepts*. Redwood City, CA: Stanford University Press.

Krajewski, M. (2011). Commodifying and embedding services of general interests in transnational contexts – The example of healthcare liberalisation in the EU and the WTO. In C. Joerges and J. Falke, (Eds). *Globalisation and the potential of law in transnational markets international studies in transnational market*. (pp 231–254). Oxford: Hart Publishing.

Lambert, M. T. (2014). *Privatization and the public good: Public universities in the balance*. Cambridge, MA: Harvard University Press.

Lisican, E. (2008). The future of IT: Hybrid jobs. *Certification Magazine (November)*. Retrieved May 4, 2015 from http://certmag.com/the-future-of-it-hybrid-jobs.

Murphy, R. (1984). The structure of closure: a critique and development of the theories of Weber, Collins and Parkin. *British Journal of Sociology of Education*, 35(4), 547–567.

O'Sullivan, J., Weiss, P., and Sharov, G. (2011). ICT certification in action, May 3, 2011 draft final report, CEN Workshop ICT skills, Retrieved May 4, 2015 from www.ict-certification-in-europe.eu.

Povalej, R. and Weiss, P. (2007). Survey of ICT certification systems for ICT professionals in Europe. *Upgrade – the European Journal for the Informatics Professional,* VII(3), 36–45.

Randall, M. H. and Zirkle, C. J. (2005). Information technology student-based certification in formal education settings: Who benefits and what is needed. *Journal of Information Technology Education,* 4(1), 287–306.

Robertson, S., Mundy, K., Verger A., and Menashy, F. (2012). *Public private partnerships in education: New actors and modes of governance in a globalizing world.* Cheltenham: Edward Elgar Publishing Ltd.

Sako, M. (1995). *Skill testing and certification in Japan.* Washington, DC: The World Bank.

Saks, M. (2010). Analyzing the professions: The case for the neo-Weberian approach. *Comparative Sociology,* 9(6): 887–915.

Sassen, S. (2006). *Territory, authority, rights. From medieval to global assemblages.* Princeton, NJ: Princeton University Press.

Schiller, D. (2000). *Digital capitalism – networking the global market system.* Cambridge, MA: MIT Press.

Sherry, M., Carcary, M., McLaughlin, S., and O'Brien, C. (2013). Actions towards maturing the ICT profession within Europe. *International Journal of Human Capital and Information Technology Professionals,* 4(1), 46–61.

Sorkin, R. A. (2011, August 29). The mystery of Steve Jobs's public giving. *The New York Times.* Retrieved May 25, 2015 from http://dealbook.nytimes.com/2011/08/29/the-mystery-of-steve-jobss-public-giving/?_r=0.

SQA. (2007). *Evaluation of the digital media and ICT vendor alliance (DIVA),* Bulletin number 30, Scottish Qualifications Authority, Glasgow. www.sqa.org.uk/files_ccc/ResearchBulletin30.pdf.

Streeck, W. (2009). *Re-forming capitalism: Institutional change in the German political economy.* Oxford University Press: Oxford.

Summerfield, B. (2007). Funding your certification. *Certification Magazine (August).* Retrieved May 4, 2015 from http://certmag.com/funding-your-certification.

Thelen, K. (2001). Varieties of labour politics in the developed democracies. In A. P. Hall and D. Soskice, (Eds). *Varieties of capitalism: The institutional foundations of comparative advantage.* Oxford: Oxford University Press.

Thelen, K. (2004). *How institutions evolve: The political economy of skills in Germany, Britain, the United States, and Japan.* New York: Cambridge University Press.

Thelen, K. and Busemeyer, M. (2012). Institutional change in German vocational training: From collectivism toward segmentalism. In M. Busemeyer and C. Trampusch, (Eds). *The political economy of collective skill formation.* (pp. 68–100). Oxford: Oxford University Press.

Tissot, P. (2004). *Terminology of vocational training policy: A multilingual glossary for an enlarged Europe.* Cedefop Reference series; 41. Luxembourg: Office for Official Publications of the European Communities, retrieved May 4, 2015 from http://www.cedefop.europa.eu/files/4064_en.pdf.

Tittel, E. (2006). Certification Top 10 lists revisited. *Certification Magazine (November).* Retrieved May 4, 2015 from http://certmag.com/certification-top-10-lists-revisited.

Tittel, E. (2014). Beware the top paying IT certifications for 2014 survey. *Tom's ITPro.* Retrieved May 4, 2015 from www.tomsitpro.com/articles/top-paying-it-certifications-2014,1-1655.html.

Tyler, K. (2004). Carve out Training? *HR Magazine,* 49(2), 52–57.

UNESCO. (n.d.). *What is the ICT CFT?* Retrieved June 20, 2015: from: http://www.unesco.org/new/en/communication-and-information/access-to-knowledge/unesco-ict-competency-framework-for-teachers/what-is-the-ict-cft/.

Weber, M. (1978). *Economy and society.* Berkeley, CA: University of California Press.

Weiss, P. and Povalej, R. (2007). Survey of ICT certification systems for ICT professionals in Europe, *UPGRADE, The European Journal for the Informatics Professional*, VII (3), pages 36–45, June, 2007.

Whitney, K. (2007). The international market for certification. *Certification Magazine.* Retrieved May 25, 2015 from http://www.nxtbook.com/nxtbooks/mediatec/cm0507/index.php?startid=7.

15 Questioning the Global Scaling Up of Low-Fee Private Schooling

The Nexus between Business, Philanthropy, and PPPs

Prachi Srivastava

The LFP Sector: The Second-Wave

In view of generally accepted claims of poor state sector quality in many countries of the Global South, the low-fee private sector has often been posited as "the poor's best chance" (Tooley 2000) against broader concerns of the state's fundamental duty to provide basic education to all (Watkins 2004). The initial emergence of the low-fee private sector and its subsequent evolution into an attractive sector for business backed by domestic and international corporate investment holds an important and divisive place as we enter the post-2015 era in global education.

As I have discussed elsewhere (Srivastava 2013), at the beginning of the international Education for All (EFA) movement, the emergence of the low-fee private sector was dismissed in high-level policy circles, and by academics and right-to-education advocates as an atomized phenomenon, fragmented and insufficient in scope to warrant concerted study. This was in view of more pressing EFA goals to ensure, quite rightly, that all children are able to access free basic education. However, what first seemed like small, disconnected, individual schools "mushrooming" in specific contexts where there was little or poor quality state provision has taken root as a phenomenon, purportedly of scale, backed by corporate actors, particularly in some parts of sub-Saharan Africa and Asia.

This has attracted widespread attention as part of a broader trend of privatization of and in education, and, quite unlike dismissals of the past, has reached the highest levels of global education policymakers, influencers, and advocates. For example, the UNESCO *Education for All Global Monitoring Report* began including a section on low-fee private schooling from the 2009 report. Global civil society actors such as the Right to Education Project, the Soros Open Society Foundations, and the Global Initiative for Economic, Social and Cultural Rights have been spurred into developing a human rights framework for private sector engagement in education. The most vehement criticism has come from the United Nations Special Rapporteur on the Right to Education who has referred to the existence of corporate-backed schools and providers in education as being indicative of "abusive practices" (United Nations 2014) of the private sector, calling on states to sanction them:

89. By definition, business is profit-oriented. Education is all the more attractive since it denotes a certain respectability, which can be projected to disguise business interests, fraudulent practices and corruption […]

90. As regulators, States must sanction abusive practices by private education establishments.

(United Nations 2014)

Given the earlier dismissive response of the academic and global policy community, the urgency expressed just a decade later to examine the potential centrality of the sector as inimical to equitable access to education for all is remarkable. In essence, we are entering a "second-wave" in our understandings and analyses of the low-fee private sector, as is the sector in its evolution.

I argue that the second wave sees a shift from "one-off mom-and-pop teaching shops" in schooling micro-ecosystems (individual villages, slum communities, and urban neighborhoods), to their coexistence with corporate-backed school chains and service providers. These chains operate as part of a micro-system within themselves, across geographical boundaries beyond the local (across districts, cities, regions, and countries). The entry of "big" corporate capital, both domestic and international, and the emergence of an ecosystem of allied service providers for this sector (education microfinance institutions; rating systems; scripted curriculum delivery systems; education technology providers (low- and high-tech, etc.)), many of which are also corporate-backed or run, are markers of institutional evolution (DiMaggio and Powell 1983). Thus, though the scale and reach of the low-fee private sector may not be as grand and wide as the operators purport, the second wave is strongly entrenched within increased corporate engagement, business practice, and commercialization. And this warrants serious attention.

The second wave seems comprised of at least three intertwining and enabling trends, resulting in the emergence of corporate-backed low-fee private school chains and service providers in the Global South. Of these, this chapter will focus on the first two, in the main:

- mobilizing discourse and filtering evidence – in particular, morphing the metaphor of the market to illogical consequence;
- the opening up of domestic formal education spaces through state-sanctioned public–private partnership (PPP) arrangements, and framing mental models accepting of the discourse of "partnership";
- increasingly opaque, intertwined, and complex sets of "new/non-traditional" non-state private actors operating in education in the Global South, with direct or arm's length corporate connections that operate by blurring the lines between "doing business," profit-making, and "doing good" (Ball and Olmedo 2011).

These arguments are posited against three caveats. First, claims of "scale" put forward by the corporate-backed low-fee private sector should not be taken at face value.

In fact, when we examine the reach and numbers of some of the most publicized chains, we find the total numbers to be minuscule as a proportion of state provision.

Second, the corporate-backed low-fee private sector does not operate equally across all areas of the Global South. As a concerted business venture with desired results on investment, we see the emergence of this second wave primarily in lower-middle/middle-income countries with significant "buzz" around the engine of economic growth. India, with its relatively stable political climate and as one of the top five largest world economies, is a favored location.

Finally, the act of "doing good" may be broadly termed "philanthropic," but is of a nature quite different from traditional non-profit grant-making philanthropies in the "business of charity." Many of the non-state actors (venture philanthropies, social entrepreneurship firms, corporate social responsibility units, etc.) involved with the diffusion of corporate-backed low-fee private school chains and their allied service providers operate with mental models framed by, and the modalities of, the "business of making money" with an added offshoot of "doing good." This is similar to Ball and Olmedo's (2011) characterization of "creative capitalism," or "an approach where governments, businesses, and non-profits work together to stretch the reach of market forces so that more people can make a profit, or gain recognition, doing work that eases the world's inequities" (Microsoft 2008 quoted in Ball and Olmedo 2011: 84).

Morphing the Metaphor of the Market and Filtering Evidence

The emergence of the second wave of the evolution of the low-fee private sector and its research is linked to strong enabling discourse that "morphs" (Cowen 2009) the metaphor of the market and filters evidence. A number of recent reviews raise queries about the low-fee private sector, and point to inconclusive evidence on relative achievement, inputs, and affordability (see Day Ashley et al. 2014; Mcloughlin 2013; Srivastava 2013). Overlooked work includes that of influential low-fee private sector advocate and investor James Tooley, and his colleagues' own scholarly and refereed published research which is technical in tone and, when closely read, reveals important nuances.

On relative achievement, their work in Kenya and India showed that private school students did not universally achieve better results in every subject, taking account of background variables (Dixon et al. 2013; Tooley et al. 2010). On equity concerns, their work in Nigeria and India showed that the most disadvantaged, described as orphans, migrants, and financially unstable families, could not afford the "low" fees charged (Tooley and Dixon 2005b). Finally, their work revealed education corruption at the highest levels, showing that such schools in India gained recognition through bribery (Tooley and Dixon 2005a). These findings are similar to results of other studies in contexts including Ghana, India, Nigeria, Malawi, and Pakistan, among others (Akaguri 2011; Chudgar and Quin 2012; Fennell and Malik 2012; Härmä 2009, 2011; Ohara 2013; Rose 2005; Rose and Adelabu 2007; Srivastava 2007, 2008).

Despite much contrary research evidence, including that from his own work, Tooley's "catchy" journalistic commentary, grey and informal reports, and book on his "personal journey" into the "education of the poor" (Tooley 2009) have been highly publicized. This work has caught the attention of high-level policy circles and networks of non-state private actors. Nambissan and Ball's (2010) detailed analysis suggests that this is a result of Tooley and his network's policy entrepreneurship par excellence on school choice and the low-fee private sector in deep and far-reaching transnational networks.

Recommendations include establishing public and private voucher schemes, education service companies for school improvement and accreditation, education microcredit/loan companies, and "the liberalization of the regulatory environment regarding private ... schools making a surplus" (Tooley and Dixon 2003: 22), acknowledging that this may, in fact, be illegal. These have inspired many second-wave low-fee private sector players to act. Examples referring to Tooley's work, in particular, include India's Centre for Civil Society advocating state-subsidized vouchers to access low-fee private schools; Gray Matters India creating a school performance system for "affordable private schools"; co-founder of Omega Schools Ken Donkoh starting a chain in Ghana (eventually in collaboration with Tooley); and IDP Foundation's Rising Schools Program, a micro-credit initiative for the sector in Ghana.

The decided enthusiasm about the low-fee sector is not based in sentiment alone. It is infused with the motivation *to actively create* a global market for the corporate-backed low-fee private sector. This is helped by extending the metaphor of the market and the reach of its "Three Musketeers" – branding, competition, and profit: "Assisting the market in the creation of educational brand names ... is another possible area for outside action – for philanthropy, investment, and aid if required to satisfy investors of the viability of the market" (Tooley 2009: 260).

The potential for investors to capitalize on establishing branded chains and services to the sector, with a focus on replication and standardization, is key. Tooley asserts, "school chains with names such as EasyLearn or Virgin Opportunity could be as reliable as, say, Sainsbury's [supermarkets] or Boots [pharmacies]" (Wilby 2013). Bridge International Academies, purportedly the world's largest chain of low-fee nursery and primary schools, bills itself as "the Starbucks" of schools in developing countries (Olopade 2013).

In this idealized market, "competition would be a chief spur." Unbranded or unchained schools "could suffer or go out of business," or others could "soon enter the market establishing competing brand names" (Tooley 2009: 261). There is little consideration for what would happen to children in instances where they are attending schools that close and others do not step in to fill the gap.

The profitability of low-fee private schools even as relatively small, single operations by individuals without the backing of "big" capital, was noted early on: "running a school even for low-income families was potentially a profitable undertaking, with estimated profits of about 25 percent in the year of [school] recognition" (Tooley and Dixon 2003: 19). The profitability of scaling-up the sector did not go unnoticed. In 2012, Pearson, owner of the Financial Times, and the world's largest educational publisher, launched the Pearson Affordable Learning Fund (PALF), a $15 million fund to invest in the low-fee private sector across Asia and Africa (Tran 2012). PALF has quite possibly, and with speed, become the most influential player in supporting the scaling up of the corporate-backed low-fee private sector. "In January 2015 we [PALF] announced Pearson will invest a further $50 million over the next 3 years" (PALF 2015). Michael Barber, PALF's Chief Education Advisor, and reportedly "an old friend" of Tooley's (Wilby 2013), stated in an interview on *BBC HardTalk*: "It's absolutely for profit. But get this right – it's important to demonstrate profit because we want other investors to come in" (Barber quoted in Riep 2014: 264). As Riep (2014) notes, demonstrating profitability is key to attracting investment in the early attempts to create a market in this sector.

For those with interests in the corporate-backed low-fee sector and for advocates of increased private provision, the impetus to draw big capital into the fold is a welcome development. Acknowledged state sector dysfunctions in many countries are proposed as the impetus to expand the low-fee private sector, rather than actively injecting capital to improve the state sector. For example, Michael Barber asserts: "The question every education leader needs to answer is: 'How do we get every child in this district, city, state, province or country a good education as soon as possible?' Low-cost private education is an important part of the answer, in almost every country in the developing world" (PALF 2015).

However, the current discourse framing the development of the low-fee private sector morphs the metaphor of the market to such degree that there is little consideration of whether the claim to a fundamental right and the provision of a social good to the economically and socially disadvantaged are really comparable to middle-class supermarkets, pharmacies, and coffee shops. Even Milton Friedman, the revered champion of the marketization of education, conceded the role of the state in ensuring basic education for all. He noted two peculiarities of education as a good, which add to the complications of treating markets in education as pure competitive markets.

The first was related to what he termed, "neighborhood effects." These are "circumstances under which the action of one individual imposes significant costs on other individuals for which it is not feasible to make him[/her] compensate them, or yields significant gains to other individuals for which it is not feasible to make them compensate him [/her]" (Friedman 1962: 85–86). In other words, education has social consequences beyond the individual. The effect, for example, of choices made by one group of parents at a specific point in time that lead to school closures can have resounding effects for other children in the present, and for future children. This can lead to deleterious effects on society.

The second was termed as the "paternalistic concern for children and other irresponsible individuals" (Friedman 1962: 86). There is the need for the state to be involved in education (particularly in developing countries) where schooling may not be universal, making it compulsory to some minimal level, and enforcing that compulsion to uphold children's right to education. In addition, there may be equity concerns regarding mechanisms that disproportionately benefit relatively advantaged groups.

Nonetheless, the corporate-backed expansion of the second-wave of the low-fee private sector, sometimes with the financial support of bilateral agencies and multilateral development banks, exists (e.g. Bridge International Academies). This is despite inconclusive evidence and amid calls against profiteering and, in certain cases, is in contravention of legal frameworks. Bridge International Academies, which receives funding from the UK Department for International Development (DFID), the International Finance Corporation (IFC), and the CDC (the UK's development finance institution), openly admits it: "Technically, we're breaking the law," as stated by Chief Strategy Officer Shannon May in an interview with the *Times Education Supplement* (Exley 2013).

The primary strategy for keeping costs "low" across the sector is the common practice of hiring teachers at below the minimum wage in some instances, or, in most cases, certainly below the teacher's state salary scale (India, Pakistan, Ghana, Nigeria, etc.) This is against labor laws. There are laws against the commercialization of schools and running schools for a profit (India). There are additional concerns that such operators may receive undue taxation benefit and the acquisition of land at much below market rates in certain contexts (Pakistan, India). Despite this, the scaling up of the corporate-backed sector is enabled by the tacit and willing involvement of government and international agencies through the mental models and modalities of partnership.

Scaling up: Tacit "Partnerships" and PPP Modalities

The involvement of certain non-state private actors – corporate actors, in particular – may be more immediately explained by a commercial motive. However, scaling up the corporate-backed low-fee private sector is many times tacitly, but also explicitly, enabled by national governments and supported by bilateral and multilateral agencies, most recently, under the modalities of PPPs and the discourse of "partnership."

The argument here resists the idea that the second wave of the low-fee private sector naturally evolved as the result of default due to state sector dysfunction. While areas of consensus between sympathizers and critics of the low-fee sector are few, as the first wave of low-fee private sector studies emerged, both groups seemed to initially agree that spontaneous, "de-facto privatization" of education emerged because of state failure (Tooley and Dixon 2006), a response that "grew by default rather than design" (Rose 2003: 80). I contend that there has been inadequate provision of state schooling in many contexts, but privatization (or slices of privatization), which may once have been a default strategy, is becoming the strategy of design. This is specifically the case with PPP modalities, which, in particular, have enabled the evolution of the second wave of the low-fee private sector, keeping the centrality of partnership discourse in mind.

Partnership constitutes the education buzzword *du jour*. Cornwall explains: "buzzwords gain their purchase and power through their vague and euphemistic qualities, their capacity to embrace a multitude of possible meanings, and their normative resonance" (2007: 472). Their ability to signify what is *en vogue* is ensconced within a logic of taken-for-grantedness and can "cloud meanings ... through a language of evasion" (Cornwall 2010: 3). Currently, "partnership" is as "ubiquitous as *community*, evoking much the same warm mutuality" (Cornwall 2007: 475). But, it is precisely its ubiquity that renders "partnership" "a floating empty signifier" (Burgos 2004).

In an attempt to more radically define the term, Pickard (2007) suggests that:

> *partnership* denotes a special relationship between equal participants, or yes, partners, who enjoy a distinctive bond of trust, a shared analysis of exist-ing conditions in society, and thus in general a common orientation of what needs to be done *to construct a more just, equitable, and democratic world.*
>
> (575, emphasis added)

However, the social justice ideal mentioned above is conspicuously missing from most discussions in favor of the vagaries of partnership as "a universal – almost a neutral – value upon which all specific agents and governments in general, would agree" (Burgos 2004: 58).

I argue that the seemingly convivial mutuality of the term "partnership" obscures the fundamentally altered mode of governance under PPP modalities, particularly with the introduction of new/non-traditional (and for-profit) non-state private actors in education. While the partnership discourse normatively neutralizes the involvement of profit-motivated actors in particular, state-sanctioned PPP modalities may insert them in complex, opaque, and intertwined arrangements, in which the motivations of individual actors may not resonate. Despite this, the notion of mutuality persists.

This notion of mutuality enables PPP modalities to be legitimized, in spite of lessons from countries with longer histories of PPP-friendly institutional frame-works that large-scale PPP arrangements are riskier for the public sector as there are fewer actors to bear the risk, but also that they operate with vested interests against those of the public, can lead to more complicated regulatory frameworks not less, and that they have the potential of becoming "abusive" if the stronger partner dominates (Coulson 2005; van Marrewijk et al. 2008).

India, Pakistan, and Uganda are examples of countries that have instituted PPP arrangements relatively recently for non-state actors (including, in some cases, private entrepreneurs or "edupreneurs," corporates, and international organi-zations) to take over the management, operation, and establishment of schools. Words such as "nurture," "encourage," and "facilitate" are repeatedly used in gov-ernment documents to outline desired action regarding PPPs and the involvement of non-state actors. These arrangements and the accompanying discourse fuel evolution of the second wave of the low-fee private sector by design, not default.

In 2007, Uganda's Ministry of Education and Sports (MOES) adopted a PPP policy to universalize secondary education. In the MOES vision, PPPs are posi-tioned as vehicles through which quality education can be achieved (MOES, n.d. section "The Department's Mission and Vision"). A PPP program has been launched with the aim of: "Identifying private schools to partner with government in implementing USE [universal secondary education]" (MOES, n.d., section "Programmes"). This has enabled external non-state actors to set up schools in Uganda and apply for state funding.

In Pakistan, the Sindh Education Foundation launched the "Promoting Private Schooling in Rural Sindh Project" in 2008, designed in collaboration with the World Bank. The scheme aimed to support 1000 new private schools in underserved areas in 10 districts (Sindh Education Foundation n.d.: 7). "Entrepreneurs" were invited to establish lower-fee private schools in rural areas but were barred from charging tuition fees to students. Schools were meant to receive a subsidy of Rs. 350/month/boy and Rs. 450/month/girl enrolled. This model is predated by the Punjab Education Foundation's Foundation Assisted Schools program, which runs along similar lines (Punjab Education Foundation 2014).[1] Recently, the All Private School Management Association appealed to the government to view low-fee schools in Sindh outside the scheme as necessary partners in expanding education access. It asked for government grants to fund these private schools to "salvage their crumbling" finances (The *International News* 2014), as they were unsustainable without them.

My analysis of India's Tenth, Eleventh, and Twelfth Five Year Development Plans showed that the broader macro-planning process successively facilitated PPPs in education, and decreased the role for the state in education financing, management, and regulation (Srivastava 2010; Srivastava et al. 2013). Verger and Vanderkaaij (2012) provide a compelling analysis in the Indian context of the use of PPPs as political instruments of "reform." This is despite the limited role officially accorded to the private sector in the Government of India's *Sarva Shiksha Abhiyan* (Education for All) program, which has focused on expanding state provision since 2000. Under an unspecified "PPP mode," the PPP discourse has been sufficiently broadened to allow a range of actors with different motives to enter the schooling space. This included opening up the sector to private companies under their philanthropic arms to start/run low-fee private schools, including a host of international non-state actors.

Positioning low-fee private schools as PPP initiatives is a notable shift in policy discourse and practice, which should not go unnoticed. In the countries cited above, traditional models that could be likened to public–private arrangements before the term was *en vogue* did not include the possibility of corporations or individual "entrepreneurs" running schools, or schools running for a profit. Instead, these were usually community run, or run by a charity, religious order, or trust (private-aided schools, *madrasas*, missionary schools, etc.) under very different regulatory environments and compulsions.

In the first wave of research on the low-fee private sector, the language of PPPs was neither used to describe low-fee private schools, nor were such schools thus conceptualized. Conversely, until very recently, none of the research on low-fee private schools (including Tooley's) positioned them as PPPs. It focused instead on their for-profit or unregulated/unrecognized nature which fell outside the regulatory framework of most countries. In essence, the "PPP creep" in the low-fee private sector normalizes and encourages the expansion of a sector that, until recently, was seen as usurping state regulation, and in certain contexts, still does.

Scaling up (?)

As is apparent from the discussion thus far, evidence of initiatives in the second wave in the sector is nascent. Available information is fragmented and opaque, and concentrated in a small range of countries in the Global South, and on a relatively small number of actors. This makes it difficult to map the evolution of the sector, its size, and to draw broad conclusions. Nonetheless, a few notable examples are presented here. For the purposes of this discussion, and given its influence, we focus on PALF, specifically on its portfolio of education chains (Table 15.1).

According to Pearson's earlier website, it "makes minority equity investments in for-profit companies to meet a growing demand for affordable education services" (Pearson plc 2012: para 1). As mentioned above, as of January 2015, Pearson announced a further $50 million investment in addition to its initial $12 million over the next three years. According to PALF, "This is a testament to Pearson's commitment to educate children in the developing world and brings our total assets under management to $80 m[illion]."

PALF has a portfolio of 10 investments in what it calls "affordable education services," more specifically, in chains and ancillary service providers. Of these, six are school chains from pre-school to secondary, and one is a chain of private tuition centers focusing on secondary school exam preparation. The remaining three are investments in education technology and learning materials.[2] Geographically, four of the investments are in India, and the rest are spread out in Ghana, Kenya, Nigeria, Philippines, South Africa, and Tanzania. Crucially, what constitutes "affordable learning" for PALF is neither precisely defined, nor consistently applied, as a cursory look at the fees charged by its chain operators reveals.

Of these, Omega Schools and Bridge Academies International are best known. In 2008, while a student, Ken Donkoh, a native of Ghana, and previously an employee of the World Bank and IFC, approached Tooley with a business plan (Riep 2014). As relayed by Donkoh and Tooley to me in personal communications, Omega started with the investment of personal capital, until PALF took a stake in Omega Schools in 2013. This allowed the chain to expand to 38 schools and reportedly to 20,000 students. In 2013, Tooley predicted 100 schools with 50,000 students by 2014 (Wilby 2013). This does not seemed to have materialized at the time of writing, and may point to the potential limits of scalability.

As of June 2012, Pearson is reported to have invested in Bridge. Its "Academy-in-a-Box" approach is marketed as having "re-engineered the entire lifecycle of basic education, leveraging data, technology, and scale" to keep quality up and prices low (Bridge International Academies 2013). From its first academy in 2009 in Kenya, Bridge had 359 schools in 2014, and plans to expand to Uganda and Nigeria in 2015. According to the Omidyar Network, one of its investors, Bridge plans to operate in at least 12 countries across sub-Saharan African and India, and have more than 10 million students by 2023 (Omidyar Network n.d.).

Though it is premature to make definitive claims based on available information, we can, nonetheless make a number of initial observations. First, it is clear that chain operators are linked to a number of various kinds of actors, included

Table 15.1 Pearson Affordable Learning Fund (PALF) portfolio of chains

	Country	Sector	Stated Scale	Published Fees	Estimated Fees as Proportion of Min Wage/ Unskilled Wage*	Organizational Links+	Type of Linked Actor+
APEC Schools	Philippines	Secondary	13 schools[x]	Grade 7: P 24,850/yr Grade 8: P 25,350/yr Grades 9–12: N/A	Grade 7 and 8: 15% Grades 9–12: N/A but likely higher	• Ayala Corporation • PALF	Corporate group (holding company)
Avanti Learning Centres	India	Secondary private tuition	12 centers [5 stand-alone centers; 7 in-school centers (Chennai and Tibetan schools)]	Unclear	N/A	• Echoing Green • Draper Richards Foundation • Pan IIT Alumni • UnLtd India • PALF • Personal investors	-Social enterprise/ impact investment -Not-for-profit -Personal investors
Bridge International Academies	Kenya (Uganda, Nigeria for expansion)	Elementary	359 schools; +100,000 students	~$5/month	8% (As proportion of stated target group: families living on maximum $2/day)	• Bill Gates • CDC • DFID • IFC • Khosla Ventures • Learn Capital • NEA	-Venture capital and private investment firms -Bilateral aid agency -Bilateral donor bank

(continued)

Table 15.1 (continued)

						• Novastar • Omidyar Network • PanAfrican Investment Co. • Rethink Education • PALF	-Personal investors
Lekki Peninsula Affordable Schools	Nigeria	Elementary	N/A	N/A	N/A	• Unclear • PALF	Unclear
Omega Schools	Ghana	Elementary	38 schools; 20,000 students	41%	~$0.65/day	• Personal investors • PALF	-Personal investors
Spark Schools	South Africa	Elementary	5 schools (+ 1 for expansion)	62%	R 17,955/yr	• eAdvance • ISASA • PALF	-Education management company -Private schools association
Sudiksha Knowledge Solutions	India	Pre-school	23 pre-schools	N/A	N/A	• ~Unclear (Franchise model) • PALF	-Private investors

Source: All data extracted from PALF and organizational websites. Last verified March 2015.

Notes:

* Calculated in the currency used by the provider. Latest lowest wage rates were used. South Africa (farming and agriculture, March 1 2014 – February 29, 2015); Philippines (mean of four groups, 2015); Ghana (local daily wage rate, May 1, 2014 – May 30, 2015); Kenya (lowest wage 2014–2015). Monthly rate calculated on 30 working days, and on the basis of one full-time adult worker.

+ The organizational links may not be exhaustive, as not all data may be publicly available. Some websites were more developed than others.

x A news report states that APEC plans to expand by adding 11 new schools by the end of 2015.

an expanded array of new/non-traditional non-state private actors, sometimes alongside government, not-for-profit, and aid agencies in complex arrangements. The relationship between the actors is opaque, their roles, and their influence on the chain operator is unclear. In many instances, they are sets of investors, but not always (SPARK schools). While Bridge, the largest operator, also has the largest and most diversified sources of funding, this is not true of Omega, the second largest. Much more concerted analysis is required to make sense of the links, and to ascertain whether or to what degree each operator would be part of a network.

Second, claims of scale are over zealous. It is unclear if this is a marketing ploy by chain operators to inspire confidence in attracting PALF and other investors; mobilizing discourse by PALF to gain global legitimacy; or plain naiveté and misplaced optimism. Simple observation reveals that, with the exception of Bridge, the actual number of schools/centers for each operator is quite small. They constitute a minuscule proportion of total provision in these countries, as well as a minuscule proportion of public provision. Simple calculations would reveal these to be much below one percent.[3] Even in Bridge's case, coverage would constitute approximately 1.8 percent as a proportion of public provision in Kenya with 19,397 public primary schools, and less if this included the total number of primary schools.[4]

Third, published fee rates were difficult to obtain publicly. Only APEC, Bridge, Omega, and SPARK published their fees. In the case of APEC, only rates for the first two years (Grade 7 and 8) were available, even though the schools run until Grade 12. Based on APEC's increasing fee structure between Grade 7 and 8, it would be reasonable to assume that this continues until the end of the cycle. Finally, other than in Omega's case, it was unclear if the fees charged represented the total out-of-pocket costs households would need to pay. SPARK provided a breakdown of tuition, stationery, and registration fees, and, although uniforms and a meal plan were mentioned, costs were not available.

Finally, all operators frequently used terms such as "affordability," "disadvantaged," and "bottom of the pyramid" on their promotional websites. The analysis here shows that this can be severely questioned by: (a) the paucity of information and lack of transparency on the fee structure and fee amounts; (b) any specific operationalization of what is meant by "affordable"; and (c) estimates showing published fees as a proportion of local daily/minimum wage rates.

There is no universally agreed figure on what constitutes "affordable" expenditure on education. Estimates here are provided as a general rule of thumb. A more detailed cost analysis with average numbers of wage-earning members in families among the bottom quintile in specific country contexts, and comparisons with costs of accessing public providers would need to be conducted.[5] However, as the bulk of literature on household education expenditure confirms, families in the bottom quintile are highly sensitive to income and other insecurities (i.e. health, food price shocks, seasonal migration, etc.), and are unlikely to be able to access fee-paying providers for any sustained period. It would be hard to argue that Omega Schools and SPARK, in particular, whose costs amount to 41 percent and 62 percent respectively, as a proportion of local daily/minimum wage rates *per child*, would be affordable to this group, even if estimates included two full-time adult workers.

This raises serious questions about how and on what basis PALF judges affordability and invests in school chains; and, further, how chain operators raise money in the name of reaching disadvantaged children in the Global South. This analysis assumes urgency where public monies in such initiatives are directly invested by bilateral agencies, or where domestic governments subsidize such providers in PPP arrangements either through their own funds or through direct budgetary support via official development assistance. We must seriously question whether the expanded array of new/non-traditional non-state private actors in complex arrangements with non-profit, government, and international donors facilitated by PPP arrangements can lend itself to the potential capture of those spaces by actors engaged in creative capitalism who are in the "business of making money," without necessarily doing the "good" they purport to.

Acknowledgments

This work was conducted as part of a larger research project on the role of non-state actors and the right to education, funded by a grant from the Social Sciences and Humanities Research Council of Canada.

Notes

1 The Sindh Education Foundation and the Punjab Education Foundation were established by the government as semi-autonomous and autonomous institutions, respectively.
2 These are Zaya (India) "'LabKit' solution [which] includes ClassCloud, an adaptive learning platform that can store and deliver digital content in both online and offline environments" and "End-to-end solution that includes tablets pre-loaded with curriculum content, a classroom projector, a Wifi router, content storage, teacher training, and a classroom management tool"; Experifun (India) providing science experiments and learning materials; and Ubongo (Tanzania) "a social enterprise that creates interactive edutainment for learners in Africa" geared to teaching math through "edutoons" on television.
3 Estimates for Sudiksha and Avanti are difficult to provide as public data on the number of registered private tuition centres and pre-primary centres are unavailable.
4 Based on official data available from Kenya Primary Schools Data 2007, Kenya Open Data Initiative.
5 This may not be possible in the case of private tuition centres.

References

Akaguri, L. (2011). *Quality low-fee private schools for the rural poor: Perception or reality? Evidence from southern Ghana.* CREATE Pathways to Access Research Monograph No. 69. Brighton: Centre for International Education, University of Sussex. Retrieved from May 31, 2015 http://www.create-rpc.org/pdf_documents/PTA69.pdf.
Ball, S. J. and Olmedo, A. (2011). Global social capitalism: Using enterprise to solve the problems of the world. *Citizenship, Social and Economics Education*, 10(2), 83–90.

Bridge International Academies. (2013). Approach [Model]. Retrieved March 8, 2014 from http://www.bridgeinternationalacademies.com/approach/model/.

Burgos, R. B. (2004). Partnership as a floating and empty signifier within educational policies: The Mexican case. In B. M. Franklin, M. N. Bloch, and T. Popkewitz (Eds), *Educational partnerships and the state: The paradoxes of governing schools, children, and families.* (pp. 55–82). New York: Palgrave Macmillan.

Chudgar, A. and Quin, E. (2012). Relationship between private schooling and achievement: Results from rural and urban India. *Economics of Education Review,* 31(4), 376–390.

Cornwall, A. (2007). Buzzwords and fuzzwords: Deconstructing development discourse. *Development in Practice,* 17(4/5), 471–484.

Cornwall, A. (2010). Introductory overview – buzzwords and fuzzwords: Deconstructing development discourse. In A. Cornwall and D. Eade (Eds), *Deconstructing development discourse: Buzzwords and fuzzwords.* (pp. 1–18). London: Oxfam.

Coulson, A. (2005). A plague on all your partnerships: Theory and practice in regeneration. *The International Journal of Public Sector Management,* 18(2), 151–163.

Cowen, R. (2009). The transfer, translation and transformation of educational processes: And their shape-shifting? *Comparative Education,* 45(3), 315–332.

Day Ashley, L., Mcloughlin, C., Aslam, M., Engel, J., Wales, J., Rawal, S., Batley, R., Kingdon, G., Nicolai, S., and Rose, P. (2014). *The role and impact of private schools in developing countries: A rigorous review of the evidence.* Final report. Education Rigorous Literature Review. UK Department for International Development. Retrieved from: https://www.gov.uk/government/uploads/system/uploads/attachment_data/file/307032/Private-schools-2014.pdf.

DiMaggio, P. J. and Powell, W. W. (1983). The iron cage revisited: Institutional isomorphism and collective rationality in organizational fields. *American Sociological Review,* 48(2), 147–160.

Dixon, P., Tooley, J., and Schagen, I. (2013). The relative quality of private and public schools for low-income families living in slums of Nairobi, Kenya. In P. Srivastava (Ed.), *Low-fee private schooling: Aggravating equity or mitigating disadvantage?* (pp. 83–104). Oxford: Symposium Books.

Exley, S. (2013). Schools – "technically, we're breaking the law." *Times Education Supplement.* 8 November 2013. Retrieved from: https://www.tes.co.uk/article.aspx?storycode=6373280.

Fennell, S. and Malik, R. (2012). Between a rock and a hard place: The emerging educational market for the poor in Pakistan. *Comparative Education,* 48(2), 249–261.

Friedman, M. (1962). *Capitalism and freedom.* Chicago: University of Chicago Press.

Härmä, J. (2009). Can choice promote Education for All? Evidence from growth in private primary schooling in India. *Compare,* 39(2), 151–165.

Härmä, J. (2011). *Study of private schools in Lagos.* Education Sector Support Programme in Nigeria Assignment Report, Report No. LG: 303. Lagos: ESSPIN/UKAID.

International News, The (2014, 20 February). Call to get low-cost private schools back on their feet. Retrieved March 7, 2014 from http://www.thenews.com.pk/Todays-News-4-233790-Call-to-get-low-cost-private-schools-back-on-their-feet.

Mcloughlin, C. (2013). *Low-cost private schools: Evidence, approaches and emerging issues.* Economic and Private Sector Professional Evidence and Applied Knowledge Services (EPS-PEAKS) Topic Guide. Retrieved May 31, 2015 from http://r4d.dfid.gov.uk/Output/194091/.

Ministry of Education and Sport [MOES], Republic of Uganda. (n.d.). Departments [Private schools and institutions]. Retrieved March 8, 2014 from http://education.go.ug/data/smenu/50/Private.

Nambissan, G. B. and Ball, S. J. (2010). Advocacy networks, choice and private schooling of the poor in India. *Global Networks*, 10(3), 324–343.

Ohara, Y. (2013). The regulation of unrecognised low-fee private schools in Delhi and the Right to Education Act. In P. Srivastava (Ed.), *Low-fee private schools: Aggravating equity or mitigating disadvantage?* (pp. 1–18). Oxford: Symposium Books.

Olpade, D. (2013). Pop-up schools could radically improve global education. *Wired*. Retrieved March 31, 2015 from http://www.wired.com/2013/11/schoolinabox/.

Omidyar Network. (No date). Portfolio [Bridge International Academies]. Retrieved March 8, 2014 from http://www.omidyar.com/portfolio/bridge-international-academies.

PALF. (2015). *Pearson Affordable Learning Fund*. [Homepage]. Retrieved from: https://www.affordable-learning.com/ Last accessed: June 10, 2015.

Pearson plc. (2012). PALF overview. Retrieved March 8, 2014 from http://www.affordable-learning.com/the-fund.html#sthash.Y2CW8B3X.EslIXehp.dpuf.

Pickard, M. (2007). Reflections on relationships: The nature of partnership according to five NGOs in southern Mexico. *Development in Practice*, 17(4/5), 575–581.

Punjab Education Foundation. (2014). PEF Departments, FAS Department [Foundation Assisted Schools (PEF-FAS)]. Retrieved March 8, 2014 from http://www.pef.edu.pk/pef-departments-fas-overview.html.

Riep, C. B. (2014). Omega schools franchise in Ghana: 'Affordable' private education for the poor or for-profit-profiteering? In I. Macpherson, S. Robertson, and G. Walford (Eds), *Education privatisation and social justice: Case studies from Africa, South Asia, and South East Asia*. (pp. 259–278). Oxford: Symposium Books.

Rose, P. (2003). From the Washington to the post-Washington consensus: The influence of international agendas on education policy and practice in Malawi. *Globalisation, Education, and Societies*, 1(1), 67–86.

Rose, P. (2005). Privatisation and decentralisation of schooling in Malawi: Default or design? *Compare*, 35(2), 153–165.

Rose, P. and Adelabu, M. (2007). Private sector contributions to Education for All in Nigeria. In P. Srivastava and G. Walford (Eds), *Private schooling in less economically developed countries: Asian and African perspectives*, 67–88. Oxford: Symposium Books.

Sindh Education Foundation. (n.d.). *Promoting private schooling in rural Sindh: A public-private partnership project based on per-child subsidy model*. Sindh Education Foundation, Government of Sindh. Retrieved May 31, 2015 from http://www.sef.org.pk/pdf/current_initiatives/PPRS_Brochure.pdf.

Srivastava, P. (2007). *Neither voice nor loyalty: School choice and the low-fee private sector in India*. Research Publications Series, Occasional Paper No. 134. New York: National Center for the Study of Privatization in Education, Columbia University. Retrieved May 31, 2015 from http://www.ncspe.org/publications_files/OP134_2.pdf.

Srivastava, P. (2008). The shadow institutional framework: Towards a new institutional understanding of an emerging private school sector in India. *Research Papers in Education*, 23(4), 451–475.

Srivastava, P. (2010). Public–private partnerships or privatisation? Questioning the state's role in education in India. *Development in Practice*, 20(4), 540–553.

Srivastava, P. (2013). Low-fee private schools: Issues and evidence. In P. Srivastava (Ed.), *Low-fee private schooling: Aggravating equity or mitigating disadvantage?* Oxford: Symposium Books.

Srivastava, P., Noronha, C., and Fennell, S. (2013). *Private sector study: Sarva Shiksha Abhiyan*. Report submitted to DFID (India). Retrieved May 31, 2015 from http://www.prachisrivastava.com/uploads/1/9/5/1/19518861/srivastava_et_al._private_sector_study_ssa_india.pdf.

Tooley, J. (2000). Private education: The poor's best chance? *UNESCO Courier*, 53(11), 24.

Tooley, J. (2009). A beautiful tree: A personal journey in how the world's poorest people are educating themselves. Washington, DC: Cato Institute.

Tooley, J. and Dixon, P. (2003). *Private schools for the poor: A case study from India*. Reading: CfBT. Retrieved May 31, 2015 from: http://cdn.cfbt.com/~/media/cfbtcorporate/files/research/2003/r-private-schools-for-the-poor-india-2003.pdf.

Tooley, J. and Dixon, P. (2005a). An inspector calls: The regulation of 'budget' private schools in Hyderabad, Andhra Pradesh, India. *International Journal of Educational Development*, 25(3), 269–285.

Tooley, J. and Dixon, P. (2005b). Is there a conflict between commercial gain and concern for the poor? Evidence from private schools for the poor in India and Nigeria. *Economic Affairs*, 25(2), 20–26.

Tooley, J. and Dixon, P. (2006). 'De facto' privatisation of education and the poor: Implications of a study from sub-Saharan Africa and India. *Compare*, 36(4), 443–462.

Tooley, J., Dixon, P., Shamsan, Y., and Schagen, I. (2010). The relative quality and cost-effectiveness of private and public schools for low-income families: A case study in a developing country. *School Effectiveness and School Improvement*, 21(2), 117–144.

Tran, M. (2012, July 3). Pearson to invest in low-cost private education in Africa and Asia. *The Guardian*. Retrieved May 31, 2015 from http://www.theguardian.com/global-development/2012/jul/03/pearson-invest-private-education-africa-asia.

United Nations. (2014). Sixty-ninth session. Agenda item 68 (b) Promotion and protection of human rights: Human rights questions, including alternative approaches for improving the effective enjoyment of human rights and fundamental freedoms. Right to education. Report of the Special Rapporteur on the right to education, Kishore Singh. A/69/402. September 24, 2014.

van Marrewijk, A., Clegg, S. R., Pitsis, T. S., and Veenswijk, M. (2008). Managing public–private megaprojects: Paradoxes, complexity, and project design. *International Journal of Project Management*, 26(6), 591–600.

Verger, A. and S. VanderKaaij (2012). The national politics of global policies: Public–private partnerships in Indian education. In A. Verger, M. Novelli and H. K. Altinyelken (Eds), *Global education policy and international development: New agendas, issues and policies*. (pp. 245–266). Bloomsbury, London.

Watkins, K. (2004). Private education and 'Education for All'—or how not to construct an evidence-based argument: A reply to Tooley. *Economic Affairs*, 24(4), 8–11.

Wilby, P. (2013, November 12). Professor James Tooley: A champion of low-cost schools or a dangerous man? *The Guardian*. Retrieved May 31, 2015 from http://www.theguardian.com/education/2013/nov/12/professor-james-tooley-low-cost-schools.

16 Economy, Business, and First Class

The Implications of For-Profit Education Provision in the UAE

Natasha Ridge, Susan Kippels, and Soha Shami

We adopted the airline model of economy, business, and first class to make top-notch education available based on what families could afford.
Sunny Varkey, GEMS founder and managing director
(Rai, 2014: 1)

The discovery of oil in the 1960s marked the beginning of rapid social and economic development in the Arabian Peninsula. Key to this development was large numbers of expatriates who were needed to work across all sectors due to small national populations (National Bureau of Statistics 2010). This resulted in an influx of expatriates and their families, which created a need for schools to educate their children. With government education policies across the Gulf restricting access to public education largely to citizens, the majority of expatriate families were required to send their children to private schools (Moujaes et al. 2011). As a result, private education providers, in particular for-profit ones, flourished in the region and none more so than GEMS (formerly known as Global Education Management Systems) (Alpen Capital 2014).

GEMS is currently the largest private education management company in the world, with annual revenues exceeding USD $500 million (Sharif 2013). In its home country of the United Arab Emirates (UAE), the GEMS corporation currently educates approximately one-quarter of all private school students in Dubai (Shabandri 2013), and globally nearly 100,000 children attend its schools (GEMS MEA Sukuk Limited 2013). The company runs over 70 schools in countries such as the UAE, the United States (US), the United Kingdom (UK), Kenya, and India (GEMS Education 2014a) and employs over 11,000 teachers, administrators, and support staff worldwide (GEMS Education 2014b; Ernst and Young 2014). The Founder and Managing Director of GEMS Sunny Varkey embraces a philosophy of "you get what you pay for," embodied by his statement above of providing economy, business, and first-class education (Rai 2014). Hayden and Thompson (2013) have therefore compared the GEMS enterprise to a hotel chain for the way it offers various levels of service at different price points.

This chapter examines the GEMS group, its approach to education, and its impact on key stakeholders in the UAE. Utilizing a combination of network and document analysis, supplemented with interviews, the chapter provides a detailed view of GEMS, including its corporate structure, marketing practices, and networks of influence. The chapter argues that the for-profit company has philosophies and practices that lead to social segregation, widening disparities between rich and poor and, due to its market dominance, exposes the UAE government and residents to significant risks if operations should suddenly cease.

The Development of GEMS: From a Single School to a Global Conglomerate

What we know now as the GEMS conglomerate, estimated by Forbes (2014) to be worth USD $1.8 billion, began with a single school in Dubai. K. S. Varkey and his wife Mariamma founded the first school (Our Own English High School) in 1968 (Hamdan 2012). In 1980, Our Own English High School had 350 students, and the couple's 23-year-old son, Sunny Varkey, took over management of the school (Rai 2014). By 2014, Varkey had managed to grow Our Own English High School to over 9,000 students and expand his educational operations, under the banner of GEMS, to ownership of 40 other schools in the UAE (GEMS Education 2014c; School Improvement Partnership n.d.).

Alongside the expansion in the number of schools, Varkey established a parent company, the Varkey Group Limited (Ltd.), to oversee a complex web of associated companies that provide a range of services for the schools, from construction to operations to transportation. Figure 16.1 provides an overview of the numerous companies in which the Varkey Group Ltd. is invested. This figure was constructed using information from the GEMS MEA Sukuk Prospectus (2013), an auditors' report entitled, GEMS Menasa (Cayman) Limited and its subsidiaries: Consolidated financial statements (Ernst and Young 2014), annual reports from the Varkey Foundation and Everonn Education Ltd. (Report and Financial Statements 2013; Everonn Education Ltd. 2012), affiliated entity websites (Everonn Education Ltd. 2014; Everonn India Foundation 2015; Chicago Maintenance and Construction Company [CMC] 2014; GEMS Learning Trust 2015), and various news sources (Everington 2014; Bhatia 2011).

If we examine Figure 16.1, we see that GEMS MENASA TopCo, a company registered in the Cayman Islands, is the parent company of GEMS MENASA (Cayman) Ltd. Sunny Varkey's two sons have key roles in this company with Dino holding the position of Director and Group Chief Operating Officer while his other son Jay is the Director of Business Development (GEMS MEA Sukuk Limited 2013). GEMS MENASA (Cayman) Ltd. is the holding company for the majority of all the education enterprises, more commonly referred to as GEMS. Under this company fall a number of partially and wholly owned subsidiary companies, including individual schools, school management companies, transportation companies, and an education consulting business. While, legally, all of these companies are partially or majority owned by GEMS, they are managed as separate entities. Chief Executive Officer (CEO) Saeed Al Mutafiq runs GEMS Education, which is responsible for schools and school operations, while GEMS

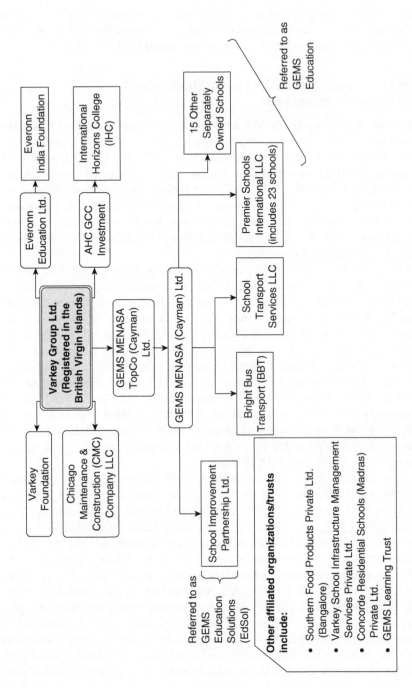

Figure 16.1 Corporate structure of the Varkey Group[1]

Education Solutions, the consulting and international arm of the company, is run by CEO Chris Kirk. Bright Bus Transport and School Transport Services LLC, although appearing to be separate entities with separate websites in the GEMS Sukuk Prospectus (GEMS MEA Sukuk Limited 2013), are operated by the same Managing Director, M. L. Augustine.

In addition to these entities, other noteworthy companies in the Varkey Group connected to its education business but not owned by GEMS MENASA, are:

- *The Varkey Foundation*
  The Varkey Foundation was established in 2011 and registered in the UK as "a not-for-profit organization that builds new classrooms and centers of learning, addresses global teaching capacity and seeds excellence and innovation in the next generation of educators" (GEMS Education 2015). The honorary chairman of the foundation is former US President Bill Clinton and advisory board members include Bertie Ahern, former Prime Minister of Ireland, and Lim Hwee Hua, a former minister in the Singapore Parliament.
- *Everonn Education Ltd.*
  Everonn is an education company in India that purports to have thousands of education and training centers operating in 27 of the 29 Indian states (Everonn Education Ltd. 2014). In April 2011, the company came under much scrutiny after its founder and managing director was arrested for allegedly bribing an income tax official (*The Economic Times* 2011), a scandal that also led to the resignation of the chairman of the board. Despite these and other issues, in September 2011 the Varkey Group decided to invest in Everonn. It began with acquiring a 12 percent stake in the company (Hindu Business Line 2011), later increasing this to become the majority shareholder, owning 43 percent of the company as of 2013 (The *Economic Times* 2013).
- *AHC GCC Investment*
  In 2014, GEMS acquired a minority stake in AHC GCC Investment, a holding company that owns Dubai's International Horizons College (Everington 2014). The college was opened in 2014 and provides students with a two-year academic program that offers pathways to enrollment in select university programs in the US or India (Everington 2014).
- *The Chicago Maintenance & Construction (CMC) Company LLC*
  This company was founded in 1978 in the UAE and was one of Varkey's first businesses. CMC is a construction, interior, and facilities management company that has over 2,200 employees, and its website highlights a number of projects that are directly linked to GEMS schools in the UAE (CMC 2014).

The extensive and diverse range of companies held by the Varkey Group work together to ensure that all aspects of school operations are performed by an entity that is owned or operated by the conglomerate. There are at least ten separate incorporated entities under the Group, in the UAE, UK, and elsewhere, with the holding and two parent companies registered in the offshore tax havens of the Cayman and British Virgin Islands.

Crafting Credibility through Networks

Alongside the expansion of its business and investment activities, GEMS also employs a sophisticated marketing approach to convey and maintain credibility with key stakeholders. This approach relies heavily on the development of a network of high profile individuals and recognized organizations.

Networks are important for the success of any business, and this is no less true in the case of GEMS. The Varkey family, and Sunny Varkey in particular, have been actively developing influential connections that stretch across nations and sectors. By doing so, not only is credibility implied, but doing business is also that much easier. To gain a better understanding of GEMS' global reach across different sectors, two types of social network diagrams were used. The first, Figure 16.2, maps Varkey's individual ties whereas the second, Figure 16.3, depicts GEMS' overall corporate connections. Both figures were developed based on Ball's (2008) discussion of education policy networks, which outline the relationships and flows of influence among people and organizations in the field of education.

Of critical importance to GEMS' continued success are the personal relationships that Varkey has been actively involved in fostering with key political figures, organizations, and corporations across the globe. Figure 16.2 depicts an unweighted network of the direct connections between Varkey and various politicians, CEOs, educators, and international organizational leaders. All connections were determined based on publically available news articles written between the years of 2007 and 2015 and the GEMS Education website.

Varkey's connections range across sectors, from political to non-governmental to corporate and, of course, to educational. Some of the most notable and influential political figures include the ruler of the emirate of Dubai, His Highness Sheikh Mohammed bin Rashid Al Maktoum, former US President Bill Clinton (official GEMS and Varkey Foundation partner), former UK Prime Minister Tony Blair (official GEMS and Varkey Foundation partner), Queen of Jordan, Rania Al Abdullah, and former Deputy Prime Minister of Australia, Mark Vaile (advisor/consultant for GEMS).

In the non-government sector, Varkey is also linked to many individuals from high-profile organizations, such as Rebecca Winthrop from the Brookings Institution, Irina Bokova, Director General of the United Nations Educational, Scientific and Cultural Organization (UNESCO) (see Box 16.1 for a more detailed discussion of this relationship), Jeremy Fryers of the World Economic Forum (WEF), and Andreas Schleicher of the Organisation for Economic Co-operation and Development (OECD). He is also closely linked with the International Baccalaureate Organization (IBO), through three connections: George Walker (former Director General of the IBO), Jeffrey Beard, and Greg Crafter.

Varkey's contacts in the private sector are no less impressive. Close business ties exist between him and chief executives of multinational corporations such as Bill Gates and Anoop Gupta of Microsoft and Talal Al Zain of PineBridge Investments. Less surprising, but worth noting, are the connections with private education providers that Varkey has established. These include leaders of other

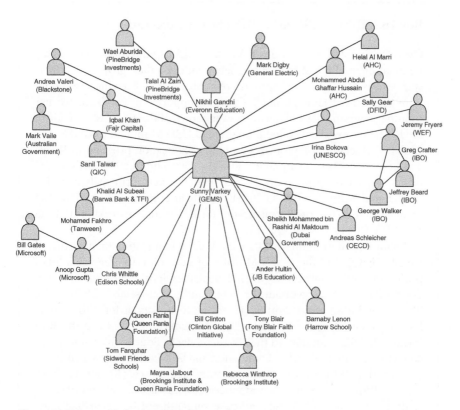

Figure 16.2 Sunny Varkey's personal network

Sources: GEMS Education website; Finance Sharing 2013; EMEA Finance 2014; Sambridge 2013; Everington 2014; the Free Library 2012; Dubai Cares 2008 and related news links.

large for-profit education providers such as Chris Whittle of the Edison Schools, Anders Hultin of JB Education, and Nikhil Gandhi of Everonn Education. This strong network of people from the political, non-government, corporate, and education sectors provides both Varkey and GEMS with much needed influence when it comes to conducting business.

If we now examine the organizational network of the overall GEMS group, the picture becomes even more complex and the network more wide ranging. Beyond Varkey's personal network, the GEMS organizational network connects the entity to partners from across the education, information technology (IT), non-profit, and government sectors in at least 16 countries. Figure 16.3 shows an undirected weighted network of influence using the Harel-Koren Fast Multiscale (Cline 2014) for GEMS. GEMS is the focal node and holds a degree centrality of 11, where degree centrality represents the number of actors outside of GEMS that are connected to GEMS. In other words, 11 nodes are directly linked to GEMS, off

Box 16.1 The GEMS/Varkey/UNESCO connection

Over the last five years, Sunny Varkey, GEMS Education, the Varkey Foundation, and UNESCO have widely publicized their growing relationship. One could argue that key to this relationship have been the large donations that Varkey has made to UNESCO in support of its youth and teacher training programs. Two of the more well known of these gifts were made in 2011, when the Varkey Foundation granted USD $1 million to UNESCO's Global Partnership for Women's and Girls' Education program in Kenya and Lesotho (2012) and another undisclosed amount to UNESCO's school principal leadership program to train 10,000 school principals in India, Ghana, and Kenya (UNESCO 2013). Shortly after this, in 2012, UNESCO named Varkey a Goodwill Ambassador for Education Partnerships (GEMS Education 2014d; UNESCO 2014).

Following on from this, in 2013, the Varkey Foundation then partnered with UNESCO and the UAE's Ministry of Education to organize a high-profile, invitation-only conference in Dubai, the Global Education and Skills Forum (GESF), to target both the public and private sector (GESF 2015). The key ambition of this Forum, according to Varkey, is for it to become known as the "Davos of Education" (GEMS Education 2013). At the 2014 forum, UNESCO announced the "Business Backs Education" campaign in cooperation with the Varkey Foundation and GEMS, which asked corporations to "double their giving to education-related causes" (Kamenetz 2014). The resulting press from this announcement was significant and positive, again positioning GEMS and Varkey as philanthropists rather than businessmen with the UNESCO relationship at the front and center.

which further connections are made. The network was created based on the list of 116 speakers who presented at the inaugural GEMS-organized GESF in Dubai in 2014, as well as Varkey's personal connections mentioned in Figure 16.2. For the purpose of simplifying the figure, only speakers from entities that have had two or more individuals speak at the GESF event were included in the network (GESF 2014). Personal connections to Varkey (as depicted in Figure 16.2) from two or more individuals of the same entity are also included in the network. First-level connections are represented by the organization name (e.g. IBO, Clinton Global Initiative, or Brookings Institution) or category (e.g. government, IT companies, or education companies) and secondary levels use individual names. Weights were assigned to each of the nodes on the basis of nodal degree. That is, nodes that have higher degrees are larger than those with smaller degrees.

As can be seen in Figure 16.3, GEMS is directly linked to twelve representatives from Global Education First Initiative, five from UNESCO, three from the IBO, two from the OECD, two from AHC GCC Investment, two from the Brookings

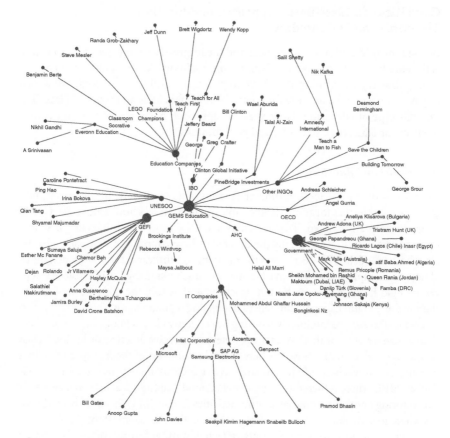

Figure 16.3 GEMS' corporate network of influence

Source: Gems Education website.

Institution, and two from the Clinton Global Initiative. GEMS is also linked to representatives of sixteen governments, six IT companies, five education companies, and four other international non-governmental organizations (INGOs) outside of the ones already mentioned. This shows the extensive network that GEMS has developed across different sectors and its potential for leveraging support globally. It also shows the vast governmental network needed for setting up schools in new countries and locations. The INGO and think tank partners lend legitimacy to GEMS through their high-profile work promoting child rights and education for all. Such connections not only make it easy to do business, but also attract parents and future investors, both of which are crucial to GEMS' continued operations.

However, despite GEMS' success in carefully constructing its image and cultivating a network of high-profile organizations and individuals, the story differs considerably at the stakeholder level, in particular for educators, students and their families, and governments. The next section explores this in more detail.

Casualties of a Class-Based Approach to Education: The Impact on Stakeholders

Beyond the international conferences and the impressive public relations machine is the core business activity of GEMS, running schools. As we have seen, if parents want a first-class education they have to pay more, and those who cannot afford to pay more will have to settle for what Varkey refers to as an economy class, or a no-frills type of education. However, this approach has implications and consequences for educators, students, and governments.

The Impact on Educators

In order to operate schools at different price points (economy, business, and first class) (see Table 16.2 for more detailed information on fees and structures), GEMS needs to keep costs down. Teacher salaries are the most expensive part of school operations and thus are naturally the first area where educators are impacted by the class-based model. Table 16.1 shows the salary ranges for teachers of different nationalities (an example of the "free" market at work) at schools in the UAE. Western teachers are paid more than non-Western teachers, and, within the non-Western group, there are also significant pay differences depending on nationality. Thus, South Asian teachers, who are predominately working in economy class schools, can be paid less than a quarter of what their Western counterparts receive at a first or business class school (see Table 16.2). Those teachers at the bottom end of the pay spectrum, that is South Asian teachers, often can barely cover their living expenses (George 2011; Sankar 2010). There is therefore, a greater likelihood that these teachers engage in private tutoring or other income generating activities (Farah 2011) that have been shown elsewhere to contribute to poor quality teaching in the classroom (Bray 2007).

Teachers working for GEMS are also affected by other features of the class-based system, such as higher student–teacher ratios (as shown in Table 16.2, where economy class schools have class sizes in some cases almost double those at the first class schools) and heavier workloads in lower fee schools (Nazzal 2014b). This should not come as a surprise, however, as, in 2014, GEMS commissioned other research on the "efficiency" of education. The Efficiency Index report,[2] which examined the efficiency of education in 30 countries, stated that larger class sizes and reduced teacher salaries could actually increase education efficiency in some cases (Dolton et al. 2014; Coughlan 2014). Downplaying the importance of education quality, it declared: "efficiency [of education] is a very important metric to consider—some

Table 16.1 K–12 average expatriate teachers' salaries in the UAE

Teacher Nationality Group	Estimated Monthly Salary Range (USD)
South Asian	700–1,400
Non-Gulf Arabs	2,200–2,750
Western	2,750–4,100

Sources in order of appearance: Sankar (2010); Ridge et al. (forthcoming); Nazzal (2014b).

countries may wish to prioritise efficiency over quality. For others, the opposite is true. Country context will dictate this" (Dolton et al. 2014: 25).

The Efficiency Index report was met with heavy criticism. With respect to its methodology, Belfield (2014) analyzed the work and found that "the report serves to distract policymakers … and the model's predictions are far beyond what is reasonable or feasible" (Belfied 2014: 6). The ethos of the report was also troubling as it reflected its sponsor's philosophy of education as a business.

Finally, the infrastructure differs considerably between tiers of schools (see Table 16.2) which affects both students and teachers. The limited outdoor spaces in the economy class schools and the lack of the most high-tech facilities found in first class schools, such as robotics labs, mean that teachers are constrained in terms of what they can teach. In particular, teachers of physical education, creative arts, and technology are impacted by a lack of facilities.

Thus, the combination of low salaries, large class sizes, and poorer facilities in economy class schools makes work for teachers in these schools much more difficult than for their counterparts working in the upper class ones. The combination of these factors, however, not only impacts the lives and health of teachers, but also the learning and futures of the students that they teach.

The Impact on Students and Families

Varkey's airline analogy, quoted at the beginning of the chapter, is in essence supporting the notion that, despite the class of school they attend, all students will arrive at the same destination, but some of them will get there in better style than others. However, as many people will be aware, education does not quite function in the same way as an airline. While it may be true that, in the UAE, the majority of students will graduate from high school, regardless of which school they attend, the opportunities that they have had, or not had, will certainly impact their engagement in school (Fullarton 2002), the quality of university they attend (Berkowitz and Hoekstra 2011), and their future career outcomes (Mincer 1974). This is particularly true for students who require extra attention, such as those with learning difficulties or those who struggle with English as a second language (Benz et al. 2000; Engstrom and Tinto 2008).

Table 16.2 below details a sample of 9 out of the 28 GEMS schools in Dubai (GEMS Education 2014a) to illustrate what more money buys in terms of facilities and teacher–student ratios for different student nationalities at these schools. It is evident from the table that students attending the premium or first class schools enjoy smaller class sizes and superior facilities, with one school even having its own planetarium. These schools also have better paid, better trained, and, in theory, more motivated teachers, which thus impacts the learning and achievement of students as well. In addition, GEMS' premium schools are more likely to be attended by Western expatriates (Knowledge and Human Development Authority 2014a-i) and wealthy families; in turn, these groups are able to access more influential social networks, often referred to as "old boys" networks, that will be of use later in life (Nann et al. 2010).

Table 16.2 Economy, business, and first class K–12 schools in Dubai

	School Name	Tuition Fees (USD)[1]	Largest Student Nationality Group(s)	Largest Teacher Nationality Group(s)	Teacher/ student ratio	Facilities[2]
First Class (USD 16,001+ for annual tuition)	GEMS World Academy - Dubai	22,300	UK	American and Canadian	N/A	Swimming pools, auditorium, planetarium, symphony center, garden, design technology lab, language labs, tutoring rooms, Discovery World (library with science, robotics, and design technology), athletic track, all-weather artificial pitch, tennis courts, gymnasium, fitness center, and indoor climbing wall
	Dubai American Academy	19,500	American	American and Canadian	1:12	Swimming pools, theater/auditorium, soccer field, weight training room, gymnasiums, covered playgrounds, both covered and uncovered tennis courts, and library media centers
	Jumeirah College - Dubai	16,500	UK	UK	1:12	Swimming pool, multi-purpose hall, interactive whiteboards, digital projectors, iPad trollies, communication and resource center, music suites and practice rooms, drama studios, tennis/netball courts, and grassed playing fields

Business Class (USD 8,001– 16,000 for annual tuition)	GEMS Wellington Primary School - Dubai	12,700	UK	UK	1:15	Swimming pools, climate controlled gymnasium, and Astroturf field
	GEMS Royal Dubai School	11,100	UK	UK	1:15	Swimming pools, multi-purpose hall, interactive whiteboards, artificial sports field, tennis, basketball and netball courts, dance studio, and creative learning zone
	GEMS Modern Academy - Dubai	10,100	Indian	Indian	1:16	Swimming pool, auditorium, squash courts, basketball courts, tennis courts, running tracks, and Astroturf field

(continued)

Table 16.2 (continued)

	School Name	Tuition Fees (USD)[1]	Largest Student Nationality Group(s)	Largest Teacher Nationality Group(s)	Teacher/ student ratio	Facilities[2]
Economy Class (less than USD 8,000 for annual tuition)	GEMS Winchester School - Dubai	4,300	Indian	Indian and Pakistani	1:16	Auditorium
	Our Own High School - Al Warqa'a	2,300	Indian	Indian	1:22	Play area, math lab, and bookstore
	The Westminster School - Dubai	2,000	Non-Gulf Arab and Pakistani	Non-Gulf Arab, Pakistani, and Indian	1:17	Covered play areas, activity rooms, and craft rooms

Source: KHDA (2014a–i), phone calls with individual schools, and www.gemseducation.com.
1 Tuition for 8th grade fees during the 2014–15 academic year are listed, with the exception of GEMS Wellington Primary School – Dubai where 6th grade fees are listed.
2 The following facilities have been omitted as they are common across schools: computer labs, science labs, cafeterias, art and music rooms, medical centers, and libraries.

Parents in the UAE are therefore faced with a dilemma when choosing a school, as most would like to give their children the best education available, yet many will only be able to afford a cheaper option. GEMS, however, appears untroubled by the challenges facing some parents when it comes to paying school fees. In an interview about education in the UAE, Varkey acknowledges the tension between finding both a high quality and an affordable school but tells parents that it is unfortunate if they cannot afford the better quality school, stating:

> Parents can very well see which are the schools that are good, outstanding, fair, or not good. And, accordingly, they can choose a school ... So if you put your children in a school that you can't afford then you can't grumble. You understand what I'm saying? You must choose a school that you can afford.
>
> (Buller 2013: 1)

Figure 16.4 below shows there is a relationship between fees and rankings in Dubai, meaning that, when parents are unable to pay higher fees, they are most likely receiving a lower quality education. While the association is not as strong as would be expected, there is still a meaningful correlation with an upward-sloping line of best fit.

In 2014, as part of a strategy to avoid paying the two percent fees on credit and debit card payments, GEMS partnered with the National Bank of Abu Dhabi (NBAD) to launch a special GEMS/NBAD credit card as the sole means by which parents could pay school fees (Nazzal 2014a). Parents who chose to pay with cards other than that are now charged the two percent bank transaction fee, as opposed to the company paying the fee which was the case before, thereby adding another cost for parents.

Beyond the GEMS/NBAD credit card, parents are also pressured by existing economic conditions in the UAE. With salaries not keeping pace with inflation

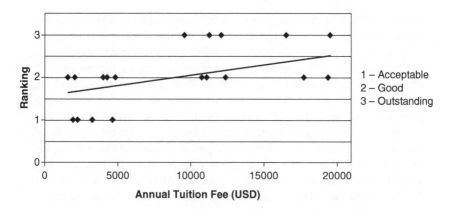

Figure 16.4 Relationship between GEMS 4th grade schools fees and rankings in Dubai, 2013–2014

Sources: www.gemseducation.com and http://www.khda.gov.ae/en/dsib/reports.aspx.

rates in the UAE in recent years, disposable incomes are shrinking and parents are struggling to pay off school fees (Al Sayegh 2013a; Sophia 2014). This is particularly true as school fees were reported to be experiencing higher rates of inflation at 5.6 percent in 2013 than other sectors (Al Sayegh 2013a). According to one article, one in five families in the UAE allocates over 30 percent of their monthly household budget to school fees (Dhal 2013). However, based on earlier research it was found that Western families, with higher incomes, working in the UAE are typically on packages where the employer covers the school fees and their spending on education amounts to only 10 percent of their annual incomes. In contrast, the situation is far worse for expatriate Arab and South Asian parents, who are typically covering the cost of their children's education themselves (Ridge et al. 2014), and thus, could be spending even more than 30 percent of household income on their children's education.

GEMS parents also had concerns about transportation costs, with one parent we interviewed explaining that they pay an additional USD $2,200 per semester for transportation.[3] In addition to the fees associated with transportation, depending on the country, GEMS also charges nonrefundable application fees and additional fees for extracurricular activities (GEMS MEA 2013; GEMS Education 2014e).

However, it is not only the fees and additional costs that act as a barrier to access for students, as there is also the question of places available. Currently, there is a shortage of school spaces across the UAE, with Dubai running at close to 90 percent capacity (Shabandri 2015), and thus a rise in school fees may force parents out of a particular school only to find that there are no other available places in the same fee bracket (see Box 16.2 for an example of this).

Box 16.2 Fee increases at GEMS modern high school

In 2009, GEMS Modern High School, a school in Dubai with over 2,000 students, primarily from India, announced that it was going to raise school fees by 90 percent over two years, ostensibly to meet rising rental charges (Al Najami 2009a). Despite attempts by parents to reverse the decision, all efforts failed and fees were raised (Oatway 2009). Parents appealed to local education authorities and to their embassies, arguing that they had already gone through numerous fee hikes initiated by GEMS without seeing any positive change, but nothing was done (Lewis 2009). Parents were faced with the situation of either choosing to pay the higher fees or looking for another school, though the majority of schools in similar fee brackets were already filled to capacity (Al Najami 2009a). Some families were eventually forced to consider sending their children back to their home countries for schooling (Ahmad 2009; Al Najami 2009b). Similar concerns have transpired at other GEMS schools surrounding fee hikes, following that incident (Francis 2012; Sankar 2013).

While Varkey's airline metaphor, which claims that all students will arrive at the same destination regardless of how luxurious the trip has been, may sound plausible at face value, it is clear that, for families in the economy school option, there are real opportunity costs both in terms of the quality of education and of financial security through being exposed to sudden fee hikes or additional charges for activities. In Dubai, where GEMS educates over 55,000 students (Shabandri 2013) with most of these in low-fee (economy) schools (KHDA 2014a-i), there are also issues of sustainability that will not only affect educators and families but also the state.

The Impact on the State

The final, and no less important, stakeholder impacted by GEMS is the state. With a severe shortage of low-fee school places (approximately 20,000 Pakistani children from low-income families in the UAE were not enrolled in school in 2014 (Ahmed and Nazzal 2014)), the risk of having more children out of school if other low-fee schools shut down is very real. Despite the large demand for schools at this fee level, there is, according to GEMS, very little profit to be made from low-fee private schools in the UAE. Varkey has publically declared that GEMS hopes to stop operating its low-fee schools in the UAE in the long run stating:

> It is impossible to run a good school with fees as low as Dh [UAE dirhams] 6,000 [USD $1,630]. If the KHDA [Knowledge and Human Development Authority, the education regulatory body in Dubai] does not allow us to restructure fees, no school charging fees below Dh 15,000 [USD $4,080] will survive in the UAE. In ten years they will all be gone ... We have been pushing the KHDA to allow us to increase fees so that we can run these schools successfully.
>
> (Sankar 2012: 1)

While the UAE government is not obligated to provide free, public schooling for non-citizens, the implications of having an inadequate supply of affordable schooling options for its low to medium-wage workers should not be underestimated. For the UAE to continue to develop and be able to attract skilled workers from South Asia, the Middle East, and South East Asia, it needs to have education options for their children. Many workers from India, where wages have been steadily rising, have said that it would be better for them to relocate back to India as they would have more disposable income and be able to get their child into a good school (Bouyamorn 2015). Thus, the state needs to think carefully not only in terms of maintaining social cohesion but also economic wellbeing.

Sustainability is also something that should be a concern for the government, particularly in Dubai where a single company, GEMS, controls approximately a quarter of the market. The USD $200 million lawsuit against a subsidiary of GEMS in New York (Halligan 2014) raises questions about the company's viability outside of the UAE, in which it has a monopoly-like market advantage and the support of significant political connections. In 2013, GEMS took out a USD $545 million loan from UAE banks (Mathew 2013) and also had an Islamic bond offering which raised USD $200 million for the company (Reuters 2013), both of which increased the company's debt obligations.

Finally, the company has been embarking on a sale-and-leaseback scheme with some of its schools in order to raise more capital (Al Sayegh 2013b). In this scheme, the company sells the school to an investor and but leases it back from them and continues to operate it. However, these types of schemes have been criticized. In 2011, in the UK a large nursing home operator became unable to meet its rental commitments to the company it had sold and leased back from, and thousands of elderly Britons were facing eviction as a result (Wachman 2011). In the event that GEMS cannot meet the financial obligations from its bond offering, leaseback schemes or loans, it is possible that schools in the UAE will close and that tens of thousands of children will be displaced, echoing the demise of Edison Schools in Philadelphia (Saltman 2005) and of JB Education in Sweden (Smith 2013).

The state, therefore, also has the potential to be negatively impacted by GEMS on two main fronts. Firstly, the looming shortage of low-fee schools if the company keeps closing these schools down has the potential to negatively impact the lower paid end of the skilled labor market and, secondly, there is significant risk posed to thousands of students if the company goes into liquidation or faces financial troubles.

Conclusion: Shareholders vs. Stakeholders

> *Education, then, beyond all other devices of human origin, is the great equalizer of the conditions of men – the balance-wheel of the social machinery.*
>
> (Horace Mann, Education Reformer 1849: 24)

When education is viewed as merely another business or way for a corporation to make profit, it loses its very essence. As for-profit education companies, such as GEMS, continue to make headway across the world into the highly lucrative and largely untapped global education sector, governments need to think beyond the immediate gains, such as the provision of more schools or outsourcing the management of schools, and see the inherent conflict of interest in the for-profit, privatized provision of a public good. In his book, *The Corporation*, Bakan (2004) writes that the first priority of any corporation is profit and that it is the responsibility of shareholders to maximize profit, explaining:

> Unlike public institutions, whose only legitimate mandate is to serve the public good, corporations are legally required to always put their own interest above everyone else's. They may act in ways that promote the public good when it is to their advantage to do so, but they will just as quickly sacrifice it – it is their obligation to do so – when necessary to serve their own ends.
>
> (Bakan 2004: 117–118)

Education management companies such as GEMS are necessarily committed to making profits above all else. For-profit education companies are not altruistic ventures set up to serve a need or to cater to a deficit. Rather, they are commercial entities dedicated to generating profits. While the needs of their shareholders may coincide with the needs of key stakeholders at times, there is no guarantee that this will always be the case, and it is precisely with reference to this point that governments need to take heed.

When education is described as having economy, business, and first classes, then it has automatically stopped being what education reformer, Horace Mann, described above as "the great equalizer of the conditions of men." In Varkey's reimagining of education, the rich get the best education while the poor will get the worst. The GEMS group evidences no concern for the social consequences of this tiered approach and of the destabilizing effect that any disruption or changes to its operations could have on local communities and the state at large. For Varkey, education in the UAE is viewed more as a privilege than a right, and, if people cannot afford it, they do not deserve it.

In the GEMS vision of education, the school marketplace becomes much like a mall where you can find high, medium, and low-priced clothing shops. Those with more income are able to purchase the more expensive, better-made clothes, while those with the lowest income levels are only able to buy the cheaper, inferior goods. As we saw earlier in the chapter, in a first class education students not only have smaller class sizes, better trained, and better paid teachers but they also have more facilities, more extra-curricular activities, and as a result more opportunities to access better quality higher education. Poorer families will receive the inferior good and, rather than education serving as the great leveler, it will in fact exacerbate existing inequalities. Through its economy, business, and first class approach to education GEMS has privileged the wealthy family over the poorer one.

The GEMS case, however, serves far more broadly as a cautionary tale for what happens when education is largely considered to be a private rather than a public good. To return to Varkey's airline analogy, while it is good for the consumer to be able to choose between first, business or economy class, whether or not they travel in first or economy class makes no impact on the people around them; it is a private good yielding private benefits. Education however is not the same; the quality and level of a person's education does have an impact on the people and communities in which they are situated, in terms of crime rates, health, longevity, and productivity among other things. In order to ensure long-term social stability and sustainable economic growth, the world needs equitable education systems, that is, ones in which everyone rides in first class.

Notes

1 The Varkey Group corporate structure is complex, with companies registered around the world. Figure 1 provides the most basic structure of the company and a few of its affiliated education related entities based on publically available data.
2 The Index measures efficiency in terms of test scores and resource use, and is analyzed in terms of teacher wages and pupil–teacher ratios (Belfield 2014).
3 The interview was conducted in 2014.

References

Ahmad, P. F. (2009, January 28). *Your comments*. Comment posted to http://gulfnews.com/news/gulf/uae/education/90-hike-in-school-fees-leaves-parents-perplexed-1.1720.

Ahmed, A. and Nazzal, N. (2014, September 8). Around 20,000 Pakistani children in the UAE don't go to school. *Gulf News*. Retrieved May 31, 2015 from: http://www.gulfnews.com/news/gulf/uae/education/around-20-000-pakistani-children-in-the-uae-don-t-go-to-school-1.1382466.

Al Najami, S. (2009a, January 27). 90% hike in school fees leaves parents perplexed. *Gulf News*. Retrieved May 31, 2015 from: http://www.gulfnews.com/news/gulf/uae/education/90-hike-in-school-fees-leaves-parents-perplexed-1.1720.

Al Najami, S. (2009b, February 4). Parents protest outside Dubai Modern High School over fee hikes. *Gulf News*. Retrieved May 31, 2015 from: http://www.gulfnews.com/news/gulf/uae/education/parents-protest-outside-dubai-modern-high-school-over-fee-hikes-1.1716.

Al Sayegh, H. (2013a, May 27). More than half UAE residents say salaries not keeping pace with cost of living. *The National*. Retrieved May 31, 2015 from: http://www.thenational.ae/business/industry-insights/economics/more-than-half-uae-residents-say-salaries-not-keeping-pace-with-cost-of-living.

Al Sayegh, H. (2013b, November 23). Gems sells long lease of Dubai school to fund global expansion plan. *The National*. Retrieved May 31, 2015 from: http://www.thenational.ae/business/industry-insights/property/gems-sells-long-lease-of-dubai-school-to-fund-global-expansion-plan.

Alpen Capital. (2014). *GCC Education Industry*. Retrieved May 31, 2015 from: www.alpencapital.com/downloads/GCC_Education_Industry_Report_July_2014.pdf.

Bakan, J. (2004). *The corporation*. London: Constable & Robinson.

Ball, S. J. (2008). New philanthropy, new networks and new governance in education. *Political Studies*, 56(4), 747–765.

Belfield, C. (2014). Review of the efficiency index. *National Education Policy Center*. Retrieved May 31, 2015 from: http://www.nepc.colorado.edu/thinktank/review-efficiency-index.

Benz, M. R., Lindstrom, L., and Yovanoff, P. (2000). Improving graduation and employment outcomes of students with disabilities: Predictive factors and student perspectives. *Exceptional Children*, 66(4), 509–529.

Berkowitz, D. and Hoekstra, M. (2011). Does high school quality matter? Evidence from admissions data. *Economics of Education Review*, 30(2), 280–288.

Bhatia, A. (2011). Early days of Varkey schools: It was a management challenge. *Gulf News*. Retrieved June 1, 2015 from: http://www.gulfnews.com/news/gulf/uae/general/early-days-of-varkey-schools-it-was-a-management-challenge-1.410266.

Bouyamorn, A. (2015, March 9). Construction workers returning to India as UAE living costs soar and wages rise back home. *The National*. Retrieved June 1, 2015 from: www.thenational.ae/business/economy/construction-workers-returning-to-india-as-uae-living-costs-soar-and-wages-rise-back-home.

Bray, M. (2007). The shadow education system: Private tutoring and its implications for planners. Retrieved March 18, 2015 from: http://www.unesdoc.unesco.org/images/0011/001184/118486e.pdf.

Buller, A. (2013, July 3). Exclusive interview: GEMS chairman Sunny Varkey talks profits and philanthropy. *Gulf Business*. Retrieved May 31, 2015 from: http://www.gulfbusiness.com/2013/07/full-excusive-interview-gems-chairman-sunny-varkey-talks-profits-and-philanthropy/#.VBfme1fZSZR.

Chicago Maintenance and Construction Company. (2014). *Profile*. Retrieved March 10, 2015 from: http://www.chicago.ae/company/company-profile/.

Cline, D. (2014, November 10). *Using NodeXL to do social network analysis: A workshop*. Presentation, University of Oregon. Retrieved March 18, 2014 from: http://www.academia.edu/9095985/Using_NodeXL_to_do_Social_Network_Analysis_The_Pericles_Workshop.

Coughlan, S. (2014, September 4). Bigger classes for budget efficiency. *BBC News*. Retrieved May 31, 2015 from: www.bbc.com/news/education-29063679.

Dhal, S. (2013, May 1). School fees cost UAE expats up to 30% of income. *Gulf News*. Retrieved May 31, 2015 from: http://www.gulfnews.com/news/gulf/uae/general/school-fees-cost-uae-expats-up-to-30-of-income-1.1178213.

Dolton, P., Marcenaro-Gutierez, O. M., and Still, A. (2014). The Efficiency Index. *GEMS Education Solutions*. Retrieved May 31, 2015 from: www.gemsedsolutions.com/efficiency-index.

Dubai Cares. (2008, November 17). Dubai Cares receives AED 10 million donation from Sunny Varkey. *Dubai Cares*. Retrieved June 5, 2015 from: http://www.dubaicares.ae/en/news/media-library/news-releases/dubai-cares-receives-aed-10-million-donation-from-sunny-varkey.html.

EMEA Finance. (2014, October 16). Interview: Fajr Capital CEO Iqbal Khan. *EMEA Finance*. Retrieved June 5, 2015 from: https://www.emeafinance.com/live/actual/news/2458-interview-fajr-capital-ceo-iqbal-khan-2578.

The Economic Times. (2011, November 14). *After trouble over founder's arrest, Everonn Education Ltd in the red*. Retrieved May 31, 2015 from: http://articles.economictimes.indiatimes.com/2011-11-14/news/30397473_1_everonn-education-q1-net-profit.

The Economic Times. (2013, February 20). *Everonn Education terminates Centum Learning acquisition from Bharti Group*. Retrieved June 1, 2015 from: http://www.articles.economictimes.indiatimes.com/2013-02-20/news/37200524_1_p-kishore-everonn-education-nikhil-gandhi-s-skil-infrastructure.

Engstrom, C. and Tinto, V. (2008). Access without support is not opportunity. *Change: The Magazine of Higher Learning*, 40(1): 46–50.

Ernst and Young. (2014). *GEMS Menasa (Cayman) Limited and its subsidiaries: Consolidated financial statements*. Retrieved May 31, 2015 from: www.rns-pdf.londonstockexchange.com/rns/8868N_-2014-7-31.pdf.

Everington, J. (2014, June 2). New horizons for Varkey with stake in Dubai college. *The National*. Retrieved June 1, 2015 from: www.thenational.ae/business/property/new-horizons-for-varkey-with-stake-in-dubai-college.

Everonn Education Limited. (2012). *Annual report 2011–2012*. Retrieved June 1, 2015: from www.everonn.com/images/Annualreport-11-12.pdf.

Everonn Education Limited. (2014). *About Everonn*. Retrieved October 12, 2014 from: www.everonn.com/about_everonn.html.

Everonn India Foundation. (2015). Welcome to Everonn India Foundation. Retrieved March 9, 2015 from: www.everonnindiafoundation.org.

Farah, S. (2011). Private Tutoring Trends in the UAE. *Dubai School of Government*. Retrieved June 1, 2015 from: www.mbrsg.ae/getattachment/e4e5fbc8-c95c-46f6-8cbb-f31a33dbd6dc/Private-Tutoring-Trends-in-the-UAE.aspx.

Finance Sharing. (2013, July 1). The First Investor, Qatar Insurance Company and Tanween form partnership with GEMS Education. *Finance Sharing*. Retrieved June 5, from: http://financesharing.com/the-first-investor-qatar-insurance-company-and-tanween-form-partnership-with-gems-education/.

Forbes. (2014, September 15). #1033 Sunny Varkey. Retrieved June 1, 2015 from: www.forbes.com/profile/sunny-varkey/.

Francis, M. S. (2012, September 6). 9% fee hike by Gems school shocks parents. *Emirates 24/7*. Retrieved June 1, 2015 from: www.emirates247.com/news/emirates/9-fee-hike-by-gems-school-shocks-parents-2012-09-06-1.474450.

Fullarton, S. (2002). Student engagement with school: Individual and school-level influences. *Australian Council for Educational Research*. Retrieved March 9, 2015 from: http://research.acer.edu.au/cgi/viewcontent.cgi?article=1030&context=lsay_research.

GEMS Education. (2013). *Press Releases*. Retrieved October 15, 2014 from: www.gemseducation.com/media-centre/press-releases/Global-Education-and-Skills-Conference-GESF-to-be-held-annually-in-the-UAE-following-the-inaugural-event-and-will-become-The-Davos-of-Education/543.

GEMS Education. (2014a). *List of our schools*. Retrieved August 17, 2014 from: http://www.gemseducation.com/our-schools/list-of-our-schools.

GEMS Education. (2014b). *How will we achieve our target*. Retrieved October 25, 2014 from: www.gemseducation.com/MENASA/parents/contents.php?pageid=132.

GEMS Education. (2014c). *Our Own English High School—Dubai*. Retrieved October 15, 2014 from: www.gemseducation.com/our-schools/list-of-our-schools/Our-Own-English-High-School-Dubai/33.

GEMS Education. (2014d). *Press articles*. Retrieved November 2, 2014 from: http://www.gemseducation.com/MENASA/parents/contents.php?pageid=3888\.

GEMS Education. (2014e). *Fee structure and program*. Retrieved November 15, 2014 from: www.gemseducation.com/MENASA/parents/contents.php?pageid=4896.

GEMS Education. (2015). *The Varkey Foundation*. Retrieved March 3, 2015 from: www.gemseducation.com/philanthropy/.

GEMS Learning Trust. (2015). *Our Governance*. Retrieved March 17, 2015 from: www.gemslearningtrust.org/contents.php?pageid=6044&submenuid=7262&parentid=1180.

GEMS MEA Sukuk Limited. (2013, November 19). *Prospectus*. Retrieved June 1, 2015 from: http://www.dfsa.ae/Documents/Official%20List/DB%20v1%20Project_Platinum%20Final%20Clean%20Prospectus%20for%20stamp-off.pdf.

George, J. (2011, February 2011). Asian teachers want pay parity. *Emirates 24/7*. Retrieved June 1, 2015 from: www.emirates247.com/news/emirates/asian-teachers-want-pay-parity-2011-02-22-1.359221.

Global Education and Skills Forum. (GESF). (2014). *Speakers*. Retrieved October 12, 2014 from: https://educationandskillsforum.org/.

Global Education and Skills Forum. (GESF). (2015). *About*. Retrieved March 4, 2015 from: https://educationandskillsforum.org/about/.

Halligan, N. (2014, July 14). US developer lodges $200m lawsuit against Dubai's GEMS. *Arabian Business*. Retrieved June 1, 2015 from: www.arabianbusiness.com/us-developer-lodges-200m-lawsuit-against-dubai-s-gems-557790.html#.VP6hWXyUcok.

Hamdan, S. (2012). Building an education empire. *Global Citizen*. Retrieved June 1, 2015 from: http://issuu.com/global-citizen/docs/global-citizen-09.

Hayden, M. and Thompson, J. (2013). International schools: Antecedents, current issues and metaphors for the future. In R. Pearce (Ed.), *International Education and Schools: Moving Beyond the First 40 Years*, 3–24. London: Bloomsbury Academic.

Kamenetz, A. (2014, March 17). $1 million global education 'Nobel in teaching' announced. *Washington Monthly*. Retrieved June, 2015 from: http://www.washingtonmonthly.com/college_guide/blog/1_million_global_education_nob.php.

Knowledge and Human Development Authority. (2014a). *Inspection Report: The Westminster School – Dubai.* Retrieved October 15, 2014 from: http://www.khda.gov.ae/DISB/AttachmentDownload.aspx?DOC_ID=lJOqw3tftfk%3d.

Knowledge and Human Development Authority. (2014b). *Inspection Report: GEMS Modern Academy.* Retrieved October 14, 2014 from: http://www.khda.gov.ae/DISB/AttachmentDownload.aspx?DOC_ID=xxK1KateA%2bI%3d.

Knowledge and Human Development Authority. (2014c). *Inspection Report: GEMS World Academy.* Retrieved October 14, 2014 from: http://www.khda.gov.ae/DISB/AttachmentDownload.aspx?DOC_ID=B5JoYtScURA%3d.

Knowledge and Human Development Authority. (2014d). *Inspection Report Jumeirah College – Dubai.* Retrieved October 14, 2014 from: http://www.khda.gov.ae/DISB/AttachmentDownload.aspx?DOC_ID=wl%2bXi09efMA%3d.

Knowledge and Human Development Authority. (2014e). *Inspection Report: GEMS Royal Dubai School.* Retrieved October 14, 2014 from: http://www.khda.gov.ae/DISB/AttachmentDownload.aspx?DOC_ID=JL1iQuC4x6I%3d.

Knowledge and Human Development Authority. (2014f). *Inspection Report: GEMS Wellington Primary School.* Retrieved October 14, 2014 from: http://www.khda.gov.ae/DISB/AttachmentDownload.aspx?DOC_ID=NCQKhE81%2foc%3d.

Knowledge and Human Development Authority. (2014g). *Inspection Report:* GEMS *Dubai American Academy.* Retrieved October 14th 2014 from http://www.khda.gov.ae/DISB/SchoolInspectionReportRD.aspx?EN=1&SID=262&FP=36492&INID=1605.

Knowledge and Human Development Authority. (KHDA). (2014h). *Inspection Report: GEMS Winchester School.* Retrieved October 14, 2014 from: http://www.khda.gov.ae/DISB/AttachmentDownload.aspx?DOC_ID=2yNMV6um4nU%3d.

Knowledge and Human Development Authority. (2014i). *Inspection Report: Our Own High School - Al Warqa'a.* Retrieved October 14, 2014 from: http://www.khda.gov.ae/DISB/AttachmentDownload.aspx?DOC_ID=x1D2bUysPU0%3d.

Lewis, K. (2009). School stands firm on fee increase. *The National.* Retrieved June 1, 2015 from: www.thenational.ae/news/uae-news/education/school-stands-firm-on-fee-increase.

Mann, H. (1849). *Twelfth annual report.* Dutton & Wentworth.

Mathew, S. (2013, April 21). Dubai GEMS Education Obtains $545 million loan for expansion. *Bloomberg Business.* Retrieved June 1, 2015 from: www.bloomberg.com/news/articles/2013-04-21/dubai-s-gems-education-obtains-545-million-loan-for-expansion.

Mincer, J. (1974). Schooling, experience, and earnings. *National Bureau of Economic Research (NBER).* Retrieved March 9, 2015 from: http://www.nber.org/chapters/c1767.pdf.

Moujaes, C. N., Hoteit, L., and Hiltunen, J. (2011). *A decade of opportunity the coming expansion of the private-school market in the GCC (Booz & Company publication).* Retrieved May 16, 2013 from: http://www.booz.com/media/file/BoozCo-Private-School-Expansion-GCC.pdf.

Nann, S., Krauss, J., Schober, M., Gloor, P. A., Fischbach, K., and Fuhres, H. (2010). The power of alumni networks – success of startup companies correlates with online social network structure of its founders. *Working Paper No. 2010-00: MIT Center for Collective Intelligence.* Retrieved March 10, 2015 from: https://www.academia.edu/2851206/The_Power_of_Alumni_Networks-Success_of_Startup_Companies_Correlates_With_Online_Social_Network_Structure_of_Its_Founders.

National Bank of Abu Dhabi (NBAD). (2014). *NBAD GEMS Titanium Card.* Retrieved March 8, 2015 from: http://www.nbad.com/en-ae/personal-banking/cards/credit-cards/gems-titanium.html.

National Bureau of Statistics. (2010). *Population estimates 2006–2010*. Retrieved March 10, 2015 from: http://www.uaestatistics.gov.ae/ReportPDF/Population%20Estimates%20 2006%20-%202010.pdf.

Nazzal, N. (2014a, May 6). GEMS schools to charge fee for credit card payments. *Gulf News*. Retrieved June 1, 2015 from: http://m.gulfnews.com/news/uae/education/gems-schools-to-charge-fee-for-credit-card-payments-1.1329079.

Nazzal, N. (2014b, September 2014). Low pay, low morale in Dubai private schools. *Gulf News*. Retrieved June 1, 2015 from: http://gulfnews.com/news/gulf/uae/education/low-pay-low-morale-in-dubai-private-schools-1.1379175.

Oatway, L. (2009, January 30). Protest as school hikes fees by 90%. *The National*. Retrieved June 1, 2015 from: www.thenational.ae/news/uae-news/education/protest-as-school-hikes-fees-by-90.

Parent Relations Executive. (2014). *GEMS Education*. LinkedIn. Retrieved November 1, 2014 from: https://www.linkedin.com/jobs2/view/17303697.h.

Rai, S. (2014, April 14). Billionaire education entrepreneur Varkey takes his Dubai school chain worldwide. *Forbes*. Retrieved June 1, 2015 from: www.forbes.com/sites/saritharai/2014/04/02/chalk-a-block/.

Report and Financial Statements. (2013). The Varkey GEMS Foundation. Retrieved March 10, 2015 from: http://apps.charitycommission.gov.uk/Accounts/Ends19/0001145119_AC_20130331_E_C.pdf.

Reuters. (2013, November 2013). Dubai's GEMS compromises on size, price with $200m sukuk. Retrieved June 1, 2015 from: www.arabianbusiness.com/dubai-s-gems-compro-mises-on-size-price-with-200m-sukuk-526687.html#.VP142XyUcok.

Ridge, N., Kippels, S., and Shami, S. (2014). *Private education in the absence of a public option: The cases of the UAE and Qatar*. Privatisation in Education Research Initiative.

Ridge, N., Shami, S. and Kippels, S. (forthcoming). *Arab Migrant Teachers in the United Arab Emirates and Qatar: Challenges and Opportunities in Arab Migrant Communities in the GCC*. Doha: Georgetown University Doha.

Saltman, K. (2005). *The Edison Schools: Corporate schooling and the assault on public education*. Routledge, New York.

Sambidge, A. (2013, November 6). Dubai's GEMS sells school campus to US money manager. *Arabian Business*. Retrieved June 5, 2015 from: http://m.arabianbusiness.com/dubai-s-gems-sells-school-campus-us-money-manager-525417.html.

Sankar, A. (2010, June 15). Teachers at GEMS unhappy with pay increase. *Gulf News*. Retrieved June 1, 2015 from: http://www.gulfnews.com/news/gulf/uae/education/teachers-at-gems-unhappy-with-pay-increase-1.641283.

Sankar, A. (2012, December 19). Schools charging less than Dh15,000 could close: Varkey. *Xpress*. Retrieved June 1, 2015 from: http://www.gulfnews.com/about-gulf-news/al-nisr-portfolio/xpress/schools-charging-less-than-dh15-000-could-close-varkey-1.1121381.

Sankar, A. (2013, January 16). Bus fee hike in GEMS schools. *Gulf News*. Retrieved June 1, 2015 from: http://www.gulfnews.com/news/gulf/uae/education/bus-fee-hike-in-gems-schools-1.1133521.

School Improvement Partnership. (n.d.). *Bridging private and public education: A GEMS company*. Retrieved March 10, 2015 from: www.gemssip.com/download/sip_brochure_web.pdf.

Shabandri, M. (2013, May 14). Private schools a big business. *Khaleej Times*. Retrieved June 1, 2015 from: http://www.khaleejtimes.com/kt-article-display-1.asp?section=education nation&xfile=data/educationnation/2013/may/educationnation_may19.xml.

Shabandri, M. (2015, January 6). Private schools in Dubai are almost full. *Khaleej Times*. Retrieved June 1, 2015 from: www.khaleejtimes.com/kt-article-display-1.asp?xfile=data/educationnation/2015/January/educationnation_January5.xml&section=educationnation.

Sharif, A. (2013, March 27). World's biggest private school operator GEMS seeks $1 billion. *BloombergBusiness*. Retrieved June 1, 2015 from: www.bloomberg.com/news/articles/2013-03-27/world-s-biggest-private-school-operator-gems-seeks-1-billion.

Smith, L. (2013). Sweden's top free schools provider to close, in blow to Education Secretary Michael Gove. *The Independent*. Retrieved June 1, 2015 from: www.independent.co.uk/news/education/education-news/swedens-top-free-schools-provider-to-close-in-blow-to-education-secretary-michael-gove-8640111.html.

Sophia, M. (2014, December 11). UAE salaries not keeping up with inflation- report. *Gulf Business*. Retrieved March 10, 2015 from: http://gulfbusiness.com/2014/12/uae-salaries-keeping-inflation-report/#.VP8HgeGvw5w.

The Free Library. (2012). Welcare, City Hospitals to be renamed. *The Free Library*. Retrieved June 5, 2015 from: http://www.thefreelibrary.com/Welcare,+City+Hospitals+to+be+renamed.-a0302148247.

The Hindu Business Line. (2011, December 21). *Varkey Group buys 12% stake in Everonn Education*. Retrieved May 31, 2015 from: http://www.thehindubusinessline.com/industry-and-economy/info-tech/varkey-group-buys-12-stake-in-everonn-education/article2735276.ece.

UNESCO. (2013). *Monitoring of programme implementation for regular programme and extrabudgetary resources as at 31/12/2013*. Retrieved March 7, 2015 from: http://unesdoc.unesco.org/images/0022/002269/226953E.pdf.

UNESCO. (2014). *Designation ceremony of Sunny Varkey as UNESCO Goodwill Ambassador*. Retrieved October 12, 2014 from: www.unesco.org/new/en/unesco/events/major-events/?tx_browser_pi1[showUid]=6355&cHash=cbc4e71df5.

Wachman, R. (2011, July 16). Southern Cross's incurably flawed business model let down the vulnerable. *The Guardian*. Retrieved June 1, 2015 from: www.theguardian.com/business/2011/jul/16/southern-cross-incurable-sick-business-model.

Index